CIRCLE OF WINNERS

MUSIC IN AMERICAN LIFE

A list of books in the series appears at the end of this book.

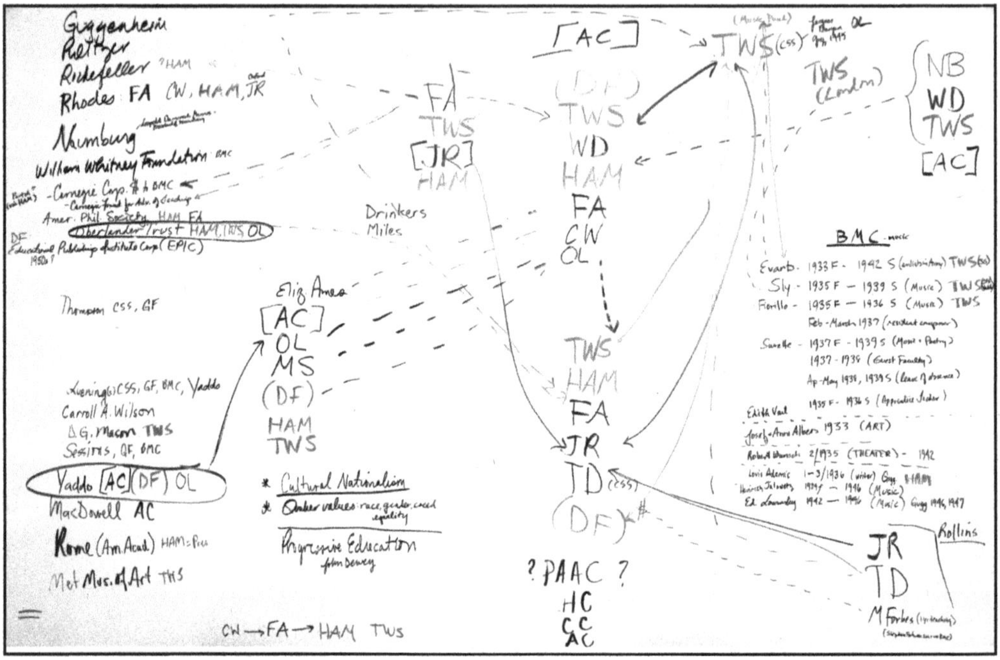

Guggenheim
Pulitzer
Rockefeller
Rhodes FA CW, HAM, JR
Naumburg
William Whitney Foundation
Carnegie Corp.
Amer. Phil. Society HAM FA
Oberlander Trust HAM, TWS OL
Educational Publishing Institute Corp (EPIC)
Thompson CSS, GF
Carroll A. Wilson
D.G. Mason TWS
Sessions, GF, BMC
Yaddo [AC] (DF) OL
MacDowell AC
Rome (Am. Acad.)
Met Mus. of Art TWS
CW → FA → HAM TWS
[AC]
TWS
TWS (London)
NB
WD
TWS
[AC]
FA
TWS
[JR]
HAM
Drinkers
Miles
TWS
WD
HAM
FA
CW
OL
Eliz Ames
[AC]
OL
MS
(DF)
HAM
TWS
* Cultural Nationalism
* Quaker values: race, gender, creed equality
Progressive Education
from Dewey
TWS
HAM
FA
JR
TD (CSS)
(DF)
? PAAC ?
HC
CC
AC
BMC
Evarts 1933 F - 1942 S
Sly 1935 F - 1939 S (Music)
Fiorillo 1935 F - 1936 S (Music) TWS
Feb - March 1937 (resident composer)
Sunelle 1937 F - 1939 S (Music + Poetry)
1937 - 1938 (Guest Faculty)
Edith Vail
Josef + Anni Albers 1933 (ART)
Robert Wunsch 2/1935 (THEATER) - 1942
Louis Adamic 1-3/1936 (writer)
Heinrich Jalowetz 1939 - 1946 (Music)
Ed. Lowinsky 1942 - 1946 (Music)
Rollins
JR
TD
M Forbes

CIRCLE OF WINNERS

How the Guggenheim Foundation Composition Awards Shaped American Music Culture

DENISE VON GLAHN

UNIVERSITY OF ILLINOIS PRESS
Urbana, Chicago, and Springfield

1 2 3 4 5 C P 5 4 3 2 1
∞ This book is printed on acid-free paper.

This book was published with support from the General Fund of the American Musicological Society, supported in part by the National Endowment for the Humanities and the Andrew W. Mellon Foundation, as well as a grant from the Henry and Edna Binkele Classical Music Fund.

Frontispiece: Visualizing the Guggenheim Foundation network in 2012. Image by the author.

Library of Congress Cataloging-in-Publication Data
Names: Von Glahn, Denise, 1950– author.
Title: Circle of winners : how the Guggenheim Foundation composition awards shaped American music culture / Denise Von Glahn.
Description: Urbana : University of Illinois Press, 2023. | Series: Music in American life | Includes bibliographical references and index.
Identifiers: LCCN 2022056908 (print) | LCCN 2022056909 (ebook) | ISBN 9780252045097 (cloth) | ISBN 9780252087226 (paperback) | ISBN 9780252054419 (ebook)
Subjects: LCSH: John Simon Guggenheim Memorial Foundation—History. | Music—Endowments. | Music—North America—20th century—History and criticism. | Music—Latin America—20th century—History and criticism.
| Surette, Thomas Whitney, 1861–1941.
Classification: LCC ML26 .J644 2023 (print) | LCC ML26 (ebook) | DDC 780.797—dc23/eng/20221130
LC record available at https://lccn.loc.gov/2022056908
LC ebook record available at https://lccn.loc.gov/2022056909

for my sisters
Carol and Janet,
and my friend
Kathy

Contents

Acknowledgments

Although my name appears as sole author of this book, *Circle of Winners* reflects the work of dozens of musicians, scholars, librarians, archivists, administrators, colleagues, graduate assistants, students, friends, and family members who have participated in its creation. For over a decade they have functioned as my own Guggenheim network. Although I kept a running list of people who deserved acknowledgement, I know that someone whose casual remark shifted my focus or whose simple question clarified what I needed to say will go unnamed. I apologize.

Some people's impacts are obvious, and I begin with them: Ellen Taaffe Zwilich asked the question that got me started on the project; Laurie Matheson, director of the University of Illinois Press, patiently guided and encouraged its investigation, and Mariah Mendes Schaefer shepherded it through its penultimate stage. Tad Ringo has seen it through to completion. Edward Hirsch, president, and André Bernard, vice president, of the John Simon Guggenheim Memorial Foundation cautiously permitted my intrusion into the foundation offices, arranged a workspace, and allowed me to consult select composer files. Financial support from The Copland Fund for Music made my early-stage research trips to the Guggenheim's New York offices possible.

Over the years I traveled to many archives and libraries where I consulted undigitized records, letters, reports, and audio materials that filled in holes in the foundation's materials. Heather South, archivist at the Western Regional Archives in North Carolina, welcomed and assisted me during multiple on-site visits to the Asheville facility; she helped me navigate the voluminous Black Mountain College collection and located additional documents that she believed would be useful. The Friends Historical Library at Swarthmore College houses documents in the Frank Aydelotte Papers that are essential for any scholar studying the John

Simon Guggenheim Memorial Foundation. Unfettered access at the Western Regional Archives and permission to cite Frank Aydelotte's presidential papers at Swarthmore allowed a fuller story to be told than would have been possible without them. I am grateful to Christopher Densmore, curator of the library, and archivists Patricia O'Donnell and Susanna Morikawa for their assistance when I first visited in 2012 and for answering queries in the interim. Leslie Perrin Wilson and, after her retirement, Anke Voss, archivists at the Concord Free Public Library in Concord, Massachusetts, made my work with the Surette Papers in the William Monroe Special Collections both pleasant and productive. I appreciate their gracious, expert, and timely assistance on site and in cyberspace. George Boziwick, former chief of the Music Division at the New York Public Library for the Performing Arts at Lincoln Center, and librarians in the Manuscripts and Archives Division of the New York Public Library assisted me with the Otto Luening Papers and Yaddo Records. The New York Public Library is another essential repository for materials related to the Guggenheim Foundation. Staff at the American Philosophical Society in Philadelphia, the Historical Society of Pennsylvania, and the Honorary Degree Records Office at the University of Pennsylvania helped locate information related to Henry Allen Moe, the Drinker family, and additionally to Thomas Whitney Surette. Ruth Solie shared a rare copy of *Accademia dei Dilettanti di Musica, 1930–1960*, Henry S. and Sophie H. Drinker's formal record of the guests who attended and the music that was sung at their in-house singing parties. Robin Rausch, head of reader services in the Music Division, Library of Congress, has been a thoughtful sounding board and a steady source of ideas, encouragement, and advice in this book project and multiple prior ones. Her help with the library's collections of Copland, Seeger Family, and Antheil papers among others, and especially during the recent pandemic, was invaluable. What started as a shared professional curiosity that focused on the MacDowell Colony and Amy Beach years ago has become a treasured friendship. Sarah Dorsey, music librarian at the University of North Carolina at Greensboro, regularly lent her imaginative ear and insights at all stages of this project and never wavered in her belief that it would come together. This book exists in part because I couldn't bear to disappoint her. Laura Gayle Green, head of the Warren D. Allen Music Library in the College of Music at Florida State University, has demonstrated creativity, patience, and good humor throughout the years finding recalcitrant documents. When traditional paths didn't yield results, Laura Gayle deployed her personal network of librarian colleagues across the country to hunt down the information. This book has benefited in untold ways from "LGG's" presence.

I am grateful to the Society for American Music, which programmed the first paper of mine on the topic of this book for its 2013 conference, and to Andrew Granade for asking a question about Harry Partch that underscored for me just how important Thomas Whitney Surette was to the course of high-art U.S. music culture in the first half of the twentieth century. I thank Carol Oja for conference lunches and dinners where we talked about our common interests in American music culture and the institutions that supported it. I appreciate that she put me in touch with her former student Michael Uy, who shared his work on the NEA and the Rockefeller and Ford Foundations before its appearance as his 2020 book *Ask the Experts*.

I have been gifted with extraordinary graduate students. I continue to appreciate the clear-headed intelligence, thoughtfulness, and friendship of Stephanie Stallings. Work on her 2009 dissertation "Collective Difference: The Pan-American Association of Composers and Pan-American Ideology in Music, 1925–1945" first caused me to appreciate the multi-directionality of cultural flows. I could not have anticipated the full resonance of that idea or imagined its application in this project prior to exploring the Copland-Chávez relationship. Laura Moore Pruett, first a student, has become an expert Americanist in her own right and a trusted ear. Her honesty and candor provide invaluable reality checks for me. For a decade a series of graduate assistants has created searchable annotated databases for thousands of photographed documents, located and organized information beyond that which I had found, made wise suggestions on chapter drafts, and thought out loud with me about the book in classes, seminars, and casual meetings. *Circle of Winners* would not exist without the extraordinary help of Megan MacDonald, Dana Terres, Ashley Geer Hedrick, Hannah Crider, and Abby Rehard. I offer you my sincerest thanks and hope that work on this book allowed you to witness the application of lessons I strove to impart in classes and seminars. Amy Bradley, whose master's and doctoral musicology committees I chaired, is now a professional project consultant, writing coach, and editor. We have worked together on parts of this project since 2016 and on others in between, and most recently she has been the person to review and organize what I sent to the University of Illinois Press. She is an invaluable assistant, a second pair of eyes and ears, a scrupulous editor, an imaginative problem solver, and a good friend. I would not have made my deadlines without her.

During the lengthy gestation of this project the Florida State University College of Music supported me on multiple occasions with research-focused semester leaves. I also received a major grant from the Committee on Faculty Research Support at the university for this project. The most recent of two semester-long sabbaticals made the final stages of manuscript preparation possible. I appreciate the time and financial support offered by my university, but even more important, I'm grateful for a culture within the College of Music Musicology Area that generously encourages individuals to pursue their passions and interests regardless of how unorthodox they may seem to others. My faculty colleagues, Sarah Eyerly, Charles Brewer, Michael Bakan, Frank Gunderson, Eduardo Lopez-Dabdoub, Paddy League, and Maria Ryan, provide an ever-present sounding board and cheering squad. They are a consistently creative and cordial cohort. I know that it is rare and not to be taken for granted. Colleagues outside my immediate area have generously encouraged this project and me as well. Thank you, Marcia Porter, Heidi Louise Williams, and Rachel Lumsden: Each of you has taken a specific interest in this work and prodded me to finish it. My former deans, Patricia Flowers and Michael Thrasher, believed in the value of my scholarly work and made my sabbaticals possible and productive. I miss their wise and humane counsel and know how fortunate I was to benefit from both of these extraordinary administrators and people.

Friends of many years, Sherry Williams and Tammy Kernodle, continue to buoy me with their long-distance listening hearts. Their voices provide comfort. Our friendships only deepen with the passing decades. Irene Trakas and Veronica Donnelly support me daily with their close-by caring. I'm lucky to have these women in my life, far and near. It was my deepest wish that Kathy Strickland had lived to see the completion of this project. She was cheering from the sidelines from its beginning and until her end. She passed away in the summer of 2020 after a brief illness. We were friends for forty-two years. In our last conversation I promised I'd send her a copy of the book.

My family anchors me and reminds me of the wholeness of life. My mother, Lorraine, who celebrated her one hundredth birthday in April 2022, my sisters, Carol and Janet, my daughters, Peggi and Tracy, my sons, Haynes and Evan, and my daughters-in-law, Claire and Courtney, are at my core. I'm grateful for Johanna, my inherited granddaughter, and her always inspiring multimedia artistic imagination, and "Mr. Dan," a family member by marriage, who endured a detailed explanation of the process by which the book had come together only to ask why it was important. Leave it to an engineer to cut to the chase. Since I last wrote acknowledgments, Tessa Merritt Cooney has joined the clan. She, like her father and uncle before her, reminds me of the value of wonder and the assumption of goodness that we're all born with. When the world weighs heavy, I only have to think of Tessa and her unbridled enthusiasm for everything and everyone around her to believe that there is hope. There has to be.

For over twenty years my husband, Michael Broyles, has provided a unique combination of love and support. Whether accompanying me on research trips, engaging in dinnertime debriefings, or challenging my thinking, he's there and rooting for me. He has never been anything but my champion. During my six years as Musicology Area Coordinator, Michael remained serene in a greater confidence than mine that once my administrative tour of duty was over, my brain would still be able to think long thoughts. And then he shared my joy when I discovered he was right. He has been the essential link in my network.

CIRCLE OF WINNERS

INTRODUCTION

Circle of Winners has been a work-in-progress since the spring of 2008. That was when Ellen Taaffe Zwilich visited my graduate seminar on Music and Institutions and asked why the John Simon Guggenheim Memorial Foundation wasn't among the organizations we were studying. My response that the foundation's papers were not available for consultation inspired Zwilich to investigate that practice. As a recipient of a Guggenheim Fellowship and a member of the foundation's board, Zwilich inquired on my behalf. Months later, I conducted personal talks with foundation administrators concerning the nature of my interests, the files I wanted to consult, the time frame during which I and the foundation offices were available to do the work, and my need for funding, all of which delayed the start of the project. In the intervening years, however, the focus of the study morphed many times. What eventually began in 2010 as an exploration of six early composer awardees and their fellowship experiences became a study of the little-known original music advisor, Thomas Whitney Surette. His curious background and involvements altered the study again, first to one focused more on the foundation's administrators and their networks of associations, and later to the ways the Guggenheim Foundation exemplified a successful philanthropic institution. Only after nearly a decade of research and reflection did the various aspects of the project coalesce into a history of the early years of the foundation's composition awards, 1925 to 1940, and what a study of six awardees said about the role the Guggenheim Foundation played in shaping the nation's "high-art" music culture. In the interim, there have been multiple other scholarly projects—presentations, articles, essays, and books on other topics—but rather than distract me completely from this inquiry, they broadened my understanding and appreciation of the agents and the agendas of the individuals and institutions that wield power. *Circle of Winners* has become a study of one way a slice of our culture is made.

* * *

As they have always been, papers related to applicant files held by the John Simon Guggenheim Memorial Foundation remain closed and confidential. There is no publicly accessible collection, archive, or finding aid, and there are no staff members dedicated to their management. Individual requests to consult materials are handled on an ad hoc basis by the vice president and secretary of the foundation, André Bernard. There is no place set aside in the New York offices for anyone but staff to work. Twenty-first-century foundation officers honor promises made to referees almost a century ago that their letters of evaluation would be held in confidence, and they are. In my case, were it not for the intercession of Zwilich I never would have been able to consult the materials I did. Her belief in this project allowed her to argue that a history of the music composition awards needed the consultation of relevant materials. I hope that this study has not made her regret her involvement on my behalf. That said, I saw no file that had not been vetted thoroughly by Bernard, with any pages he considered controversial or compromising removed. I am grateful to the foundation for trusting me with what it allowed me to access and for its hospitality on the multiple occasions when I visited its offices. I am left wondering, however, who gets to decide what are appropriate historical documents for scholars to consult? How does the excision of any evidence compromise the histories we tell? Does a surfeit of sources guarantee a fuller story?

In an ironic twist, the numerous redactions from composers' files compelled me to locate resources at many other institutions so I could fill in obvious missing pieces. I likely learned much more than was redacted. Evidence is seldom found in one place, and it is plentiful in the case of the Guggenheim Foundation if one has the time, resources, and tenacity to hunt it down. In that regard it is not a project for an untenured faculty member in need of a quick book. It might not even be the project for a senior faculty member unless he or she has a strong obsessive streak and longevity on his or her side. I am grateful to the Aaron Copland Fund for Music, Inc., for providing a grant to jump-start my original Guggenheim Foundation research. I could not have afforded to travel to or stay near the foundation's Park Avenue offices without it. Unlike the successful composer applicants who were expected to "meet with Mr. Surette," I do not live close by.

The generous and eager cooperation of dozens of archivists, researchers, and friends curious to learn about the early years of the foundation for themselves made this project a collaborative effort of an unusual kind and duration. Consultation of resources that reside in Frank Aydelotte's presidential papers at Swarthmore College, Henry Allen Moe's papers at the American Philosophical Society in Philadelphia, the collection of materials related to Thomas Whitney Surette and his Concord Music School held by the Concord, Massachusetts, Free Public Library, the papers of various composers and organizations at the New York Public Library and the Library of Congress, papers in the Sophia Smith Collection at Smith College, and the nearly limitless resources on Black Mountain College housed at the Western North Carolina Historical Association Archives in Asheville made this a more complete study by far than it could have been had I drawn from the foundation's papers alone. It also prolonged the project by many years because trips had to be squeezed into the weeks or months not consumed by teaching and administrative duties and then altered completely by Covid. I'm grateful that all of the major players in the Guggenheim story had a sense of their own historical importance and kept their papers, and for the many scholars who have worked on parts of this story, knowingly and unknowingly, whose intellectual efforts have provided context, details, and thoughtful evaluation unavailable elsewhere.

* * *

In 2025 the John Simon Guggenheim Memorial Foundation celebrates its one hundredth anniversary. Since its beginnings in 1925, it has grown from an ambitious family-business–funded philanthropy—an alternative to the model of individual personal patronage that dominated previous arrangements between supporters and those supported—to a venerated competitive award-granting institution of high culture. Dedication to a mission that was uniquely inclusive at the time, one that promised to support fellows in "the advancement and diffusion of knowledge and understanding and the appreciation of beauty" regardless of "distinction on account of race, color, or creed," has earned the foundation approbation, gratitude, and loyalty from thousands of awardees, and rightly so.[1] For a century it has supported and shaped aspects of the nation's intellectual and artistic life while simultaneously engaging in its own version of cultural diplomacy. Cultivating advantageous relations for the family's mining and refining businesses and the nation's hemispheric interests, especially with Central and South American countries, was never far from its founders' thinking even if such goals weren't foregrounded in official announcements describing the foundation's original purpose. In a statement of intent issued on February 23, 1925, Senator Simon Guggenheim clarified an additional distinguishing feature of his plan: to have the foundation provide fellowships "for older students of proved ability, and for women as well as men."[2] From the start, the clause referencing women set his organization apart from others whose practices, if not always their stated policies, aimed assistance exclusively at men. Despite their official inclusion, however, for myriad reasons women were not equally represented across award categories in the early years.

Although private arrangements between individual benefactors and composers and artists continued to be made throughout the twentieth century and exist to this day, starting around 1900 institutionalized philanthropy assumed an increasingly important role in the United States. The Guggenheim Foundation was among the vanguard of those that supported artists and musicians. It developed a model for the selection process whereby all applicants submitted a written application, provided required documentation of their personal and educational background, listed their accomplishments and plans, and had multiple recognized experts write confidential letters of endorsement on their behalf. There were exceptional applicants for whom the process was streamlined significantly, as the case of Carlos Chávez reveals later in this book. Confidentiality was and remains a near-sacred tenet of the process. In many award categories, applying for a fellowship often meant trusting one's fate to a largely anonymous panel of adjudicators whose deliberations took place in secret, whose criteria were unknown, and whose decisions were final and uncontestable. In the early years especially, all power resided within a system designed, shaped, and enacted by a small circle of like-minded insiders. Waiting to learn one's destiny became part of the application ritual, although that did not discourage some applicants from continuing to press their case while deliberations were taking place.

From the beginning, winning a coveted prize carried more than a financial stipend. A marketing plan crafted by the founders and put in place in late 1924 through discrete announcements in high-circulation newspapers introduced the concept of the foundation's fellowships to the public and generated a buzz. Before announcing a single winner, the foundation characterized the awards as uniquely esteemed. An award from the John Simon Guggenheim Memorial Foundation, it asserted, would provide an unmatched imprimatur and cultural cachet for the recipient: By extension, universities that included numerous Guggenheim winners among their faculty would be more prestigious. The plan, designed with the input of elite university administrators who had been consulted in the earliest days of the Guggenheims' fact-finding and feasibility studies, assured that their interests, their institutions, and their applicants would be privileged without that needing to be stated or consciously acted on. In reality, applicants reaped both economic and cultural capital from being named fellows, and the foundation as well as the fellows were empowered by such claims. Such has remained the case to the present.

In 1925 the John Simon Guggenheim Memorial Foundation music composition award was among fifteen initial categories of awards that were granted; the other categories were general nonfiction, classics, history-British, history-Renaissance, literature-English, literature-medieval, religion, botany, chemistry, mathematics, medicine, neuroscience, political science, and psychology. An additional fifteen categories were added in 1926, and eleven more in 1927. It would be the foundation's practice over the years to regularly add award categories as new fields emerged, thereby increasing its reach and the likelihood of attaining the goal of advancing and diffusing knowledge so boldly articulated in its mission statement. In the first fifteen years the foundation solidified its administrative personnel, chose advisers and advisory board members, instituted and refined policies, cultivated useful contacts and pipelines, selected early fellows, continuously expanded its sphere of influence, responded to challenges from within and without, and claimed its place as a new type of American institution: a strategically positioned, increasingly powerful, large private philanthropic network with international interests, resources, and ambitions.

For all its scrupulous attention to organizational details, however, the foundation operated within a social and cultural environment that was beyond its control and frequently unsympathetic to the Guggenheim family. It emerged amid the decade that saw the passage of the Nineteenth Amendment, as well as a tragic personal event that was the immediate inducement for its creation: the death of a child. Within five years of its founding, the Great Depression altered the nation's financial landscape. Quotas limiting Jews' participation in a range of organizations were imposed with impunity. If each individual is a unique product of his or her environment, then an institution, with its roster of stakeholders, is a composite of various histories, experiences, connections, and environments, and they all shape the result. And such was the case with the John Simon Guggenheim Memorial Foundation.

The foundation's assets were secured by the family's enormously successful and varied mining-related enterprises. Like other nineteenth-century titans of industry, the Guggenheims exploited the nation's natural resources as they built its infrastructure and their personal fortune. The first industrialists, like the first pioneers, operated with the tacit assumption that resources were unclaimed and unlimited, as endless and available as the land they traversed. With immediate gains so dazzling, and government policies encouraging growth at any cost, few businessmen paused to consider the long-term human or environmental consequences of their actions, or if they did, they ignored their findings.[3] In the nineteenth century U.S. capitalism didn't encourage selflessness or deferred gratification any more than it does today; it would have been a rare captain of industry who voluntarily postponed or sacrificed profits by thinking about the results of business practices beyond those enjoyed on the spot. From our vantage point in the third decade of the twenty-first century, it is hard to accept or forgive the lack of imagination, foresight, or concern exhibited for the environment by rapacious businessmen, but we need only consider how difficult it is today to convince fully informed industrialists of the benefits of long-game thinking even when consequences are known, acknowledged, and experienced.

In the decades surrounding the turn of the twentieth century the Guggenheim family boldly navigated the fear-filled politics and xenophobia of the time. Racial epithets were hurled at them because of their Jewishness as often as slurs were directed at African Americans and Italian and Chinese immigrants, if for different reasons. The family's wealth made them prime targets for focused resentment and cheap characterizations. Creating a foundation that announced it would not discriminate was an extraordinary move for any philanthropic organization in the 1920s, but it was especially so when the patrons themselves were often denied full participation in society because of their "race." Quotas aimed at restricting the number of Jews attending educational institutions, vacationing at tony resorts, or enjoying elite club memberships affected the Guggenheims directly.[4] Starting with its very first year, however, the foundation awarded fellowships across disciplines to people of color, Jews, Christians, women, and men, with no specific assumed philosophy or stated aesthetic agenda required.

Aware that it needed a reliable supply of qualified applicants, especially in the critical early years, in the months prior to its debut in 1925 the foundation sought advice from and forged alliances with a carefully chosen group of prestigious educational institutions and their administrators. Forming another tight circle within which the foundation operated, the earliest members of the Educational Advisory Board came from this same group of university personnel. In awarding the first fellowships, with few exceptions the foundation turned to those it knew to help decide the winners: the well-placed educational leaders who had supported their endeavor. It is little surprise that large numbers of awardees came from their institutions.

The Guggenheim Foundation was and remains its own private, confidential, and largely impenetrable world, but it operates within an array of high-culture institutions and shares many of their assumptions and behaviors. In her 1995 book *Rationalizing Culture: IRCAM, Boulez, and the Institutionalization of the Musical Avant-Garde* Georgina Born observed the dearth of scholarship focused on individual high-culture institutions; she offered a corrective with this paradigmatic study of the French music research institute. Subsequent studies of the MacDowell Colony by Bridget Falconer-Salkeld (2005), George E. Lewis's study of the African American musicians' collective AACM, the Association for the Advancement of Creative Musicians (2008), the edited collection of essays on the American Academy in Rome by Martin Brody (2014), and most recently Michael Uy's exploration of the Ford Foundation, the Rockefeller Foundation, and the National Endowment for the Arts (2020) have reinforced Born's argument that only by recognizing the embeddedness of cultural systems, values, and hierarchies within the practices of individual institutions do we understand the multitextuality of social relations between institutions and their cultures.[5]

Deciding early on that the Guggenheim Foundation's music awards would go to composers rather than others involved in musical culture—instrument makers, performers, teachers, impresarios—reduced the number of women and people of color in the pool of applicants. Limited access to university-level training in composition in the United States until the second half of the twentieth century eliminated the majority of Black and female applicants from serious consideration for any music composition fellowship. In addition, for decades adjudicators for such awards were overwhelmingly white, Western males: Born called them the "key animateur[s] or protagonist[s] in artistic development" at the Institut de Recherche et de Coordination Acoustique/Musique, the computer music research center founded in Paris in 1977 and directed by Pierre Boulez.[6] The same applied to those who decided the early Guggenheim Foundation music composition awardees. The judges were all male and, except for Latin American composers who had won their own fellowships and were called upon to evaluate others, they were all white. Both institutions assured applicants of confidentiality at all stages of the process. Ideally, confidentiality encouraged honest assessments of applicants without fear of hurt feelings or retribution, but it could also provide a veil behind which questionable criteria, incomplete evaluations, and unjustified judgments hid.[7] As Born observed, confidentiality can protect and perpetuate unchallenged "dominant aesthetic codes" as well as prevent fully informed histories from being written.

Beyond the tangible product that may or may not result from fellowship time focused on creative work, both organizations promised something initially less tangible but far more valuable over the long term: legitimation, authority, status, privilege, and power, and in some cases increased financial rewards. The Guggenheim Foundation engineered and understood the desirability of its imprimatur, carefully controlled its circulation, and created a demand for the "brand."[8] In return, those making the awards maintained their cultural power and continued the dominant aesthetic codes. The circularity of the process is reinforced but risks closing in on itself.[9]

Born's study of the French center illuminates the concentric contexts within which cultural institutions function and bolsters her argument that such scholarship is valuable. I see it as one model for this study of the early Guggenheim Foundation music composition awards. *Circle of Winners* considers the guiding principles of the original foundation and the ways they were imagined, enacted, tested, and modified to accommodate individual applicants and the rapidly changing culture of the 1920s and 1930s. Ultimately it illuminates the impact that the Guggenheim Foundation has had on one small sector of musical life in the United States and within the Western hemisphere.

* * *

Circle of Winners is more a historical study than a musicological one despite its focus on U.S. music culture and discussions of six composition award winners. It is broadly informed by archival work, biographical methods, and institutional theory. Chapter 1, "The Family," situates the Guggenheims, the patriarchs who emigrated from Switzerland to the United States in 1848 and established the various businesses that ultimately brought their family to a position of unrivaled economic clout. It surveys the challenges they faced as Jews in an overwhelmingly Christian nation, the impact of World War I, white fears of rampant immigration, the nation's growing interest in its neighbors in Mexico and South America, and philanthropic practices at the time.

Chapter 2, "The Foundation," focuses on a single year, 1924, when initial organizational issues were tackled and key administrative personnel were identified and appointed. The chapter illuminates the basic challenges they faced conceptualizing a music composition award program in particular. With no similarly ambitious philanthropic organization available to model how one identified, selected, or nurtured young composers, and with none of the original organizers possessing musical expertise of any kind, the founders of the John Simon Guggenheim Memorial Foundation were challenged to envision, organize, and oversee an operation of such size and ambition.

Chapter 3, "The Advisors," focuses on Thomas Whitney Surette, the man appointed to serve as music advisor to the foundation, a position he held for fifteen years. Surette was not a professional musician, he had no earned degree or university appointment in music, and he was not a known composer. By comparison with advisors for other award categories, who were traditionally credentialed and recognized experts and practitioners in the fields they advised, Surette was a decidedly curious choice. For several reasons, however, not the least of which were Surette's availability, proximity, and connections through his wife's well-placed Philadelphia family, he emerged as an acceptable if not optimal choice. The story of Surette's tenure provides insights into the ways in which little-known, questionably qualified individuals can become impactful culture makers when given the opportunity and left unchallenged.

Chapter 4, "The Network," provides an aerial view of the network of professional relationships and associations that was carefully built by foundation organizers, especially Frank Aydelotte, president of Swarthmore College, and Henry Allen Moe, who was initially appointed secretary of the foundation. Before institutional theory and network theory were recognized scholarly tools, the John Simon Guggenheim Memorial Foundation pioneered the thinking and techniques that would become codified in their philosophies. The chapter reveals some of the earliest challenges faced by the new foundation as it systematically crafted an advantageous leadership role for itself in an ever-enlarging web of professional, artistic, and government-related organizations.

Chapter 5, "The College," looks at the founding of Black Mountain College as an experimental educational endeavor whose creation was thoroughly intertwined with members of the extended Aydelotte family and their aspirations. In the brief and hurried months of the college's germination in the summer of 1933, organizational work was carried out at the Foundation's New York office under Moe's watchful eye. Supporters were identified using Aydelotte's and the foundation's connections. Although Black Mountain College did not share an official or legal association with the foundation, Aydelotte, Moe, Surette and their associates invested extraordinary amounts of time, energy, and resources in the North Carolina school. Chapter 5 provides a pre-history of what we think of as "Black Mountain College" and the artistic experimentation for which it became famous in the late 1940s and early 1950s.

Chapter 6, "The Winners," focuses on six early music composition awardees and considers their relationships with foundation insiders and the people who championed their causes, the processes of their selection, their fellowship work, and their places in American (writ large) music culture today. On the surface, Aaron Copland (awards: 1925, 1926), Roger Sessions (awards: 1926, 1927), Ruth Crawford (award: 1930), George Antheil (awards: 1932, 1933), William Grant Still (awards: 1934, 1935, 1938), and Carlos Chávez (awards: 1938, 1956) appear to exemplify the foundation's commitment to awarding fellowships "without distinction on account of race, color or creed, scholars, scientists and artists of either sex in the prosecution of their labors," and I originally chose the individuals precisely because of their diversity. A deeper exploration of the composers' experiences with the foundation, however, complicates any superficial or uncritical reading of their selection.

The final chapter, "Concluding Thoughts," looks back to assess what the early composition awards accomplished for American musical culture at the time, and forward to consider the impact of the John Simon Guggenheim Memorial Foundation on the contemporary music scene. I review the ways in which it simultaneously borrowed, created anew, and reinforced what are today touted as best practices for guaranteeing institutional success. I also reflect on how the Guggenheims' business interests in the mineral-rich lands of the far western United States and in Central and South America informed and advanced the diplomatic and aesthetic aspirations of the United States as it strove to be a good neighbor. The chapter concludes with a reflection on the foundation and its sources of wealth: How do we in the twenty-first century understand the origins and responsibilities of wealth, whether defined by personal privilege, real property, financial security, or unfettered opportunity for education and advancement? What is a scholar's responsibility when someone else's questionably gained wealth becomes a potential source of funding for conducting one's own work? Knowing we can't undo the past, how can we respond to it in honest and productive ways? *Circle of Winners* doesn't presume to have the answer, but I hope that this study can keep the question alive.

1

THE FAMILY

When family patriarch Simon Guggenheim (1792–1869) and his family arrived in Philadelphia, Pennsylvania, from Lengnau, Switzerland, in 1848, he and his son Meyer Guggenheim (1828–1905) took up the only trade that didn't require significant capital investment: They peddled essential household goods to wives in the city and surrounding areas. Quickly recognizing that controlling both the manufacture and the distribution of their best-selling products—stove polish and coffee essence—would increase their profits, the two expanded their business to involve more family members and include the production of the polish and the essence. Four years after immigrating and saving enough money, Meyer Guggenheim married Barbara Meyer, who had traveled on the same ship with the Guggenheims when they came to the country. Between 1854 and 1873, Meyer and Barbara Meyer Guggenheim had eleven children including a set of twin sons, one of whom, Simon (1867–1941), would start the John Simon Guggenheim Memorial Foundation in 1924.[1]

Meyer's family steadily prospered, not with an eye toward philanthropic endeavors but with the twin goals of economic success and financial freedom, conditions denied to Jews living in Switzerland at the time. It is doubtful that the patriarch Simon could have imagined the size of the fortune his family would eventually accumulate. He and his wife Rachel had lived modestly in Philadelphia, and although there was little possibility that the Guggenheims would be welcomed into the elite circles of the original Protestant families who had also come to Pennsylvania seeking religious tolerance, opportunities for advancement were significantly greater there than they had been in the ghetto of Lengnau, where law and practice kept Jews from owning property and businesses or entering various trades and industries.

In 1869, the year his father Simon died, forty-one-year-old Meyer became head of an ever-enlarging family, and the Golden Spike was driven at Promontory, Utah, linking the Central Pacific and Union Pacific railroads and by extension the nation's many private and public rail systems. Railroads revolutionized transportation, expedited the conveyance of raw materials from remote extraction sites to central processing locations and then to their final destinations for distribution, and made possible the conquest of the continent including the removal of many of its indigenous inhabitants. Over the years Meyer Guggenheim diversified his activities. Using the same strategy that he and his father had employed twenty years earlier, identifying and supplying necessities, Meyer reinvested his profits in an increasingly lucrative series of businesses. He opened a grocery store, provided clothing and materials for the Union Army, became a successful spice merchant, founded the American Concentrated Lye Company to capture the market on the manufacture and sale of soap, purchased critical shares in a connector railroad needed by Jay Gould to complete his dream, the Missouri Pacific line, and with his wife's family connections in Switzerland began a lace and embroidery import business.[2] By the late 1870s Meyer Guggenheim had formally brought his seven sons into his enterprises, which he named M. Guggenheim's Sons. Good timing, good (business) instincts, and good luck allowed Meyer to participate in the nation's expansionist crusade, which, starting at the beginning of the nineteenth century, was the result of natural resource discovery, extraction, and exploitation, all made possible by the railroad.

Despite the steady increase in the family's financial security, the business venture that would eventually catapult the Guggenheims into the ranks of the nation's monied, if not social, elite was none of these. In 1881 Meyer bought a $5,000 stake in a pair of lead and silver mines located just outside Leadville, Colorado: the A.Y. and Minnie mines. As Guggenheim biographer John H. Davis explains: "He bought the interest from an old Quaker acquaintance, Charles D. Graham, a grocery-store owner and speculator in Western mineral lands, who had borrowed to buy his two-thirds interest and then couldn't pay half the note when it was due."[3] Meyer purchased one-half of Graham's holdings, thus acquiring a third interest in the mines. This would be Meyer's smartest business move, the one that secured his family's future.[4] It was also the first documented financial interaction of the Guggenheim family with Philadelphia Quakers.

Meyer would have been familiar with and respected the business acumen of the many Quakers who, over the years, had lived in and around Philadelphia: The city had Quaker roots as much as Boston had Puritan ones even if the Quaker population had diminished significantly since the city's founding. He would also have appreciated their professed belief in the equality of people regardless of religion or creed, a quality that distinguished Quakers from other

Christian sects at the time.[5] Joseph Wharton (1826–1909), a contemporary of Meyer's and a prominent Philadelphia Quaker, was a successful industrialist. He had co-founded what would become Bethlehem Steel in 1857 and then created the nation's first university business school, which today bears his name, at the University of Pennsylvania in 1881. Meyer's youngest son, William, graduated from the university, a school that prided itself on its practical as well as philosophical curriculum.[6] In addition, in 1864 Wharton, along with other family members and Quaker friends, founded Swarthmore College; he served as its president from 1883 to 1907. From the beginning, Swarthmore enrolled both men and women, because equality of the sexes was also a basic tenet of the faith.[7] Connections with Quakers and an appreciation of their values seem to have remained strong among the Philadelphia-based Guggenheims. In 1924, when Meyer's son Simon, now a former senator from Colorado, sought a man to head his foundation, he appointed Frank Aydelotte (1880–1956), who had been serving as president of Swarthmore College since 1921. Not a Quaker himself but respecting, supporting, and implementing their beliefs, Aydelotte maintained both positions until 1939, when he left the college presidency to assume the directorship of the Institute of Advanced Study in Princeton. He kept his appointment as chair of the Educational Advisory Board at the Guggenheim Foundation even after leaving the institute in 1947, all the time building a large network of academic and philanthropic associations for himself and the foundation. The mission statement of the John Simon Guggenheim Memorial Foundation, drawn up in 1924, affirmed and even bested values central to Quakerism. It would insist on the equality of all fellowship applicants regardless of race, religion, gender, or creed.

Though he had no knowledge of mining or experience in the industry but understood the need for these natural resources to a growing nation, Meyer's speculation yielded a windfall. Davis explains why: "The ore in them, though highly refractory, was nevertheless found to have a higher silver content than any of their neighboring properties. In fact, they had the highest silver content of any mine in Leadville."[8] Meyer had secured his family's future, but he was not satisfied. Despite earning close to three-quarters of a million dollars in 1888 from his mining interests alone, Guggenheim once again recognized that the greatest financial benefits accrued to those who controlled all aspects of a business. He begrudged profits lost to those who smelted his premium ore. Drawing heavily on his own resources, Guggenheim partnered with Edward R. Holden, who owned a smelter in Denver, to form the Philadelphia Smelting and Refining Company. As Davis observed: "Before the mines were exhausted they would yield the Guggenheims over $15 million. . . . It was the first step toward the Guggenheim's control of the smelting industry in America."[9] Within a few years, the Guggenheims, father and sons, sold the lace and embroidery import business and focused their energies on the lucrative field of mineral extraction, refinement, and sales. Stationing his sons Benjamin (b. 1865) and William (b. 1868) in Colorado so that the family had its own men on the ground overseeing operations, Meyer controlled the business first from Philadelphia and then from New York, where the family moved its headquarters in order to be closer to the new financial center of the nation.[10]

When Meyer died in 1905, he left a large fortune controlled exclusively by his seven surviving sons. His was the quintessential rags-to-riches American story. Many poor immigrants achieved financial success, but few would own a success story quite like Meyer Guggenheim's. Although being Jewish presented fewer obstacles to the Guggenheims in their new homeland than it had in Switzerland, they would not be allowed to forget their "alien" race in their adopted nation. In a world of nineteenth-century American capitalists, captains of industry, and less flatteringly "robber barons," populated by Astors and Carnegies, Fricks and Goulds, Harrimans, Huntingtons, Mellons, Morgans, Rockefellers, and Vanderbilts, Calvinists, Episcopalians, Northern Baptists, and Moravians, the Guggenheims stuck out for their Jewish ancestry.[11]

In the early decades of the twentieth century, the word *race* was used as often to distinguish Jews (the alien race) from Christians as to differentiate Blacks from whites. The word's more exclusive usage, identifying people along color lines, is a relatively recent practice and is continually morphing, as the increasingly common usage of *brown* to characterize the skin tone of multiple ethnic groups attests.[12] Racial distinctions depend on social practices and political exigencies as well as national policies, and they change over time. Jews, alternately referred to as "Israelites" and distinguished by some at the time from Hebrews, were excluded from participation in most of the fraternal organizations and clubs that were home to others of similar economic class. This was the case for the Guggenheims despite their fortune's being made in business ventures like those of the insiders, including natural resource extraction and railroads. Jewish Americans were frequently turned away from hotels and resorts; one such incident attracted nationwide attention thanks to a story that ran in the *New York Times*. In June 1877 the successful New York financier Joseph Seligman and his family were refused accommodations at the Grand Union Hotel in Saratoga Springs, New York, by order of Henry Hilton, although they had vacationed there multiple times before. The *Times* screamed: "a sensation at saratoga. new rules for the grand union. no jews to be admitted—mr. seligman, the banker, and his family sent away."[13]

The Seligman incident replicated the quotidian racism experienced by numerous private citizens at the hands of small companies. When, however, an event involving famous, wealthy individuals occurred, it illuminated, as never before, behaviors heretofore quietly endured by an entire group of people. "The Seligman Scandal," also known as "The Seligman-Hilton Affair," was the first antisemitic incident in the United States to capture the public's attention; it would become part of Guggenheim family history when in 1894 one of Meyer's sons married a daughter of the Seligmans.[14] While it energized some, including Henry Ward Beecher—who knew Joseph Seligman and preached a sermon provoked by the encounter—to tackle the issue, it also affirmed other business owners who already practiced discrimination. Racial discrimination directed at Jews and African Americans (as well as Italians, Chinese, and Irish), was woven into the nation's social fabric.[15] Antisemitism was part of the culture navigated by the Guggenheim family in Switzerland and in the United States.

By the early years of the twentieth century the Guggenheims were the wealthiest Jewish family in the United States and among the wealthiest families in the nation, period.[16] Their business interests extended from the Yukon to Mexico and Brazil, Bolivia and Chile, Angola and the Belgian Congo (now named the Democratic Republic of the Congo), and Malaysia. They controlled the global mining industry; they could not be ignored. Today, what was once Meyer's family-run business is a diversified global enterprise, administered by family and non-family members, with assets in the hundreds of billions of dollars.

In the years surrounding World War I, the Guggenheims' Latin American mining interests meshed seamlessly with the nation's twin concerns for the security of the Western hemisphere against possible incursions by Axis powers and its designs on foreign natural resources; they also capitalized on what Carol Hess has described as a growing popular fascination with the spiritually rich cultures found south of the U.S. border.[17] Relations between the United States and its Latin neighbors were complex, however. On January 16, 1917, a telegram sent by the German Foreign Office to its diplomat in Mexico City instructed Ambassador Heinrich von Eckardt to urge Mexico to side with Germany and the Axis powers if the United States entered the war. The so-called Zimmermann Cable, which was intercepted and decoded by British intelligence, warned of imminent increased submarine warfare against the United States and promised the return of parts of Texas, New Mexico, and Arizona to Mexico at the war's conclusion if Mexico joined forces with Germany. The 1917 proposal was not an isolated threat against the hemisphere, however, because Germany had attempted to build on growing international discontent and incite discord between the United States and Mexico as early as 1914. With the Zimmermann proposal Germany hoped to distract from, disrupt, and delay U.S. troop support and aid to England and France long enough to defeat their armies. Confirmation of the authenticity of the communiqué and its release to the public by President Woodrow Wilson on February 28, and further confirmation by Zimmermann himself, the high-ranking civil servant who had sent the original note, ultimately convinced the United States to declare war on Germany on April 6. Although the "Good Neighbor Policy" became the official U.S. position in 1933 with the administration of Franklin Delano Roosevelt, its seeds were firmly planted sixteen years earlier by Wilson. Given that the Guggenheims' mining business was dependent for its profits on the cheap labor available to the south, it behooved the family to support the nation's position against the Axis powers. Continued access to rich Central and South American sites depended on maintaining the existing hemispheric balance of power, however imbalanced it was. The nation's business and national interests were aligned.

Pan-American thinking had its start with Simón Bolívar and was formalized when the leader called a Pan-American conference in Panama in 1826. In 1904, according to Stephanie N. Stallings, "the U.S. government . . . appropriated the term 'Pan-American' in the [Theodore] Roosevelt Corollary to the Monroe Doctrine."[18] The movement achieved what Hess has referred to as "the 'golden age' of Pan-Americanism" in the 1930s and 1940s.[19] The Guggenheims were positioned to take advantage of the confluence of politics and economics, and so was the foundation. The earliest organizers' letters to discuss a foundation focused on "transmarine education" attest to a specific interest in South American exchanges.[20] In April 1924, the Guggenheims' general counsel recommended consulting with the "Director of the Pan-American Union in Washington, D.C."[21] In his "Second Letter of Gift," dated June 7, 1929, Simon Guggenheim clarified his intentions for involvement in the Americas. He explained that in the first letter "we purposely . . . did not limit the operation of the Foundation to this country. We had in mind then what we desire to make effective now by this new endowment, namely, to assist in increasing the interaction among the American republics, each upon the other, in the arts and sciences, in education, and in the learned professions."[22]

Beyond recognizing business interests, the international turn evident in the Guggenheims' expanded program reflected the nation's new status as an important creator and consumer of culture. The tide of influence that had coursed so powerfully westward from Europe to the Americas for centuries changed in the interwar years in large part because of World War I, and the John Simon Guggenheim Memorial Foundation would be at the front edge of that new wave. Acting on the realization that cultural currents flowed in all directions, north and south as well as east and west, the foundation would ultimately disseminate the art, music, dance, and technology of the Americas, writ large, to the world.[23]

The senator made no apologies for his family's economic interests in the American hemisphere: "My brothers and I have long been engaged in commerce with many of the republics to the south of the United States, and we know that there are no longer any important factors of economic isolation separating us. But a similar commerce of things of the mind, of spiritual values, is yet to be accomplished. It is Mrs. Guggenheim's and my hope that this new fund may assist in supplying that great need."[24] Within the context of a family business philosophy that privileged profits above all else, former senator Simon Guggenheim demonstrated unusual sensitivity to the variety of peoples and cultures that made up the "republics to the south" when he explained:

> We are proceeding in the conviction that we have much to learn in those countries that are our elder sisters in the civilization of America and much to give their scholars and creative workers. That is fundamental to our thinking on this subject. Nor must we fall into the easy error of grouping them all together in our thinking under the general term 'Latin American republics'; for they are as individual as our own country is individual, and each will make her distinctive contribution to the commerce of the mind that we contemplate.[25]

It is ironic that the alien Simon Guggenheim could acknowledge the distinct "elder sisters" of Central and South America and their potential contributions to "the commerce of the mind" when his family business appeared to be untroubled by exploiting the natural resources of the lands belonging to the same international siblings. At the same time, the U.S. government was encouraging the homogenization of remaining Native American peoples to preserve what was left of the once distinct and variegated "American Indian" populations at home.[26]

With an initial gift of more than three million dollars and a second gift of one million dollars, the foundation's assets grew close to five million dollars and enabled the establishment of the Latin American program.[27] In 1929 the John Simon Guggenheim Memorial Foundation officially launched its Latin American fellowship awards and used the opportunity for cultural exchange and education to promote the "national priority" of "north-south amity."[28] Given the location of so many of the family's mining and smelting operations, it is not surprising that in the program's first years of operation Mexico emerged as the Latin American country to receive the most awards by a significant margin.[29]

For the Guggenheims, commerce was the model, whether considering raw materials or ideas. They understood access to any type of product as the right of anyone with means. When it came to the John Simon Guggenheim Memorial Foundation, it could provide the means to access ideas by the broadest range of fellows, and that was a noble undertaking. Modern scholars of colonialism, however, have an easy target in the Guggenheim family's business philosophy when it is applied to the seizure of others' resources—intellectual, cultural, or natural—for personal gain. Enormous wealth guaranteed that the family enjoyed the most favorable conditions for its business operations at home and abroad.

Years earlier, in 1907, the same mining wealth had bought Simon Guggenheim a different kind of resource, his Colorado senatorial seat, which the successful candidate unabashedly acknowledged in public speeches that were published.[30]

As Davis explained, being a senator from Colorado was "not an unrealistic ambition" for a Guggenheim, "especially since the greatest political issue of the day was silver, and Colorado was a silver state, and Simon Guggenheim's family owned the choicest silver mines in Colorado."[31] Using gifts, promises, and threats Simon secured what no other Guggenheim brother possessed: a high elected position. The seventh surviving son of Meyer and Barbara became Senator Guggenheim.

At the same time the nation worked to strengthen relations with its southern neighbors, it endured growing fears of unchecked immigration, the headline-grabbing red scare, and continuing rampant antisemitism: All three were related to increasing numbers of Eastern European Jews fleeing pogroms in their native countries. In a period of three years, 1919–1921, the Palmer Raids, conducted by the Department of Justice, aimed to intimidate and capture anarchist radicals, many of whom were identified as Jewish; almost 250 high-profile "disruptive people" (alien anarchists), including the writer and political agitator Emma Goldman, were deported to the Soviet Union under the provisions of the Alien Act of 1918; and the Emergency Immigration Act (also known as the Emergency Quota Act) was put into effect. Elite private universities responded in kind and enacted their own unofficial quota systems by limiting the number of Jewish students admitted: Harvard, Yale and Princeton could elect to fill their classes with "legacy" students, the sons of former students, thereby leaving little room for those without the proper family ties and Protestant bloodlines. It is ironic, given current notions of undesirable populations, that no citizens from Latin American countries were restricted from entering the United States as a result of the 1921 Immigration Act. It wouldn't have served the nation's economic or political interests at the time to exclude them.[32]

Beyond the economic, political, and social conditions that affected the Guggenheim family and its business enterprises, more specific forces acted on the creation of the John Simon Guggenheim Memorial Foundation. The immediate impulse was the desire on the part of Simon and Olga Hirsch Guggenheim (1877–1970) to memorialize their son John Simon (1905–1922), who had died suddenly of mastoiditis at age seventeen the spring before he was to start college.[33] They hoped "in some sense to continue the influence of the young life of eager aspiration."[34] The tragedy prompted the couple to invest some of their share of the family fortune in the creation of an international, philanthropic memorial unlike any existing in the nation at the time. They endeavored to honor their child by supporting intellectual work that they imagined he might have pursued were he to have had the chance. In alignment with their own interests and the ones they had hoped to cultivate in John Simon, they were especially eager to support artists and musicians; in doing so, they also distinguished their foundation from existing organizations.[35]

Although the previous two generations of the family hadn't shown any philanthropic inclinations, early on Simon and Olga Guggenheim exercised a penchant for public-spiritedness.[36] When they married at the Waldorf Astoria in Manhattan on Thanksgiving Day, November 24, 1898, they celebrated by providing Thanksgiving dinners for five thousand of the city's poor children. In honor of their first son's birth in 1905 they donated money to the Colorado School of Mines for a building that would bear the family's name. When their second son was born two years later, the couple donated money for a law school building at the University of Colorado. Like Joseph Wharton, who had started investing in educational institutions in his hometown of Philadelphia fifty years earlier, the Guggenheims directed a significant portion of their discretionary resources to educational enterprises. The John Simon Guggenheim Memorial Foundation would be their most famous and enduring gift to a broad educational project.[37]

Now that he was a member of Congress's "millionaires club," Simon Guggenheim and his family could help shape political policies that favored their various business enterprises from a position inside the government.[38] As is typical with the well-heeled today, the Guggenheims bought their way into the club.

In 1896 William Jennings Bryan had excited Democratic National Convention attendees with a rousing speech arguing for the moral superiority of a bimetal monetary standard (silver *and* gold rather than gold exclusively). He had predicted that "the producing masses of the nations and the world . . . the laboring interests, and the toilers everywhere" would risk crucifixion "on a cross of gold" if the opposition were to win.[39] In 1907, Simon Guggenheim could take advantage of Colorado's continued economic dependence upon its silver wealth: To fight for a bimetal standard was to fight for Colorado. That many miners lost their lives (had been "crucified") in mining accidents or died early deaths because of the grueling twelve-hour days of dangerous work required of them was a known risk. Latching on to the sensitive topic, Guggenheim campaigned on the promise of an eight-hour day, and he delivered, at least for a brief time after his election. Shortly after taking office, however, the twelve-hour day returned. Miners who had voted for Guggenheim were justifiably incensed.

By 1910 the family's strategic business practices had become the subject of derision, as the poem "The Gobbling Guggenheims," which first appeared in the *Washington Times* in 1910, attests:

> The Guggenheims will get you if you don't watch out;
> They're gobbling all the coal lands of the West and North and South.
> It simply is appalling when you think what they're about.
> They'll surely gobble everything inside the earth and out.

They've gone into Alaska and optioned all the coal;
They've searched the mountains over and gobbled all the gold.
The water rights they do not own are very few, I'm told;
In fact this clan of Guggenheims is growing all too bold.

In Denver, Colorado, they own the whole blamed town.
The copper mines they cabbaged and nailed securely down.
The state was bought by Simon, and he did the job up brown.
For he wears the senate toga now and owns our Washington.

It really looks a good deal like they'd gobble all in sight.
On top the earth or under it, so fearful is their might.
They'll gobble all there is to get and turn you inside out.
The Guggenheims will get you if you don't watch out.[40]

With the venerated patriarchs of the family instilling in their progeny the belief that the accumulation of wealth (privilege, power) trumped all else, clever criticisms, poetic or otherwise, meant little. Recognizing that approval was unlikely for members of this alien "clan," the family had steeled itself against condemnation; it would not yield to public opinion, although it would work hard to shape it. Starting in 1924, as Simon Guggenheim turned his attention to creating the foundation that would bear his son's name, he recognized that it behooved him to win the approval of at least certain circles of potential supporters. With economic, political, and most important, personal motivations animating the creation of the foundation, it was set to succeed.

In the early decades of the twentieth century institutionalized philanthropy was not yet formalized or practiced on a large scale. From the beginning it looked different from its European progenitors, evolved as they had been from the church, then courts, the patronage of minor nobility, and governmental programs. In the United States philanthropy increasingly became the responsibility of those whose fortunes owed their existence to railroads, extractive industries, and capitalism.[41] It depended almost entirely on a combination of providers: wealthy individual patrons who supported artists and composers whose projects aligned with their own tastes, the most famous of them Isabella Stewart Gardner (1840–1924), Jeannette Thurber (1850–1946), Elizabeth Sprague Coolidge (1864–1953), Blanche Walton (1871–1963), and Gloria Vanderbilt Whitney (1875–1942), among others; a few small private funds whose existence and selection process were not publicized; and local churches, groups, clubs, and societies dedicated to the arts. The National Association of Women's Music Clubs provided some of the most important early support for musical culture in the nation by cultivating an interest in music among its members and sponsoring local performances of what members considered morally uplifting music. They later bankrolled competitions to encourage and award young American composers, but on a completely different scale.[42]

From the start, the Guggenheims imagined something different, a philanthropic foundation that was larger, better endowed, self-consciously more prestigious, formally and centrally administered, connected to a network of academic institutions in the United States and abroad, and meant to endure for the ages. As with all of their enterprises, they thought big. Since nothing the size or scope of what they imagined existed in the United States, they looked elsewhere for ideas. Two exemplars existed: the Rhodes Scholarship program and the American Academy in Rome. For myriad reasons, one provided a more adaptable model than the other.

In 1924 the Rhodes Scholarship program offered an attractive template for the aspiring foundation, in part because many of the original planners were Rhodes scholars themselves; they were familiar with its operations and had remained engaged with the program in leadership roles. As G. Thomas Tanselle explained in his chronology of the foundation, on February 25, 1924, "Carroll A. Wilson (general counsel to Guggenheim Brothers, a former Rhodes Scholar, and a scholarly bibliophile) wrote to Frank Aydelotte (President of Swarthmore College, former Rhodes Scholar, and American Secretary to the Rhodes Trustees), asking him his advice about a plan that was developing in Simon Guggenheim's mind for an appropriate memorial to his son John Simon."[43] Like Cecil Rhodes, Simon Guggenheim was interested in a large-scale educational initiative and could fund it with his mining wealth.[44] Although the Guggenheim Foundation took a cue for its structure and operations from the Rhodes Scholarships, which Senator Guggenheim said he wanted to "supplement" in his original February 23, 1925, statement announcing the establishment of the foundation, significant differences marked the Guggenheim project, not the least of which was the inclusion of women and older students in the applicant pool. In addition, whereas Rhodes scholars were required to attend Oxford University, the alma mater of the scholarships' founder, Cecil Rhodes (1853–1902), Guggenheim Fellows had greater freedom to spend their award year anywhere their work required, although originally there was an assumption that it would include European study. As Tanselle explained, "About eighty percent of the annual budget would be used to allow young men and women from the United States to pursue their work in Europe, and the other twenty percent would be used to bring South Americans to the United States." Tanselle quoted Wilson as saying, "I gather from my talk with [Senator Guggenheim] that so far as the 80 per cent is concerned, he is interested first in extending the benefits of his gift to persons of musical and artistic ability, or along other lines more remote from pure scholarship, and second, that he wishes these benefits to be applied wherever in Europe proves to be best suited to the particular beneficiary, rather than have them confined to a single country or specific institution."[45]

Like Simon Guggenheim, Cecil Rhodes had also been a political figure. Rhodes served as prime minister of the Cape Colony in South Africa from 1890 to 1896 and was committed to British imperialism and training of world leaders, goals that he saw as integral to achieving world peace. Such a position lent a more overtly political agenda to his eponymous scholarship program from its beginnings in 1903. Guggenheim never characterized his hopes for his foundation in such singularly imperialistic or universalist terms, although he was idealistic regarding what his foundation could accomplish on behalf of the nation. From the beginning, the Guggenheims' desire to memorialize their son conferred an additional moral and humane purpose on their enterprise. Their focus on music and the arts was personal and distinctive.

Guggenheim hoped that support from the foundation would "increase, at least to some degree, the vitality and effectiveness of American education."[46] His own educational experiences were quite different from those of Rhodes. Simon Guggenheim and his brother Benjamin were both graduates of Central High School in Philadelphia and Union Business College, later renamed Peirce School of Business Administration, also in Philadelphia. Through the efforts of his foundation appointees, however, the senator became sensitized to the difficulties endured by American college and university faculty who, after having earned a sabbatical, often couldn't take advantage of the opportunity because of inadequate compensation. Guggenheim observed that European educational systems offered faculty "greater opportunities" to "remain productive scholars." "It is my hope," he wrote, "that this Foundation will do something to provide a similar opportunity for young men and women in the United States."[47]

Like Rhodes, Guggenheim envisioned an institution with global impact. He could easily embrace Rhodes's desire to "promote leadership marked by public spirit and good character, and to 'render war impossible' by promoting friendship between the great powers."[48] It was while the United States was emerging as an international player that Senator and Mrs. Guggenheim envisioned the nation's scholars, composers, and artists as benefiting the entire world. The Guggenheims' insistence, among other things, that their awards be available to scholars, scientists and artists (and primarily to artists and composers), and to both men and women, distinguished their plan at the outset from the British model: Among other restrictive criteria, neither artists nor women were considered for Rhodes Scholarships.[49] The intentional absence of a stated aesthetic agenda also differentiated the foundation from what might have been a more obvious model, the American Academy in Rome, although it could be argued that in the early years a clear musical-aesthetic preference for avoiding high levels of dissonance characterized the majority of the foundation's music composition fellows.

The American Academy in Rome began offering multi-year residential fellowships to composers in 1921. Its insistence on classical artistic values above all others, however, provided the Guggenheims with a model of what *not* to do with their own composition awards.[50] The co-founders of the academy also included men who had made their fortunes in railroads and extractive industries, although the Jewish mining barons were not among them. The names of the academy's founders read like a who's who of nineteenth-century industrialists: Carnegie, Frick, Morgan, Rockefeller, and Vanderbilt.[51] Henry Clay Frick, Henry Walters, James Pierpont Morgan, and Cornelius Vanderbilt each contributed $100,000, as did Harvard University.[52] The sheer number of unrelated stakeholders supporting the academy also distinguished it from the Guggenheim enterprise.[53]

As a residential program, the site of the academy was all-important. According to Brody, the Italian hillside provided both visual inspiration and spiritual reinforcement for the aesthetic agenda.[54] The visual paean to the past was the perfect environment for encouraging in-kind architectural and musical responses. If the rallying cry of the Futurists was to destroy museums and relics of the past, the American Academy was there to make sure they were preserved forever. If the goal was not to "Europeanize" American composers per se, the hope was that a thorough commitment to traditional European genres, structures, and processes would provide the most effective framework for an American voice to develop.

In her essay "'Picked Young Men,' Facilitating Women, and Emerging Composers," Carol Oja considers "the deep stylistic conservatism generally advocated—in some respects even mandated—by the Academy."[55] Quoting from a 1923–1924 annual report summarizing the values of the architecture program at the academy, Oja attested that it was "'founded upon a settled belief' based on 'the unquestionable acceptance of the supremacy of the arts of classical antiquity and the Italian Renaissance, to the exclusion of all other styles and periods.'"[56] Beyond its devotion to classicism, it was also decidedly anti-modern.

Candidates demonstrated their allegiance to the academy's conservative project by proving their mastery of traditional Western genres and forms. Application materials had to include "two compositions, one for orchestra either alone or in combination such as a sonata for violin and piano, a trio for violin, 'cello and pianoforte, or possibly for some less usual combination of chamber instruments." Compositions had to confirm "facility in handling the larger instrumental forms, such as the sonata form or free modifications of it." To that end, "a sonata for pianoforte or a fugue of large dimensions will be accepted." To clarify that the academy was not a training ground for merely talented amateurs or aspiring composers but a residential program for those who had already achieved a high level of technical prowess, the rules stated that the committee would not consider "songs and short pianoforte pieces."[57] Instead, "the award [would] be made only to a musician of exceptional promise already thoroughly trained in technique."[58]

Beyond clear aesthetic preferences, additional requirements limited the pool of acceptable applicants, distinguishing it even further from the Guggenheim Foundation. Only "unmarried men who are citizens of the United States" were eligible. Oja summarizes: "As a matter of explicit principle, then, a select group of young men were handed the keys to an exclusive club. In fact, the homogeneity of the fellows was narrowly defined: there were no Jews, no African Americans, no women. The first two bans remained unstated, and the final one was a founding principle, repeatedly articulated over the years."[59]

The first composers-in-residence embodied the American Academy's aesthetic agenda: Leo Sowerby and Howard Hanson (1921–1924), Randall Thompson (1922–1925), and Wintter Watts, who overlapped with Thompson during his residency years (1923–1925), favored more traditional genres and even sacred and choral music composition. Insistence on such an agenda is noteworthy given the decade in which the academy's music composition fellowships were first awarded. In a period more famous in the art world for the anarchical activities of the Surrealists, Cubists, Expressionists, Dadaists, Fauvists, and Futurists and in music for the modernists and ultra-modernists, dissonant counterpoint and machine-age music, the project of the American Academy was in every sense a rearguard action.

The John Simon Guggenheim Memorial Foundation music composition awards aspired to be different. It is hard to imagine that the family's lived experiences as Jewish residents of Quaker-founded Philadelphia and as outsiders in a frequently hostile and overwhelmingly Christian nation did not play a role in shaping their mission. From the beginning there would be no requirements that prevented fellowships from being awarded to Jews, Gentiles, African Americans, Caucasians, Mexicans, Argentines, men, women, married people, or single applicants. There would be no aesthetic litmus test, although the values of the limited number of academic institutions that provided the initial feeder system for the foundation determined to a large extent who was most likely to obtain an award and what their artistic preferences would be. It is possible that had the original administrators engaged a musical advisor with strong composing credentials of his own and a clear alignment with a school or tradition, there might have been a greater emphasis on a particular style of work, but as readers will learn, they did not.

In a study that concludes with a discussion of six early Guggenheim composition fellows, it is hard to argue that the John Simon Guggenheim Memorial Foundation insisted on an aesthetic criterion that approached in its prescriptiveness what was required for consideration by the American Academy. If the academy privileged the values of the conservative Austro-Germanic classical symphonic tradition, in the first fifteen years of its existence the Guggenheim Foundation had closer ties to a burgeoning Franco-American aesthetic and then a Pan-American one, both encouraged and reinforced by the Conservatoire Américain, Nadia Boulanger, and Aaron Copland. Emerging as it did in a decade that celebrated having survived the twin traumas of World War I and a devastating flu pandemic, the Guggenheim Foundation promised an opportunity for more expansive musical thought. One hundred years after the foundation made its first composition awards, the nation's music culture still feels the effects of those early choices in the composers it celebrates and the histories that get written, and those that don't.

2

THE FOUNDATION

The emergence of the John Simon Guggenheim Memorial Foundation in early 1925 was the result of no less than one full year of intense, systematic, and thorough preparations. Its action plan combined proven business practices employed by the founders of a global mining empire with sophisticated research and administrative skills honed by established scholars in leadership positions at colleges and universities across the United States. Ultimately, the foundation owes its longevity and impact to its reliable funding, strategic agenda, attention to detail, and allegiance to its original mission.

The twelve-month effort involved the focused work of three men in particular besides Simon Guggenheim: Carroll A. Wilson, Frank Aydelotte, and Henry Allen Moe came on board as plans coalesced and needs arose. Wilson, chief legal counsel to the Guggenheim Brothers, helped hatch the idea for the foundation idea alongside the senator. With Simon and Olga Guggenheims' permission he initiated talks with Frank Aydelotte to oversee the range of issues associated with the start-up phase. Using his considerable experience with educational and philanthropic endeavors and his international network of friends and associates, Aydelotte took charge. Within a few months, and on the senator's and Wilson's approval, Aydelotte engaged Henry Allen Moe, initially on a trial basis but ultimately as a full-time employee; Moe was known to both Wilson and Aydelotte. Using all the means at his disposal, Aydelotte, later joined by Moe, studied existing educational philanthropic organizations and compared their various missions to identify holes and avoid duplication. They assessed information on the demographics served, and eventually conducted personal interviews with dozens of university presidents, deans, and administrators at institutions located in the Northeast, along the Atlantic Seaboard, and in the Midwest to learn how a new organization of the kind the Guggenheims imagined could best serve the goal of supplementing and supporting transmarine education.

Early on, Aydelotte turned to Raymond Walters, his personal assistant at Swarthmore College, to help procure and organize the information he needed. It was, in fact, Walters's data that provided a starting place for the work Aydelotte and Moe carried out. In 1932 Walters would accept the presidency of the University of Cincinnati, but in 1924 he was Swarthmore's utility player, teaching English while also serving as registrar and dean of men.[1] As Robert Earnest Miller explains, Walters had collected annual reports from educational institutions starting in 1919 and earned a reputation for his expertise in statistical analysis. (In 1946 a *Cincinnati Enquirer* story would refer to Walters as "the nation's 'statistician laureate of higher education.'"[2]) Armed with Walters's data, Aydelotte identified the most promising university administrators for consultation. He and Moe traveled widely, gathering responses to a series of questions, with the former closely supervising the latter.[3] Moe's near-ceaseless reconnaissance work on behalf of the nascent foundation in the summer of 1924 became an extended job interview. Aydelotte corresponded with Wilson over the course of the year and provided general updates on his findings. Until Aydelotte was fully committed to the venture and Guggenheim was fully committed to him, he dealt almost exclusively with Wilson. Thereafter, when it came to specific matters relating to the foundation, Swarthmore's president talked directly with the senator. It was a tight, closed circle, and the hierarchy was clear: Moe answered to Aydelotte, who answered to Wilson, who answered to Guggenheim.

The scope and the compressed timeline of the project demanded vision, clarity of purpose, efficiency, and especially fortitude. In an age that preceded air travel, email, social media, and Internet searches, information was gathered in person and interviews took place only after logging hours on trains shuttling between nearby and not-so-nearby cities. Letters and telegrams, often more than one in a single day, kept the principal players informed about the findings and the overall state of preparations throughout 1924. Scrutinizing why and how these men were chosen to shape the new foundation, and evaluating what their impact would be on the music composition fellowships in particular, illuminates the many ways the John Simon Guggenheim Memorial Foundation modeled how successful institutions think.[4] With a single, but key, exception, everyone was in place to select future music composition winners by October 1924; the man destined to become most important to that process, Thomas Whitney Surette, was added in January 1925. As will become evident, he was unlike Wilson, Aydelotte, and Moe in significant ways, and not without consequences.

* * *

Although the foundation bears the name of the Guggenheim family, the specifics of its mission were shaped and guided in the very earliest days by Carroll A. Wilson, an attorney, bibliophile, and published literary scholar whose role in the foundation's genesis has remained largely unknown to all but the innermost circle.[5] According to documents in the Frank Aydelotte Papers at Swarthmore College, by February 1924, Wilson, general counsel for the Guggenheim Brothers family business, had already been in talks with former senator Simon G. Guggenheim and his wife Olga Hirsch Guggenheim regarding some type of memorial for their son.

Wilson had enjoyed a wholly elite education. Although generations of his male relatives matriculated at Colby College in his home state of Maine, Carroll Wilson attended the more prestigious Williams College in Massachusetts (1903–1907), where he graduated in the top five of his class, and went on to Harvard Law School. He left Harvard after a single year to take up his Rhodes Scholarship at Worcester College, Oxford University, where he earned a degree in civil law in 1911. He returned to the United States and set up practice, but soon after that went to work for the Guggenheim family business.[6] Wilson never forgot his three years of studies at Oxford. Despite having a thriving legal practice, he would carve out respected positions in the scholarly and the business worlds, writing studies of Thomas Hardy and Oliver Wendell Holmes and directing multiple corporations and companies within the Guggenheim mining empire. Regardless of his legal responsibilities, Wilson's scholarly bent predisposed him to think along the lines of educational endeavors. When given the opportunity to help shape a memorial for the Guggenheims' son, Wilson guided the couple to consider Cecil Rhodes's scholarships as a model and to look to other Rhodes awardees to facilitate the creation of an American counterpart to the British program. Without Wilson's guidance, it is unlikely the Guggenheims would have imagined the memorial the way they did or embraced the Rhodes model.

Wilson needed a person with a vision similar to his own, with an impeccable educational pedigree, strong ties to the academy, and a commitment to progressive pedagogy to realize his plan. He identified Frank Aydelotte, a friend and fellow Rhodes Scholar. Aydelotte had earned a bachelor's degree from Indiana University in 1900 and an M.A. from Harvard in 1903. In 1905 he was named a Rhodes Scholar and attended Oxford. He returned to the United States to take faculty positions first at Indiana, where he taught from 1908 to 1915, and then at MIT. In 1921, when he assumed the presidency of Swarthmore, he became the first non-Quaker to lead the college run by the Religious Society of Friends just outside Philadelphia, where the original Guggenheims had settled. Aydelotte was committed to educational reform, which, he believed, required small seminar-style classes taught by experts in their fields, like those he had enjoyed at Oxford. By his second year as president he instituted changes that resulted in Swarthmore's Oxbridge-tutorial-style honors program. Over the next few years he made equally radical changes to campus social life, most noticeably, perhaps, eliminating fraternities and sororities.

Aydelotte's zeal for all things Oxford matched Wilson's and fueled his loyalty to the Rhodes Scholarship program and his desire to support it from his U.S. home base. Over a period of forty years he served as secretary of the Rhodes Alumni Association, editor of its magazine *The American Oxonian*, and American secretary of the Rhodes Trust. In 1917 he became the chief administrator of the Rhodes Scholarship program in the United States. It is a testament to Aydelotte's intellect, vision, energy, administrative skills, and large network of admiring colleagues that he would be able to hold down simultaneously his considerable responsibilities to the Rhodes program, his presidential position at Swarthmore, and that of chair of the Educational Advisory Committee at the Guggenheim Foundation, the title he negotiated in 1924. He kept the foundation position until 1950 and only resigned as chief administrator of the Rhodes Scholarship program in 1953, when failing health necessitated that he do so.

The value of education was clear to Simon Guggenheim, if indirect, and he had cherished the idea of an elite imprimatur for his lost son.[7] Surrounding himself with Rhodes Scholars likely provided some degree of comfort and validation. The senator's four older brothers, Isaac, Daniel, Murry, and Solomon, had benefited from lengthy studies in Switzerland, where they polished their German skills, acquired continental refinements, and learned every aspect of the embroidery business, which had been among the first of the family's large-scale commercial ventures. Simon's education was more singularly practical: After he attended a local high school and business college, Simon was sent to Spain by his father Meyer for two years to develop language skills that would be useful to the family's mining business, which increasingly trained its sights on Central and South American nations.[8] If Simon Guggenheim's senatorial seat distinguished this son from his brothers and secured a respected place within the family, his affiliation with these accomplished Rhodes Scholars through a memorial for his son guaranteed his reputation in American educational culture. Listening to Carroll Wilson would be among Simon Guggenheim's smartest career decisions; it sealed his place in history. Twenty-two months after his son's death, planning for a memorial foundation began in earnest in early 1924.

FEBRUARY

On February 25, 1924, Wilson wrote to Frank Aydelotte to introduce the idea of the foundation. At the time Wilson tapped him, Aydelotte was American secretary of the Rhodes Trustees and intimately knowledgeable about the details of that organization's day-to-day operations.[9] In this initial communication Wilson projected a yearly income for the foundation of $500,000. He explained that the donor imagined spending 20 percent of the income to bring young men from South America to the United States for general education purposes, and the remaining 80 percent to support European study for young American men and women.[10] According to Wilson, the donor was "interested first in extending the benefits of his gift to persons of musical and artistic ability, or along other lines more remote from pure scholarship." From this it is evident that the idea of a focus on music and the arts came from the Guggenheims. This will be important to remember because the merits of such an emphasis would be both championed and challenged by early consultants; the criteria for judging worthy applicants would become the topic of extended debate. Wilson closed by explaining, "[The] whole matter has come as a surprise to me," but he thought that the two men could "be of real assistance to the donor in working out his plans for the use of this money."[11]

In a letter dated two days later Aydelotte agreed to Wilson's invitation to meet one of the "Messrs. Guggenheim," whom Wilson had not identified specifically. He also expressed his support of the idea of scholarships focused on musicians and artists and acknowledged that all he had learned from his administration of the Rhodes Scholarships in the United States could be useful. Wilson had been vague about the donor because the senator was not eager to be identified as the source of the funding; and in the earliest interviews with academic leaders the donor's name was not divulged. There are many possible reasons for his reluctance, and they are shared by large numbers of moneyed people, but among those at work in the case of the Guggenheims' dream foundation might have been a hesitancy to reveal the Jewish ancestry of the donors. Given the antisemitism of the time and the racist treatment the family had endured, it is likely more than coincidence that the men Simon chose to be the face of his foundation were all white Protestant Christians, members of the racial and religious ruling class.

Finding a day for Guggenheim and Aydelotte to meet proved problematic because both men traveled regularly, and their planned trips eliminated all of March and most of April. The postponement proved advantageous to everyone, however, for it allowed Wilson, in long-distance consultation with Aydelotte, to create what would become a thirty-page report for the senator titled "Suggestions for the John S. Guggenheim Foundation."[12] Although not all the original ideas survived, this report reveals basic values and goals that shaped the foundation. It also discloses motivations less reflective of its idealistic mission, perhaps, but in keeping with the business ethos of its founding family.

APRIL

Wilson's report, dated April 10, acknowledged the Guggenheims' original demographic target, "boys and girls" their son's age (late teens), and the source of funds as "his money": the three-million-dollar seed money that would have been John Simon's inheritance had he not passed away two years earlier. Wilson applauded the Guggenheims' "devotion," which would allow young recipients to "enjoy educational benefits in his name." He addressed the larger topic of recognizing the need for education, for understanding Europe, and for "the broadening and bettering of the mental and social equipment of selected Americans." Given the still-raw wounds of World War I, a desire to understand Europe made sense.

Then Wilson referred to Simon Guggenheim's less talked about but clearly formative interest in South America, which he identified as "your main idea." Although not recognized today as being among the founders' key motivations, the Guggenheims' mining business and memorial foundation were inextricably entwined. As the chief counsel explained, in addition to providing "a better education for the boy—which we naturally assume is more needed by South Americans than by others," the foundation would create the opportunity to nurture "a better feeling toward the United States by South Americans, a result much needed, and toward which there is much general talk, but little concrete constructive effort." Wilson recognized potential gains for the Guggenheims' personal image abroad and the corrective the foundation might provide when he noted: "The name of Guggenheim will become to South Americans the symbol of educational opportunity and mutual understanding, rather than of profit from their natural resources."

Later in the report Wilson noted additional advantages that would accrue to the Guggenheims, specifically those gained by transferring select securities to the foundation, which, he advised, would "reduce your own taxability." Wilson knew his boss: No amount of idealism or even paternal love could offset a disadvantageous bottom line. If the plan was to succeed, it would need to demonstrate wise investments and sound returns.

Wilson reviewed the structures and conditions of existing philanthropic organizations to point out their successes and failures, mentioning the Rockefeller, Juilliard, and Spelman Foundations. With access to Rhodes-related information through his association with Aydelotte, and Aydelotte's access to Walters's data, Wilson presented detailed charts showing Rhodes Scholarship winners by region of the country starting in 1919—the year Walters had begun collecting statistics—and then he interpreted the data for the senator. He boasted about the numbers of Rhodes Scholars whose names had appeared in the 1919, 1921, and 1923, editions of *Who's Who*, and noted that the current "Commissioner of Education of the United States (J.J. Tigert) is a Rhodes scholar." He explained the program's tightly organized system of selection, with state and regional committees overseen by the American secretary.

Despite so much to recommend the Rhodes system, Wilson also noted three serious limitations: Only males were eligible, the award had to be taken at Oxford, and the stipend was "not fully sufficient." Wilson pointed to an additional concern, especially important given Guggenheim's stated interest in music and art: Oxford offered no awards to young musicians and artists seeking additional training.

With the most obvious holes identified, Wilson made another observation, one that had more to do with process than with the final product. In the cases of the Juilliard and Rockefeller Foundations, Wilson reported, the failure to optimize their effectiveness was traceable to misunderstanding the need for sound mechanics and thorough promotion. "No foundation," he wrote, "regardless of how amply endowed it is[,] can succeed without publicity." It must "command a high degree of publicity in the press and in educational circles. Wilson didn't see any of these obstacles as insurmountable to the new foundation:

> In short, the ultimate success of your very fine idea about a scholarship memorial to your son depends (in my judgment) very largely on the mechanics that you apply to carry out that idea. . . . Your difficulty will be in making your scholarship known through the United States, getting a large number of the right sort of young men and women to apply for the opportunity, and properly selecting the cream of your candidates. Despite the excellence of the idea, and the benefits afforded, experience shows that they will not succeed unless they are generally known and talked about.

Having surveyed the field, identified the opportunities, considered the structures of existing programs, and reviewed the details of stipend amounts and tenures, Wilson proceeded to suggest ways to organize Guggenheim's memorial foundation. Based on the Rhodes model of personnel headquartered in various locations, Wilson initially imagined the senator's foundation as having something similar. He acknowledged that this was "a task of real magnitude" that required a general organizing secretary and suggested a salary of between $7,500 and $10,000 for that person. He proposed a permanent man in Europe, "a European secretary," to oversee operations once the initial organizing work was complete. That person would act as a "moral guardian" of the American students abroad. He also advised hiring a "South American Secretary" who should consult with the "director of the Pan-American Union in Washington."

Responding directly to the senator's desire for a scholarship program that focused on music and the arts, Wilson's "Suggestions" addressed the unique "mechanics" and challenges associated with selecting fellows in those fields. It is noteworthy that music and art are the only disciplines discussed at length in this report or identified as potentially problematic in the early months of the foundation's organization. With no other general educational philanthropic organizations supporting practitioners in these fields and no models to follow, the Guggenheim Foundation had to invent the rules. It is impossible to know whether Wilson reflected his own concerns or Guggenheim's when he talked about the need for a more decentralized selection process when it came to the arts. As Wilson imagined it, a state- or region-oriented, rather than a centralized, selection process might mean "we get a decent amount of Western red-blooded materials to leaven the Eastern more-cultivated lump."[13] Wilson assumed that Guggenheim did "not want to confine [his] scholarships in music and art to the Eastern States only . . . [but] wish[ed] them to be country-wide in scope, and to have a country-wide appeal." And then he offered reasons why local selection committees might be preferable, although the idea was quickly dropped.

From the beginning, conceptualizing how to evaluate music and art applicants appeared to be problematic. Wilson argued that development in music and art didn't necessarily require a college degree and so suggested that Guggenheim might want to reserve a certain number of fellowships for "very exceptional cases." As Wilson understood it, there was no way to assess "the less measurable lines of musical and artistic ability" or budding talent, and he explained:

> The standards here are entirely different from the standards of ordinary scholarship. In music, it is very difficult to segregate the person with great natural talent from the person with little real ability but elaborate previous education. In art, real achievement along one line, for example, modern painting, might have absolutely no appeal to a committee of selection composed of recognized experts in the classical school. In both, any definite standard of ability such as success in the classroom, laboratory, or examinations is lacking.

He concluded that the organizing secretary would need to rely on advisors in music and art.

Today's practicing musicians and artists will readily acknowledge the role personal predilection plays in preferring the works of a composer or painter, a school or a movement, but it's unlikely that they would see any selection process as completely free of basic standards or criteria by which to judge potential applicants: technical mastery is measurable; knowledge of one's medium is apparent; possession of certain skills is clear. Wilson, on the other hand, believed, "You are hunting for a potential genius, and you cannot, as far as I know, find him with any yardstick. Your committee of selection will have to weigh intangibles and exercise the utmost care not to be guided by considerations which appeal to their own prejudices."[14] That he did not recognize the subjective judgments, the "intangibles," that play a role in all human assessments speaks to the power of the notion of the artistic genius, of the rationalist argument, and of the allure of objectivity so long associated with the sciences. It also reflects unfamiliarity with the subject. Wilson's (and, it would turn out, Aydelotte's and Moe's) complete inexperience with music meant they would depend more heavily on their music advisor than on advisors in other fields.

With decentralized national committees seemingly not an ideal solution for all award categories, Wilson outlined an alternative plan that gave select universities the power to choose Guggenheim Fellows. In this iteration of the process fellowships would supplement existing university travel awards. To minimize favoritism for one's own students he suggested, "Any committee should exclude officials of specific colleges."[15] In this scenario, Wilson observed, "Your difficulties of selection are done." As regards resources, the foundation could match university contributions three to one, thereby freeing Guggenheim monies to support still more fellows. He suggested that all scholarships be divided equally among men and women. This is an admirably progressive idea given the all-male makeup of the inner circle of founders and the overwhelmingly male university leaders asked for advice. After brief consideration, the idea of equal, fixed numbers of awards for men and women was also dropped.

Wilson offered his thoughts on age limits and marital status: There should be no fixed age limit, although twenty-five was too low a cutoff and single and married applicants should be treated equally. He quoted a section of "The Rhodes Will": "No student should be qualified or disqualified from election to a scholarship because of his race or religious opinion," and reflected that "this is valuable." As if to provide additional evidence of his own commitment to such thinking, he told Guggenheim about his participation in a Rhodes Scholarship selection committee for a scholar-at-large position the previous fall: A "brilliant young Jew from Missouri who wants to become a rabbi" was their unanimous choice. Race, religion, and ethnicity would be sensitive issues for Guggenheim, although it appears he never threw his weight behind an individual applicant or attempted to influence the selection process in any way.

Wilson's personality, proclivities, and position as legal counsel to the Guggenheims informed a final series of suggestions he made regarding finances and language. He raised the question whether committee members should be paid; advised against stipulating a fixed amount for awards in light of the unknowns associated with future costs of living; and reminded Guggenheim that extreme care should be taken with wording his deed of gift, which would be scrutinized by "candidates and committees" alike. He advised him to consider the form the organization would take, "whether trust or corporation." Having helped shape the particulars of the foundation, Wilson focused on its legal standing in the state of New York.

On April 12, Wilson wrote to the former senator reaffirming his belief that given the Rhodes program's twenty-year record it was the best model for his foundation.[16] He also wrote to Aydelotte, assuring him that he had sent the report and informing him that he had succeeded in arranging a dinner for Guggenheim and Aydelotte at the Hotel Ambassador. Aydelotte's April 25 letter to Wilson agreeing to the May 1 date shows the two men working together to guarantee that Aydelotte made a good first impression. Given the positions held by both men, their attention to all aspects of the dinner meeting suggests what they believed was at stake. Aydelotte arranged his train schedule in order to meet Wilson at the Harvard Club in New York, where he could change clothes and the two men could talk before heading to the Ambassador. He assured Wilson that he would be "armed with certain suggestions as to men and a tentative scheme of organization." He also confirmed that he had studied Wilson's report and liked the idea of working with existing traveling fellowship programs at colleges as a way to get the new foundation up and running as quickly as possible. Aydelotte understood that Guggenheim wanted swift results, and he couldn't fathom an alternative scheme "that could be set up [and] would so quickly take on national importance." More like a nervous groom than the president of a college, Aydelotte asked Wilson about proper dress. A handwritten note in the margin inquires: "Do I wear black tie or white? i.e. dinner jacket or tails?"[17]

MAY

Events moved quickly. As part of his effort to secure Guggenheim's approval Aydelotte produced a two-page typed document titled "Suggestions for Organization" that included a list of names penciled in at the end representing all those he had considered as potential assistants. Henry Allen Moe's name was among them. In a letter sent to Aydelotte on May 5, Wilson referenced their conversation at the Harvard Club and informed Aydelotte that on his recommendation, the Guggenheims wanted him to lead the foundation. He also explained his own role as "confidential messenger" to Swarthmore College, where he would endeavor to sell their plan to Aydelotte's employers.[18] As Thomas Tanselle and colleagues explain, despite Guggenheim's and Wilson's enthusiasm and Aydelotte's clear interest in the endeavor, "Aydelotte felt he could not leave Swarthmore at that time."[19]

Guggenheim was now confident he wanted Aydelotte to lead his foundation, but he also understood that it was unlikely he could persuade him to leave his prestigious and secure position for one at an untested organization with an uncertain future. And much as Simon and Olga Guggenheim controlled the foundation proper, in its embryonic stage it was still closely tied to the larger Guggenheim Brothers enterprise, and other family members needed to approve Aydelotte's appointment. Strengthening his case, the senator sought support from well-placed others including Wickliffe Rose, president of the International Education Board, founded by John D. Rockefeller Jr., and a man described as "a master in the difficult art of applying private philanthropy to the highest purposes of scientific education and research," and Beardsley Ruml, who between 1922 and 1929 directed the Laura Spelman Rockefeller Memorial Fund.[20] Both argued strongly in Aydelotte's favor. When Guggenheim presented Aydelotte's name to his family for their approval, he went armed with endorsements from incontestable experts in the field of philanthropy.

While details of Aydelotte's precise title and duties were being decided, on May 14 Wilson presented the senator with a four-page, fifteen-point plan that he had created in consultation with Aydelotte and titled "Suggestions for Chronological Working Out of Your Ideas as to Foundation."[21] The first five suggestions set the foundation on a swift course to becoming a reality: 1. Engage Aydelotte; 2. Have Aydelotte engage an assistant; 3. Make certain that the assistant can assume a leadership role after the initial start-up phase has been achieved; 4. Establish an office; 5. Immediately undertake an intensive interview and discussion campaign. Wilson's valuation of solid mechanics and targeted publicity above all else would propel the foundation from concept to entity in less than a year's time.

Over the next few months, correspondence between Wilson and Aydelotte reveals the two men using their considerable organizational and intellectual gifts to create what would debut as "an unexampled investment in America's futures," an institution that was "unique in American philanthropy."[22] Letters between Guggenheim and Aydelotte show them negotiating the terms of a contract, something the former was unaccustomed to doing with a person of Aydelotte's stature, who was himself in the habit of hiring faculty and staff. On June 19, 1924, Guggenheim sent Aydelotte a three-page statement of understanding that proposed a one-year contract at $10,000. He enumerated incidental expenses that would be covered and clarified his assumptions regarding where Aydelotte would work. On July 1 Aydelotte asked Wilson to help convince Guggenheim that a one- or even a two-year contract was inadequate, and two weeks later, on July 16, Aydelotte wrote directly to "My dear Mr. Guggenheim." He explained the need for time to adjust the original plan if that was deemed necessary, and to follow up with fellows to see how their careers unfolded after their award years. Knowing that it wasn't necessary, he reminded the Senator that he was free to terminate him at any time if he was dissatisfied. Aydelotte concluded, "Meanwhile, I am going ahead energetically with the work mapped out for this summer."[23]

The situation speaks to the different worlds the two men inhabited and their individual senses of worth. Aydelotte's experience in academia predisposed him to think in terms of longer contracts: Five or six years is now a typical span of time before a faculty member comes up for tenure, and five years is what he proposed. With as much experience administrating educational institutions as Guggenheim had running businesses, Aydelotte knew that the senator's plans required time to design, refine, and revise. Yet Guggenheim's experience in business meant that his employees served his bottom line. Maximum flexibility to terminate or redistribute human resources as needed argued against long-term commitments: A one-year contract was generous in the business world. The two men eventually agreed on Aydelotte's title, "Educational Adviser," and a three-year contract at an annual salary of $10,000, very generous remuneration at the time, especially for a part-time job and on top of his Swarthmore compensation.[24]

Aydelotte worked energetically over the summer, adhering to the schedule and plan he and Wilson had delivered to Guggenheim in mid-May. They looked for an assistant, a leader-in-waiting who could establish and maintain the foundation's New York office. Their familiarity with the basic mechanics of the Rhodes program and loyalty to its traditions and its community of scholars provided a common well from which to draw a colleague who would be sympathetic to the cause, familiar with their thinking, and share their values, both professional and personal: In August they named Henry Allen Moe. From the beginning, foundation personnel were thinking institutionally.[25] Sharing formative thought worlds helps explain the tightness of the bonds Wilson, Aydelotte, and Moe enjoyed. Similar upbringings meant their common roots went even deeper.

* * *

Aydelotte and Wilson had much in common before they experienced Oxford as Rhodes Scholars. Born seven years apart in 1880 and 1887, respectively, the two were both products of late nineteenth-century small-town America who made good. Carroll Wilson was a native of Benton Falls, Maine, a community northeast of Waterville and famous today for its Congregational Church, which boasts one of the last steeple bells produced by the (Paul) Revere Family Foundry in Charleston, Massachusetts; it was installed in 1894, when Wilson was seven years old. He would have grown up aware of his town's connection to the nation's history and the silversmith patriot.[26]

Frank Aydelotte hailed from the Midwest but was also the product of a small town: Sullivan, Indiana, a mill town. A diploma from Aydelotte's high school in Sullivan "was accepted for admission to Indiana University," about sixty miles east in Bloomington, and so he went there. He earned his bachelor's degree before striking out on his own.[27] Given Aydelotte's eventual leadership of a Quaker college, it may be noteworthy that the first settlers of Sullivan were members of another small religious sect, the Shakers. Later the town became a site along the Chautauqua circuit, hosting concerts and lectures by traveling orators. "Chautauquas," the itinerant manifestations of the permanent Chautauqua movement and sites, supplied some of the earliest opportunities for adult education in rural areas of the country. They combined a relaxed atmosphere for learning within a non-denominational Protestant environment.

Moe was also a Midwesterner. His parents had emigrated from Norway to Minnesota in the 1880s and settled in Monticello, a town that bordered the Mississippi River northeast of the Twin Cities. They were relatively new Americans when Henry was born there in 1894. Like many recent immigrants, the senior Moes embraced their adopted land with a zeal often not present in the native-born. Their belief in the power of freedom was as influential to Henry Allen Moe in his early life as his experience with the Rhodes program would become later on.[28] In 1916 Moe graduated from Hamline College, a private Methodist Church–associated liberal arts college in St. Paul, worked briefly as a reporter for a local newspaper, and then enlisted in the navy when the United States entered the war in 1917; he was twenty-three years old. By the time Aydelotte was looking for an assistant in 1924, he and Wilson already knew Moe from their work on the Rhodes Scholarships selection committee. As Tanselle explains, "they had . . . recommended [Moe] as a [Rhodes] Scholar-at Large; indeed, Wilson had conducted the interview when Moe was still in his hospital bed following the serious injuries he had received while in command of a Navy destroyer during World War I."[29] A commitment to delivering Senator and Mrs. Guggenheim a solid plan for a suitable memorial within a very short period of time motivated Wilson and Aydelotte to move quickly, and knowing Moe streamlined the process.

AUGUST

In consecutive letters written to Wilson on August 18 and 19, Aydelotte made a case for why Moe was ideal, even if he argued that Moe tended to overvalue Oxford.[30] Picking up on Wilson's earlier concern that the foundation might need to fight an East Coast bias, Aydelotte mentioned Moe's roots in the "Middle West": "Hence he has in his blood a consciousness of the size of this country, which people born on the Atlantic Seaboard find it hard to get."[31] He believed that Moe knew how to be secretary and that he also had more knowledge of Europe than did other Rhodes Scholars. He cited Moe's propensity for legal scholarship, which would give "great tone" to the work of the foundation. That he knew multiple languages and that his fiancée was a linguist strengthened his case. Although he acknowledged Moe's youth—he had only turned thirty on July 2, 1924—Aydelotte didn't see his age as an issue.

In the August 19 letter Aydelotte informed Wilson that he was hiring Moe on a trial basis. He provided his new assistant with letters of introduction to present to university administrators across the country when talking with them about the plans of an unnamed "rich man" who "wishes to found a scholarship system for American boys and girls to European universities." Moe was instructed to send written reports that he could elaborate on in personal meetings once he was done with his tour. Aydelotte, in the meantime, would speak with educators and administrators in New Haven and Boston. For a month starting in late August, Moe, under Aydelotte's supervision, met with carefully chosen college and university presidents to press the basic concepts of the plan and seek their responses to questions that Aydelotte had designed. Moe's summer fact-finding mission took him to Ohio State, Butler University, Wabash College, Carleton College, the University of Minnesota, Hamline College, Northwestern University, the University of Chicago, Indiana University, Oberlin College, (Case) Western Reserve University, and the University of Buffalo.[32] Aydelotte's and Moe's Midwest upbringings served them well. Staying close to their home turf and visiting their alma maters provided the highest likelihood of a positive reception.

Despite Aydelotte's confidence in Moe, he felt compelled to justify his novice assistant's travels to Guggenheim, who would pay Moe's expenses, and explain the value of personal interactions with well-placed university administrators. Aydelotte made his case succinctly:

> First, the obvious one that some of them would be able to contribute suggestions of value, and secondly, the psychological one, that when your plans are put into operation, they, having been in on the ground floor, will be the more interested and will therefore be the more certain to give their valuable support.[33]

Aydelotte then listed "four possible types of support [that Moe could] discuss with the people he visited," all of them still sought by university faculty today: "grants to supplement sabbatical salaries, research fellowships for advanced scholars, renewals of such awards for recipients who needed more time, and publication subsidies for work produced on the fellowships."[34] What Aydelotte did not mention was that the trip also gave him a chance to evaluate how Moe would work out; more than the foundation was on trial.

Moe quickly proved his worth by sending detailed reports to Aydelotte. Beyond providing the information Aydelotte sought, Moe also revealed a more strategic and philosophical bent: the same combination of qualities that would characterize his work at the foundation for the next four decades. Understanding that a loose collection of ideas and initiatives had little likelihood of appearing as a unique cohesive enterprise in the minds of those he was meeting, or of distinguishing the proposed foundation from other efforts, Moe encouraged Aydelotte to consider "a big, statesmanlike idea, an idea . . . that strikes the imagination, [and] is easy to grasp and to hold." And beyond a big idea, as interviewees would insist, the success of the foundation depended on selecting the right fellows.[35]

SEPTEMBER

Over the next few months, a number of those interviewed provided additional detailed written responses to Aydelotte's questions. The president of Ohio State University, W. O. Thompson, offered his September 8 letter as a "supplement" to what Moe would report. He questioned whether the scholarships could be used in industries that dealt with military or secret research without compromising the industries or the nation. He worried about "trade secrets."[36] He wondered whether the proposed scholarships would be available to Europeans studying in the United States and observed that if such awards were confined to undergraduates, then there was little that was new. In the latter case, he pointed out, "We'll fail to develop the fellowships, and friendships, and good will that I assume to be a much-desired objective in the proposal under consideration."[37] His use of "we'll" reveals that Thompson already saw himself as part owner of the project, precisely the outcome that Aydelotte had hoped for and suggested to Guggenheim. A letter from Walter D. Scott, president of Northwestern University, reminded Aydelotte to look beyond the obvious northeastern corridor for possible fellows and plumped for "the inland districts quite as much."[38] In a meeting with Wilson on September 17, Aydelotte reported on his own conversations with Abbott Lawrence Lowell, president of Harvard University, from which he "got a great deal," and with Joe Willits, founder of the International Research Unit at the University of Pennsylvania. He confided to Wilson that "the thing is rather clearing up in my mind."[39] In one of the few written expressions of concern about Moe's performance, Aydelotte reported to Wilson that because of illness, Moe's expected report had been delayed. Demonstrating the kind of goal-oriented, single-minded focus that characterized the entire operation and allowed for no weak links, Aydelotte reflected: "He appeared entirely well, but if he is not, that would be, in my opinion, a fatal objection to him."[40]

By late September Aydelotte had received Moe's report on colleges he had visited, and his fears were allayed. Believing that the document reflected Moe's ability, he sent it to Wilson for his opinion. Of those whom Moe had interviewed, Aydelotte valued the opinion of Guy Stanton Ford, dean of the graduate school and professor of history at the University of Minnesota, most highly. Many others he dismissed, characterizing them as "chaff." He pointed to Ford's endorsement of an opinion that had been gaining support over the course of the summer: that awards for more advanced scholars were what was needed and would distinguish the Guggenheim program from others.[41] This would become the foundation's practice and it has remained to this day. As a sign of the esteem in which Aydelotte held Ford, the Minnesota professor was named one of the original nineteen members of the Educational Advisory Board. Providing Wilson with a final opportunity to comment on other candidates for the secretarial position that Moe had been occupying on a trial basis, Aydelotte suggested the name of his personal assistant at Swarthmore, Raymond Walters, the man who had provided the foundation with the all-important data they had used to design their summer fact-finding interviews. But Aydelotte clearly hoped that Wilson preferred Moe, as he did.[42] The next day Wilson wrote saying he was satisfied with Moe as secretary.[43] Whether it was a part of their considerations or not, Moe possessed the all-important Rhodes imprimatur and Walters did not.

* * *

Given Simon Guggenheim's insistence that a foundation named for his son would not discriminate on the basis of race, gender, or religious affiliation, it is revealing of the larger culture to see how deeply embedded racialized and gendered thinking was among those solicited for opinions or entrusted to carry out its mission. Until the end of the process, all those interviewed were white male educational leaders. With rare exceptions, interviewees referred to potential candidates and fellows exclusively as men. In a discussion of a board of trustees, one respondent clarified that there was no need to have all members be educational experts: Men of business and public affairs should be welcome. When it came to naming advisors, interviewees recommended a group comprised of leading educational men in the country.[44] While employing a rhetorical practice typical of the time, the word also conveyed the gendered reality of the academic and business worlds in the 1920s and for decades afterward.

Racial realities revealed themselves in more oblique ways during the foundation's gestation period, and in all cases they revolved around Jewish otherness rather than Blackness. Beyond the senator's initial reluctance to reveal his name to those being solicited for advice about his plans, which may or may not have been a response to anticipated negative reactions by the Christian educational leaders who dominated the nation's academy, a curious situation arose when Moe wrote to Aydelotte and volunteered to change his name to "More" so he would not be mistaken for being Jewish. He provided a long explanation that in the Midwest no one assumed his name was anything but Norse, but on multiple occasions during his recent travels, he was "often embarrassed by the inference, until they see me, that I am Jewish." He was "tired of making explanations."[45] Either the young barrister was oblivious to the multiple antisemitic biases contained in his remarks, or he felt comfortable sharing them with his supervisor. Moe clearly believed it was important to the foundation that neither he nor it appeared to be Jewish. He proceeded to describe the derivation of his family name and the logic of changing it to "More," the "least violent" of the variant spellings. He assured

Aydelotte that the spelling change was acceptable to his family and fiancée were he to be offered the secretarial position. Moe observed that "a name might be important to the foundation in the event I became connected with it" and requested that Aydelotte change the spelling on his letters of introduction if he thought it desirable.[46] In a handwritten note at the bottom of Moe's letter Aydelotte wrote a brief response intended for his secretary to type up. The Swarthmore president admitted that he did not think how one spelled a name was important, that he had never thought of the name as Jewish, and he didn't have an opinion on what Moe should do. He would abide by Moe's decision. We can only speculate what Moe thought of being associated with a foundation whose name was Guggenheim, or of ultimately working for and being paid by a man whose family had been persecuted for being Jewish. It is an indicator of the times and perhaps the personal sensitivity, experiences, and naiveté of a young Henry Allen Moe that he would volunteer such an action. One wonders how Moe separated the mission of the foundation from his own original biases and "embarrassment" at the inference that he was Jewish once he was hired, or whether his own worldview expanded immediately and dramatically on going to work for the Guggenheims.

OCTOBER

In a report dated October 2, 1924, that Aydelotte prepared for the senator, he reviewed his findings regarding philanthropic programs in place, the regulations that governed their operations, the type and number of people eligible and served, and their successes. He acknowledged existing fellowships and scholarships but also the opportunities to meet unfilled needs: additional scholarships for women, older scholars who were past the baccalaureate degree, and those already teaching.

Aydelotte offered a possible design: a two-tiered system where junior fellowships would be combined with university support and senior fellowships that would be funded exclusively by the foundation. The latter would be for applicants who had already demonstrated an aptitude for scholarship. He suggested stipend amounts and age limits. Drawing again on his recent experience as a faculty member, Aydelotte referred to the frustrations associated with sabbaticals whose benefits "are annulled by the fact that instructors and professors can't afford to go abroad on the half salary usually granted."[47] He suggested publication subsidies as a way to circulate the work of fellows and the name of the foundation and recommended an organizational structure that included a Board of Trustees, an Educational Advisory Board, and an Executive Committee chosen from the Advisory Board that functioned as a Committee of Selection. He volunteered that his own best use would be as chairman of the Educational Advisory Board and recommended that the executive work of the organization be in the hands of a director with an office in New York. This person would be responsible for the daily operations of the foundation, take charge of publicity, receive and process applications, make arrangements with foreign universities, distribute stipends, and follow the careers of awardees.

In a two-page memo to Guggenheim written October 6, Aydelotte reviewed what he had accomplished since their meeting in the spring. He had collected statistics on philanthropic foundations, assembled detailed information, consulted approximately forty educational leaders about the plan, interviewed potential secretaries, and worked out two or three tentative proposals for his consideration. He welcomed a meeting with the senator.[48]

In an undated but still more detailed document that Aydelotte titled "Endowment for Foreign Study" he limited his recommendations and couched them in terms of the benefits that would accrue to the foundation itself:

> By setting the standards of qualification up to the highest possible point, the Foundation would necessarily designate its fellows as being very superior men and women. The fact of having held such a fellowship would come to be a very hallmark of excellence; in after years, it would be a very important part of an ex-fellow's credentials. Colleges and universities would announce in their catalogues and bulletins whenever some member was awarded such a fellowship; and it is not inconceivable that the time might come when the number of ex-fellows on the teaching staff of some institution would afford a very good index of its caliber.[49]

Aydelotte recommended focusing on one-year advanced fellowships that carried a stipend of $2,500 at first. He allowed for the possibility of renewal for a second year, and rarely for a third, or for a shorter interval, and suggested that the foundation set aside funds to subsidize publication of senior fellows' work by a well-known publisher. Books would carry the foundation's imprint on the title page. As regards junior fellowships, he recommended that the trustees take up the idea at a later date.

With the mechanics of the foundation's operation coming into clearer focus, thanks in large part to Moe's legwork, Aydelotte sought to formalize the young assistant's financial relationship to the organization. Reverting to an earlier pattern of using Wilson as an intermediary, Aydelotte wrote to Wilson urging him to petition Simon Guggenheim to pay Moe starting on October 1, rather than October 15, which was the date that had been offered. Aydelotte pointed out that Moe had already done six weeks' work with no remuneration except for travel expenses.[50] Providing an easy out if the answer was going to be no, Aydelotte explained that he understood "the boy is fortunate in a way to start in so good a position, so if you feel it is more tactful not to mention this to the senator, don't do so."[51] Wilson responded that he didn't want to press Moe's case as he was young, untested, and "does not make such a favorable impression on the first interview. . . . He's got to earn his spurs with the senator."[52]

The same day Wilson wrote to Aydelotte, October 20, Guggenheim wrote to Henry Allen Moe offering him a one-year contract, effective starting October 15, with an annual salary of $5,000 to be paid monthly. The salary was more than twice the average earned by an American in 1924. Moe was expected to devote all his working hours to managing the New York office of the foundation. He would answer to Aydelotte, who was responsible for developing policies and seeing to their execution. Moe's contract was effective until October 1, 1926, and terminable on two months' notice by either party; his precise title was to be determined. The senator invited Moe to confirm the agreement. With Moe officially on board and already engaged in the search for his own stenographer, the basic administrative team of the John S. Guggenheim Foundation was in place. Eight months after initial conversations had begun, and while interviews with educational leaders across the nation continued, the foundation was ready to turn to publicity and to filling board and advisory committee positions.

NOVEMBER

Aydelotte spent the first weeks of the month of November drafting and revising the announcement introducing "Fellowships for Advanced Study Abroad." He described the awards as "advanced" fellowships for people in the teaching and other professions who have already demonstrated unusual capacity. They would include a stipend of $2,500 and be offered without restriction to men and women, married and unmarried, with no age limit, although it was assumed that age thirty-five was the likely cutoff. The plan was to award twenty-five fellowships in 1925. Aydelotte sought Moe's input before the latter headed to the Midwest to conduct additional interviews at Ohio State, the University of Cincinnati, Indiana University, the University of Illinois, the University of Chicago, Northwestern University, and the University of Wisconsin. A letter written on November 18 by Moe's stenographer, Eva D. Rossell, to Aydelotte included the details of Moe's breakneck trip; he visited seven schools in three days.

Once again Moe produced a lengthy and detailed report of his findings. Music and art fellowships continued to be topics of discussion, with a certain Mr. Lyman, assistant to President Walter Scott at Northwestern, providing a strong dissenting opinion regarding the value of offering any such awards:

> On the face of it, it looks like the mention of music and art were made simply as a sop to the donor, and if that is not the fact, that I should exclude studies in those fields. The plan is broad and comprehensive without it, and, as far as your difficulties of

> selection go, music and art would be like a wrench in the machinery. Furthermore, you are talking the language of studies which can be approached with a scientific method, and music and art simply do not fit in.[53]

According to Moe, when he asked Scott his thoughts, the president differed mildly from his assistant, believing that the program might gain in breadth by including music and art. Moe solicited opinions about limiting applicants to American citizens, and the "sagacious" Scott thought that there would be a psychological benefit to the foundation to doing so. President Robert Vinson of Western Reserve endorsed the plan as presented and foresaw no difficulties at all in judging music and art applicants provided that suitable criteria were applied by knowing evaluators.[54]

On November 29, Moe presented Aydelotte with a twenty-two-page report on follow-up interviews he had conducted with "prominent educators" from New York City to Minneapolis. He devoted multiple pages to his second visit with Dean Guy Ford of the University of Minnesota, who offered opinions on the details of operations as well as more philosophical considerations. Ford had specific suggestions for the application: that fellows provide quarterly reports during their award years and a statement about the "social return" that the foundation could anticipate from each fellow's work. He questioned who would profit from published works and whether copyright would belong to the foundation or the author. Moe's report included Ford's lengthy reflection on music and art applicants and awards, the gist of which was that the selection of awardees should be done in an active and personal way by talking with those in positions to know who were worthy applicants rather than rely on a process of passive acceptance; this would spare potential applicants the risk of "being appalled by the application blank" and its query regarding "social return."[55] Given the acknowledged dominance of women in the nation's music culture at the time and the fears that reality raised, it is noteworthy that discussions about music were conducted exclusively by and with men.

Like a stubborn rondo theme, the question of how to attract the right musician and artist applicants and judge their accomplishments or promise returned regularly. Moe characterized the situation as the only real controversial issue, whereas in all other areas the plans were universally embraced. He framed the unique situation for Aydelotte:

> With respect to music and the other fine arts, it should be noted that, with rare exceptions, the men I interviewed did not appear to know what they were talking about. They admitted it. All seemed to be of the opinion that in music we would be swamped with applications. President Birge, who did know his ground, suggested that we cut down the number of applications in music by limiting them to fellowships in music composition. Such a requirement would doubtless make the fellowship conform to the general requirement of creative ability in all fellows. But to me, the publication

> clause is just a general method of insuring a social return from studies done under the auspices of the Foundation; and in music and the other fine arts, the return is to be calculated in a different way. It would appear that if an artist is trained by the Foundation to paint or to sing beautifully, the social return he makes is in painting or singing beautifully, even though he paints or sings for his own profit. Dean Ford agrees with that, and that, I think[,] is what President Vinson had in the back of his mind. For the reasons advanced by Dean Ford and President Vinson, I do not think that we should set aside a certain number of fellowships in music and the other fine arts. My opinion is that we should feel our way cautiously in every field, leaving our plans completely flexible, and always giving the Foundation the benefit of the doubt whenever there is the slightest ground for belief that a candidate does not measure up to the highest standards in the field in which he applies.[56]

The suggestion of President Edward Birge of the University of Wisconsin that music awards be restricted to music composition appeared to solve one problem, but it created another. In the early decades of the century any but a white male's access to advanced study in harmony, theory, and counterpoint, essential skills for Western high-art music composition, was severely limited, and it was nearly nonexistent for women or people of color. Without systematic training, there was little chance that applicants from either group could compete equally with their white male counterparts. That Ruth Porter Crawford would be the only female music composition fellow in the first twenty-one years of the award program, and William Grant Still the only African American music composition fellow for many years beyond that, speaks to the built-in biases at work in the vetting process, but chief among them was rewarding a skill that so many were discouraged from or denied the opportunity to cultivate.[57]

DECEMBER

As late as December, with many of the basic mechanics of the operation set, Aydelotte still sought ideas from educational leaders regarding the makeup of the Board of Trustees, the Educational Advisory Board, and the Committee of Selection. It was as preparations for the launch of the foundation were nearing their end that the names of high-power women educators and administrators first appeared among those consulted. Ada Comstock, president of Radcliffe College, the all-female companion college to Harvard, wrote to Aydelotte on December 5, soon after a meeting applauding the plan and praising the devotion of resources to "educational purposes." In a letter of December 7 Moe explained to Aydelotte that he would see Virginia Gildersleeve the next day. Gildersleeve was dean of Barnard College, the all-female companion college to Columbia University in New York, mere minutes away from the Guggenheim headquarters on Broadway. On December 11, Gildersleeve wrote to Aydelotte concerned that Moe did not get back to her after their very brief meeting on the eighth. Despite the slight, the dean was hopeful that the scheme would do a great deal for the fine arts in the country. To that end she offered three suggestions for Aydelotte's consideration. The first stressed the supreme importance of the selection process to the success of the organization; the second addressed the need to consider the personality as well as the skills of the fellows, part of whose responsibility as Guggenheim awardees would be to "promote international friendship"; and the last emphasized the necessity of women on the selection committee. Gildersleeve expressed her doubt that men could assess women applicants wisely, especially "from the point of view of personality."[58] Given Comstock's and Gildersleeve's geographical proximity to others who were consulted over the course of Moe's and Aydelotte's many months of travel, and the close relationships Aydelotte and Moe had cultivated with male faculty at Harvard and Columbia, it is hard not to conclude that they weren't sought out because they were women, and women attached to women's colleges. With "he" and "him" being the only pronouns used in discussions of fellowship recipients, it is difficult to avoid the conclusion that women were not taken as seriously in practice as they were in prose given the mission statement's wording.

When the first Educational Advisory Board was announced, its nineteen members included Dean Gildersleeve and President Comstock. Although Comstock had not suggested that she sought an active role on the board for herself, her appointment was prudent. By 1925 she had been acting president of Smith College (1917–1918), and president of the American Association of University Women (1921–1923), and had begun her twenty-year tenure as president of Radcliffe College (1923–1943). In the final paragraph of Gildersleeve's letter to Aydelotte, she had named the American Association of University Women as an organization that she believed could recommend worthy applicants.[59] Both women would be asked to serve on early iterations of the "Committee of Selection: United States and Canada."[60] In addition to reconsidering his positions related to race and religion, Moe would need to be educated to recognize and respect intelligent and accomplished female educational leaders who deserved a place at the table. The all-male world of his Oxford days demanded expansion.

It was in the waning days of 1924 that the name of a possible music advisor first appeared in any correspondence. In a letter written on Sunday, December 7, Moe expressed his dismay to Aydelotte that he had not been able to meet Thomas Whitney Surette the previous day but hoped to meet him next time he was in town. It is still unclear how Surette's name first came to Aydelotte's attention or surfaced as a potential music advisor, but once it did, Moe trained his sights on securing the man.

3

THE ADVISOR

Unlike Wilson, Aydelotte, and Moe, Thomas Whitney Surette (1861–1941) was not a Rhodes Scholar. In truth, he had minimal traditional formal education of any kind. He was also unlike the three original foundation figures when considered in terms of age, experiences, achievements, or goals. Moe recalled Surette in an address he would deliver to the American Academy of Arts and Sciences in 1945: "He was sixty-three years old when he first began to act as our adviser and that certainly was one strike against him." Acknowledging other liabilities, Moe pointed out that Surette "was not a composer of any consequence, he was not a rigorous historian of music." On the other hand, Moe observed, "he had time and he had unlimited interest in young composers and the future of music in the United States." He could "read a score and hear it in his mind and he had that unpredictable ability called judgment."[1] It is hard to imagine Moe's enduring a similarly qualified advisor in his own discipline, law, but he had been convinced that music was different. From the beginning a combination of the administrators' ignorance of the field and pressure to appoint someone quickly to adjudicate a category of awards that mattered deeply to the Guggenheims worked in Surette's favor. A brief consideration of who else might have served as advisor puts Surette's selection in context.

Many reasons, all of which are speculative, might have eliminated seemingly more obvious candidates from consideration. The German-born Americans Frank Damrosch and his younger brother Walter Damrosch had impeccable musical credentials and were based in New York. Sons of Leopold Damrosch, patriarch of the Damrosch dynasty, either would have brought immediate prestige to the foundation. Any Damrosch would have held his own in the company of senior scholars and university administrators eventually appointed advisors for other award categories. Their own musical obligations, however, might have precluded adding the role of foundation advisor to their workloads.

Another possibility was Daniel Gregory Mason, who taught at Columbia University. He, too, came from a musical family: Daniel Gregory was a grandson of Lowell Mason, the nation's nineteenth-century musical entrepreneur par excellence. Lowell was the patriarch of a multigenerational line of sons, nephews, and grandsons who shaped the nation's musical culture through their involvement with instrument building, music publishing, concertizing, performing, public education, and academic work. Daniel Gregory's Harvard degree and appointment at Columbia provided the academic credibility that Wilson, Aydelotte, and Moe valued. On paper, he would have fit in effortlessly with other Guggenheim advisors. His virulent and public antisemitic remarks and writings from 1920, however, which included references to "the Jewish infection in *our* music" and the "insidiousness of the Jewish menace to *our* artistic integrity,"[2] would have needed to be ignored, and that would have been difficult. Mason repeated and amplified his sentiments a decade later in his book *Tune in America: A Study of Our Coming Musical Independence*, where he bemoaned what he saw as "our whole contemporary aesthetic attitude toward instrumental music, especially in New York, [as] dominated by Jewish tastes and standards, with their Oriental extravagance, their sensuous brilliancy and intellectual facility and superficiality, their general tendency to exaggeration and disproportion." He worried that "*Our* public taste is in danger of being permanently debauched . . . by the intoxication of what is, after all, an alien art." He further elaborated on the incompatibility of Jews and Gentiles: "The Jew and the Yankee stand, in human temperament, at polar points; where one thrives, the other is bound to languish."[3] Given his beliefs regarding who is the rightful owner of the nation's musical culture, it is hard to imagine him voluntarily associating with the Guggenheim family's foundation had he been asked.

Henry Cowell was another possible candidate, but less likely, in part because of his peripatetic ways. An avowed modernist, he traveled back and forth between the East and West Coasts and abroad, concertizing while working tirelessly on behalf of musical modernism. Although Cowell was eclectic in his embrace of a variety of musical styles himself, and eagerly championed a range of composer colleagues, his relative youth and lack of formal academic credentials or proven administrative experience in 1924 could have eliminated him from consideration. With regard to temperament alone, it is hard to imagine a personality more different from the elitist, academically oriented, fully credentialed Rhodes triumvirate than Cowell, although as Surette's appointment proved, earned degrees were not essential.

Four other composers had the musical credentials, professional standing, and geographical proximity to make them well-qualified candidates, at least to an observer from the twenty-first century. Ernest Bloch, Rubin Goldmark, Frederic Jacobi, and Leo Ornstein appear not to have been considered for the advisory role, which raises several questions, not the least of which has to do with race.[4]

Bloch, a Swiss-born Jewish American, was the same age as Aydelotte, had come to the United States in 1916, and become a U.S. citizen in 1924. He shared a Swiss-Jewish heritage with the original Guggenheims. Starting in 1917 Bloch taught composition at the Mannes School of Music in the city. Its founder, David Mannes, was concertmaster of the New York Symphony Orchestra and married to Clara Damrosch, sister of Frank and Walter Damrosch. Bloch enjoyed the Damrosch imprimatur, if one degree removed. Between 1920 and 1925 Bloch served as director of the newly founded Cleveland Institute of Music and then became director of the San Francisco Conservatory of Music. His connections and his experience as a composer, teacher, and administrator meant that Bloch was well qualified to act as music advisor to the foundation. Sensitive to the burden their Jewishness had placed on generations of Guggenheims and to the resistance they met in so many quarters of their lives, it is possible that the family sought to surround themselves with non-Jews in the front offices, although it is unlikely that the Guggenheims had much to do with suggesting advisors at all. But such a reading could explain Moe's concern that his name (and he) might be mistakenly considered Jewish. If this is true, in a strange turn-around it would mean that the Guggenheims discriminated against people of their own race and faith to advantage their foundation. In 1931 Daniel Gregory Mason would describe Ernest Bloch as "long the chief minister of that [Jewish] intoxication to our public."[5] In an effort to best situate their son's memorial the Guggenheims might have decided that Bloch was too Jewish, although that is pure speculation.

Rubin Goldmark was similarly well qualified, and he was close by. Goldmark was trained as a pianist and as a composer in the United States and at the Vienna Conservatory; he also studied composition with Antonin Dvořák at the National Conservatory in New York, where Goldmark himself had taught theory and composition; his works were regularly performed and well received. Although best known today as the teacher of George Gershwin and Aaron Copland, Goldmark was an omnipresent force in the New York area as a music lecturer, theorist, and composer and perhaps most influentially, starting in 1924, as head of the Composition Department at the newly renamed Juilliard School. His Jewish ancestry and close association with Juilliard, which as an institution was increasingly associated with Jewish musicians (and disparagingly so), may have played a part in his not being considered for the music advisor position, although this also has to remain speculation.[6] Given that most advisors for other award categories had full-time academic positions or were top administrators at colleges and universities, Goldmark's faculty appointment at Juilliard would not have disqualified him; on the contrary, it would have made him typical of advisors.

A similar situation inheres with Frederic Jacobi. A composer and teacher at Juilliard, Jacobi was a founding member of the New York–based League of Composers (with which Copland would align himself on returning to the United States in 1924) and director of the American section of the International Society for Contemporary Music. He clearly had connections and standing in the contemporary music world. His European studies included work at the Paris Conservatoire and in Berlin, and in the United States he took composition lessons with Ernest Bloch and Rubin Goldmark. Like Goldmark's, Jacobi's orchestral music was frequently performed and critically applauded during his lifetime, and he was supremely qualified to act as advisor to the foundation.

Another candidate for music advisor could have been Leo Ornstein. Taken under the wing of Frank Damrosch immediately after arriving in the country in February 1906, the Russian Jewish pianist-composer trained at and graduated from the Institute for Musical Arts in 1910. In 1918 he married a New York debutante, Pauline Mallet-Prevost, whose father, Severo Mallet-Prevost, was a highly regarded international attorney. Mallet-Prevost, who was born in Mexico, founded the Pan-American Society in 1912; he served as its president between 1921 and 1927. In addition to Ornstein's own credentials and reputation, his connections to Latin America and abroad through his father-in-law could have been advantageous to a foundation eager to strengthen its reputation in Central and South America. Famous as a pianist and notorious for his ultra-dissonant, percussive, "futurist" compositions of the mid-teens, starting in about 1920 Ornstein limited his performing career and concentrated more on composing, dividing his time between New York and Philadelphia. Whether Ornstein was ever on any list of contenders is unknown. Despite his marriage into a prominent New York family, that Ornstein was Russian and Jewish and had been marketed years earlier as a musical anarchist could have made him a questionable candidate in a decade frothing with fears of "reds" and suspicious of an alien cultural coup.

The pressure to name a music advisor quickly in order to meet Guggenheim's compressed timetable, coupled with the insularity of the founders' circle and the elite academics who supported and advised them—the majority of whom were white males not immune to the antisemitism of the time—provides some rationale for Thomas Whitney Surette's appointment. Instead of aspiring to cultivate an intellectual, musical, and artistic elite to lead the nation, which was a foundation goal, however, Surette was outspokenly committed to the amateur and to music education, and he aligned with those who shared his beliefs.

He was especially close to Henry and Sophie Drinker of Philadelphia, who were music enthusiasts famous for their Sunday invitation-only singing parties, gatherings of local acquaintances who sight-read Bach chorales and cantatas that Surette attended. When not encouraging music making, Henry Drinker was a prominent attorney and, from 1922, a member of the American Bar Association's Ethics Committee. At a time of widespread xenophobia and antisemitism, even the American Bar Association was actively against admitting anyone but white Christians. In 1929 Drinker, addressing an Ethics Committee meeting, referred to "Russian Jew boys who came up out of the gutter [and] were merely following the methods their fathers had been using in selling shoe strings and other merchandise."[7] Twenty-four years later Drinker wrote a book, *Legal Ethics*, that became among the most cited texts on the topic.[8] The Drinkers used the Sunday singings to reinforce their belief in the supremacy of the European masters and the moral uplift that attended amateur music making, but a subtext of the gatherings was the reinforcement of Western Christian culture.[9] Surette's position outside the inner circle of the foundation's leaders and his identification with an old-school notion of which musical cultures mattered invites a full accounting of the man. It turns out that his outsider position was one with which he was familiar, a type of family inheritance.

A FATHER'S BEQUEST

Thomas Whitney Surette's father, Louis-Athanase Surette, was born in Yarmouth, Nova Scotia, in 1818 to Athanase Surette and Louise D'Entremont. His name was the creative conjoining of those of his parents. In Yarmouth, Louis-Athanase was tutored by the accomplished and beloved French Catholic priest Jean Mandé Sigogne (1763–1844), who had come to Nova Scotia in 1799 via London from Paris, where he had fled the Republic and its requirement that priests swear allegiance to civil authority. As Sigogne's student, Louis-Athanase was under the wing of one of the most lauded religious men in the overwhelmingly Catholic province.

Louise D'Entremont's French heritage and Louis-Athanase Surette's birth and education in Nova Scotia meant that their household was fluent in French, which, alongside English, was widely spoken in the province then as it is today. With his strong private academic credentials, Louis-Athanase taught for two years in provincial schools before pursuing a career in seamanship and relocating to Boston, where he established a business trading with the Maritimes.[10] When he moved further inland to Concord, Massachusetts, Louis-Athanase became active in local educational initiatives. His investment in his new town increased when he married Frances Jane Shattuck (1829–1913), the daughter of the prominent Concord Shattucks; she was twenty years old when she married the thirty-one-year-old Louis-Athanase on May 15, 1849.

Frances Jane's father, Daniel Shattuck, was a member of Concord's "Social Circle," a private all-male society founded in 1794 whose number was limited to twenty-five men at any one time. The society met weekly from October through March to converse and perpetuate the memory of its members, which it assured by writing biographies of those who had recently died. According to a description of the circle found on the website of the Concord Free Public Library, biographies were collected from time to time and published under the title "Memoirs of Members of the Social Circle in Concord."[11] From the beginning, membership in the Social Circle was restricted to influential Concord men; it included John Adams, Ralph Waldo Emerson, and Horace Greeley. Given the persistence of prejudices among New England bluebloods against outsiders, and especially against marriage beyond their social network, it is unlikely that the Shattucks enthusiastically welcomed their daughter's marriage to someone from the provinces who would have been considered backwards simply by dint of his roots. Louis-Athanase Surette, on the other hand, benefited significantly from his marriage into the Shattuck family. And this is important for understanding his son, Thomas, who repeated his father's pattern fifty years later when, at thirty-eight, he married the daughter of a prominent Philadelphia family.

Daniel Shattuck became Louis's first business partner. Their firm, Surette and Shattuck, endured until 1853. Two years later Louis joined forces with a good friend of the Shattucks and another prominent Concordian, Thomas E. Whitney, to form a new business called Surette and Whitney. They apparently enjoyed a sound relationship until 1866, when the company dissolved. It was midway through their partnership, in 1861, that Louis's seventh child, Thomas Whitney Surette, was born. Able to trace their connections to *Mayflower* passengers, the Whitneys had deep roots in New England, something of no small consequence in the history-conscious region. Whitneys, like Shattucks, were members of the Social Circle. By naming his son Thomas Whitney, Louis Surette simultaneously honored a business partner and bequeathed borrowed prestige to his child.

In the first twenty years of his marriage Louis was deeply involved in the life of his adopted town: He belonged to the Masons, rose to the rank of Master, and wrote a history of the Concord Lodge.[12] He served with Bronson Alcott and Ralph Waldo Emerson on the town's school committee. The value that Louis placed on education, rooted in his own tutelage under Abbé Sigogne, would be passed on to his son Thomas.

In 1866 and 1867 Louis not only chaired the local school committee but also curated the Concord Lyceum, an important responsibility in a town that took pride in its lecture series. Louis had earned the respect of the townsfolk even if his Acadian birth meant he could never be a member of the Social Circle or be fully embraced by the Concord coterie. In 1873, however, when Thomas was twelve years old, the tenuousness of Louis's position was exposed, and his borrowed social standing was rescinded. The international financial panic of that year and poor decisions that led to desperate actions caused the failure of his mercantile business and his personal ruin; he never recovered from his disgrace.

Having gained the trust of the Concord elite, Louis had been appointed treasurer of the Sleepy Hollow Cemetery Fund, a position that required that he safeguard the fund's resources. Over the course of 1873, however, it became apparent that Surette had misappropriated monies by exchanging bonds and taking a personal "loan" totaling $3,000. He was confronted with the evidence of his "defalcation" at a private meeting with select trustees who allowed him to quietly resign his position if he paid back the missing funds immediately.[13] Despite condemning his actions, the trustees responded generously to Surette's explanation that he only acted as he did under dire business pressures and to his plea that they minimize the potential embarrassment that broad public knowledge of his actions would cause his family. They decided to keep the information quiet even from other members of the association. All documents were sealed, and the trustees promised that the matter would remain confidential if Surette repaid what he had taken.

Not having $3,000 to replace the funds, however, Surette suggested a compromise that would allow him to continue his business and "restore the amount" over time. In a letter of July 1873 he explained that his wife had offered to help in any way she could, although he admitted that she was unaware of his actions.[14] He also clarified that if he was forced into bankruptcy, he could raise funds by selling some of her property or using it as security against the outstanding debt.

Unable to pay back the money he had taken, Surette declared bankruptcy within a few months of the trustees' meeting, and they commenced to procure the lost funds by transferring his wife's property. It was discovered, however, that multiple mortgages on that property and additional parcels of land far exceeded the amount Surette had stolen from the fund. Given that women typically forfeited control over their finances at the time of marriage in nineteenth-century New England, it is unlikely that Frances Jane was aware of the many liens against property that had been given to her by her family or that she had been consulted when it came to matters of business. Any lingering doubts among the elites regarding the wisdom of Frances Jane's marriage outside her social circle were answered many times over as the reality of the situation became public. They were confirmed in the wisdom of their insular social practices. The trustees grudgingly assumed parts of Louis Surette's debt with a creative combination of purchases and loans to save the family from complete humiliation and ruin. In a letter of November 18, 1873, Surette explained that he and his wife had decided to "sell all [their] Real Estate, excepting the Homestead, replace the Bonds, and afterwards pay every Concord Creditor in full."[15]

Forfeiting ownership of Shattuck property was problematic under any circumstances, but it was especially so given that Frances Jane's brother, Henry Livingston Shattuck, had gifted one of the three large houses he owned to Louis and Frances when they married. When Louis spoke of selling "all *our* real estate" he was referring in part to Shattuck property, that which Frances Jane had brought with her to the marriage. In the months and years that followed Louis was reported to be "very despondent and hardly approachable,"[16] a condition that would have cast a pall over his entire family but perhaps been especially traumatic for twelve-year old Thomas Whitney, whose name was a reminder of his father's earlier business successes.

Ruined financially and emotionally and discouraged from participation in the social circles that had previously accepted him thanks to his marriage, Louis worked off his debts with a job as a station agent at the Concord depot on the Lowell branch of the Boston and Maine Railroad, an honorable job but perhaps beneath what he'd grown accustomed to believing he deserved. His son, a young Thomas Whitney Surette, helped him there.[17] Louis-Athanase Surette lived until 1897, but there is little mention of him after 1873. One can only wonder about Louis's continuing relationships with his in-laws, his Concord friends, and his former business partners, to say nothing of his wife and children. Regardless of the trustees' promise to remain discreet, there was no hiding what had happened. Concord was a small, proud New England town and Louis-Athanase Surette, an outsider, had disgraced prominent members of that social unit.

The family's financial reversal and the resulting change in social status would have made a deep impression on the adolescent Thomas. Though as an adult Surette claimed to eschew most symbols of status, a position that suited a person whose family had lost their own, he clung to vestiges of his family's former position, and none more tightly than his name. Throughout his tenure with the Guggenheim Foundation Surette insisted on a certain old-fashioned formality and used his full name on all documents. He appeared to take pleasure in signing, almost drawing, Thomas Whitney Surette. Men within the Guggenheim fraternity regularly addressed letters to each other using first names, but letters to Surette were always addressed "Dear Mr. Surette." References to him in even the most informal internal office memos used "Mr. Surette." Perhaps their formality was a sign of respect for the older gentleman. Perhaps his family name was all that Surette could take with him from his childhood that seemed honorable, and so he insisted on using it. Like his father, he married up and benefited from another name, that of *his* father-in-law, the wealthy, world-traveling, polyglot, philanthropic engineer-industrialist Frederick Basil Miles of Philadelphia. Surette's association with the Miles family provided the framework for his future financial security and eventual work with the Guggenheim Foundation.

THOMAS WHITNEY SURETTE

When the future music advisor was born in Concord, Massachusetts, in 1861, most of the marquee Transcendentalists, Emerson, Alcott, Brownson, Clarke, Ripley, Channing, and Hawthorne, were still living. Thoreau would die in 1862. Spirits of Transcendentalism did not merely hover over the town or hang in the mists of Walden Pond, they walked the streets. Surette identified with the heroic narrative of Concord's storied past, even if he and his siblings were the first generation of Surettes to be born in the United States.

Not long after his father's business failed in 1873, Thomas Whitney Surette began to teach piano. Much to the amusement of some older Concordians, even at a young age he insisted on being called "Mr. Surette." Secure in their superiority, New Englanders didn't abide pretense, despite their own fixations on lineage and pedigree. They did value education, however, but here, too, Surette came up short. He had little formal training in music; he had little formal education at all: He had some public schooling in Concord, but there is no record that he completed high school. This situation is almost certainly the result of the family's financial straits and his need to work rather than his educability or desire. He studied piano with his sister Sarah, who may have taken lessons from Benjamin Johnson Lang, the highly regarded pianist, organist, conductor, and composer of Boston, although the date and duration of Sarah's studies are unknown, and their cost would have been burdensome.[18] Lang was acquainted with Wagner and promoted the newly founded Bayreuth Festival; he also introduced many Americans to the composer's music. Wagner would become one of Surette's favorite lecture subjects.

With more confidence than skill, perhaps, in 1882 Surette began presenting local concerts. He talked about the pieces he played, which consisted of works by Mozart and Beethoven. Over the next decade Surette's local reputation grew as he and his sister performed at the First Parish Church (Unitarian) in Concord, where he became organist. In 1887 thirty amateurs founded the Concord Choral Club with Surette as their conductor, and by 1890 there were forty-seven active members and thirty-two honorary members, including Ellen Emerson, the first child of Ralph Waldo Emerson and his second wife Lidian. A year later Surette added organ and harmony to the subjects he taught in Concord and Boston, although there is no record of his systematic formal instruction in either to that time.

Autodidacticism appears to be responsible, at least in part, for the unflattering assessments of Surette's abilities as they were reported in local papers. According to Charles W. Hefferman's sources, Surette was "not a skillful performer," he "had very little concern for technique," and his playing was "marred by wrong notes." Heffernan surmised that Surette was "unwilling to practice intricate passages." Whether he lacked the temperament, time, or interest to attend to details is impossible to ascertain, but the consensus appears to be that his playing lacked discipline.[19] To be fair, Surette needed to earn a living, and there was likely little time for perfecting technique. Years later he would express disdain for virtuosity, which, he believed, got in the way of amateur and community music making, a position shared by many who reviled the "cult of virtuosity," as it was called at the time. It may well be, however, that Surette made a virtue of necessity.

As time allowed, Surette studied canon, fugue, and instrumentation intermittently with the German-trained American composer John Knowles Paine, a professor at Harvard University. Although Surette referred to himself as a "special student" at the university, it appears that his relation to both the composer and music studies was informal and sporadic at best. Surette was simultaneously engaged in several other activities that took him far away from Cambridge, and he would have been unable to attend regular courses. Although Surette never matriculated or earned a degree at Harvard, numerous references to his educational achievements later on assign him a class year ('94) and refer to his education there.[20] Around the same time Surette became a board member of the Concord Lyceum, the organization that his father had headed twenty-three years earlier, and between 1891 and 1892 he served as its president. Lyceum-style presentations would exert a lasting influence on him, his valuation of community education, and his lecturing style in years to come.[21]

Around the same time Surette composed an operetta, *Priscilla; or The Pilgrim's Proxy* (1889), whose music owes a large debt to Gilbert and Sullivan, and later a dramatic ballad/cantata called *The Eve of Saint Agnes* (1897).[22] These and a handful of chamber works were directed expressly toward amateur musicians and promoted his goal of fostering "a love of singing."[23] Heffernan observed that "no great degree of technical proficiency is required" to perform Surette's works, whose melodies were often unoriginal.[24] Their style was vaguely chromatic and reflected a late Romantic sensibility in keeping with the times and with Paine's preferences, although Paine obviously wielded much greater skill and subtlety as a composer. Although *Priscilla* was performed in Brooklyn at the Academy of Music in 1891, Surette later dissociated himself from this work and others.[25] This was likely a smart move given their amateurish quality and his eventual elevation to a position of judgment over much more accomplished composers. In this instance Thomas Whitney Surette appears to have recognized his own limitations.

Throughout his life Surette proselytized for the cause of amateur music making, and most especially for the civic value of community singing. In this regard he had his finger on the pulse of a national movement. Over the next few decades, large community choruses formed across the country.[26] Starting in the winter of 1891, Surette assumed the position of conductor and lecturer in organ of the choir at The Hill School, a private preparatory school for boys in Pottstown, Pennsylvania, about thirty miles northwest of Philadelphia.[27] In 1892 he was appointed as a full-time faculty member there, and between then and 1894 he also taught piano and courses in choral music and music appreciation. While in Pottstown Surette founded a chamber series and became organist and choir director at the First Presbyterian Church, which was associated with The Hill School. He also conducted the Pottstown Choral Society in a performance of *Priscilla* that included musicians from Philadelphia. On leaving The Hill School, Surette held positions as organist and choir director in Baltimore, Maryland, and Patterson, New Jersey, cities equidistant from Philadelphia. Like many musicians today, he cobbled together a living doing some teaching, some playing, and some church work.

His days as a church musician came to an end, however, in 1895, when he started lecturing itinerantly for the American Society for the Extension of University Teaching (Extension Society), a private group dedicated to adult education that was headquartered in Philadelphia. The society had been co-founded by Frederick Basil Miles, a philanthropically minded businessman with a deep interest in music and continuing education. Sometime soon after he began lecturing for the Extension Society, Surette met Miles's daughter, Ada Elizabeth Miles (1869–1937), a violinist. She belonged to the Civic Club, an elite group of Philadelphia society women that sponsored cultural events including some of Surette's Extension Society lectures. Ada Miles played in the first performance of *The Eve of St. Agnes*, which took place at the Melody Club of Philadelphia. Surette dedicated the work to her, and they married in June 1899 while Surette was in the midst of a lecture tour in New Rochelle, New York.[28] Thomas Whitney Surette was thirty-eight; Ada Elizabeth Miles was thirty. Thomas's bride came from a highly regarded family in Philadelphia, much as his father's wife, Frances Jane Shattuck, had come from an established family in Concord. Both families belonged to their city's social elite.

By September 1899 Thomas and Ada were in England for an extended tour, and then they purchased a large house on Lexington Road in Concord, Massachusetts, just down the road from Surette's original family home. Ada had been to Europe before with her family, but it was Thomas's first trip and the beginning of a pattern of annual excursions abroad. While there the Surettes attended a music festival in Worcester and thanks to Miles family connections, Thomas became acquainted with Cecil Sharp, Gustav Holst, Ralph Vaughan Williams, Donald Francis Tovey, editor of Bach's and Beethoven's works, Ernest Newman, the celebrated British music critic, and Edward Elgar. Years later Sharp's influence would be evident in an anthology of folk songs that Surette helped collect. Surette's involvement with the University Extension Service in Philadelphia and his marriage to Ada Miles shaped the course of his life thereafter. Without the Miles family Surette would not have had much hope of a relationship with the John Simon Guggenheim Memorial Foundation.

THE AMERICAN SOCIETY FOR THE EXTENSION OF UNIVERSITY TEACHING

Today the idea of extension services likely conjures images of outreach programs focused on food and agriculture, home and family, the environment, and community assistance for those living in rural areas. And that is logical, given that for the past several decades extension service programs have been overseen by the federal government and are regularly associated with local or regional land-grant universities.[29] The American Society for the Extension of University Teaching, founded in 1890 in Philadelphia, however, was altogether different, although it too was dedicated to educating a broad community of citizens in settings distinctly different from the typical college or university. Despite its name, which is suggestive of some kind of national affiliation, this was a completely private enterprise dedicated to uplifting the moral character of its audiences by exposing them to arts and ideas deemed elevating by its officers. Attendees purchased tickets to hear a single talk or a brief series of lectures on various topics. Successful lecturers were those who could attract the largest audiences. There were no textbooks, assignments, or grades, and attendance wasn't taken. The Extension Society was modeled on English societies that had been in existence since the 1870s in Cambridge, London, and Oxford. It resembled the Chautauquas popular in the late nineteenth and early twentieth centuries in the United States, which Frank Aydelotte had experienced growing up, as well as the lyceum series in Concord, with which Surette had intimate knowledge. Part educators and part entertainers, extension lecturers were especially valued by those engaged in the community and settlement school movements. Frederick B. Miles was a founding force in the Extension Society, serving from the beginning as its treasurer and later as president.[30] In the first ten-year report he was singled out for special approbation for his unstinting loyalty and assistance to the cause.

The goal of the British societies had been to bring what universities offered their students to "people unable to go to the Universities." Although the American version aspired to do something similar, the ten-year report observed that the stateside society had an additional goal: It was first "necessary to awaken a desire to learn." To that end it had to "send out its missionaries."[31] Indeed, the Extension Society's rhetoric was infused with religious cum patriotic zeal. The report explained that the society was

> meant for those for whom religion is intended: for those for whom life, liberty, and the pursuit of happiness is intended. It is meant to help the ignorant who desire knowledge that they may learn wisely; to reveal to the half-educated the insufficiency of their knowledge; to rouse intellectual sluggards; to stimulate those

> who are in the right way; to bring questioning to the hearts of the self-satisfied. There is no class for which University Extension is not intended nor to which it has not ministered.[32]

Christian settlement-movement sensibilities were obvious, as were the society's privileging of earnestness and the sense of collective ownership: Its report concluded that the society had "become a social force of the first importance."[33] Its aspiration to moral uplift through education would be echoed in Surette's later rhetoric and shape his work on behalf of music.

The Extension Society originally published a magazine, *University Extension*, a newsletter called "The Bulletin," and finally a paper called "The Citizen," but by 1898 it ceased all publications with the exception of the syllabi of its lectures, which it described as "outlines for study and reading."[34] While Philadelphia was its home base, gradually the number of satellite centers increased to at least twelve, located throughout Pennsylvania, New York, and New Jersey. All of them depended on a corps of unpaid volunteers who arranged for lectures, found meeting places, sold tickets, and paid deficits. When costs exceeded the means of the on-site organizers, officers and donors made up the difference.

The initial ten-year summary report reveals the scale of the society's operation. Total expenses for the decade 1890–1900 were $330,000, of which $70,000 was covered by guarantors and special contributions. The rest was covered by fundraising initiatives, membership dues, and subscriptions. The report recommended the creation of an endowment to guarantee that lecturers could make a career of their work, but this would not happen before the society's work was taken up by other entities.

Using meeting space at the University of Pennsylvania for its summer classes, between 1893 and 1897 the society offered four-week sessions in the month of July.[35] In 1896 Surette participated in one of these sessions and got his first taste of how such a program might operate. His lecture, "What Constitutes Good Church Music?," was published the following October in the *Protestant Episcopal Review*.[36] Surette's willingness to assert what was *good* or the *best* music would be a hallmark of his style. But summer sessions were discontinued after five years because of the inhospitably hot Philadelphia weather, which affected enrollments. In what would be a prophetic statement, the Extension Society report suggested that it would leave "summer schools for cooler places." Starting in 1917, the four-week July session became the standard for Surette's summer school in Concord, Massachusetts, a town where the Sudbury and Assabet Rivers came together and canopy roads provided shade from the summer sun.

By any measure, Surette was a successful lecturer for the Extension Society. Between 1894 and 1900 he taught nearly seventy iterations of courses on ten different topics. His 1899 marriage to Ada Miles coincided with a significant uptick in the number of courses he taught.[37] Whereas in 1894 he taught five iterations of courses, in 1900 he taught thirty iterations. His courses on the great composers of the Classical and Romantic periods were offered most frequently, followed by a general course on the development of music and one on the music dramas of Wagner.

The society's report for the 1905–1906 academic year shows that during Surette's travels through Connecticut, New Jersey, New Hampshire, Massachusetts, Rhode Island, New York, and Pennsylvania more than sixty-two hundred people attended his lectures. His work with the society stoked his missionary zeal and expanded the range of his work on behalf of music education. In the brief faculty biographies provided at the top of the report, in addition to being identified as "Staff-Lecturer in Music of the American Society," Surette is also listed as "Lecturer for Columbia University."[38] Surette's association with Columbia is also intertwined with the Miles family, although in this case his father-in-law and wife acted more behind the scenes than they had with the Extension Society.

CONNECTIONS IN NEW YORK

By 1905 Frederick B. Miles had moved to New York and was living at 40 West Ninth Street in a spacious apartment on a tree-lined street in Greenwich Village, although he remained president of the Extension Society in Philadelphia. The 1905 revised edition of *Who's Who in New York* listed Thomas and Ada Miles Surette as residing at the same address as Frederick Miles.[39] By keeping their Concord home, they behaved like others of the establishment set, which spent its summers in the country or abroad but lived in New York from fall through early spring. That arrangement gave Surette opportunities he would not have enjoyed otherwise, and one of them involved acquaintance with Daniel Gregory Mason. Mason was a bona fide student of John Knowles Paine and an 1895 Harvard graduate. In 1905 Mason became a lecturer in music at Columbia University. Over time he moved through the academic ranks, ultimately becoming MacDowell Professor of Music and head of the department. He stayed at Columbia until his retirement in 1942.

In 1907 Mason and Surette collaborated on a book that reflected their shared musical values: *The Appreciation of Music: A Course of Study for Schools, Colleges, and General Readers* was among the first music appreciation texts when the topic was in its infancy. Like Surette, the Columbia professor was a champion of the German Romantic tradition; he was also a critic of jazz, modernism, and any music that suggested the popular or avant-garde.[40] A collaboration with Mason provided Surette with an elite university association; a collaboration with Surette provided Mason with access to the Miles network and the publisher, the H. W. Gray Company.[41] As Elizabeth Crouch Fitts explains, H. W. Gray had originally been "an American distributor for the English publisher Novello, Ewer & Co." but by 1906 had become "an independent firm."[42] The company published the journal *The New Music Review and Church Music Review*, which between 1906 and 1908 ran a long series of articles first by Surette, then by Mason and Surette, and finally by Mason alone.[43] It was logical and convenient that the firm should publish their book given the relation of Frederick B. Miles and Ada Elizabeth Miles Surette to the H. W. Gray Company: Father and daughter, along with Frederick S. Converse, H. Binney, and Walter Henry Hall, were co-owners of the company.[44] Just as the Miles family had enhanced opportunities for Surette's success with the Extension Society, it now underwrote his (and Mason's) publishing efforts. As Fitts clarifies, "The *NMR* focuse[d] on the conservative perspective and its composers, who were also important in leading musical education and American sacred music in the early 1900s."[45] The *NMR* and *The Appreciation of Music* became logical sites for the continuation of Surette's Extension Society lectures and for Mason's first text. Fitts concluded, "The need for education as a means for reform is a theme that recurs frequently in the *NMR*."[46] This idea was wholly in line with Surette's beliefs.

CONNECTIONS ABROAD

Over the next fifteen years Thomas Whitney Surette established associations in the United States and abroad that extended the reach of his educational initiatives. In 1907 the Surettes returned to England, where Thomas lectured throughout the countryside for the Oxford University Extension service, the English counterpart of the private American Society. On his return to the United States his association with Oxford would be cited as evidence of Surette's international regard, although no distinction would be made between Oxford University proper and the university-related extension service. There is little doubt that Surette's American lectures revealed a gift for teaching lay people about music, and his and Mason's music appreciation book would have been known in England given the connection of the H. W. Gray Company with Novello. As regards Oxford, here too his relations to the Miles family provided the essential link.

Ada's brother, Basil Miles, had graduated from both the University of Pennsylvania and Oxford University and was a highly regarded U.S. diplomat with connections across Europe including Germany, France, and Russia, as well as in England. Frederick B. Miles's earlier business connections throughout the continent and his son's prestige facilitated Surette's involvement with the English university program and with the Ancoats Brotherhood, a private Christian society focused on social reform that was founded in England in 1878. The brotherhood was dedicated to bringing lectures on art and literature to working-class people, as well as providing entertainment to its elite members.[47] Surette benefited from his marriage into the Miles family much as his father had benefited from his association with the Shattuck family. In both cases, wives' families opened doors which the father and son happily walked through.

Ada and Thomas Surette traveled in England, Germany, and France throughout 1908. They met Emperor William and Empress Augusta Victoria of Germany as the guests of Basil and Frederick Basil Miles, who both attended the formal reception in their official capacities.[48] Paris would become a favorite summer destination for the Surettes for the next three decades.[49] It was a city well known to Basil Miles, the American Administrative Commissioner to the International Chamber of Commerce in that city. When the Surettes returned to the United States in 1909 Thomas continued to lecture through the auspices of the Extension Society; this time his work took him as far as the St. Paul, Minnesota, area, where he spoke about Beethoven, Brahms, Schubert, and Schumann. When Surette lectured in Minneapolis, a reviewer from a Chicago paper mistook him for a Briton and chastised him for presuming to lecture Americans on good music.[50] It seems he had acquired a British accent while on his travels.

Although he was already in his early fifties, 1914 and 1915 became especially important years for Surette, who never stopped proselytizing on behalf of music education reform. Beginning in 1914 he developed a close friendship with Archibald T. Davison, a young choral conductor and music professor at Harvard. They eventually co-edited collections of folk songs and anthems for their Concord Series, published by E. C. Schirmer Music Company in Boston. Excited by the possibilities of an alliance with a similarly ardent music reformer, Davison invited Surette to serve on a community committee that the professor chaired whose goal was to reform the Boston public school music curriculum.[51]

A position on the committee allowed Davison and Surette to cultivate their many shared values and goals and to formalize a professional relationship. It was also at this time that the two men's names became associated with The Music Fund, a private initiative whose goal was to support music study abroad.[52] The curriculum committee endeavored to overhaul the way music was taught in American classrooms, or at least in Boston ones, by insisting on teaching only "the highest quality" music, by standardizing all grade-level goals, and by advocating for materials that Davison and Surette had collected, selected, and published. The committee rejected the current practice of using what it characterized as newly composed, "made to order, commonplace songs" with their "lifeless melodies" in favor of teaching time-tested "beautiful music," which it deemed the "best" music.[53] With very few exceptions, both men equated good music with European composers.

As expected, large numbers of trained public school music educators rejected the committee's criticisms, which one teacher called "uninformed." They took issue with rigid notions of what constituted good or bad music, which clearly favored continental repertoire, and the seemingly self-serving practices of a committee that required educators to use only its materials. Surette was the target of especially critical remarks by Peter Dykema, president of the Music Supervisors National Conference. In 1917 Dykema pulled no punches when he pronounced: "Mr. Surette's statements concerning public school music are based upon a ridiculously inadequate knowledge of music in this country."[54]

That Surette knew little about the history of American music or its vernacular traditions is almost certain. Committed as he was to European music, he appears never to have educated himself about his own nation's musical culture. From his earliest efforts as a teenager teaching piano in Concord, he championed Beethoven and Mozart. As a lecturer he focused on only the "masters" and Wagner. Although he would not have been alone at the time in ignoring or dismissing his nation's musical heritage, his position would make any posturing as an expert on American educational needs extremely hard to abide. As was likely inevitable from the start, the curriculum reform effort failed, teachers returned to choosing the materials they preferred, they re-incorporated American tunes, and the committee disbanded.

In 1915 Surette became active in the education department of the predominantly female National Federation of Music Clubs (NFMC), the largest and most powerful organization of private music teachers and amateurs in the country. The NFMC was founded in 1893 to centrally organize local amateur music clubs from Maine to Washington State. It was dedicated to promoting cultivated music in America, though not originally or necessarily American music. In April Surette became chairman of the Department of Education of the NFMC, and a month later he assumed the chairmanship of the Courses of Study project of that same department. At that time the federation numbered thousands of members who collectively taught additional thousands of private students.

Surette, determined to spread his personal musical gospel, took his most decisive step in June 1915 with the creation of his own summer school. He started small and with a clientele that closely resembled the membership of the NFMC: female private music teachers. In the summer of 1919 Walter Piston, soon to be a music student at Harvard, visited the school. Within a few years Davison became a popular guest lecturer there. As Heffernan surmised: "Davison's distinguished presence undoubtedly contributed greatly to the prestige of the Concord Summer School in the early 1920s."[55]

THE CONCORD SUMMER SCHOOL

The importance of Surette's summer school as a locus for his musical ministry is clear. For twenty-three years, from 1915 to 1938, the names Concord and Surette were synonymous in the minds of many amateur choral music lovers. They traveled like pilgrims to the town made famous by Emerson and Thoreau for a chance to listen to Surette expound on music and to sing in his summer chorus; the school operated much as today's music camps do without the more rigorous curricula the latter offer. A number of regular attendees were so devoted to the musical crusader that they called themselves "Suretters." The one-time local boy had ascended to near sainthood among his followers, although many long-time Concord residents couldn't understand why anyone would listen to the fifty-four-year-old man who, as a youth, had sold tickets at the railroad station with his disgraced father and had insisted upon being called "Mr. Surette." The Concord Summer School took advantage of its accessible and bucolic location and attracted many seeking a getaway from the heat and congestion of various nearby cities to imbibe the rarefied Transcendentalist air.

Its initial 1915 prospectus was direct and spare. It announced a "Summer School for Teachers in Methods of Teaching Music to Children." Surette identified the school's location as his home at 21 Lexington Road in Concord, Massachusetts, and explained that formal sessions would be confined to weekday mornings from June 14 to July 2 inclusive. He clarified that the object of the school was "to instruct Teachers in such methods as will make children understand and appreciate the best music" and assured attendees that "the instruction is intended to be suitable for teaching children who do not play an instrument as well as for those who do." He advised prospective students that "in addition to the attendance at the regular sessions those taking the course will be expected to work outside the class on topics assigned to them." The prospectus closed with a prompt that encouraged a quick response because "Only a limited number of Teachers can be taken." He invited interested parties to "apply to Mr. Surette" directly for particulars regarding "terms, information as to boarding places, trains, etc."[56]

The original three-week summer school attracted a dozen female music teachers, who in later correspondence were affectionately referred to as the "twelve eager ladies."[57] When enrollment eventually exceeded the space available in the Surettes' living room, the school moved to the local church. Consistent with perceptions that music belonged to the female sphere, enrolling a significant number of male students was a challenge in the school's first seven years. When twelve men finally attended in 1922 it was cause for special comment and celebration. In a letter to Mrs. K. S. Pray, one of the original students, Ada Surette acknowledged that it was "quite thrilling to have twelve *men* enrolled as students. . . . The

Figure 3.1. Thomas Whitney Surette and Ada Miles Surette leaving the Concord Summer School lecture hall in 1935. Reproduced with kind permission of the Concord Free Public Library.

singing is fine and the men's voices make it wonderful." Besides the improved sound, however, the participation of a critical mass of men conveyed a degree of legitimacy on the entire educational endeavor that a student body made up exclusively (or predominantly) of women could never achieve regardless of its attainments. At a time when music was considered too much a woman's domain to be taken seriously, the mere presence of men bestowed prestige.[58] By 1922 the school had changed significantly from what it had been at the beginning. A quick survey of the 1915 curriculum printed opposite the single-page announcement of the school's opening reflected Surette's original ambitions, basic values, and unflappable confidence in his judgement.

TOPICS

I. The teaching by ear of a large number of beautiful songs as a preparation for any musical instruction, theoretical or practical.
  [a] Elements of beauty in folk-songs as distinguished from current children's songs.
  [b] Faults in taste and sentiment; in technique.

II. The teaching of rhythm.

III. Training in listening
  [a] to rhythms,
  [b] to melodic phrases,
  [c] to modulations, etc.

IV. The teaching of musical forms as an expression not of the technique of composition, but of universal laws.
  [a] Parallel with poetic forms;
  [b] with the story.
  [c] All musical forms are dictated by the limitations and needs of human beings; no one has been created by a composer.

V. The standard of pianoforte music for children.
  [a] A repertoire for teaching.
  [b] How necessary for technical purposes is a lowering of standard?
  [c] In teaching pianoforte playing to children what besides technique should be included?

VI. The teaching of Harmony.

Regardless of the originality or wisdom of Surette's beliefs, his argument for teaching traditional (mainly European) folk music only, disparaged contemporary American composers and their works. He was certain of what constituted good taste and the components of beauty, but beyond that Surette proclaimed the existence of universal laws governing musical behavior. His confidently conservative musical values elevated Bach, Beethoven, and Brahms above all others and guided his choice of study repertoire at his summer school. Days started with the singing of a Bach chorale and ended with study of a symphony.

The 1916 prospectus suggested a more ambitious agenda and a move away from a narrow focus on music pedagogy aimed at children toward the inclusion of chamber music and a performance of Brahms's *Requiem*. Drawing on his Extension Society experience, Surette promised that performances would be preceded by informal lectures.[59] To the 1915 announcement the 1916 version added a simple statement at the bottom of the page: "Mason and Hamlin Pianos." Surette's connection to the Mason family continued, and their pianos became the official instrument of Surette's summer school from the second year on.

Although Surette attempted to differentiate the curriculum for returning and new students, the program was too informal and turnover too great to impose a graded course of study. Of the thirty-eight women attending the 1916 session, only seven were continuing students from the original twelve. Thereafter Surette made no effort to formalize his summer school.

He did, however, ask all students to familiarize themselves with a number of readings prior to arriving for school. His preference for English authors and literature was evident in the titles: "Essays on Style" (1889) by the writer and art critic Walter Pater, the novel *Evan Harrington* (1860) by George Meredith, the popular 1915 novel *Victory: An Island Tale* by Joseph Conrad, and the 1909 volume *The Romantic Movement in English Poetry* by poet and editor Artur Symons, from which students were to read the introduction and final hundred pages. The complete absence of any music-focused readings is notable. Showing his preference for masters and masterworks, Surette also required students to bring with them solo piano arrangements of Beethoven, Brahms, and Franck symphonies and promised that chamber music would also be discussed and reading assignments made.

Surette added a four-page "Historical Outline" to the 1916 flyer he circulated among his summer school attendees: a chronological listing of style periods and schools, composers and instrument makers, and a variety of anecdotal observations and assessments whose style would mark his Guggenheim Foundation applicant assessments. He characterized J. S. Bach as a "profound philosophic mind" who is "uninfluenced by Italian style."[60] He compared Handel to Bach and found the former "less profound." Regarding Haydn, he was "a naïve personality; [and his] music rustic, simple, merry—all objective." Mozart, according to Surette, was the "perfect master of his art" and Beethoven "a great man, as well as a great composer . . . [who] stands for intellectual freedom." Of the composers associated with Italian Romantic opera: Donizetti was "fluent, but not deep"; Bellini, the "same type as Donizetti, but greater"; and Verdi the "greatest Italian composer . . . more of a thinker; more persistence, and a longer life." Among composers of the German Romantic school, Surette noted that Schubert was the "son of an obscure schoolmaster; poor; friendless," but recognized that "he and Mozart [are] the two great writers of pure melody." Schumann's educational credentials were foregrounded: "Good education: Heidelberg University; interested in poetry; imbibed the ideas of Heine and Richter," but he was "not a master of the greatest forms in music." Instead, Surette pronounced Schumann's works the "best music for the piano." He understood Mendelssohn to have had a "happy, cultivated, rich family, complete education; every advantage; fluent expression in music: a clear stream, but not a deep one," and observed Chopin's "feminine nature" and his ill health. The "atmosphere of the Salon in some of his music" is clearly not a desirable quality.[61] Brahms fared much better with Surette, who characterized him as a "strong, vibrant personality" who possessed "great learning (in music); classical strength, romantic feeling; part of Beethoven, part of Schumann." Brahms "stands apart from his contemporaries and preserves the best traditions of the art."[62] Surette's thumbnail sketches reflect a breezy, confident, reductionist predisposition that when used in his advisor's role at the Guggenheim worked against applicants he was disinclined to favor.

Surette's historical outline titled "Modern Opera" gave primacy of place to Wagner and traced the composer's impact on the genre, moving it from opera (*Rienzi*) to music drama (*Tristan und Isolde*), which he understood as his "highest achievement." He recognized Wagner's influence on Puccini, who "uses some of Wagner's methods, but never rises to any great heights," and Strauss, who "outdoes Wagner in freedom of form, but in *Salome* and *Elektra* pays little heed to that necessity for repose which exists in every dramatic-musical composition."[63] Surette ended his outline with a paragraph on César Franck, who preserved "something of the medieval spirit," and a final, unusually expansive entry on Debussy. It is unique for its focus on the composer's harmonic language in the context of historical developments:

> Debussy represents another phase of the struggle to free music from the bonds of our tempered scale. Modal scale forms appear here and there in Beethoven; Brahms uses them more freely. Debussy employs at times a whole tone scale. His harmonic system is free and pliable, but he does not create a broad, stable melodic line. In *Pelleas et Mélisande* he abjures melody altogether and creates a background of ever-changing color and intensity against which the singer chants a half sung, half spoken voice part.[64]

Surette was guided in his thinking about Debussy's music by Archibald Davison and specifically by Davison's 1908 Harvard PhD dissertation, "The Harmonic Contributions of Claude Debussy," the first dissertation ever to be written about the French composer. Given what appear to be Surette's music-analytical insecurities, he would have listened to the Debussy expert. Beginning in 1919, Davison became a regular presence at Surette's summer school, first giving recitals and lectures on harmony and then assuming a larger role in the school's operation. Davison's impact can be felt in Surette's forward-looking closing remarks, which suggest unexpected curiosity about the future of music and what it might hold.

> Music is today in a state of continuous experimentation. Ravel, Schoenberg, Scriàbin, and Stravinsky combine sounds that have never been combined before; but this is the history of music. How permanent their music will be we have no

> means of knowing, but it is certain to be tested finally by the natural laws that underlie all human expression.[65]

The following summers' announcements reflected the continuing expansion of Surette's target demographic and a trend away from teaching teachers to reaching amateur appreciators, an audience like the one he had addressed so successfully in his extension lectures. Singing choral music and studying the masters' symphonies and chamber works took primacy of place, augmented by discussions of select readings from Surette's favorite literature, art history, novels, and increasingly, his own publications: his course of study *The Development of Symphonic Music* (1915), the first in a projected series of books to be published by the National Federation of Music Clubs Press that never materialized, and *Music and Life* (1917), a collection of articles that had been published previously in the *Atlantic Monthly*. He assured students that all the titles he named could be purchased at discounted prices through the Boston Music Company.

At the same time as his Summer Music School work, in the late teens and early twenties Surette continued his lecture tours, directed choral ensembles, and helped organize arts-related programs at the newly opened Cleveland Museum of Art. He worked with the museum's music program between 1918 and 1922 and contributed to the establishment of what is now the museum's Department of Performing Arts and its acclaimed arts series. Surette's increasing reputation as a crusader for music education took him back to the Philadelphia area, where, in the 1920s, he helped organize music offerings at Bryn Mawr College and put Horace Alwyne in place as piano instructor there.

By 1920 the summer school ran for four weeks, although many attendees did not stay the entire time; they came late and left early as their summer plans dictated.[66] Such flexibility reinforced the amateur music practices that Surette encouraged. In 1922, when the first men registered, Surette used the validation their presence provided in a female-phobic music culture to invite a number of guest lecturers. Drawing on his connections in the Boston area, Surette engaged Augustus D. Zanzig, supervisor of music in the Brookline public schools who also lectured at Harvard University and Smith College, and Edward Yeomans, founder of the Ojai Valley School in Ojai, California. In the spring of 1924, as the Guggenheim Foundation was coalescing, an *Atlantic Monthly* advertisement for the school named a number of new participants including the American String Quartet, Horace Alwyne, Richard Tattersall (an organist from Toronto), and William Ernest Hocking (professor of philosophy at Harvard University), whose book *Human Nature in the Remaking* Surette recommended to his students. Other men with Harvard connections joined in Surette's enterprise; G. Wallace Woodworth, for instance, a former student of Davison's, became an invaluable aid to Surette beginning in 1929 and through the final years of the school's operation.

Over the next few years, Surette's direct impact on Guggenheim Fellowship recipients was reflected in the number of Concord Summer School attendees who received music composition awards: Robert Delaney (awards in 1929 and 1930), Randall Thompson (1929, 1930), Otto Luening (1930, 1931, 1974), Walter Piston (1935), and Dante Fiorillo (championed by Surette starting in spring 1935, summered in Concord in 1936, and awarded Guggenheim Fellowships in 1935, 1936, 1937, and 1938). Without access to the names of all those who applied to the foundation for music awards, it is impossible to know whether any of the many women who attended Surette's summer school submitted an application. Since composition wasn't taught there it is unlikely that they would have been competitive if they had.

SURETTE AND THE GUGGENHEIM FOUNDATION

To return to the questions posed at the beginning of the chapter: Who, specifically, suggested Thomas Whitney Surette to Moe or to Aydelotte? How did his name first surface as a potential music advisor to the foundation? Given Surette's connections with Archibald T. Davison and the foundation's determined efforts to cultivate friendly relations with elite universities, a recommendation from Davison would have been taken seriously if it had been solicited. Surette biographer Kathleen Uhler Adams suggested Joseph Lee, a well-known Boston philanthropist, "father of the playground movement" and founder of the National Recreation Association, now known as the National Recreation and Park Association, as a possible recommender. He and Surette were close friends, and they had many of the same social goals.[67] It is also possible, given Surette's many connections in and around Philadelphia, which was Aydelotte's bailiwick and home to Henry and Sophie Drinker, that his name came up in informal conversations with those active in music circles in the city. Decades of involvement with the Extension Society, which publicized his name, as well as the Miles family's circle of professional associations and well-placed acquaintances in Philadelphia, New York, and abroad, could also have enhanced his attractiveness.

A January 14, 1925, letter from Moe to Aydelotte written after the secretary first met Surette suggests that Aydelotte did not know him personally, but it leaves open the possibility that the Swarthmore president had heard his name. Aydelotte would have known of the Miles family, if not for their involvement with the American Society for the Extension of University Teaching, then as potential donors to his institution. Moe's three-and-a-half-page single-spaced letter reveals that he was clearly taken with Surette:

> I do not know whether you know Mr. Surette personally or not, and therefore give you my opinion: If we can get him for this Foundation, I can not conceive

> of a better man. His interests are much wider than music, and he discussed with me very interestingly and with a great deal of information the relation of musical studies to studies which lead to what is generally known as a liberal education.[68]

Moe explained Surette's criticisms of the newly created Juilliard Musical Foundation: Even a "super-conservatory," according to Surette, can't provide the thoroughness of a French or English education. To correct for what he perceived as this national weakness, Surette explained The Music Fund to Moe:

> Mr. Surette told me that he, with Professor A. T. Davison, of Harvard, is Director of The Music Fund—a fund the income of which is put in their hands by the donor without any conditions attached except that it is to be used for purposes of musical education. A large part of the income, he said, they use for the purpose of sending students of music to study in Paris, and at the present time they have six there in various schools. The balance of the income is used for the purpose of aiding American teachers of music to take advanced courses in this country, in support of children's concerts, and for similar purposes. He said that students who had returned from Paris, where they spent from two to three years, had proceeded a great distance further in their studies than they would have if they had remained in the United States, and had acquired a thoroughness which he thought it was almost impossible to attain here, in addition to the cultural effects of living in Paris.

Surette's bias against training performers rather than amateurs surfaced in Moe's report to Aydelotte:

> Students sent to Paris on The Music Fund are usually persons who plan to become teachers of music, and not musical performers. I gathered, in so far as I can express it in more familiar terms, that it is a kind of "musical scholarship" that he hopes they will acquire by their studies in Paris.

Moe relayed a story told him by Surette of "a boy who was playing in a restaurant in Boston." According to Surette's account he and Davison "provided him with funds to take the regular undergraduate course at Harvard," where "he obtained A grades in practically all subjects and won a traveling fellowship in music." With that he went to Paris and studied for two years, and "now he is about to return to become an instructor under Professor Davison at Harvard."[69] Moe was uncertain about the exact nature of The Music Fund, but surmised that it "is administered in a very personal kind of way. It would appear that Mr. Surette and Professor Davison are very good pickers of musical talent."

Moe asked Surette about application processes and criteria for selection, about age ranges and limits, and what a reasonable stipend might be. Referring to his experience with Music Fund recipients, Surette offered that "a normal stipend of $2500.00 a year was ideal." This turned out to be the same figure that Aydelotte had suggested and the amount of a stipend awarded in music composition during the early years of the Guggenheim.

In early conversations, there had been the possibility of assisting awardees with publication and its costs. Surette observed that "the Carnegie Corporation was assisting in England certain composers to publish their musical compositions," but he noted that enacting such a plan in the United States would likely be more difficult "because . . . scholars in England seem to have a kind of detachment and impartiality which it seems impossible to attain here."

Although Surette claimed to value impartiality, when it came to generating an applicant pool for the new foundation, he argued against "wide publicity," favoring instead "some more quiet way." When Moe characterized Aydelotte's means of identifying Laura Spelman Rockefeller Memorial Scholars in England the previous spring as the "personal method," Surette assented, believing that "the success of the Foundation might be endangered by too much publicity." It is difficult not to wonder about the degree to which a more public call for applications and their assessment might have changed the course of U.S. art music culture starting in the 1920s. It certainly would have diluted Surette's influence over the choice of awardees.

When it came to ideas regarding the actual selection process Surette offered that

> the ideal method of selection would be to have a committee of three who had demonstrated that they could pick *men* and read credentials with intelligence, and who were geographically located so that they could meet sufficiently often to do the business of the Foundation thoroughly.[70]

Perhaps without intending it, Surette's advice regarding geographic proximity limited not only the possible advisors but the applicants as well. The frequent requests by Moe that applicants meet with Mr. Surette would have been impossible for hopefuls who lived any distance from New York. Other assumptions also affected the pool of likely applicants. Rather than simply express the gendered linguistic habits of the time, Surette's concern that advisors could "pick men" accurately reflected his assumptions and beliefs regarding who would (or should) be applying. That only one woman, Ruth Crawford, received a single award in either music composition or music research during Surette's fifteen-year tenure as advisor speaks to the weakness of the "personal method" when it came to identifying or cultivating the widest pool of potential awardees. Essentializing attitudes regarding women's abilities in the realm of music composition, music scholarship, or more general behaviors colored his and many of his informal reviewers' assessments and peppered their correspondence. Surette's unshakeable (if tenuously grounded) confidence in his abilities to "read credentials" and

Moe's confidence in Surette allowed him to assume near dictatorial power over the awards.

But even with Moe's enthusiastic endorsement Surette was not a shoo-in for the advisor's position. An April 18, 1925, letter from Frank Aydelotte to Charles Homer Haskins, professor of medieval history at Harvard and ultimately an advisor to Aydelotte and the Educational Advisory Board from 1925 to 1933, shows Aydelotte's concerns about Surette's lack of desired experience and perhaps his credentials:

> So far as Fine Arts and Music are concerned, I believe we better call on Emerson and Surette for special advice without making them members of the committee. I believe this committee would have more grasp of artistic subjects than Surette or Emerson would of general problems of research. This remark is not intended as derogatory as to either those two men, but only as to the facts about their experience.[71]

Aydelotte's early premonitions about Surette's lack of experience would prove correct a decade later when the latter championed an unknown composer, Dante Fiorillo. In April 1925, however, Aydelotte's concerns about Surette were apparently mollified, and with Moe's eager endorsement, no doubt motivated by his need to find a music advisor quickly, Surette was entrusted with the responsibility of selecting the Guggenheim Foundation's music composition fellows. Surette was also named one of the original nineteen Educational Advisory Board members, a position he maintained until his death in 1941. In 1927, when the foundation added an award in music research, Surette took charge of that as well and decided its winners. His new position simultaneously recognized, rewarded, and consolidated influence he had enjoyed elsewhere and expanded it significantly to include the network of people, organizations, and institutions that came with the Guggenheim Foundation.

4

THE NETWORK

In its first fifteen years, the Guggenheim Foundation depended heavily on existing organizations for direction: Those associated with Aydelotte in general and with Surette when it came to musical matters were especially important. But new connections were forged all the time, and Henry Allen Moe was essential to them; he ultimately became the face of the organization. Surette and Moe, with increasing help from previous composition fellows, became the principal actors deciding music fellowships. As intricate as the foundation's network became, however, behind the scenes it was always the Guggenheim Brothers' global mining business that funded the endeavor. The foundation formed a specific network nested within a larger family business network.

From the beginning Simon Guggenheim's experience in a close-knit, generations-long family enterprise informed all aspects of his thinking, but especially anything associated with the bottom line. When it came to the foundation this manifested itself as a concern with payroll: how many employees and who they would be, their responsibilities, and their cost. The senator was clear: Staff would be minimal and foundation expenses would be restricted to their salaries, costs incurred while doing their work, maintenance of an office space, and the fellowships themselves. Today the foundation's expenditures are similarly targeted.

Crucial to building the new organization's network was its first employee, Frank Aydelotte. Guggenheim had understood that his unassailable credentials and professional standing would immediately elevate the foundation in the public's mind. In 1933 Aydelotte's achievements were acknowledged in a uniquely public way when his image appeared on the cover the June 5 issue of *Time*.[1] Guggenheim appreciated that this principal actor made a difference: Almost singlehandedly Aydelotte gave the foundation credibility.

Although Guggenheim accepted that Aydelotte would divide his energies between the presidency of Swarthmore College and the foundation, in the early years he wanted Moe to be focused wholly on foundation duties. Once again thinking like a businessman, for whom loyalty to the concern was paramount, Guggenheim demanded dedicated, discreet employees. When, in April 1931, after six full years of work on behalf of the foundation, Moe asked Aydelotte for permission to serve on the board of the newly constituted Oberlaender Trust, Aydelotte consulted Guggenheim, who responded that he was hesitant to approve anything but nominal participation, fearing that outside work would interfere with Moe's work for the foundation: "I do not wish to have Mr. Moe placed in a position whereby he may not be able to give practically all of his time to our foundation. This is a policy I have personally followed in business and have always had the important officers of the Smelting Company do likewise."[2] Business practices informed foundation practices. Two weeks later Aydelotte assured him that Moe understood, but emphasized the benefits that Moe believed might accrue to the foundation if he assumed some kind of role at the trust: "At the same time he points out that his participation in the activities of the Oberlaender Trust is very useful in preventing them from encroaching on our activities and in turning over to them certain people to whom we could not give appointments."[3] The argument about encroachment is a curious one given that the Guggenheim Foundation appeared not to have been concerned about duplicating others' efforts directed at composer support. On four occasions in its first seven years, it awarded fellowships to composers who had been recipients of Pulitzer Traveling Scholarships.[4] Going forward, Guggenheim Fellows also found additional support at the American Academy. Ultimately, Moe's presence on other organizations' boards proved helpful to the foundation and to his own reputation. Although his role in the Oberlaender Trust for its twenty-two years of existence went far beyond nominal participation, he maintained enough focus on the foundation to assuage any fears that his energies or loyalties were compromised. Moe's suggestion that his participation could prevent encroachment likely appealed to the senator-businessman's territorial instincts. In truth, however, there was no real danger that the trust would intrude on the foundation's terrain given that their missions were more complementary than competitive and would become increasingly so in response to political developments of the 1930s.

By 1933 Moe had established himself as the indispensable go-between for composers seeking support not only from the Guggenheim Foundation, but also for residencies at Yaddo, and financial assistance from the Carnegie Corporation of New York and the Institute of International Education, which administered Carnegie grants. Over the years, Moe expanded his reach and became an essential actor in multiple other organizations' boards, initially, at least, with the rationale that his involvement benefited the Guggenheim Foundation. At the end of his career there, Moe had served as treasurer and director of the Association of American Rhodes Scholars and been a trustee of the Rockefeller Foundation, the Institute of Current World Affairs, the Institute for Advanced Study at Princeton, the New York State Historical Society, the Museum of Modern Art in New York, the American Academy in Rome, the American Academy of Arts and Sciences, and the Oberlaender Trust, among other organizations. After he retired from the foundation in 1963, Moe served as interim chair of the National Commission on the Humanities for one year, 1965–1966: Today it is known as the National Endowment for the Humanities. Moe was arguably the most powerful and omnipresent actor in elite academic, artistic, philanthropic, and intellectual circles, a role he had built with a combination of intelligence, opportunity-seeking, ambition, energy, and networking savvy—and it started with the Guggenheim Foundation.[5]

While over the years Moe moved closer to center stage in all foundation affairs, Carroll Wilson, like the senator, moved away from visible front-office concerns once Aydelotte and Moe were in place and Wilson had successfully incorporated the organization in the State of New York. He returned to his work as full-time chief counsel for the brothers' business concerns and served the foundation as a trustee from 1925 to 1947. Maintaining his ties to the Rhodes program, in 1946 he became director of the Association of American Rhodes Scholars. The inner circle of the foundation was extremely small and continuously revolving.[6]

The foundation's emergence at an inhospitable moment for those identified with Judaism was likely a powerful motivator for its mission statement. Immigration restrictions, quota systems, conspicuous antisemitism, the red scare, and deportations worked against many groups seeking entry to the country while serving multiple government agendas that went unacknowledged.[7] That the foundation followed the lead of the first generation of Guggenheims in the country by supplying an identified need—in this case, financial support for artists and musicians—reflected proven business practice.

World War I had challenged the nation's allegiance to German culture while it increased Americans' attraction to all things French. This political reality had a direct impact on the Guggenheim's music composition fellowships and the emergence of the Conservatoire Américain from what had been a military bandmaster's school during the war years and immediately after. The Conservatoire Américain de Fontainebleau, just outside Paris, with its most famous pedagogue, Nadia Boulanger, became *the* destination for young American composers seeking a European imprimatur and the favored academic milieu for early Guggenheim music composition fellows. At the same time, the United States increasingly understood the strategic importance of its southern neighbors in its own hemisphere. A new attitude toward Latin American culture, and the economic, political, and security benefits that awaited "good neighbors," grew from an abstract idea introduced by President Woodrow Wilson (1913–1921) to national policy under President Franklin Delano Roosevelt (1933–1945). The Guggenheim network, too, looked south with its Latin America program. When Hitler consolidated power and was named chancellor of the German Reich on January 30, 1933, the exodus of European intellectuals had already begun; the John Simon Guggenheim Memorial Foundation was well placed to help fleeing artists, musicians, and scholars through its network of associations, which it had carefully built in its first eight years. Starting in 1931, Moe's work with the Oberlaender Trust, a private philanthropy founded by a Philadelphia-area manufacturer, would be key to rehabilitating international relations and specifically "furthering a better understanding between the people of the United States and the German-speaking peoples," which had suffered as a result of the war.[8] The trust became an important node in the foundation's early network.

THE LARGER NETWORK

Prior to the foundation's deliberate network-building efforts, however, a number of educational and artistic organizations had operated separately for decades, and many of them formed associations with the Guggenheim's personnel. Typically, actors identified with one organization played roles in others as well, which kept the cast small. The Rockefeller Foundation, with which Aydelotte enjoyed close relations, remained a favored partner in philanthropic work; it also supported the Oberlaender Trust. The American Philosophical Society, founded in Philadelphia in 1743 by Benjamin Franklin, was a private, self-selecting, members-only society honoring the nation's intellectual elite from across disciplines: Election signaled prestige like that which the young Guggenheim Foundation aspired to bestow on its fellows. Aydelotte, newly installed president of Swarthmore, was elected to the society in 1923, and twenty years later Moe joined its ranks, later serving as its president from 1959 to 1970. Multiple generations of the Philadelphia-based Drinker family were members. Philadelphia remained an important hub for Guggenheim-related projects including the American Society for the Extension of University Teaching, founded in 1890, which had figured greatly in Surette's career. In New York the Carnegie Corporation, founded in 1911 by Andrew Carnegie and headquartered on Madison Avenue, less than a half-mile away from the foundation's office, became an important partner in the latter's philanthropic efforts. The Carnegie Corporation's dual focus on advancing knowledge and encouraging world peace was a good match for the aspirations of the John Simon Guggenheim Memorial Foundation.

Less apparent but nonetheless powerful associations influenced the philanthropic enterprise. "A sense of the meeting" and a "Quaker approach to conducting business that Aydelotte had found to be successful at Swarthmore" was employed at Black Mountain College, an institution created in 1933 that owed its existence to the personal efforts of Aydelotte, Moe, and the larger foundation.[9] Initial conversations regarding the founding of the college took place at Aydelotte's office at Swarthmore, and then Moe's office at the Guggenheim Foundation supplied the new school's first mailing address, much as the Guggenheim Brothers' business offices had housed the fledgling foundation's administrative space while it was still coalescing in 1924. The experimental college located in the mountains of western North Carolina aspired to a collaborative governance model like that used in Society of Friends (Quaker) meetings but failed to achieve its idealistic mission for various reasons. A sizeable Quaker contingent, what Martin Duberman called "the Quaker bloc," became active at the college in its waning years, but not even they, with their deep sense of community and many successes in postsecondary education, could sustain the institution.[10] Despite Black Mountain's demise it played a critical role in the larger Guggenheim network throughout the 1930s and the early 1940s. Given its unique relationship to the foundation, it is discussed at length in Chapter 5, "The College."

Still other established organizations enjoyed fruitful relationships with the Guggenheim Foundation. Two artists' retreats, Yaddo, in Saratoga Springs in upstate New York, and the MacDowell Colony in Peterborough, New Hampshire, became desirable summer destinations for young writers, artists, and composers. Both promised a quiet place to work and the opportunity for guests to interact within a sympathetic creative community. Guggenheim fellows-to-be and successful awardees formed friendships and partnerships at both retreats; they became tight, self-sustaining networks of their own. The efforts of Elizabeth Ames and George Peabody and others tasked with selecting summer residents at Yaddo, for instance, were especially important to composers seeking Guggenheim support in the early to mid-1930s. Ames, its first executive director, prided herself on her good track record coaching hopeful applicants for Guggenheim fellowships. Numerous letters exchanged between Ames and Aaron Copland in the Yaddo records, for instance, detail arrangements for accommodations, music activities, and suggestions for potential residents. Correspondence dating from 1933 to 1935 related to Dante Fiorillo, the composer who received four consecutive Guggenheim Awards (1935–1938), illuminates the advocacy that applicant received from Ames, Marion Sheffeld—a friend and associate of hers at Yaddo—and others who had the foundation's ear. Additional correspondence in the Yaddo collection reveals Copland's work in organizing a pair of modern music concerts at the Saratoga Springs summer retreat and identifies Yaddo as important to the creation of the Copland-Sessions Concert Series.[11] Roger Sessions was named one of two Guggenheim Fellows in 1926; the other was Leopold Damrosch Mannes.[12] Letters between Henry Allen Moe and Otto Luening (who would be awarded consecutive Guggenheim Fellowships in 1930 and 1931 and who became a major figure at Yaddo in the mid-1930s), and between Moe and other composer hopefuls, underscore the close connections between Yaddo and the Guggenheim Foundation.

The aspirations of the Pan-American Union (the Organization of American States, originally founded in 1890 then reorganized and renamed in 1902 and 1910), and the Pan-American Association of Composers (1928–1934), a small international group of modernist composers that included Guggenheim Fellow Carlos Chávez, reinforced the goals of the foundation's Latin American Program and provided an additional rationale for the undertaking. In years to come both the Museum of Modern Art and the William Whitney Foundation supported Guggenheim initiatives, especially Black Mountain College, with major financial gifts. For a remotely located college with no endowment and far from moneyed northeastern patrons, their gifts were essential to survival. These organizations are among dozens that interacted with the Guggenheim Foundation in some way.

THE PRINCIPAL NETWORK ACTORS

Reciprocity was essential to cultivating and maintaining productive partnerships at all levels of engagement. Within the specific sub-sphere of the foundation's music composition awards, however, a small number of institutional actors played especially large roles. The remainder of this chapter further probes some organizations already introduced and considers a handful of others in greater depth: Columbia University (founded 1754), Swarthmore College (1864), the Conservatoire Américain (1921), and the Oberlaender Trust (1931). Surette's Concord Summer School (1915) has already been discussed in detail in Chapter 3, but it will appear again because it supplied a summer home for various network actors and had close ties to Black Mountain College. Although these organizations are discussed chronologically by date of their founding, like others in the system, they acted in concert and as needed, especially throughout the foundation's start-up.

COLUMBIA UNIVERSITY

The physical proximity of Columbia University at 116th Street and Broadway to the foundation's first headquarters at 42nd Street at Park Avenue, and the large, common pool of academics, artists, and intellectuals that shared their New York world, determined more than simply which or whose ideas were privileged in the foundation's gestational phase.[13] For the first fifteen years of the foundation's existence, the Educational Advisory Board—those who decided on awardees across disciplines—was populated with more faculty, administrators, and degree recipients from Columbia University (as well as its sister schools, Barnard and Columbia Teachers College) than from any other educational institution, by a margin of over two to one.[14] Columbia would also play an important role in the activities of the Oberlaender Trust and the Alice M. Ditson Fund, established in 1940 at the same university. Other schools that were well represented on the board included those within a relatively close radius (or a convenient set of train connections), which made personal meetings, when desirable, easy to arrange: Harvard, Radcliffe and MIT (Cambridge, Massachusetts), Yale (New Haven, Connecticut), Princeton (Princeton, New Jersey), and Johns Hopkins (Baltimore, Maryland), and to a lesser degree those located farther west including the Universities of Chicago, Wisconsin, and Minnesota.

Proximity assured convenience, which was helpful, but it alone couldn't explain the outsized impact of Columbia and its associated personnel; it was hard to ignore its quality or that of other elite institutions in the region. With Harvard founded in 1636, Yale in 1701, Princeton in 1746, and Columbia in 1754, the four schools had hundreds of years of graduates and their progeny who were well-placed. Large numbers of their alumni were in positions of influence and remained close by their alma maters. Many had attended more than one of the institutions and brought their own intertwined networks to the foundation. Although Surette was not a graduate of any of the institutions, he could claim a connection to Columbia through a series of open lectures he presented there on the development of instrumental music and through the music appreciation textbook that he wrote with Daniel Gregory Mason.[15] Moe also enjoyed an occasional relationship with Columbia through a number of lecture engagements. Although he requested that such outside work be acknowledged in his Guggenheim contract in 1929, Aydelotte and the senator determined that any such activities would be considered on an ad hoc basis. Otto Luening and Douglas Moore (Guggenheim fellow 1934), both professors of music at Columbia (from 1944 to 1970 and 1926 to 1962, respectively), became close advisors to the foundation and evaluated music composition fellows' scores for Surette in the early years. The efforts that Surette directed at public school music reform with Archibald T. Davison and his occasional private studies with John Knowles Paine at Harvard in the 1890s provided the music advisor with connections to that favored institution as well. Harvard was second only to Columbia in terms of faculty members or administrators named to the Educational Advisory Board.

The John Simon Guggenheim Memorial Foundation enjoyed yet another close relationship with Columbia through the Pulitzer Prizes. From the start they were administered by the university as an in-house operation. Joseph Pulitzer,

Hungarian-born Jew who became a naturalized American citizen, made his fortune as a journalist and owner of multiple newspapers including the *New York World.* Upon his death, part of his two-million-dollar bequest to Columbia was used to found its School of Journalism, which opened in 1912. Starting in 1917 the Joseph Pulitzer bequest funded the awards that bear his name.

From the early years of the foundation, the uptown university and its downtown philanthropic partner were in regular communication regarding select fellows. The two organizations created a powerful unofficial mutual aid society. The closeness of their association is evident in the privately published book *The John Simon Guggenheim Memorial Foundation 1925–2000: A Seventy-Fifth Anniversary Record.* Chapter 7 of the celebratory record, titled "Prizes Won by Guggenheim Fellows," explains: "One measure of the distinction of the individuals who have been recipients of Guggenheim Fellowships is the quantity and prestige of the other honors they have been accorded." It supplies the numbers of those elected to the American Academy of Arts and Letters (located in New York), the American Academy of Arts and Sciences (located in Cambridge, Massachusetts), and the American Philosophical Society (located in Philadelphia), but it singles out the Nobel Prize (headquartered in Stockholm, Sweden) and Pulitzer Prize for naming the specific recipients. The Guggenheim Foundation takes pride in observing that "in most cases, the date of an individual's [Guggenheim] Fellowship . . . preceded the date when that person received one or both of the other honors noted here." One of the editors, G. Thomas Tanselle, vice-president of the foundation from 1978 to 2006, notes that "87 fellows have won Nobel Prizes and 203 have won Pulitzer Prizes (through 2000)."[16] The unspoken claim is that the Guggenheim Foundation was prescient in its choices because it recognized winners before they achieved greatness. This is likely true in some cases, but in others the boast is less convincing: Once a person was inside the network, additional accolades were more likely to come his or her way. Winners accumulated advantage as they moved within the circle: Moe assured that awards begat awards.[17]

The perception on the part of many outsiders that the northeastern network is a self-perpetuating and self-congratulatory closed circle of friends and supporters is hard to dislodge given the geographic and institutional concentration of early fellows and advisors. The perception remains true today despite recent focused efforts to recognize the potential and achievements of persons outside the region. In truth, in the early years the network *made* winners. It *created* high achievers. It *advantaged* a small handful of insiders—the names we recognize today—by generously supporting their early efforts, providing them with the time and money to pursue and perfect their craft away from other distractions and responsibilities, and working to find them additional support. Who else might have a place in our history books today had they been tapped, nurtured, championed, and empowered by a network the size of the Guggenheim? Which others consigned to the shadows, the footnotes, or the garbage heap of history would we study? The maxim "history is written by the victors" comes to mind.[18]

SWARTHMORE COLLEGE

American academia played a major role in the Guggenheim network from its founding, which is to be expected given the mission of the foundation to support creative and intellectual work. Unlike the established research universities whose support dominated the network-building efforts of the founding advisors, however, Swarthmore College was a small liberal arts college that focused on teaching. With its proximity to Philadelphia and all its connections to the foundation as the original home of the Guggenheim family, as well as its associations with Thomas Whitney Surette and his circle of supporters, including the Drinkers, Swarthmore functioned as the satellite campus for the foundation and continued in that role until Aydelotte resigned as its president in order to accept the directorship of the Institute for Advance Study at Princeton in 1939.

Swarthmore's Quaker heritage and especially its approach to conducting business—a practice of listening-focused conversation and consensus building—exerted their influence on Aydelotte throughout his career. The thirty-two members of Swarthmore's board, eighteen men and fourteen women, were all Quakers. The near parity of men and women, a novelty within elite institutions then and now, was in keeping with their basic belief in the equality of the sexes. The Guggenheim Foundation's mission to support both male and female fellows was aligned with this fundamental Quaker tenet, even if its own board of trustees consisted, overwhelmingly, of white males, and the goal was not consistently realized in the music composition award category for many decades. Attitudes toward gender parity did not, however, transfer to racial equality among the first Quakers in the United States. The contradiction of the Quakers' early participation in and benefit from the slave trade is a part of Friends history that was not addressed during Aydelotte's tenure at Swarthmore, which failed to admit African American students until 1945, six years after he left.[19] The foundation's resistance to promoting any single aesthetic agenda, however, aligned with the Quakers' non-doctrinaire and accommodating religious beliefs.[20] Although Aydelotte was not a member of the Society of Friends during his presidency, he regularly participated in meetings at the meeting house on campus. According to his biographer, Frances Blanshard, who taught at Swarthmore: "He rarely spoke first, preferring to develop someone else's idea, often waiting until the end of a meeting to bring the train of thought as a whole into unity."[21] Blanshard explained that Aydelotte claimed to have resisted joining the Society of Friends because he assumed that if he and the managers disagreed about "something he thought important" it "would be less painful if he were not" a Friend. "His relations with the Managers would be on a more impersonal basis if he were not a member."[22] Regardless of what appears to be a thin rationale for remaining outside the society, it is telling that, coincident with Aydelotte's resignation from Swarthmore, he formally requested to join the Meeting and in 1945 became a member of its Board of Managers. Blanshard concluded: "Indeed, he was a natural Quaker."[23] It would have been impossible for Aydelotte to enjoy his lengthy tenure as president had he not been perceived as temperamentally aligned with the school's values. The foundation's progressive mission statement, which Aydelotte helped enact, mapped easily onto the majority of Quaker beliefs and vice versa.

CONSERVATOIRE AMÉRICAIN

The role played by the Conservatoire Américain looms large within the context of the early foundation's music network. In the first fifteen years of its operation, fourteen of thirty-two Guggenheim composition fellows traveled to Paris and to the Palais de Fontainebleau to study with Nadia Boulanger.[24] Those who didn't study privately with the doyenne were nonetheless impacted by Conservatoire's values through their connections to Walter Damrosch, the most famous American promoter of the institution. In 1918 he and Francis Casadesus had responded to a request from General John J. Pershing of the U.S. army to improve American military bands' musicianship and discipline, and thereby military morale, by creating a summertime bandleaders' school. The general had been impressed with French military bands during his time serving as commander of the American Expeditionary Forces stationed on the Western Front in the final year of World War I. As Kendra Preston Leonard explains: "This school for Army bandmasters, named the École Américain du Chef de Musique, opened for the first time in the summer of 1919. Its goals were straightforward: to train army musicians, as instructed by Casadesus and Damrosch, in the areas of theory, counterpoint, harmony, and solfege—areas of study often brushed aside by American bands."[25] In 1922 Pershing ordered that the name "Pershing's Own" be attached to the U.S. Army Band.[26] Damrosch wanted a similar educational opportunity for his New York Symphony Orchestra musicians, and numbers of them headed to Paris. The band masters' summer program morphed into what we know today as the Conservatoire Américain, a three-month summer school with a clear pedagogical focus.

Starting with Aaron Copland, the first music composition fellow to attend the Conservatoire and study privately with Boulanger, a near steady stream of awardees meant that there were only two years between 1925 and 1940 when Boulanger did not work with at least one Guggenheim winner: 1931 and 1936. The stock market crash caused some belt tightening in 1931 and a single composition award went to Otto Luening (his second). He worked on his only opera,

Evangeline, during his fellowship year, but he did not go abroad. Another single award was made in 1936, to Dante Fiorillo, the second of his four consecutive awards. He spent part of that year at Black Mountain College. Despite Fiorillo's failure to capitalize on the foundation's well-established connections, the political climate after the war was propitious for cultivating Franco-American relations in general and for encouraging what Leonard quotes Walter Damrosch as seeking: "artistic solidarity" more specifically.[27]

The French school took advantage of the moment: It relished donning the mantle that German conservatories had worn during the nineteenth century, that of the premier European destination for Americans pursuing musical training.[28] Its promise of advanced music education for both men and women in an intense summer session where faculty were those who taught at the Paris Conservatoire during the regular academic year conveyed immediate prestige. American women, who were not enthusiastically welcomed into their own nation's academic music programs, and especially not into composition classes, flocked to the school for this reason and many others.[29] The imprimatur of a French *diplome* or *prix* proved irresistible to hundreds of Americans eager for a European credential.[30] For decades, claiming that one had studied in Paris, or at the Conservatoire Américain, or most especially with Nadia Boulanger, was the equivalent of a stripe on one's sleeve.

The roots of the close alliance between the foundation and the Conservatoire Américain were simultaneously vast and deep; they anchored the fledgling foundation and contributed to the cachet of the French institution as well. By dint of General Pershing's status, his role in the creation of a world-class army band was known widely. Damrosch's encouragement of the American army band was common knowledge among New York's moneyed elite, and the conductor successfully solicited their support for his new French-American summer music school. Pershing's early involvement added a patriotic sheen to the undertaking: Partnering with the Conservatoire Américain underscored the alliance between the two nations, something close to the general's heart, and that association would be transferred to the foundation.

Surette provided another part to the foundation's complex French root system. His administration of The Music Fund, which sent students to Paris starting in the early 1920s, and which Moe referenced in his January 14, 1925, letter to Frank Aydelotte, brought the city and the Conservatoire to the foundation's attention prior to its initial award cycle. Surette's many trips to Paris, his interest in music education, and his facility with the French language made him a valuable contact for the foundation; it could rely on him to stay abreast of developments at the Conservatoire, either when discussing potential students with Boulanger or, more likely, on the regular European sojourns that he took with his wife. The summer sessions offered there, with their focus on pedagogical topics and skills, reinforced the Concord Summer School's mission and its commitment to broad musical training rather than to virtuosic performers or individual composers, despite the two schools' significantly different cultural contexts.

According to Kathleen Uhler Adams, starting in 1923 Thomas and Ada Surette regularly visited Boulanger when they were in Paris; they developed a friendship and Surette "recommended the students most interested in piano and composition [who attended his school] to devote some time to studying with her." Adams concluded, "There were many who went to Paris from Concord."[31] Correspondence between Surette and Dorothy Brewster Smith, who attended Surette's summer school in 1925, illuminates how the process worked for one student who did just that. Smith earned a bachelor's degree in music with honors from Smith College in 1925. Already interested in composition, she wrote a musical drama, "Poltarnees," that was performed at her college commencement. In a series of exchanges starting in May 1925, Surette first encouraged Smith to attend his school, which she did; in December he advised her to continue her composition work. The next month, January 1926, he declared, "You are just ready to go now." Convinced that there was no place that offered equivalent training for composers in the United States, Surette was confident she would appreciate "the enormous difference between studying here and studying there."[32]

Surette's letters to Smith throughout 1926 and 1927 reveal his familiarity with Paris and with Boulanger's teaching regimen. He comfortably advised Smith about the lack of sunlight in wintertime, how to find housing through the Paris offices of the American University of Women, approximate living costs, and the best approach to Boulanger. He assured Smith that he had already mentioned her name to Mademoiselle. Surette spoke with the tone of an advisor accustomed to being listened to. He was well acquainted with both his student and the prospective teacher: "You would, of course, go to her Wednesday evening informal class meeting in which there is singing and playing of new compositions, etc., and I suppose you would take lessons in Composition and bring things for her to see, and I should say that you would want to go into a class or perhaps two, but all that would be settled when you got there." In the final paragraph he offered one more bit of encouragement followed by a final dig at American colleges and faculty. "I hope that you will go to Paris. I think, as I have thought all along, that it is just the thing for you, and that you, having been in schools and college for a matter of I suppose seven or eight years and now living in your own town have only touched the rim of things in spite of these magnificent, flambulgent, [*sic*] and ne-plus-ultra, excelsior, and all that sort of thing professors."[33] Despite the numerous elite intellectual associations Surette had cultivated over his sixty-four years, his lack of earned academic credentials appears to have stuck in his craw and made him defensive and given to taking pot shots. He clearly reconciled that position with his acceptance of an honorary doctorate from the University of Pennsylvania in 1934. Smith took Surette's advice and went to Paris to study with Boulanger beginning in 1926.[34]

In a February 1927 letter, Surette encouraged Smith to stay another year and offered to "write that persuasive letter to your parents" securing their support for her to do so.[35] Surette was confident in his powers to influence the senior Smiths. Once again, however, he had critical things to say; this time he dismissed American culture in general: "Of course, in Paris, a person can be an individual. Over here he or she is simply like a person in a large hotel identifiable only by the number of his room. The flattening-out process which takes place here in a person of any individuality is the worst element of American life."[36] Surette's concern with cultivating the individual would be something he shared with John Andrew Rice, one of the founders of Black Mountain College, an institution with which he became deeply involved starting in 1933.[37]

In a letter to Smith written in November 1927, Surette asked her to learn Boulanger's thoughts about Honegger's *Le Roi David*, and encouraged her to publish, "preferably in Paris." It was at this point, however, that Smith began to question her commitment to studying with the French pedagogue, and Surette wanted to know why her "faith in harmony and counterpoint was waning."[38] Comfortable advising not only Dorothy Smith but also her sister Gertrude (nicknamed Trudle)—who had also attended Surette's summer school, was currently enrolled at Smith College, and would study with Boulanger herself—the self-appointed guardian of his "children" questioned Trudle's motivations for choosing a thesis topic. Never lacking in opinions regarding what was and wasn't "right," Surette's confidence grew with his foundation affiliation and the authority vested in it.

By the mid-1930s Surette had expanded his advising activities beyond informal suggestions in personal letters to something of a one-man academic placement service for former Suretters and Guggenheim fellows seeking college and university positions. A young Otto Luening, for one, benefited multiple times from Surette's personal intercession and advocacy, as discussed below. It is one of the many ironies surrounding Thomas Whitney Surette that he would assume such a keen interest in American academic music departments given his disdain for the professoriate and the system in which they operated, and his minimal experience with any of it. As Surette's engagement with musical life at Black Mountain College will demonstrate, he was perhaps better suited to idealistic statements than to practical implementation.

Once Surette was music advisor to the Guggenheim Foundation there would be many who went to Paris from New York as well as from Concord. As Adams had observed, two years before being appointed music advisor or approving Copland for a fellowship, Surette had already promoted Boulanger and the Conservatoire to his own Concord students. When Boulanger came to the country to premiere Copland's Symphony for Organ and Orchestra in January 1925, Surette was in the audience, and he met with his pedagogue friend and her protégée. Boulanger was eager to advance the Conservatoire and herself, and Surette was, no doubt, pleased to have a prestigious connection and a ready nominee; his appointment to the foundation provided the ideal conduit and association for the pedagogue and the advisor. Both accumulated advantage from their membership in the inner circle.

Documents in the Copland files at the Guggenheim Foundation reveal how Surette's preferred personal style of identifying applicants worked in the early years. In a brief letter written to Copland soon after the premiere of his organ symphony, Moe acknowledged receipt of the young composer's inquiry regarding the foundation's fellowships. He also explained that the foundation was still in the organizational stages, but when the information was ready, he'd happily send it to him. Copland received a second letter from him just three days after the Boston performance, in which Moe referred to a pamphlet that explained the foundation and its plan to support study abroad.[39] In a letter that Copland wrote in March addressing the advisor as "My Dear Mr. Surette," the young composer inquired as to "what conditions must be fulfilled in order to be a successful candidate," and closed by offering congratulations "on [his] appointment as one of the trustees for the Fund"; he sent his kind regards to Mrs. Surette.[40] Like his French composition teacher, Copland understood how to build advantageous relationships and networks. He appreciated the potential of personal associations with the Conservatoire Américain, Nadia Boulanger, Yaddo, the John Simon Guggenheim Memorial Foundation, and Thomas Whitney Surette, and he cultivated them all.

Copland wrote to Surette on April 15 to assure him that he had begun securing letters of endorsement, as the new advisor had suggested, and he was still awaiting others. As an indication of Copland's naïveté and ambition, he inquired whether Surette would write a letter of recommendation on his behalf, which would have been unnecessary given Surette's role as the advisor in charge of selecting fellows. Or perhaps Copland didn't understand that the music advisory board in 1925 consisted of Thomas Whitney Surette alone, who would have been writing to himself. In closing, Copland thanked him for his "invaluable help and advice in what is for me an extremely important matter."[41] On April 25 Moe wrote to Copland informing him that his name had been proposed as a candidate for a fellowship. Given the foundation's original plan to award the first fellowships starting in 1926–1927, Moe asked Copland to explain why an earlier appointment was necessary. Copland's response that his livelihood depended on it would have been true of many composers and artists at the time. On Friday, May 1, Moe sent

Copland a telegram asking whether it was possible for him to meet with Surette at the foundation offices on Monday at eleven. Over the next few days Copland supplied a budget outlining estimated costs for the 1925–1926 year and all other documentation required, including a health certificate. Having recently spent three years in Paris, Copland explained that he preferred not to take the entire fellowship year abroad and outlined instead a plan that had him in New York for six months followed by six months in Europe. Asking for special permission to ignore one of the major goals of the fellowship program was potentially risky, but with Surette's endorsement and the official May 26 report, which argued for the wisdom of Copland's plan and Surette's belief that supporting him would be good not only for the composer but for American music, Boulanger's pupil became the first recipient of a John Simon Guggenheim Memorial Foundation award for music composition. With the Guggenheim network in place to promote its awardees, the appointment helped make Copland a star and Boulanger the star teacher.

Moe sent a congratulatory letter to Copland on May 29, 1925, and on June 1 Copland formally accepted. Later that year Copland set a poem by Edwin Arlington Robinson for four-part *a cappella* women's chorus and dedicated "The House on the Hill" to Thomas Whitney Surette. The piece was ideal for singing at Surette's summer school, where the student population was still overwhelmingly female.[42] The network connecting the Guggenheim Foundation, the Conservatoire, Boulanger, Copland, and Surette was securely anchored. It would hold fast until a changing political landscape and another war tested its strength. It's easy to understand why Henry Allen Moe would write enthusiastically in favor of Surette's being named to the advisory board. Knowing nothing about music himself, Moe could trust the impressive Parisian connections that Surette supplied and assume that music fellowships were in good hands. In Surette's case, connections trumped credentials.

It was, however, the foundation's first composition fellow who ultimately proved to be among the most powerful actors in its musical network. Copland's 1924 return from Paris couldn't have been timed better: It simultaneously announced the start of his career just months before the first call for Guggenheim applications appeared, advertised Boulanger's formidable credentials as both performer and pedagogue, and argued for the value of the Conservatoire as a destination for future Guggenheim composition fellows. The January 11 and February 20, 1925, performances of Copland's Symphony for Organ and Orchestra by the New York and Boston Symphony Orchestras, respectively, with Boulanger as soloist, had provided a visible link between the French school, the Parisian pedagogue, the young American composer, and the newly created foundation. That Walter Damrosch and Serge Koussevitzky conducted the premieres in New York and

Boston, respectively, conferred a degree of prestige upon the twenty-four-year-old composer that would have been impossible for other fellowship hopefuls to duplicate. Positive reviews and broad coverage of the performances in the Northeast lightened the burden of any advisor tasked with assessing Copland's worthiness: The press had already done the job. Those involved in the premiere—Damrosch, Koussevitzky, and Boulanger—were among eight referees who wrote on Copland's behalf for the Guggenheim fellowship. Edward B. Hill, a Harvard professor, Lawrence Gilman, music critic for the *New York Herald Tribune*, Rubin Goldmark, Copland's former teacher in New York, Clarence Adler, a faculty member at the Institute of Music Art, and Arthur Hartmann, a violinist and old friend of Claude Debussy, rounded out the applicant's references. Over the next twenty-six years Koussevitzky became one of Copland's greatest champions, Copland's sphere of influence grew, and his relationship with Boulanger became legend.[43] The seeds of what Virgil Thomson called "Copland's commando unit" were firmly planted, and the foundation would tend the soil.[44]

THE OBERLAENDER TRUST

Within five years' time the Boulanger-Guggenheim network was securely in place, thanks in large part to Copland's numerous professional relationships with like-minded composers and supportive institutions. By 1930 seven Guggenheim music composition fellows enjoyed some association with Boulanger; they traced Copland's steps and headed to Paris. As the Franco-American alliance was strengthening, however, efforts were also under way to restore cultural relations with Germany, which had been decimated by World War I, and address long-resonating anti-German sentiments that continued through the 1930s. The Oberlaender Trust, the eponymous philanthropic organization founded by Gustav Oberlaender in 1931, provided a different kind of intellectual and artistic opportunity for those it supported and another link in the expanding Guggenheim network. And this one didn't include Copland.

The same postwar political environment that provided ideal conditions to cultivate an enthusiastic Franco-American alliance also stimulated large numbers of German Americans to reassert their presence. As cultural descendants of the recent aggressor nation, some felt the need to rehabilitate the reputation of their former home. Between 1820 and 1870 approximately eight million German immigrants had come to the United States; in 1920, 1.7 million German-born immigrants lived in the country. Their cultural practices thrived in tight-knit communities where various German dialects were the primary languages spoken and German music making continued in the dozens of Männerchöre and Saengerbunds that existed wherever large populations of German-speaking immigrants settled.[45] Beyond pressures from within to recognize German culture, it was hard to keep such influences at bay when the Weimar Republic was so eager to be friends. Starting in the early 1920s the German government vigorously sought to repair relations with the United States; a devastated economy and the court of public opinion made Germany an eager courtier. Among the many private German efforts and organizations created to encourage cultural ties was the Carl Schurz Vereinigung, established in 1926. Using the name of a German American war hero, reformer, senator, and statesman, the organization was as much a vehicle for cultivating advantageous business relations between the two nations as it was an effort to encourage the appreciation of German culture by American citizens.

When, in April 1931, the German-born Gustav Oberlaender (1867–1936) of Reading, Pennsylvania, deeded a gift of one million dollars to the Carl Schurz Memorial Foundation to establish the Oberlaender Trust, he clarified that "the Oberlaender Trust be considered an integral part of the work of the Carl Schurz Memorial Foundation, Inc.," whose purpose was to increase understanding between peoples of the United States and Germany."[46] He would accomplish his goal by sending "American citizens to the German speaking countries for research, studies and surveys."[47]

Oberlaender had made his fortune as president of the Berkshire Knitting Mills Company in Reading, but he was fully committed to the arts and humanities, passions he had cultivated in his youth while studying in Cologne and Dusseldorf. Once in the United States, Oberlaender formed close associations with other German immigrants and developed interests in opera and music more broadly.[48] His love of music became evident in the continuous support his trust provided to large numbers of American musicians and scholars working on German music topics in the early years of the trust, and the many émigré musicians and scholars he brought to the country during the war years.[49]

In 1931 Oberlaender directed the Schurz Foundation to appoint four trustees, in addition to himself, to the newly formed trust: Carl Ackerman, dean of the School of Journalism at Columbia University, Haven Emerson M.D., emeritus professor of public health at Columbia University, Wilbur K. Thomas, the executive director of the American Friends Service Committee,[50] and Henry Allen Moe.[51] Some of the same institutions that enjoyed close relations to the Guggenheim Foundation, Columbia University and the Society of Friends in particular, exerted their influence on the Oberlaender Trust as well. According to Hanns Gramm, a regular attendee at board meetings, Thomas had overseen "the far-flung philanthropic activities of the Quakers in the United States, as well as in many foreign countries where suffering from the effects of the First World War prevailed."[52] Quaker influence on the board only increased when Oberlaender died in 1936 and Alfred G. Scattergood of Philadelphia took his spot.

Scattergood, like Thomas, was also a leader in the postwar relief efforts of the Friends while additionally serving as president of the Friends Hospital, trustee of the Pennsylvania Hospital, and chairman of the board of the William Penn Charter School, the world's oldest Quaker school.[53] The placement of Quakers and those associated with them in the highest administrative positions of the Oberlaender Trust announced a set of values and ways of conducting business familiar to Moe and the foundation.

Oberlaender explained that the five trustees should "enjoy powers of an absolute owner in regard to the handling and expending of funds, subject only to the limitations of the charter and to such limitations as expressed in the present letter or in the Deed of Gift."[54] He charged the trustees with "expending the principal and interest of this Trust within twenty-five (25) years from now [April 1931]" but allowed for the possibility that unforeseen circumstances might make that impossible. In that case it was acceptable to extend the period, but not beyond an additional fifteen years.[55] As it was, the trust fulfilled its charge and ceased operation in 1953, thereby completing its task well within the period that Oberlaender stipulated.

It is worth noting that the Oberlaender Trust's activities were also to "be carried on without regard to race, creed, color or sex, and free from religious, political and social discrimination."[56] The two foundations' inclusive views were unusual at the time and arrived at from different starting positions, but it is almost certain that Moe had a hand in shaping the trust's statement, much as Aydelotte had had a hand in shaping the foundation's. Moe's influence on the trust was more powerful than any imagined threat the trust posed to the Guggenheim Foundation, as he had suggested might exist when arguing for the reasonableness of his involvement in the trust. The distinctions between the two organizations became increasingly apparent when Adolf Hitler was named chancellor of Germany. The family behind the Guggenheim Foundation claimed no foreign allegiances, unless it was to nations whose mineral riches made them particularly attractive to their mining business interests. The Oberlaender Trust, on the other hand, had identified itself with and promoted German culture. The appeal of traveling for extended periods of time to Germany diminished significantly, however, with increasing knowledge of the Führer's actions, and national opinion turning against the country once again. In such a climate it behooved the trust and its parent organization the Carl Schurz Memorial Foundation to clarify any relationship they had to the German Vereinigung. The seriousness of the situation was spelled out in a January 21, 1935, article published in the *New York Times* that reported on a protest filed by twelve relatives and friends of Carl Schurz. They objected to the use of Schurz's name by any group "in connection with organizations maintaining friendly relations with the Nazi State of Adolf Hitler," and then they named the Carl Schurz Vereinigung in Berlin and the Carl Schurz Foundation in the United States. Regarding the U.S. foundation, the co-signers noted: "The latter continues to aid German universities and otherwise deal with the despotism which has succeeded in the Republic of Weimar." They pointed to the grotesquery of using the name of one who "was a rebel against the despotism of the King of Bavaria and the King of Prussia, [who] took up his sword against them and escaped with his life only by a miracle." They reviewed his service to the United States as a diplomat, as an abolitionist, and as a "champion of freedom for the Negro, justice and freedom for the Indians, and tolerance and freedom of liberty and action for every sect and group in our democracy." They cited his friendship with Jews and his condemnation of antisemitism. They evoked his commitment to the "Lincoln doctrine that 'no man is good enough to govern any other man, without that other man's consent.'" And in case their wishes were not clear, they spelled out their concerns and their demands: "Justice to this man, to his life and his noble teachings, makes it impossible for us to withhold the most vigorous and outspoken protest against the use of his name in connection with the societies we have cited. We earnestly ask that it be immediately discontinued."[57]

The original goals of the Schurz Foundation and the Oberlaender Trust were modified as allowed by the founder's charge to the board. Gramm summarized the situation: "With the approach of the war, the Trustees adopted as the major feature of their work the assistance of American institutions of higher learning in their efforts to add to their faculties desirable displaced German and Austrian scholars who had sought refuge in the United States from political persecution."[58] As will be seen, this modification had direct consequences for Black Mountain College. Gramm explained how the new arrangement worked:

> The Oberlaender Trust adopted the policy of making grants to American universities, colleges and similar schools who wished to put a certain displaced scholar on their faculty but were unable to find the means in their budget to pay his salary. In these cases, the Trust usually contributed all or part of the salary for an initial period until the newcomer had proved his value to the institution, justifying the provision of his future remuneration in the budget of the college. Ordinarily, no grants were made to these scholars directly, but rather to the institution who wanted the man and applied to the Trust for assistance. This proved a very wise policy, since it placed the responsibility of selection on the institutions, who undoubtedly were the best judges of their needs, and willing to invite the displaced scholar into their faculties rather than give the appearance that he was pressed upon them. More than 300 individuals were placed in this manner, and the Oberlaender Trust spent over $317,000 in pursuit of this program.[59]

Ultimately, of all the trust's expenditures, the grant program to American academic institutions was its most costly initiative. That said, the trust didn't act on its own in this effort. The Rockefeller Foundation partnered with the trust and provided "grant-in-aid," and a number of other organizations including the "Emergency Committee in Aid of Displaced Foreign Scholars, the American Committee for Christian Refugees, the American Friends Service Committee, the YMCA in New York and Philadelphia, the American-Jewish Committee, and the Catholic Committee for Refugees in New York," among many others, contributed to the effort.[60] It was the Emergency Committee named above that brought the Russian Jewish émigré musicologist Edward Lowinsky to the country and arranged for his faculty position at Black Mountain College.[61] This would have been done with Moe's knowledge and involvement.

The favored academic institutions that had been cultivated by Aydelotte and Moe starting in 1924 on behalf of the nascent foundation were present in force at the trust, along with dozens of other American educational and performing institutions. Their concentration in the Northeast and along the East Coast, with few exceptions, is not surprising. Gramm's history includes an appendix that lists "Institutions and Individuals who received grants from the Oberlaender Trust to facilitate the professional re-establishment of scholars displaced by the Hitler regime in Germany and Austria."[62] Bryn Mawr College, Columbia University, Harvard University, Johns Hopkins University, the Longy School of Music, the New School for Social Research in New York, New York University, Swarthmore College, the University of California, the University of North Carolina at Chapel Hill, the University of Pennsylvania, and Yale University each absorbed multiple émigrés across a range of disciplines.

Twenty-first-century musicologists might be surprised to learn the names of some of the scholars who came to the country as a result of the Oberlaender Trust: Willi Apel, Manfred Bukofzer, Karl Geiringer, Otto Gombosi, Paul Hindemith, Heinrich Jalowetz, Curt Sachs, and Leo Schrade, to name only a handful of refugee intellectuals and artists who became foundational figures in American music scholarship. Many moved between appointments before settling down. Altogether, 198 institutions created positions for émigré scholars, artists, and musicians whose abilities were valued highly enough to risk creating positions for them and suffering the ire of American-born musicians and scholars who might easily have felt overlooked or displaced in their own country because they did not enjoy the advantage of Guggenheim network support.

Moe wielded significant influence over a broad range of Oberlaender Trust activities, but he assumed an especially important role in music-related initiatives. As Gramm reports: "In all its decisions on musical projects, the Trustees were greatly assisted by the competent advice of their colleague, Mr. Henry Allen

Moe, who took a special interest in this subject and served as a link between the Oberlaender Trust, the various government agencies, and the American Music Center."[63] Moe had no more background or training in music at the time of the trust's founding in 1931 than he did when the Guggenheim Foundation was forming in 1924. He had, however, formed a close association with Surette and been present at interviews the advisor conducted with applicants that took place in Moe's foundation office. Moe solicited Surette's advice at the Oberlaender Trust, and Surette was happy to give it. The Guggenheim Foundation's musical judgments informed the Trust's.

Surette was not Moe's only mentor in musical matters at the trust, however. There was a better trained composer whom Moe could consult, if in a less formal way, and he was safely within the Guggenheim network. Perhaps responding to Aydelotte's early concerns about Surette's suitability for membership on the Guggenheim's Educational Advisory Board or recognizing the autodidact's limitations when it came to evaluating scores, Moe welcomed the input of a favored associate of Surette's: Otto Luening. The three-time Guggenheim awardee was often recruited to assess composers' applications. Over the years, he became a regular, if shadow, presence in numerous Guggenheim network endeavors: His name surfaces in relation to Yaddo, the Concord Summer School, the Oberlaender Trust, and Black Mountain College, as well as the Guggenheim Foundation's music composition award competitions, as will become evident in Chapter 6.

Surette and Moe repaid Luening for his informal but essential consultations with their indefatigable efforts to place him in an academic position, and they succeeded multiple times. In correspondence from 1932 Surette named the University of Pennsylvania and Bennington College as possibly having positions, although he ultimately conceded that Henry S. Drinker was unable to secure funding for a position at Penn. In that same year, however, thanks to Surette's efforts, Luening headed to the University of Arizona, where he stayed just two years before returning to the Northeast and Bennington College in Vermont. Luening built the performing arts program at the new women's college, along with Martha Graham, who taught six-week summer sessions there for fourteen years from 1934 to 1948; he remained at Bennington until 1944.[64] Luening moved a last time, to Columbia, where he became famous for his pioneering electronic and tape music work with Vladimir Ussachevsky. Shortly thereafter Ussachevsky would be awarded one of two Guggenheim Fellowships: the first in 1956, and the second in 1960. Luening remained at Columbia until his retirement in 1970. From the late 1920s onward, he was a supporting cast member of the Guggenheim actor-network who benefited significantly from his association with it.

Loyalty to the foundation meant that Luening would take care of his Guggenheim colleagues as he had been taken care of. In a 1938 letter to Douglas Moore (a 1934 Guggenheim Fellow), Luening informed him that Reed College, a small, progressive private liberal arts school in Portland, Oregon, was "looking for a general utility man in music."[65] Preferring to stay within the favored northeastern orbit and close to his Long Island birthplace, however, Moore waited it out and accepted a position in 1940 at Columbia, where he stayed until 1962, rather than head west.[66] When Luening accepted his position at the same uptown university four years later, he closed a circle of connections.

Luening was clearly a favored member of the network when he wrote a letter to Surette in 1937 referring to a conversation with Moe that included "a little chat about the Oberlaender Trust." This was before Luening helped found the American Music Center in 1939, a non-profit members organization dedicated to promoting music by American composers, or went to Columbia.[67] Of the six co-founders of the American Music Center, three, Aaron Copland, Quincy Porter, and Otto Luening, were Guggenheim Fellows.[68] It was seemingly impossible to found a music-related organization in the Northeast in the 1930s without involving people connected to the Guggenheim Foundation.

5
THE COLLEGE

The Black Mountain College made famous by the presence of John Cage, Merce Cunningham, David Tudor, Robert Rauschenberg, and Buckminster Fuller and associated with the first "happenings" and the geodesic dome prototype is, in fact, a latter-day incarnation of a school that first coalesced in the late summer of 1933 at the home of Frank Aydelotte. Cage and Cunningham first came to Black Mountain in April 1948 and spent six days; they returned in 1952 and 1953 and secured their places in the Guggenheim network: Cage was awarded a Guggenheim Fellowship in 1949, and Cunningham received awards in 1954 and 1959. Fuller came to the college only once, to direct a summer institute in 1949, and David Tudor joined in summer institutes for three consecutive years, 1951, 1952, and 1953. Tudor overlapped with Stefan Wolpe, who participated in summer institutes at the college from 1952 to 1956 and was awarded music composition Guggenheim Fellowships in 1962 and 1970. Infamous, idealized, and impactful as these marquee residencies were when it came to popularizing the college and securing its place in American arts historiography, they don't reflect the original school, the one that Aydelotte and Guggenheim personnel had supported and made possible. There is an entire history that pre-dates their celebrity residencies, and the Guggenheim Foundation was closely, if unofficially, involved.

Although the two entities never established a legal relationship, the college was the direct result of Aydelotte's efforts to assist his sister Nell and Nell's husband, John Andrew Rice. Rice was a Rhodes Scholar 1911–1914 and so was known to the inner circle. He was also a Guggenheim Fellow (1927) and a charismatic former classics professor at Rollins College in Winter Park, Florida. Despite being deeply ensconced in the academy, Rice saw himself as an educational maverick. Without Aydelotte's intervention and benevolence, his personal financial support, administrative expertise, and connections to far-flung philanthropic and educational worlds, Black Mountain College never would have been founded or lasted as long as it did. Bruno Latour's assertion that actors are not "substitutable" describes Frank Aydelotte in relation to Black Mountain College: No one else could have accomplished what he did for the school. He remained involved in its affairs long after Rice had broken ties with the school and his family.[1]

* * *

Rice and a small group of students and faculty colleagues including theater professor Robert Wunsch and engineer and mathematician Theodore (Ted) Dreier had left Rollins College amid a widely publicized dispute regarding faculty governance, curricular reform, and academic freedom. Rice, who was at the center of the controversy, was invited to leave. When Rice challenged their action, and Rollins was unable to resolve their differences, the American Association of University Professors intervened, heard the complaint, and voted in support of Rice. Choosing to quit after being fired, exonerated, and reinstated, however, Rice and Wunsch drove to Swarthmore, Pennsylvania, to meet with Aydelotte to discuss their vision of a new independent, arts-focused learning community more in line with Rice's experiential and Socratic pedagogical preferences. Ted Dreier joined Rice at Aydelotte's presidential home to strategize. Aydelotte assisted Rice, Wunsch, and Dreier with identifying moneyed northeasterners, who together invested the minimum $14,500 required to underwrite the new college corporation. Nell Aydelotte Rice signed as one of its three incorporators, legally binding the larger family to the enterprise.[2] Aydelotte remained an interested supporter for the duration of the school's existence, even if he was officially an outsider. It was Aydelotte's, Moe's, and (in matters related to music) Surette's indirect but essential connections to Black Mountain College that dictated its relation to the foundation and assured its position within the Guggenheim network.

Malcolm Forbes, who had taught with Rice at Rollins for one year, became the largest initial investor: He contributed $10,000 of the needed sum. Stephen Forbes, the son of Malcolm's half-sister, became the single largest ongoing investor between 1932 and 1948. Forbes family money built facilities, paid salaries, and covered unpaid loans through the 1940s.[3] Like the Guggenheim brothers' family-run business, Black Mountain College depended on the extended Aydelotte family and its friends for its creation, personnel, and sustenance. Unlike the Guggenheim family, however, the small circle of families supporting Black Mountain College had neither the depth of financial resources nor the singleness of purpose that characterized Meyer Guggenheim and his progeny, who controlled all aspects of their business through the early twenty-first century.[4]

According to Black Mountain historian Mary Emma Harris, in the summer of 1933 "advice and support were solicited from leaders in the arts and education including Thomas Whitney Surette, founder and director of the Concord Summer School of Music; John R. P. French, Sr., head of the Cambridge School; and Henry Allen Moe, secretary of the John Simon Guggenheim Memorial Foundation, who let the College founders use his New York office as their summer [1933] headquarters." Given the foundation's chain of command, such activities had to have been approved by Aydelotte, who would have directed Moe to share his office space. The Cambridge School had been established in 1886 to prepare young women for admittance to Radcliffe College. When John French was appointed headmaster in 1931 the school moved from Cambridge to Weston, Massachusetts, and became a regionally recognized progressive coeducational boarding school that granted students rule-making power. Its emphasis on cooperative government suited Rice, who had rejected the hierarchical administrative structure at Rollins.[5]

Within months of the dramatic exodus from Rollins, Rice and his followers relocated to the mountains of North Carolina, where the Blue Ridge [Christian] Assembly buildings, now emptied of their summer lodgers, awaited them. Thomas Whitney Surette, unique among the foundation's actors in lending his name to the college letterhead, became a member of the founding Advisory Council and was listed among members of the non-stock Black Mountain College Corporation.[6] Given the disdain he directed at the American academy and its traditional teaching methods and curricula, the college likely looked attractive. It promised a place dedicated to cultivating artistically aware individuals, like the environment he believed existed only in Paris. From the beginning, however, the now seventy-three-year-old Surette found himself playing a larger and much different role than he likely imagined and having to deal with realities of academic life that he had never encountered. He became increasingly out of step with the community. It was only because of the devoted efforts of Ted Dreier, a personal friend and dedicated Concord Summer School attendee, and Henry Allen Moe, whose involvements with the college grew, that Surette didn't resign from its board or sever his ties to the place on several occasions, starting as early as the fall of 1936. Given Surette's decades-long campaign to develop musical tastes anchored in the "best" European traditions, it is hard to envision a greater incongruity between the self-styled Old World urbane fish and his new rural mountain waters.

* * *

In 1933 Black Mountain was imagined with full-time, tuition-paying resident students, a two-semester school year, and a permanent faculty, even if notions of what constituted a course, and how grades and degrees were conceived and conferred, were less traditional than elsewhere. The Oxbridge concept of tutorials, which Rhodes Scholars and Swarthmore students enjoyed, provided a model for the academic program, and logically so, with Rice in charge and Aydelotte and Moe in the background. But Black Mountain College was also a product of both the American progressive education movement that had begun in the nineteenth century and the unique cultural conditions that characterized the 1930s. In her exhaustive study of the college, Harris observed:

> Black Mountain College was conceived at a critical moment in American and international history. The crisis that precipitated the college's founding occurred simultaneously with the appointment of Adolf Hitler as chancellor of Germany in January 1933, with the closing of the Bauhaus by the Nazis, and with the beginning of the persecution of artists, intellectuals, and Jews on the European continent. The United States was in the depths of the Great Depression. A Bank Holiday had been declared, and the American public was waiting to see whether the newly elected president, Franklin Delano Roosevelt, would fulfill his commitment to put the American people back to work.[7]

But this reality was also accompanied by a new idealism. Deep in the fourth year of the Depression, Black Mountain College aspired to provide an alternative to Old World rote methods of teaching and learning. It promised to privilege conversation above all, communal responsibility, hands-on, experiential learning whether in the studio or on the farm, attention to physical, mental, and spiritual being, governance by consensus (a "sense of meeting"), and music and the arts. John Rice was acquainted with John Dewey, who had been professor of philosophy at Columbia University from 1905 to 1930 and fully embraced the American pragmatist's educational philosophy, which acknowledged the central importance of experience and art in the process of creating a sound democratic society. Dewey visited the college two times in the period 1934–1935, and according to Martin Duberman, "soon after his second visit accepted an offer to become a member of its Advisory Board."[8] Beyond offering a "praise quote" solicited by Ted Dreier in 1940 to lend credibility to the college, however, agreeing to have his name listed would be the extent of Dewey's involvement.[9]

The school faced a number of challenges. Surette's preference for doing things "the personal way" might have worked for administering his small and private Music Fund or his four-week summer school, but it was not a strategy for organizing a progressive liberal arts college with aspirations for membership in the national academic community. The ongoing Depression kept people focused on necessities, and too few organizations responded favorably to requests for financial support. The William Whitney Foundation was among a handful that did, but only in the early years since it focused on "giving support to projects in their initial stages rather than on a continuing basis."[10] Of the founders, Theodore Dreier came from a wealthy, progressive family that appreciated the arts. But not even his connections and money could sustain the endeavor.[11] Personality clashes and jealousies among faculty, meager and unequal compensation with no obvious rationale for the disparities, the swift formation of factions, oversight by a small circle of remote actors with other full-time responsibilities, the perceived impracticality of an arts-based institution at a time of national financial collapse, and the stresses caused by the constant threat of insolvency doomed Black Mountain to a steady state of uncertainty and vulnerability from the beginning.[12] Despite the missteps, lost opportunities, and challenges, however, for brief periods of time over a couple of decades students and faculty learned from each other in an atmosphere of stimulating collaborative creativity, and many who attended in its later years recalled their time at Black Mountain College as being life-changing.[13]

The institution never aspired to train virtuosic musicians or mentor professional composers; in this regard it shared goals with the Concord Summer School, Henry and Sophie Drinker's Sunday Sings, the University Extension Society's lectures, and the community music and chorus movements that enjoyed nationwide popularity at the time.[14] To various degrees they all focused on providing sound pedagogy and cultivating an appreciation of "the best" uplifting music, all with an eye to strengthening "universal" values.[15] But this was not the purpose of the Guggenheim Foundation music composition or music research awards. They were intended to encourage and cultivate the nation's artistic and intellectual elite: Receipt of one of the fellowships brought status to the awardee; the success of the recipient returned glory to the foundation. It was a model feedback loop founded in and aspiring to high-art elitism. Despite his drift toward more populist music, Aaron Copland remained committed to the Guggenheim's original cultivated music mission.

When Rice and Dreier identified music and the arts as central to their educational community, Aydelotte and Moe encouraged them to consult Surette: his views concerning music education were, in reality, more in line with those of the college than with those of the foundation. Applying his personal strategy to designing a music program and hiring faculty, Surette turned to his engineer friend, Ted Dreier.

Dreier was familiar with Surette's musical goals and embraced them enthusiastically. "The thing we want most in music," Dreier explained, "is someone who will be good at leading the singing, and I have hopes that the entire group will join in. . . . But I think we ought to start it as a tradition at the very beginning and that it will play an important part in the success of our group life and activities."[16]

Dreier solicited and then seconded Surette's opinions regarding appropriate music faculty; rather than offer independent ideas, Dreier provided an echo chamber for Surette. As was his practice at the Guggenheim Foundation when assessing music fellowship applicants, Surette required personal meetings with potential music teachers. Once again geographic proximity, time, and resources were necessities for those wanting to be considered.

The Concord Summer School ethos was transferred wholesale to the college. Music à la Surette translated to compulsory group singing, chamber music practices and performances, and folk dancing. The content of basic music appreciation classes was shaped by Surette and delivered by faculty who kept his favored Germanic masterwork-focused repertoire and narrative in the forefront. No other classes were allowed to conflict with basic music classes, and everyone was expected to participate, because everyone, it was argued, could make music. Contributions of songbooks whose costs were subvented in part by The Music Fund guaranteed that Surette's approved collection and scores for works by Bach, Wagner, and Brahms became the standard texts.[17]

The range and impact of Surette's involvement in the early years of musical culture at Black Mountain were evident not only in the use of his songbooks but also in the decisive role he played in selecting the three musicians appointed to teach at the college: John Evarts, Dante Fiorillo, and Allan Sly. Evarts became the all-purpose music teacher and song leader, a position of essential importance in Surette's concept of a cohesive school community. Sly was the more public-facing pianist-performer, and Fiorillo would function unofficially as the composer-in-residence. The college became Fiorillo's destination for his first Guggenheim Fellowship year. While each man brought different expertise and experiences to the college, their interactions and combined effect suggest the larger musical environment that Surette imagined. Dreier wrote regularly to Surette and Moe reporting on musical activities and so played a powerful role in evaluating the success of the undertaking. The imbricated worlds of Surette's summer school, the foundation, and the college emerge in their stories.

Surette's school provided a training ground and conduit for Black Mountain College music instructors in much the same way as the Conservatoire Américain supplied and trained numerous early music composition award winners. Evarts and Sly, both university graduates and Concord Summer School attendees, enjoyed the longest tenures among music faculty at Black Mountain College prior to Heinrich Jalowetz (whose appointment in 1939 was the result of Henry Allen Moe's work on behalf of the Oberlaender Trust). Evarts joined the faculty at the school's inception in the fall of 1933 and stayed through the spring of 1942, when he enlisted in the army. Sly taught music at the college between the fall of 1935 and the spring of 1939. It was Sly's public performance of a composition purportedly written by Fiorillo that would test Fiorillo's credibility, put into question Sly's judgment, potentially jeopardize the existence of the struggling college, and strain the patience and resources of Guggenheim personnel.

The pianist, violinist, and composer John Evarts had studied music at Yale (1926–1930), in Munich and Berlin in 1930 and 1931, and at the Concord Summer School for multiple years starting in 1932. During that time, he became a devotee of Surette and his gospel of amateur music making. At age twenty-five Evarts began a nine-year tenure at Black Mountain where he was remembered later as a beloved presence. He was also a relatively effective fund-raiser for the college, which made his decision to enlist in the army a source of distress. On May 21, 1941, the newly appointed rector, Robert Wunsch, and secretary, Frederick Mangold, drafted a letter arguing for Evarts's deferment for a year because of his fundamental importance to the school. As a result, Evarts taught through the spring of 1942 and then willingly joined up. He eventually became a celebrated "agent of reeducation" in postwar Germany and later worked with UNESCO.[18]

The extent to which Surette oversaw all aspects of music at the college, and especially Evarts's work, is evident in the steady stream of detailed correspondence that Surette exchanged with Ted Dreier throughout the school's first year, 1933–1934. Multiple members of the Dreier family, including Ted, had attended the Concord Summer School, and all shared Surette's belief that the college's success depended on group singing. In September, before any teacher was hired, Surette told Dreier that the school needed some singing books and recommended his own 1931 *Home and Community Song Book*, which had been sponsored by Better Homes in America, Inc., and the National Recreation Association and compiled with Archibald T. Davison.[19] The table of contents reflects the then-current favorite repertoire of white, Christian Americans, replete with patriotic and minstrel songs, folksongs of the British Isles, and over twenty chorales, hymns, and carols including "Ye Christian Heralds" and "Onward, Christian Soldiers." As community singing and songbook scholar Esther M. Morgan-Ellis has shown, Surette's songbook was thoroughly in keeping with dozens of song collections that were published starting in 1913. There was nothing particularly distinctive about his compilation.

Dreier agreed that the book was necessary although the school couldn't afford to buy copies for students. On another matter, as a sign of the times, Dreier mentioned "a young Jew of a nice type who has given concert performances with piano, violin, and viola who is out of a job and whose family are worried about him." Dreier explained that "without his knowing about it [the young man's family] would pay his room and board just to make sure that he had a job." Under those circumstances, Dreier suggested, the college could "afford to take him on

BETTER HOMES IN AMERICA INC. EDITION

CONCORD SERIES No. 19

Revised and Enlarged

THE HOME AND COMMUNITY SONG BOOK

BY

THOMAS W. SURETTE

AND

ARCHIBALD T. DAVISON

Sponsored by

BETTER HOMES IN AMERICA, INC.

&

NATIONAL RECREATION ASS'N

Vocal Edition

(Words and Voice parts only)

The pianoforte accompaniments for the songs in this book are contained in the "Complete Edition" Concord Series No. Two.

E. C. SCHIRMER MUSIC CO.

221 COLUMBUS AVENUE BOSTON, MASS.

CONTENTS

No. PAGE

PATRIOTIC AND NATIONAL SONGS (Nos. 1–10)

1 America 1
2 The Star-spangled Banner 2
3 Columbia, the gem of the ocean 3
4 The Battle Hymn of the Republic 5
5 America, the Beautiful 6
6 Dixie Land 7
7 Yankee Doodle 9
8 Old Folks at Home 10
9 My Old Kentucky Home 11
10 Old Black Joe 12

FOLK-SONGS (Nos. 11–74)

11 Home, Sweet Home 13
12 Auld Lang Syne 14
13 Annie Laurie 15
14 Flow gently, sweet Afton 16
15 Juanita 17
16 Good-night, ladies! 18
17 Aunt Dinah's Quilting Party 18
18 Over the banister 19
19 There is a tavern in the town 20
20 Upidee 22
21 Shenandoah 23
22 Caisson Song 25
23 The Jolly Miller 26
24 The Coasts of High Barbary 26
25 The Foggy Dew (English) 27
26 Blow away the morning dew 29
27 Swansea Town 30
28 The Keeper 31
29 Flowers in the Valley 32
30 Heave away! 33
31 Spanish Ladies 34
32 O no, John! 35
33 Drink to me only with thine eyes 36
34 All through the night 37
35 Saint David's Day 37
36 March of the Men of Harlech 39
37 The Ash-grove 41
38 Oh, why camest thou before me 42
39 Hark! the Summons 43
40 The Monks' March 44
41 Hunting the Hare 45
42 Loch Lomond 45
43 Ye banks and braes o' bonnie Doon 46
44 Bonnie Dundee 47
45 The Hundred Pipers 48
46 The Campbells are comin' 50
47 Turn ye to me 51
48 The winter it is past 52
49 The Minstrel Boy 52
50 The Meeting of the Waters 54
51 The Foggy Dew (Irish) 54
52 Has sorrow thy young days shaded? 55
53 The Galway Piper 56
54 Believe me, if all those endearing young charms 57
55 The Fanaid Grove 58
56 Down by the Sally gardens 59
57 Avenging and bright 60
58 Oh, Mary, thy laugh was sweet 60
59 My gentle Harp 61
60 Song of Lorraine 62
61 The Miracle of St. Nicholas 62
62 There was a little maiden 63
63 The Parable of the Sinful Rich Man 64
64 March of the Kings 65
65 Good-night 65
66 The mansion we builded 66
67 Prayer of Thanksgiving 67
68 Mother Volga 68
69 Song of the Volga Boatmen 68
70 My Sun (*O Sole Mio*) 69

iii

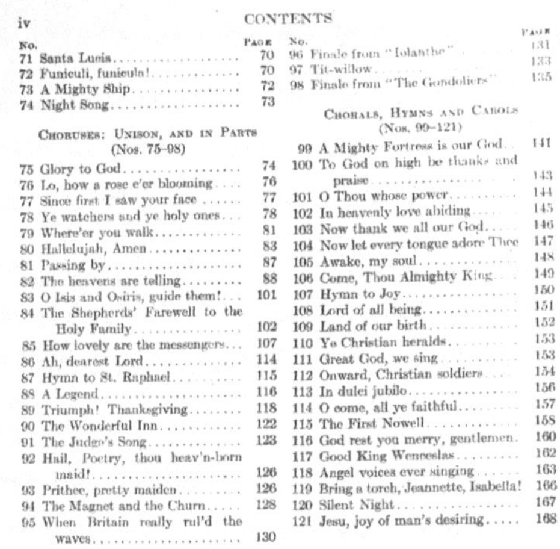

iv CONTENTS

No. PAGE

71 Santa Lucia 70
72 Funiculi, funicula! 70
73 A Mighty Ship 72
74 Night Song 73

CHORUSES: UNISON, AND IN PARTS (Nos. 75–98)

75 Glory to God 74
76 Lo, how a rose e'er blooming 76
77 Since first I saw your face 77
78 Ye watchers and ye holy ones 78
79 Where'er you walk 81
80 Hallelujah, Amen 83
81 Passing by 87
82 The heavens are telling 88
83 O Isis and Osiris, guide them! 101
84 The Shepherds' Farewell to the Holy Family 102
85 How lovely are the messengers 107
86 Ah, dearest Lord 114
87 Hymn to St. Raphael 115
88 A Legend 116
89 Triumph! Thanksgiving 118
90 The Wonderful Inn 122
91 The Judge's Song 123
92 Hail, Poetry, thou heav'n-born maid! 126
93 Prithee, pretty maiden 126
94 The Magnet and the Churn 128
95 When Britain really rul'd the waves 130
96 Finale from "Iolanthe" 131
97 Tit-willow 133
98 Finale from "The Gondoliers" 135

CHORALS, HYMNS AND CAROLS (Nos. 99–121)

99 A Mighty Fortress is our God 141
100 To God on high be thanks and praise 143
101 O Thou whose power 144
102 In heavenly love abiding 145
103 Now thank we all our God 146
104 Now let every tongue adore Thee 147
105 Awake, my soul 148
106 Come, Thou Almighty King 149
107 Hymn to Joy 150
108 Lord of all being 151
109 Land of our birth 152
110 Ye Christian heralds 153
111 Great God, we sing 153
112 Onward, Christian soldiers 154
113 In dulci jubilo 156
114 O come, all ye faithful 157
115 The First Nowell 158
116 God rest you merry, gentlemen 160
117 Good King Wenceslas 162
118 Angel voices ever singing 163
119 Bring a torch, Jeannette, Isabella! 166
120 Silent Night 167
121 Jesu, joy of man's desiring 168

Figure 5.1. Title page and table of contents from *The Home and Community Song Book*, Concord Series No. 19, by Thomas W. Surette and Archibald T. Davison (Boston, MA: E. C. Schirmer, 1931).

as an extra." Although singing was primary, chamber music making was also an important aspect of Surette's ideal program and he was eager to find people who could wear multiple musical hats.[20]

Regarding the songbooks, Surette assured Dreier that he could get him "Singer's Edition" books for forty-five cents, although he recommended the "big edition with pianoforte accompaniment for ninety cents." Surette was also "glad to see the young Jew . . . if he wants to come out here," and asked Dreier for his name and address so that he could make some inquiries concerning the man. "Out here" in this case was Concord, Massachusetts, a more difficult destination for anyone to reach than the Guggenheim Foundation's New York offices. Surette appreciated Dreier's personal way of doing things and agreed that they did "not want to take anybody without either seeing him ourselves or having someone we can depend on see him as in our small group where so much will depend on our pulling together it will be important not to have bad misfits."[21] Dreier and Surette reinforced each other's thinking.

Given the origins of the college and the relationships of its founding personnel to the most important foundation administrators, connections with the latter were impossible to avoid. Early in September 1933 Dreier had directed Surette to note that his address in New York "will be care of Guggenheim Foundation, 551 Fifth Ave," which was the address for all correspondence sent to and from John Rice as well. Dreier mentioned the perceived closeness of the relationship between school and foundation in a parenthetical remark: "It has been rather amusing the way everybody jumps to the conclusion that the Guggenheims are backing us,—quite natural, but entirely unpremeditated!"[22] If not premeditated, the connection was obvious, welcome, and advantageous to the college, and no one discouraged others from assuming some kind of endorsement. The actions of Aydelotte, Moe, and Surette were, in fact, a form of endorsement that bequeathed the foundation's prestige to the school. And the connections were used: In 1935 Rice asked Aydelotte about the eligibility of Black Mountain College students for consideration as Rhodes Scholars despite the school's newness and lack of accreditation, and five years later Moe sent Fredrick Mangold, the school's secretary, a list of new Guggenheim Fellows to consider as possible faculty members.[23] The original connections that bound the foundation men together remained; they merely added Black Mountain College to their concerns, and Surette brought his Concord Summer School to the mix. It became another pool from which he drew music faculty.

As a summer school attendee, John Evarts had a distinct advantage: He was well known to the person who was most important in deciding music faculty appointments. But their relationship was not without challenges. Surette monitored Evarts's effectiveness as a song leader to a degree that today would be characterized as intrusive, micromanaging, and potentially undermining. Unbeknownst to Evarts, Surette sought constant updates from Dreier on Evarts's progress, although Dreier was not a trained musician. The relationship of Dreier to Surette resembled that of Moe to Surette. In both cases men with no musical expertise were invited into evaluation processes that far exceeded their backgrounds by someone whose own credentials were problematic.

Dreier became Surette's man on the ground. On November 8, 1933, just weeks after the school first opened, Dreier responded to Surette's inquiry about Evarts's work in a four-page, single-spaced letter. His opening gambit set an ambivalent tone: "You asked how Evarts was getting on with the music. I should say fairly well. There are some things that are quite bad, I think, but they are mainly due to inexperience and lack of confidence. He is well liked and I don't see why there isn't a good chance that he may improve a lot." Dreier then criticized Evarts's rehearsal techniques, including his practice of going over the parts one by one, which, he concluded, took "most of the desire for singing out of people by his over-eagerness to lead them" and the absence of any attention to diction. He mentioned how many times various members of the community gathered to sing each week but was concerned that none of the songs they had learned to date were in good shape or possessed "any delicacy of expression." Having spent the bulk of his assessment criticizing Evarts's lack of attention to what Dreier believed were the most important aspects of group singing, he finished by complimenting the musician's abilities to function as a one-man chamber ensemble:

> Friday evenings after the singing, we usually have dancing. This consists of ordinary dancing and of country square dancing which one or two of the faculty learned to do in Florida. These are always great fun. The orchestra, of three or more pieces, consists of Evarts, and Evarts and Evarts, all at the piano, and he really does nobly.[24]

Dreier's assumptions regarding the proper frequency of group singings were consistent with Surette's belief that "music will weld the society together," music being defined as amateur choral singing of approved repertoire, and the society being the community at Black Mountain. Little value was attached to perfecting technique, virtuosity, improvisatory skill, or accuracy; the goals were informed enjoyment and fun and, ultimately, a more cohesive and uplifted society. Dreier's and Surette's concerns about Evarts's work are ironic given that Evarts was the only fully credentialed, trained musician of the three. A similar presumption informed Dreier's brief comment on dancing, which speaks to the different aspirations for the musical arts at Black Mountain in the age of Surette when compared to those that came to characterize the college fifteen years later, in the age of Cage and Cunningham.

As early as September 1933, Dreier had sounded out Surette regarding who might teach dancing. Dreier explained that some good people had suggested Ted Shawn, and he had spoken with him. Shawn and his wife Ruth St. Denis had established themselves as globally aware dancers when they founded what would become the Denishawn School in 1915. Together they promoted a holistic view of dance as an activity integral to everyday life, a philosophy that could have complemented Surette's belief in choral singing as essential to a sound society. By 1933 Shawn and St. Denis had separated and parted ways, but Shawn had founded an all-male dance troupe with students from Springfield College in Massachusetts, where he taught. Dreier was clearly impressed by Shawn and made a strong case for him as a faculty member in an early lengthy letter written before the November 8 missive.[25]

Dreier admitted his initial worries that Shawn's attitude might be too professional for the college, but then shared his delight when he discovered that Shawn was "really quite extraordinary: the things he told us about his ideas might many of them have come out of our own mouths or yours." What most impressed Dreier was that Shawn understood dancing "from the point of view of its relation to the broad culture and education, its place in the life of the ordinary person who would never be interested in it professionally." Clearly taken with the dancer, he assessed Shawn as "a person with a great pioneering spirit, willing to undergo great hardship and able to meet it with a spirit of confidence that he can overcome whatever difficulties he encounters." He told Surette that Shawn was going to visit the college that week and encouraged him to meet and talk with Shawn.[26]

Dreier was sensitive to Surette's fears about the professionalization of music at the college and the potential threat that hiring a well-known figure might suggest. Someone of Shawn's caliber could easily shift the balance of influence away from Surette and toward professionals. Disparagement of virtuosity was an established position in American music culture starting in the mid-nineteenth century, when a steady stream of European performers toured the nation, but it is hard not to think that part of Surette's suspicion of professionalism and virtuosity was the result of his own tenuous grip on musical accomplishments.[27]

Dreier made his case for Shawn as delicately as possible, anticipating Surette's objections. He addressed the possibility of "undesirable publicity" resulting from Shawn's fame, but he believed that Shawn was sensitive to the environment the college sought to create. He also assured Surette that Shawn's troupe wouldn't cost the school anything because they would simply use one of the cottages as a home base between engagements and pay for their meals while on campus.[28]

Dreier was hesitant to suggest that he had changed his position regarding the desirability of folk-dancing only, so he took his time laying out the evolution of his thought for Surette.

> We had thought that the best way to approach the matter of dancing would be through folk-dancing (I am not clear how much of this Shawn does), though I have always felt that folk-dancing usually brought limitations that I did not feel should be present. It is hard for me to describe what I mean clearly, but it is somewhat as though there were nothing ahead in the way of music after singing folk-songs.

> These do naturally lead to other things, but I do not see where folk-dancing leads. Perhaps the trouble is due to my very inadequate knowledge and experience.[29]

Surette was clearly concerned by the prospect of Ted Shawn's involvement with the college and wired Dreier in advance of sending his own lengthy letter a few days later. He advised against "any connection with professional dancers" and pointed to the reasons Dreier had suggested in his own letter. Surette feared that "the college is bound to be advertised by him whether he wishes it or not or whether you do or not, and it may give a name to something peculiar, which is not what you want." Surette didn't elaborate on what might be "peculiar" about a connection with Shawn, but he provided a detailed response to what he considered Dreier's wrong-headed thinking about folk dancing, which Surette saw as "a thing entirely satisfactory in itself." Once on the subject of dancing, Surette took the opportunity to comment on "expressive dancing":

> The human body as I see it is not like the mind. With music, you can go on developing the imagination and mind and emotion, but when you try to do it with the body in the form of dancing, you get into all sorts of ridiculous situations. The ordinary person is not capable of doing with dancing what he can do with music. His body is not good enough. If he tries to go on, he gets into what is called 'expressive' dancing and becomes ridiculous.
>
> There are so many of these forms of expressive dances going on in the world and nearly all of them depend on specialized bodily training and on a good physique. Most of them lead to nothing but indefinite ambiguity.[30]

With little effort Surette could have learned a lot about the Denishawn School and its associations with the nation's modernist dance movement.[31] Given Surette's devotion to Old World repertoire, if not Old World pedagogical practices, however, Shawn's modernist credentials alone might have unnerved Surette, but he didn't elaborate. He urged Dreier to continue with folk dancing and, if need be, have it led by someone "on [his] own staff if there is anybody capable of doing it." It is one of the many ironies of Surette's authority in all matters related to the arts that, possessing no expertise in dance but eliminating Shawn from consideration as a college faculty member, he removed a potential source of artistic credibility and financial stability for the arts-focused institution. Dreier accepted Surette's opinions regarding what was appropriate for the arts at Black Mountain College as Moe accepted Surette's evaluation of composer applicants for the Guggenheim wards. Neither man easily questioned Surette's judgment in the fields where he exercised oversight.

Dreier's letters kept Surette informed of Evarts's progress as a choral conductor; woven within the criticisms were occasional positive remarks. In January 1934, however, in a rare demonstration of pluck, Dreier speculated that the problematic situation with singing at the college wasn't wholly Evarts's doing, although he acknowledged that Evarts's conducting left much to be desired. Students, he observed, weren't happy singing the same songs so often; they wanted to sing "rousing college songs." The absence of any such songs in Surette's songbook meant that the problem lay in part with Surette. The issue appears to have been dropped. In a later letter Dreier informed Surette that Evarts would likely be continued for a second year because he did two things very well: "He has gotten several of the younger boys really interested in music apparently, through his appreciation course; secondly, his playing of dance music is wonderful."[32] It was clear that Evarts had made a place for himself at the college, although Surette would not relinquish oversight and Dreier's continuing ambivalent reports only encouraged Surette's involvement.

As the first school year neared its end, Dreier's concerns for Evarts's musical development and personal financial situation caused him to ask Surette to permit Evarts to attend the Concord Summer School once again, apparently assuming that he would attend at no cost. If Dreier had expected Surette to offer free tuition (which he did for the Dreier, Rice, and Aydelotte families on multiple occasions), he was disappointed. Surette responded with a suggestion that the college participate in some kind of cost-sharing arrangement. Given its always tenuous finances, however, even the smallest expense placed dangerous pressures on the solvency of the entire operation. But Surette did not give away his songbooks or the Summer School experience although the Guggenheim Foundation and Black Mountain College provided him with forums to expand his sphere of influence (and streams of income) beyond what he could have accomplished on his own. An arrangement was made, and Evarts went back to Concord that summer. He worked on his choral directing techniques, and after a rocky first year, Evarts succeeded at the college, soon joined by Fiorillo and Sly. The crisis that unfolded with the two men at its center turned everyone's focus away from any real or imagined shortcomings John Evarts might have possessed to more critical concerns: the credibility of the college, the liability of the Guggenheim Foundation, its process for selecting Fellows, and the reasonableness of Thomas Whitney Surette as music advisor to both organizations.

* * *

In order to understand Dante Fiorillo's place at Black Mountain College and his role in the larger Guggenheim network, one must acknowledge both the foundation's and the composer's connections to Yaddo, the artists' retreat where he had enjoyed residencies in the fall of 1933 and 1934. Despite almost immediate and widespread concern about the unsettling impact "his troubles and his ill health" had on the Yaddo community during his first stay, Executive Director Elizabeth Ames and her associate Marion Sheffeld became Fiorillo's advocates.[33] Fiorillo, the son of Italian immigrants, had grown up in Lower Manhattan. His musical training consisted of lessons at the Greenwich House Music School, part of the Greenwich Settlement House, which was dedicated to serving the large immigrant population living in the overcrowded neighborhood. It opened in 1902 and began offering music lessons in 1906. The separate music school was established eight years later. Fiorello studied cello and began to compose under the guidance of Enrique "Hank" Caroselli, a Uruguayan violinist who became head of the school.

When he arrived at Yaddo in 1933, Fiorillo lacked not only the more typical academic and artistic training most retreat attendees possessed but also their social skills and refinements, which put him at a disadvantage.[34] Nonetheless, his innate musical skills appeared obvious, second only to his textbook artistic temperament. Ames and Sheffeld wrote long, sometimes testy letters to each other exchanging opinions about how best to encourage Fiorillo and to Moe arguing that Fiorillo's unique gifts deserved care, cultivation, and most of all, financial support. Along with Wallingford Riegger (a participant in the first two Yaddo Festivals of Contemporary American Music in 1932 and 1933), and Walter Piston (an early recipient of a grant from Surette's Music Fund and a Guggenheim Fellow in 1935), Ames and Sheffeld volunteered practical assistance to Fiorillo with his Guggenheim Foundation application. His first attempt was unsuccessful, but when Fiorillo won an award in 1935, he wrote to Ames thanking her for all she had done to make his fellowship possible.[35] Yaddo could provide an incubator and a springboard for Guggenheim Fellows.

It is unlikely that Surette would have valued a connection to Yaddo. His taste in music differed greatly from what was celebrated at its first two music festivals despite the fact that Copland supervised them. Their emphasis on new music by American composers reflected a set of values foreign to Surette, who had little use for either American or contemporary music beyond the folk songs he'd included in his *Home and Community Song Book*.[36] It's possible, however, that Fiorillo's music was traditionally expressive enough to be appreciated by Surette, and Piston's endorsement would also have carried weight since Surette approved of Piston. Copland wrote a letter in support of Fiorillo's application, a cautious endorsement of the composer as a "'genius' of sorts." While acknowledging that Fiorillo was a "'special case,'" Copland also praised his "uncanny facility in the composition of music" including "feats of memory, [and] feats of musical juggling, which are really phenomenal." He strove to make a balanced assessment of Fiorillo's musical abilities with his behavioral abnormalities. Sensitive to the extreme financial pressures of the time, Copland advocated for Guggenheim support, which he hoped might relieve some of Fiorillo's stress and allow him to achieve much-needed balance. Recognizing that the foundation could be "'taking a chance,'" he thought the risk was worth taking.[37] Copland's observations convinced Moe and Surette, both of whom remained loyal supporters of the Foundation's first composition fellow. It appears that no one was willing to let slip the opportunity to be counted among those who discovered and saved a genius. Surette was swayed by Fiorillo and his advocates and recommended his name to the board for a twelve-month music composition fellowship to start in the spring of 1935.

Minutes of the March 13, 1935, meeting of the Standing Committee of the Educational Advisory Board reveal the uniqueness of Fiorillo's case. On the Trustees' acceptance of the Board's slate of nominees, an understanding was reached by Moe, Aydelotte, Fiorillo, and his parents that a small amount of money would be taken from Dante's stipend each month and directed to Mr. and Mrs. Fiorillo to help ameliorate their financial distress.[38] The aim was to free the composer from such worries. The original arrangement did not cost the foundation anything additional, and the award remained consistent with the foundation's goals of directing all its resources to its fellows' artistic and intellectual development and restricting administrative costs. As it turned out, Fiorillo's 1935 fellowship commenced four years of Guggenheim support for the talented but troubled composer: His award was renewed in 1936, 1937, and 1938, and in 1939 Columbia University awarded Fiorillo a $1500 Pulitzer Traveling Scholarship, thanks to the intercession of Moe.

Support for Fiorillo ranged from financial relief for him and his parents, material assistance that included supplying staff paper, personal assistance that involved procuring his passport, making travel arrangements, storing his manuscripts in Moe's office safe, providing milk during his stay at Black Mountain, and at one especially precarious moment, securing and paying for medical care for the composer.[39] From 1935 to 1939 foundation personnel were intermittently consumed by the needs of this promising awardee while the foundation risked becoming a one-stop social services provider. But it was not the Greenwich House, and it was never its intention to function as such. Fiorillo's presence took its toll on everyone involved.

Although Fiorillo's fellowship was for study abroad and as late as the summer of 1935 the hope was he would go to Italy, his parents' home country, difficulties in proving his U.S. citizenship delayed securing a passport and kept him stateside.[40] Foundation leaders worked to find an alternative destination for Fiorillo. In September, at Surette's instigation, Black Mountain College became that place.[41] Part of his fellowship stipend would offset the costs of room and board and a cottage in which to compose. Although Rice feared that Fiorillo was unstable and presented a gamble, a concern he expressed as early as June 1935, he was overruled. Though neither a student nor an official member of the faculty, Fiorillo remained in Asheville for the 1935–1936 school year and returned for five weeks, February 4 to March 15, 1937, during a subsequent Guggenheim Fellowship year.

Fiorillo arrived within weeks of Allan Bernard Sly, a pianist and composer whose educational background and professional preparation were more typical of traditional college faculty. With Surette supervising from a distance through Ted Dreier, faculty members Evarts, Sly, and Edith Vail, a young "apprentice" teacher recommended by Surette, delivered the music program for the 1935–1936 school year. Surette had met with Vail in July 1935 and written Dreier to announce that she would fit well at the college. Three days later Dreier responded to Surette thanking him for the "excellent time at Concord" and for offering his assessment of Vail, as well as agreeing that Sly was a "great find."[42] Although Surette encouraged Sly's appointment, Sly would never be as susceptible to Surette's or Dreier's oversight as were Evarts and Fiorillo. It is possible that Sly's British background provided a kind of imprimatur that Surette wouldn't challenge.

Sly had been born in Reading, Berkshire, and was educated at the University of Reading and then at the Royal Academy of Music in London. There he studied piano with Evlyn Howard-Jones, a champion of Delius and a highly regarded interpreter of Brahms, and composition with Benjamin Dale and Gustav Holst, the latter of whom was enamored equally of Wagner and English folksong. Sly embraced Holst's eclectic tastes and would use his knowledge of English folk music to assist in Black Mountain's community singing and dancing. He had emigrated to North America from England in 1930 and taught at the Toronto Conservatory of Music before moving to Black Mountain College, where he stayed until 1939. From there he moved to the College of William and Mary, from which he eventually retired. Once in the United States, Sly attended the Concord Summer School a total of four times. In the summer of 1936 he also enjoyed a residency at Yaddo, where he composed multiple works including the song "Evening Sky," which was performed by Otto Luening and his wife Ethel, an accomplished soprano. Sly's English pedigree and accent supplied a soupçon of Old World authority and polish to the pianist despite his being only a year older than his colleague John Evarts.

Understanding the idealistic and complex, if fraught, arts community at the college is only possible because of the volumes of primary and secondary materials that exist concerning all aspects of the school. Books by Martin Duberman and Mary Emma Harris, a dissertation by Anna Hines, and thousands of pages of personal papers and school documents housed at the Western Regional Offices of the North Carolina State Archives in Asheville create a thick, multi-layered, and multi-perspectival image of Black Mountain.[43] The musician seldom showcased in typical Black Mountain scholarship, however, is Sly. Harris positions him in relation to Rice and to the Bauhaus printmaker Josef Albers, who taught at the school, but she also recognizes interactions between Sly, Dreier, Evarts, and Fiorillo. Hours' worth of tape recordings made by Sly in 1971 that are housed at the Western Regional Archives supply a unique perspective on the people and the place.

Harris's summary of Sly's involvements provides a sense not only of his work but also of the larger musical culture of the college, a topic seldom talked about in relation to Evarts, who was tasked primarily with teaching classes, accompanying, and building community through choral music:

> Allan Sly started an instrumental ensemble, which in the fall of 1935 boasted four violins, two flutes, a clarinet, a cello, and a piano. It was later expanded to include a viola, a trombone, and other instruments; and in 1936 Xanti Schawinsky [who joined the faculty that year on Albers's urging as an instructor in the arts] augmented this ensemble with the soprano saxophone he had used in the Bauhaus band. If the proper instruments were not available for a particular piece of music, Sly would transpose the music for those that were. He also made bamboo pipes, a popular teaching device in England, and taught the students to play Bach chorales as well as other tunes. Members of the faculty and students gave concerts on almost every Saturday night on which there was no other scheduled event. The college even performed Paul Hindemith's *Plöner Musiktag* (1932), a series of instrumental and choral pieces written for amateur musicians to be performed in one day, beginning with a reveille of brass instruments and ending with an evening concert of instrumental music.[44]

Beyond his responsibilities to the college, in Sly's first year he composed a symphony that was given a run-through by the newly formed North Carolina Symphony and taught English country dances to Evarts's accompaniments.[45] When Albers objected to Sly's instructions for dance movements and gestures, which the artist believed weren't appropriately smooth and fluid, Sly held his ground, explaining that he grew up with them and studied with Cecil Sharp, the celebrated collector of English folk song and dance music. Unwilling to remain on the sidelines any time an opportunity to spar with Albers arose, John Rice attacked him for challenging Sly. Sly remembered "Rice's peculiar arrogance," which made many encounters "shouting matches."[46] In contrast, Sly admired Albers's abilities as a teacher and respected his standing in the art world through his close connections to Walter Gropius and the Bauhaus School. He believed, however, that Albers's allegiance to German aesthetics and practice dominated his thought and practice and that Black Mountain needed to balance that with the English background he brought to the community. In a humorous aside he wondered if "perhaps [Albers] hadn't forgiven England for thwarting the Kaiser's plans."[47] Sly, no doubt, brought his own brand of arrogance to the college, where he was perceived by some as being impatient with beginning students. That said, his multifarious musical abilities and British reserve made him an ideal presence in an often volatile music-and-arts-focused enterprise that relied on a small, fractious faculty to deliver a wide variety of offerings.

Sly encouraged the work of his colleagues and played Fiorillo's pieces in public. Harris cites Sly's successful performance in Toronto of Fiorillo's Concertino for Piano and Strings, which the pianist described as "an extremely beautiful and effective piece . . . [an] absolutely delightful work." According to Sly, Fiorillo decided he didn't like the work and withdrew it. The absence of many of Fiorillo's pieces appears to be the result of the composer's withdrawing or destroying them, as was his wont.[48] In addition to publicizing Fiorillo's music, Sly's concert provided a kind of homecoming for the former Toronto teacher, and he was enthusiastically received. In an interview with Harris in the late 1970s Sly offered that he "loved playing" Fiorillo's music and enjoyed his style: "It seemed to flow from a deep well of Italian fecundity, with facility. It reflected an easy mastery of established musical customs, idioms, forms, to show a spontaneous use of counterpoint, and of the varieties of instrumental style."[49] On another occasion, he credited Fiorillo with introducing him to Yaddo and explained that his "involvement with Dante was at a fairly deep emotional level. I was completely crazy about his compositions, as much of them as I knew, or the music which I had to believe or assume was his."[50] The two men became close friends, and Sly worked to put Fiorillo's music in front of big-name conductors and ensembles on multiple occasions.[51] He also credited Fiorillo with "initiating us into music calligraphy." The need for arrangements that suited the instrumentation available at the college, and the small number of published copies they could afford, meant that music had to be hand-copied by students and faculty. Fiorillo's contribution made the "enormous amount of copying music being done . . . better to read and much easier and quicker to write." In this way, Sly positioned Fiorillo as an asset to Black Mountain's musical life. His advocacy of Fiorillo would have been appreciated by Guggenheim Foundation personnel, who were always eager to have their fellows promoted.

Sly also praised John Evarts, who "every Saturday night . . . played for dancing" and recognized that Evarts "got the entire community involved in musical experiences: choruses, chorales, listening with great, close attention[;] . . . these things went on bringing the whole group together."[52] Looking back at his time at Black Mountain, Sly acknowledged that Evarts had contributed an enormously valuable element to the life of the place from the beginning. As regards Surette, Sly recognized that the "old man" had a lot to do with music at Black Mountain through John Evarts "and through cordial visits which he and his wife often made."[53] But he also identified Surette as a "man of certain limitations," which any "experienced musician" would have recognized. As a case in point, Sly recalled that when the pianist Helen McGraw played a recital of exclusively French and Spanish music, Surette made "a sour face" and commented, "No Bach, no Beethoven, no Brahms." Sly surmised that the evening "wasn't for him," although the rest of the community was grateful for her beautiful program.[54]

Although Sly recalled that a visitor had remarked on the "almost domestic character" of music making at the school, he was quick to distinguish that character from the quality of the music. "I might say that if we in our music fell short of professionalism, I do think that we left mediocrity far behind. And we were rather conscious of that."[55] In clarifying his role in the musical life of the college, Sly explained that he "was focused rather keenly on the music" instead of larger community affairs. While not wanting to "come across as self-centered," in 1971 Sly believed that the focus on the college community may have allowed historians to overlook his influence. If Sly's recorded interviews are his attempt to write himself into history and expand on what he believes have been scholars' partial accounts, that reality doesn't change the main points of the recollections he recorded or their import for understanding the place: His remarks avoid self-aggrandizing historicizing. More important, however, they reveal the vulnerability of a network when it exceeds its grasp or cannot control the behaviors of its most demanding constituents.

From a distance of many decades, it is easy to forget that both the foundation and the college were relatively young institutions in the mid-thirties: The Guggenheim Foundation would celebrate its tenth anniversary in 1935, and Black Mountain College was not quite two years old. In 1929, when Senator Guggenheim had warned against involvements that could dissipate one's energies, he was concerned that outside commitments would distract Moe from his duties at the foundation. Between 1935 and 1939, however, the whole leadership and staff of the foundation were distracted by one composition fellow. Ironically, it was Sly's efforts to plump Fiorillo that exposed the depth of the latter's erratic behavior and the potential culpability that even an unofficial involvement with the college presented to the foundation. Although all the details won't ever be known, enough have surfaced to provide a basic outline of what transpired.[56]

As an accomplished concert pianist and promoter of Fiorillo's music—perhaps the only professional musician who had studied several of his scores in a systematic way for public performance—Allan Sly was in a unique position to appreciate the details of his compositional voice and style. When he observed certain irregularities, that fact alone might not have been a cause for concern; many artists, especially developing ones, explore multiple styles as they hone their craft, although in the case of composers there is usually an audible soundprint that resists complete erasure. It was, however, the combination of composerly inconsistencies with Fiorillo's practice of exchanging his scores with European composers that raised alarms. Sly explained:

> There was a peculiar set of, what we could call, anomalies about Fiorillo's scores. If I remember rightly, somewhere in the basement we had a sort of sub—post office and I think someone came up from the village to run that post office during certain hours of certain days. Well in and out of that post office there was a good deal of sending and receiving of musical scores that were wrapped up by and to Fiorillo. And what he told us about all this activity was that he was exchanging scores with composers all over the world, all over the world where there are composers, that is, and I do remember that he mentioned the name more than once of Kaminski: a composer in Berlin that I have read about; I don't know his work, but he was a prominent composer in the 30s in Berlin and I don't know what's happened to him since. But he was supposed to be exchanging scores with that composer and with others.
>
> And then after a few months of such references he began to tell us that in some cases he'd written compositions and had allowed these other composers to publish them in their names. And in one instance he put in front of me a very elaborate lengthy, twenty-minute long romantic, high-romantic, fantasy-like work for piano, which was so complex that it took three and four staves to notate some of it.
>
> This was engraved but there was no title page. In place of the title page there was, what would have been perhaps on the first, left-hand page, spread out two sides of ruled paper in Dante's scrawly handwriting. And so one would play two pages of Dante's scrawl and then play the rest of the piece from the engraved, printed score. And if one knew the available European publications of those days, one certainly would have identified it as the old Universal Edition of Vienna. . . . It was a very highly honored publisher, and anything engraved by that publisher was to be taken seriously.[57]

Sly's intimate knowledge of European editions reflected his background, training, and professionalism. The handiwork of established publishing houses was easily distinguishable by its characteristic fonts, spacing and layout, print clarity, paper types and colors, bindings, covers, and accuracy. Universal Editions had been founded in Vienna in 1901 and had a distinct look. The visual dissonance that Sly described required an explanation.

> Now Dante's story was that this particular composer had bought the piece from him [Fiorillo] and then published it under his own name. Well, with that information, I played the piece, and I played it several times and each time Dante said I was getting closer to the real spirit of the thing. Since we were inclined to take things at their face value, we assumed that . . . it never occurred to us that this was

> not the truth, that this was Dante's piece, and that this composer from . . . on the European continent had had it published under his name. But for some reason the front page was missing. That's why Dante had written it out from memory.[58]

Sly's candor about his and the Black Mountain community's credulousness suggests, perhaps, the depth of everyone's desire to believe in their resident genius, or at least the person being presented as one by persons associated with the Guggenheim Foundation. Sly's integrity and reputation, however, were publicly questioned when the reality of the situation was exposed. Thirty-five years after the revelation he shared his thoughts:

> Well I played that piece at Yaddo . . . in 1936, and the Gordon String Quartet, a very well-known quartet in those years, was present and they listened. But in the conversation afterwards a few people began to smell a rat, and somebody poked around, and they came up with the idea that this composition was the work of Egon Kornauth. So I looked him up in an encyclopedia and there is such a composer. He had been a repetiteur, that means a coach, a general musical factotum, backstage of the Vienna opera for some years, and he had toured America as an accompanist with some well-known singers. He also, could very well be a composer of considerable attainment.[59]

In fact, Kornauth *was* an Austrian composer, conductor, and pianist of considerable attainment and fecundity. He and his music would have been known in and around German-speaking Europe, as well as in select tour destinations around the globe including Indonesia in 1928–1929 and South America in 1934–1935. That Kornauth's works were unknown to many in North America, including Sly, didn't negate the reality that his music was familiar to a few of those in attendance at Saratoga Springs. The cordial relationship enjoyed by Yaddo and the Guggenheim Foundation, and the pride Yaddo took in that connection and especially in its musical events, meant that what happened at the concert in upstate New York didn't stay there. The years-long efforts of Yaddo personnel and attendees to champion Fiorillo and the openness of the foundation to their ideas meant that both were implicated in the ruse: a case of guilt by association. Fiorillo's and Sly's affiliations with Black Mountain College, the experimental school that was perceived as having some connection to if not endorsement by the Guggenheims, only deepened the foundation's culpability. And Sly, the pianist responsible for performing the suspect piece, was personally exposed and professionally compromised. As he recalled:

> Now, I'm convinced that particular composition must have been the work of Egon Kornauth, published by Universal, and for some reason, that I don't understand, I'm not a student of abnormal psychology, I can't understand it, but Fiorillo wanted

> that, wanted us to believe that he had written it. And I swallowed it hook, line, and sinker and made a fool of myself at Yaddo doing so.[60]

Starting the next school year, with the Yaddo debacle behind him, Sly focused on learning a piano sonata by his former teacher Benjamin Dale. He took no chances when it came to the work's provenance; there was no question who wrote the sonata. Dale's Sonata in D minor, op. 1 (1902–1905) would become his most famous work and is, according to Lisa Hardy, considered by some "the first outstanding British piano sonata."[61] In 1971 Sly described the piece as "a great long, massive work; it takes about thirty-five minutes to play, which is long for a piano sonata in those years. It's very Edwardian in its style, something like Elgar, reminiscences of Grieg, Balakirev perhaps, very colorful, goes all over the piano, takes an enormous amount of physical energy to learn it and practice it and play it." Sly remembered that when he presented it to the Black Mountain community everyone "listened attentively and with respect for the work" except Fiorillo, who attacked both him and the work, saying that it had a weak sense of form. In light of Sly's characterization of Fiorillo's own compositions as structurally conventional, it's unsurprising that Fiorillo would have taken issue with a two-movement sonata: Beyond ignoring the typical number of movements, Hardy explains, the second and final movement is a loose set of variations that blends the typical slow, scherzo, and last sections of a large-scale sonata structure in one extended virtuosic statement. Given what had transpired months earlier, however, Sly was not inclined to patiently explain the more unusual structure or possible precedents.[62]

> Well, that was too much for me, and a little shouting match developed. I don't think I've indulged in many shouting matches with people, but I told him I thought that was a very Fascist point of view, and then someone came in and tried to cool the thing by pointing out that that was a rather loaded word, perhaps there could be a better word than Fascist. But it did arouse my ire to have . . . played that work under Dante's trickery in Yaddo, to have made a fool of myself and then play this extremely fine work, which incidentally has a very fine sense of form, and have Dante say it had a weak sense of form. This was a little bit too much, and perhaps it's this particular uncertainty of Dante's personal dependability, credibility, that has brought him to become somewhat eclipsed as time has gone on until no one has heard of any of his work.[63]

The confrontation reveals the deep, if often unspoken, tensions in the college community, where the larger political situation was never far from people's minds or frames of reference. In an earlier context, when Sly had characterized Fiorillo's musical style as drawing from the deep well of his family's Italian heritage, he had cast that national association positively. But with civility strained and mid-1930s politics front and center in everyone's mind, Fiorillo's lineage provided an easy connection to Fascism, the authoritarian political system in place in Italy since 1922. Fiorillo's presumptuous criticism would also have reminded Sly of Fiorillo's reliance on musical structures inherited from the German masters, and Germans were not necessarily held up as artistic models at the moment, either, especially by a British subject. When Sly recorded his recollections more than thirty years later, the encounter excited still-raw memories and caused him to recall questions he'd had earlier about Fiorillo's veracity:

> If the work which he claims he wrote and sent to Kaminsky, who said it was his, if it was by Dante, it was an entirely different style from the Kornauth piece. I remember it was a concerto for piano with about eleven instruments . . . and it was a very angular and dissonant work, very sparse. Every note counted; I learned it, I never had a chance to play it, but I learned the piano part and had enormous admiration for the piece. I'm now fairly convinced that that has to be one of Kaminsky's works. But that was another work that Fiorillo tried to sell me as one of his. To persuade me that it was his.[64]

Despite Sly's sense of betrayal, he generously acknowledged the quality of Fiorillo's Concertino for Piano and Strings, which he had played in Toronto:

> I have never come close to finding any composer except Dante that could have written that. I think it was an extremely beautiful and effective piece, and unbeknownst to Dante, I held on to the pencil score from which I later constructed a four-hand version of the string part, so that when I play[ed] that work in public out in Illinois with two colleagues, a six-hands, two pianos version, it went very well there. But I didn't dare put on the program in print what it was; I had to hide the identity of the thing because I didn't want to get into trouble, as I had at Yaddo. But I can only say that that Concertino is an absolutely delightful work, and I think it has to be Dante's. Why the Kaminsky and Kornauth episodes had to come into the picture, I can't imagine.[65]

Starting in late September 1936, Moe and Luening, as well as a handful of others, corresponded regularly about the Fiorillo situation. Before people knew how long it would drag on, they remained relatively light-hearted: Moe suggested that he, Luening, and Surette conduct a "séance" about Dante.[66] In November Moe explained that he and Surette were determined to get a first-rate performance of Dante's music in the coming season, and he urged Luening to contact the conductor Eugene Goossens.[67] In December Luening assured Moe that he was awaiting a response from Goossens, but then he shared his own puzzlement over Fiorillo's music: He couldn't "detect the man's complete musical personality."

Luening observed: "He has so many sides, almost as though different people had written some of the works." He wanted a chance to "look at quite a few of his works" and compare them side by side.[68] In the meantime, Randall Thompson referred to a Fiorillo symphony that was being reviewed, presumably by himself, with a "liquor supply intact."[69]

With the current crisis challenging Surette's increasing, and increasingly obvious, limitations (physical, emotional, intellectual, and musical) and strengthening his resolve to pull back from all college commitments, which he had announced he wanted to do months earlier, Moe turned more and more to Luening for help. Luening had been a close friend and confidante of Moe's and Surette's since 1928, the year before he won his first Guggenheim Fellowship, so he provided a natural link to the original advisor. While Surette maintained his official advisor's role with the foundation and had the final say on all music fellowship decisions through 1940, in Luening Moe found an accomplished and respected composer and musician who was up to the task of evaluating Fiorillo's works and those of others.

In January 1937 concerns deepened as Luening informed Moe of his suspicions that Fiorillo had committed a similar fraud with works by Berthold Goldschmidt, a German Jew whose compositions were banned by the Nazis. Goldschmidt had emigrated to England in 1935 and written to Luening about his experience with Fiorillo. Goldschmidt's lyrical style would likely have appealed to Fiorillo and perhaps made it easy to pass off as his own if that was his intention.[70] Luening confessed to Moe that the unfolding situation was "almost too fantastic to consider." Having been among Fiorillo's champions early on, Luening conceded that he may have been mistaken and needed to include himself with the others who had been duped.[71]

Initially relieved to have identified Black Mountain as the place to send Fiorillo, Moe now had to contend with the increasing number of people who were aware of the situation besides himself, Luening, and Surette: Rice, Dreier, Sly, the whole college community, and various residents at Yaddo. Correspondence between Dreier and Moe mentions the range of people impacted by and involved in managing the resonance of what had occurred. In the final paragraph of a letter from early February 1937 that is devoted wholly to the Egon Kornauth matter, Moe acknowledged that Sly would be in a difficult position, as would all who knew what had happened. He hoped that number would remain relatively small, but his concerns revealed a man aware of the potential damage that awaited individuals and institutions if anyone appeared to have been party to a fraud.[72] That everyone involved had some connection to the Guggenheim Foundation likely made Moe feel especially vulnerable. Public exposure and potential embarrassment also likely resonated loudly with Surette, who would have recalled his father's self-inflicted fall from grace fifty years earlier. In a letter to Dreier, Moe's normally confident, logical, and efficient prose broke down as he expressed his uncertainty: "I am so unsure in my mind about the matter that I have no advice to offer. I think the whole story has not become known to anyone; that is to say, I don't think anyone knows the whole story understandingly. I think that, but I really don't know what to think and all that I know I want is time to get to the bottom of it."[73] Despite Fiorillo's habit of destroying his music, throughout February Dreier, Moe, and Luening worked to gather as many of Fiorillo's scores as they could find to compare with pieces known to have been composed by others. They created various feints to entice Fiorillo to send his scores to one of them so they could be studied or preserved in Moe's office safe, which is where the foundation's secretary had also kept Fiorillo's passport when it was finally issued in the late summer of 1935.

In early February 1937 Dreier wrote to Moe with news that after months of expecting Fiorillo and his wife Mary to appear at the college they had finally arrived and were "in good shape." And then he explained:

> I did not know until yesterday when I talked with Allan Sly that Dante had been trying to get the Egon Kornauth piece back from him. He had held on to it as he had wanted to play it. I suggested to him that, since he was the only one who had actually seen the two copies side by side, it might be a good idea to send it to you so that someone else could also make a comparison.[74]

Dreier informed Moe of his plan to tell Fiorillo, if he asked for the piece, that it was not there; he also assured Moe that Sly had agreed not to say anything as long as Fiorillo didn't "bring the matter up." But then Dreier provided additional background information about Fiorillo's behavior that he had observed the previous year, and it clarified what likely happened:

> You may also be interested to know that last year Dante was in constant correspondence from here with young German composers whom he asked to exchange works with him (manuscripts or hand copies, of course), saying that he would try to get them published and performed in this country. He used to get various people here who can talk German to help him write his letters.[75]

Moe assured Dreier that "Sly's word about the identity of the piece I sent him with the one he received from Dante is enough for me I am sure."[76] Containing the potential fallout from the incident devolved to Guggenheim personnel: It was, after all, their foundation that had bestowed its valuable imprimatur on Fiorillo, thereby endorsing the man and his creative work. Given the heroic efforts they had already expended in providing him with financial stability, a place to work, and a support system of individuals committed to his success, to say nothing of dozens of hours of focused attention by office staff whose responsibilities included working with *all* fellows, not just music awardees, the Guggenheim Foundation took what appeared to be an unusual next step. Rather than disassociate or distance itself from the compromised composer, the foundation made no apologies and offered no public statement; it kept things quiet and turned inward. It also doubled down on its support. The strategy of containment was in the foundation's best interests, as well as those of its progeny Black Mountain College and its associate Yaddo. But to think that self-interest was the only motivation for handling the matter confidentially would be to deny more compassionate considerations that might also have been at play.

The foundation's response was unexpected; in March 1937 the board approved the reappointment of Fiorillo to a third fellowship year. This time, however, the Guggenheim Foundation trustees, including Simon and Olga Hirsch Guggenheim, added a proviso to the renewal: It vested a committee of four, Aydelotte, Surette, Luening, and Moe, with "complete supervisory authority" over all matters related to Fiorillo's fellowship.[77] Moe took charge of consulting with and informing the committee of any developments. At the May meeting of the trustees, Moe reported that he had engaged Herbert "Harry" Stack Sullivan, the most celebrated psychiatrist of the day, to treat Fiorillo. Sullivan's focus on the connections between environmental factors and behavior and his practice of considering individuals within their networks of relationships was ground-breaking at the time.[78] With the approval of the trustees, Sullivan's $506 fees to date were paid, and other funds, not to exceed $750, were encumbered to cover bills presented by the doctor for treatment of Fiorillo during his 1937–1938 Fellowship year.[79] With Moe's guidance and input the committee monitored Fiorillo's progress, the foundation board approved payments to Sullivan, and everyone planned their next steps. Having cast Fiorillo's actions as likely manifestations of a medical condition requiring treatment rather than criminal behavior deserving prosecution, the foundation positioned itself as progressive, charitable, and caring. By supporting its troubled fellow, it deflected criticism of his reappointment and its confidential handling of the matter.

Correspondence between Luening and Moe, especially, confirms the committee members' awareness of public opinion. In July Luening acknowledged that Fiorillo's story was well known and talked about by a number of people, but in general the remarks seemed to be generous in spirit, which lessened their negative impact on the foundation and the college.[80] The foundation awarded Fiorillo a fellowship yet a fourth time in 1938, continued to pay for his medical care, and with the help of Sullivan found a way to finally send him abroad in summer of 1938 for a total of five weeks.[81]

The foundation had taken extraordinary steps to assist Dante Fiorillo, including showing unprecedented concern for his psychological health at a time when mental illness was not discussed and counseling was not widely available. Sullivan was a pioneer in his field: He helped found the professional journal *Psychiatry* in 1937 and in 1943 was among the founders of the William Alanson White Institute of Psychiatry, Psychoanalysis, and Psychology in New York, the first private institute of its kind. Psychoanalytic counseling would only emerge as a widely applied and then approved therapy in the 1940s.[82] And so the foundation's actions raise the question, why? It strains credulity to imagine that it was so concerned with its reputation that it wouldn't risk a relatively small storm of bad publicity swirling around a single music fellow, although concerns with public perception were always in the forefront of Moe's mind. This is not to minimize the possibility that if Fiorillo had been charged with and proven to have committed criminal fraud on an international scale, there could have been repercussions involving the U.S. government, something any philanthropic organization would strive to avoid. It is equally hard to believe that the Board of Trustees feared financial reprisals it couldn't afford. Through their global business activities the Guggenheim family was familiar with the courtroom, and their pockets were deep. It was unlikely that a lawsuit involving a composer's actions would bankrupt the organization, although it might tarnish the foundation's and especially Moe's reputations for a period of time. He was still an ambitious young man in the late 1930s, and building his personal network of associations likely lessened his tolerance for risk.

It is possible that more personal motivations informed the Guggenheims' decision to take the course they did. Here it is necessary to engage in generous speculation, because no written records exist to confirm or refute what they might have thought. The Guggenheim Foundation was originally created by Simon and Olga Guggenheim to honor the memory of their first son, John Simon, whose life was cut short by illness. It is possible that they didn't want to jeopardize his name or legacy with a public airing of Fiorillo's difficulties and so were inclined to keep things in-house. In 1937, however, they may also have felt charitable toward Fiorillo, in part, because of personal experience with their second son, George Denver Guggenheim. Despite his less-than-stellar academic record, in 1929 George had graduated from Harvard University. But according to family members and business associates who knew him, George seemed a lost soul with little focus or direction. His personal wealth removed the need for planning for his future, something that often motivates those with fewer resources; it bankrolled an indulgent lifestyle. According to John H. Davis, those who knew George Guggenheim concurred he was "erratic, rebellious, and very high-strung."[83] Pressure to be both first *and* second son to the demanding senator and to conform to parental expectations—to buckle down, assume a leadership role in the family business, and most important, to deliver a male heir to an extended family rich in female offspring—likely exacerbated his emotional state. Rumors about George's "equivocal" company—"call girls, bootleggers"—and homosexual orientation were commonplace. Although his official address was his parents' Park Avenue apartment, he "really lived at 146 Central Park West . . . with a man."

In addition to environmental factors contributing to his high-strung temperament, in the 1930s homosexuality was regularly pathologized and characterized as a medical condition in need of a cure. According to Davis, "physicians were consulted, and he was given insulin shock treatment, which made him worse. He became acutely paranoid, suspicious of everybody." Davis's sources reported that George attempted suicide multiple times "and a male nurse was assigned to keep him under constant guard." The Guggenheims, no doubt, endured every parent's nightmare, feeling helpless on the sidelines as their child careened toward self-destruction. That the senator and his wife transferred some of their concern for George to Dante Fiorillo is not beyond the realm of possibility. Renewing Fiorillo's fellowships and providing him with medical care may have seemed a humane course of action given personal experience with their own troubled child. Although with Sullivan's professional care the Guggenheims appear to have helped Fiorillo, ultimately, they were unable to rescue their second son: George Denver Guggenheim committed suicide in a New York hotel on November 9, 1939.[84]

Upon the conclusion of Fiorillo's fourth Guggenheim Fellowship an article appeared in the May 2, 1939, *New York Times* announcing a new source of support for creative endeavors. The article "Lincoln Play Wins a Pulitzer Award" named accomplished playwrights, novelists, historians, biographers, poets, journalists, newspaper reporters, and cartoonists, all of whom had been chosen as recipients of prizes for their laudatory work "in letters and journalism" by the trustees of Columbia University in accordance with Joseph Pulitzer's endowment to the Graduate School of Journalism there. At the end of the article, two "scholarships," one in music and one in art, were also announced. In the case of the music scholarship the Guggenheim network was once again at work, although no mention was made of the foundation's involvement. The paragraph read: "Dante Fiorillo of Westwood, N.J. received a scholarship of $1,500 awarded 'to the student of music in America who may be deemed the most talented and deserving, in order that he may continue his studies with the advantage of European instruction, on the nomination of a jury composed of members of the teaching staff of the Department of Music in Columbia University and of the teaching staff of the Institute of Musical Art.'"[85] As was the case with the Guggenheim Foundation, the music scholarship jury consisted of people who were within the network and close at hand, internal adjudicators from the teaching faculties of Columbia University and the Institute of Musical Art.[86] In July 1939 Fiorillo would turn thirty-four, and he was not a student anywhere, nor did he present himself as such. But as in all matters related to Dante Fiorillo, truths were stretched, liberties were taken, and special accommodations made. There was nothing typical about the man or the foundation's interactions with him.

On May 26 the *Milwaukee Journal* picked up the *Times* story with a headline that screamed, "Escaped Slums with Music That Won Pulitzer Prize: Violinist 'Soul Mender' Inspired Young Italian to Compose 1938 Award." No distinction was made between the established winners of the literary Pulitzer Prizes and Fiorillo, who won a scholarship to "continue his studies." In the story Fiorillo became a twenty-nine-year-old Italian rising from the "dirt and the noise and the unhappy life of the tenements" in New York, despite his American birth. John Lear, the article's author, cited a "Society of Professional Musicians" award from Yaddo and "then four Guggenheim fellowships" as evidence of the accomplishments of the prize winner and claimed that Fiorillo's works had "been played all over the world" and in New York's Town Hall. He noted Fiorillo's "entirely native" ability and pointed out that he had "never studied composition." Lear's Horatio Alger story concluded with an homage to the Greenwich House music school and its teacher, Hank Caroselli, whom Fiorillo credited with rescuing him with music and inspiring him to compose.

Fiorillo's life story was rewritten, mostly by creative adjustments and redactions. Moe had done what he could to help the composer, while his secretary, Josephine Leighton, and her assistant Mrs. Daugherty handled constant requests, communiqués, and paperwork in person, by phone, and by mail related to "the interminable affairs of Dante."[87] Surette would pass away in 1941 having never regained his health after a paralyzing stroke in December 1938, but he too had done his best to marshal his resources and connections on Fiorillo's behalf. In October 1935 Surette had consulted Dreier and Moe regarding clearing up Fiorillo's debts and throughout that fall regularly strategized with Dreier about how best to handle Fiorillo.[88] In early 1937 Surette had suggested that the English composer Ralph Vaughn Williams review Fiorillo's Sextet and a choral piece "Yahveh," both of which Fiorillo had submitted as part of his application for a fellowship renewal. The English composer recommended an extension of the fellowship, citing the music's "character and invention," even if it was "rather undisciplined at present." Vaughan Williams applauded the "melodic invention" of the Sextet but described it as "overlaid occasionally with unnecessary detail." He found that "Yahveh" was most effective when simplest, concluded that Fiorillo had less experience writing for chorus than for orchestral forces, and hoped he would dispense with the stilted text setting, pointing out that "Why hidest thou from me" was "not English." In a letter to Moe that summarized Ralph Vaughan Williams's remarks, Leighton also referenced Harold Bauer's review of Fiorillo's Suite. Acknowledging his regard for Surette's opinion, Bauer did not see evidence of "a superior gift."[89] Later, Surette inquired about the possibility of Fiorillo's visiting Vaughan Williams, to which the Englishman responded: "Please send your young man to me—any friend of yours will be welcome."[90] There is no record whether the two men ever met during Fiorillo's five-week summer sojourn to Scotland and England in 1938.[91]

Fiorillo's name surfaced a few times between the late 1930s and the early 1950s. In 1938 Ralph Kirkpatrick performed Fiorillo's Concerto for Harpsichord and Strings among a number of other composers' works. He described those by Oboussier, Schmitt, Levy, Piston, and Fiorillo as "almost completely idiomatic . . . the harpsichordist has little difficulty in realizing their musical intentions."[92] References to Fiorillo's music appeared in the 1940s: One mentioned "a group of songs with string quartet accompaniment, a sonata for 'cello and piano, and two songs" that were performed at a Composer's Forum-Laboratory afternoon session;[93] another cited his removing a piece listed on the printed program of a Carnegie Hall concert series when he explained that "Music of Youth" was "written when he was about 18 and was no longer characteristic of his style."[94] In 1949 Fiorillo's piece "Furia" was played at a young people's concert given by Dean Dixon and the American Youth Orchestra to "show the children how to count beats."[95] In the spring of 1950 Fiorillo's name appeared in connection with two music-related events: the first an "informal affair," an "inaugural concert of the newly formed New York Association of Philharmonic Scholarship Committee Winners," where his Concerto for Clarinet and Strings was performed, and the second a free concert given as a tribute by friends of the cellist Fred Camelia, who had died two months earlier at the age of forty-one. At that event Fiorillo's "Madonna and Child" was performed.[96]

Fiorillo taught composition privately, and sometime in the late 1940s he founded the Educational Publishing Institute Corporation (EPIC), headquartered at 200 Bleecker Street in New York, his home address. An ad for EPIC with its listing of choral and band pieces underscores the educational focus of the company, which was in keeping with the composer's deep gratitude to his Settlement School music training. Much like Louis-Athanase Surette, about whom little was heard after his 1873 troubles,[97] Fiorillo passed away in Brattleboro, Vermont, in 1995, having all but faded into obscurity.[98]

* * *

There is no evidence to suggest that Fiorillo's association with Black Mountain College caused its more systemic difficulties, although the disturbances he created would have distracted and drained administrators' energies and potentially

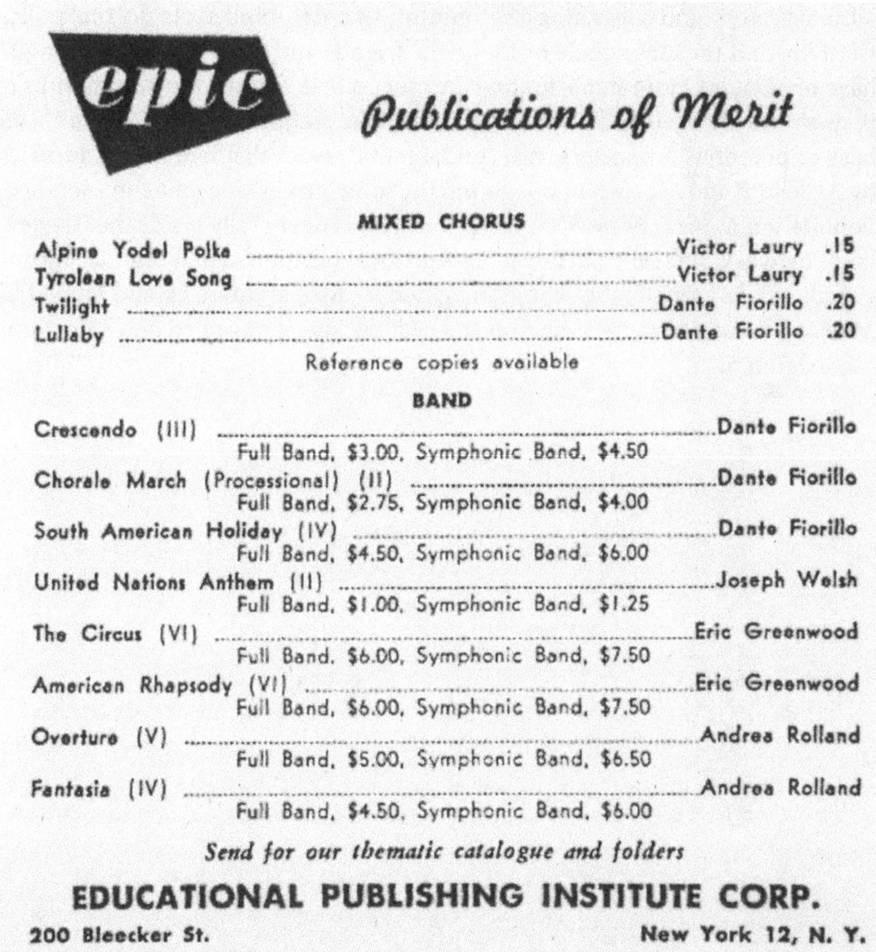

Figure 5.2. Educational Publishing Institute Corporation (EPIC) advertisement as it appears in Peter Nelson-King's blog post "The Illusory Trail of Dante Fiorillo," September 26, 2013. http://re-composing.blogspot.com/2013/09/the-illusory-trail-of-dante-fiorillo.html.

discouraged donors. For the length of its existence, the college struggled to realize and sustain itself in large part because of its diffused motivations, the self-imposed rush to open its doors before it had established a realistic plan for delivering its idealistic vision, the unfavorable financial climate of the early 1930s, and a pattern of appointing inexperienced if enthusiastic insiders as leaders. Had the eager founders been more deliberate in clarifying their mission, formulating and articulating the need for their institution, identifying reliable patrons and sources of income in strained economic times, engaging widely experienced administrators, and cultivating a community of open-minded faculty that pulled from beyond the close circle of founders' friends and family, the school might have opened on more stable footing and succeeded. But the too-few months of preparation didn't allow for broad and thoughtful planning or buy-in from a wide base of potential supporters, two fundamental issues that had been addressed by Aydelotte and Moe when imagining the John Simon Guggenheim Memorial Foundation in 1924. Black Mountain College was never fully inside the Guggenheim network, nor fully outside it. Its equivocal position kept it foundering and unfocused. Eventually the school imagined by Rice and Dreier, and tended by Moe and Surette, disappeared; over the next decade, it morphed into something quite different.

6

THE WINNERS

Between 1925 and 1940 the foundation awarded thirty-five different composers a total of fifty-five fellowships for creative work in music. Through the mid-1970s, music composition fellows often received more than one award. The term "renewal" was used loosely to describe them: Ten of the first twelve awardees received renewals in the form of consecutive years of support. Renewals didn't require the fellow to formally apply a second time but, rather, to write to Henry Allen Moe prior to the next application deadline expressing a wish to continue his or her work. Moe took the request to the Advisory Board, which made a recommendation that included a suggested dollar amount, it was approved by the trustees, and was sent to Surette for his consent. Renewal requests of this type were regularly approved. On other occasions additional awards were spaced out over a period of years—usually the second (a renewal) soon after the first, sometimes followed by a third many years later: Otto Luening won awards in 1930, 1931, and 1974; David Diamond in 1938, 1941, and 1958; and Ernst Bacon in 1939, 1942, and 1964. Through the mid-1930s, at least, the foundation's practice was not to support composers with more than two awards, but that changed with Dante Fiorillo's four awards, and then starting in the late 1950s it was not uncommon for previous winners to come back a third time, as shown above. Once chosen, awardees continued to benefit from the foundation's favor financially and professionally.

There were clear feeder systems for composition fellows in the early years, as well as a small handful of individuals whom aspiring and existing fellows were wise to cultivate; connections to Boulanger, Copland and Copland's teacher Rubin Goldmark, Surette, and the Damrosch family were helpful. Many composers enjoyed other connections: At least four of the early winners—Roger Sessions, Bernard Rogers, Quincy Porter, and George Antheil—studied with Ernest Bloch, but Sessions and Rogers had also studied with Boulanger, and Bloch and Boulanger knew each other from Paris. Bloch's work at the Mannes School put him in direct contact with the Damrosch family.[1] In the early 1930s Porter and Antheil were associated with Yaddo, where Copland was an important presence.[2] Few early composition fellows had no obvious connections to network associates. This was due in large part to Surette's insistence on a personal way of doing things and a pattern of having winners recommend the most promising applicants. But it also reflects the reality of how young institutions and especially inward-turning ones operate: They rely overwhelmingly on those they know in their immediate sphere. Figure 6.1, which lists early music composition fellows, their fellowship years, and some obvious affiliations, shows the impact that a few decider-actors had in determining the foundation's early awardees.

As the figure makes clear, Boulanger and Copland (and, by extension, Yaddo) exerted outsized influence over who was granted the opportunity to refine his craft, cultivate his art, and impact U.S. concert music culture in the foundation's first fifteen years.[3] Given Surette's early associations with both and their relationship with Walter Damrosch—thanks to his conducting the premiere of Copland's Organ Symphony in 1925 and his involvement establishing the Conservatoire Américain—it follows that the names appearing most often between 1925 and 1940 are Boulanger, Copland, Damrosch, and Surette, with Yaddo providing a locus for networking among winners and aspirants. Copland's first teacher, Rubin Goldmark, appears twice more in the chart, first in relation to Carl McKinley, his Harvard-trained student, who won fellowships in 1927 and 1928, and second with Paul Nordoff, another two-time awardee (1933 and 1935), who worked with Goldmark at the Juilliard School. Given the tightness of the foundation's intertwined circle of actors and winners, it is noteworthy when anyone outside its confines was awarded a fellowship. But the foundation's mission statement may have worked in the outsiders' favor. In light of the original commitment to "promoting the advancement and diffusion of knowledge and understanding and the appreciation of beauty, by aiding without distinction on account of race, color or creed, scholars, scientists and artists of either sex in the prosecution of their labors,"[4] it likely became obvious five years after Copland's first music composition fellowship that it had not selected anyone in this category who wasn't a white male.[5] This was not the case in other award categories, where women and people of color had been named fellows starting in 1925 and continued to be selected regularly thereafter. The minimal number of women and nonwhite composition awardees could be explained in many ways, including significantly reduced opportunities to pursue the advanced training needed to be competitive composer applicants. But in the case of the music awards, the close-knit feeder system, the absence of a board of expert advisors equivalent to those choosing other categories' winners, and the specific agenda of Thomas Whitney Surette played a disproportionate role.[6] Even when he was not deciding awardees on his own, Surette's choice for who should assist in the review process meant his values were at work.

Of the thirty-five composers awarded fellowships during Surette's fifteen years as music advisor, a single woman, Ruth Porter Crawford, two Latin Americans, Juan José Castro from Argentina and Carlos Chávez from Mexico, and one African American, William Grant Still, were not white males. With her formal training at the American Conservatory of Music in Chicago, Ruth Crawford was an extremely well-prepared and accomplished applicant. She was known from performances of her music at many concerts including those sponsored by the League of Composers and the Copland-Sessions concerts. Castro and Chávez benefited from the Guggenheim Foundation's Latin American, Caribbean, and Canadian program; in addition, Chávez was close friends with Copland and Edgard Varèse and had connections to the Pan-American Association of Composers (PAAC).[7] He was well known within Manhattan music and art circles and beyond in the United States thanks to his robust conducting tours. William Grant Still was among two of the least well known early fellows within the Guggenheim network, although he was championed by Howard Hanson, a respected presence among American composers who had won the first Prix de Rome, the American Academy in Rome's music composition prize, in 1921.

Crawford, Still, and Chávez could boast connections with Varèse, who cofounded the International Composers Guild (ICG) in 1921 with Carlos Salzedo and the PAAC in 1928 after the demise of the ICG.[8] Henry Cowell became its acting president in 1929, when Varèse left the United States to return to France for three years. Crawford was on its board, and so she benefited from the connection.[9] By 1931 the ICG had performed three of Still's works, two of which were conducted by Hanson, who conducted other pieces by Still at different venues as well. From his base at the Eastman School of Music in Rochester, New York, Hanson was deeply enmeshed in promoting U.S. music beyond Manhattan. Walter Damrosch was closely associated with the American Academy in Rome and had been elected a trustee in 1921; he had a fellowship named in his honor, the one that Roger Sessions would win. Regardless of the degree to which Varèse offended people with his "not altogether latent anti-Semitism," "pig-headed individualism," and generally dictatorial manner, he was a presence in the New York musical scene, and an endorsement from him would have carried weight.[10] The formation of the League of Composers in 1923, with which Copland became closely associated when he returned from Europe and in whose journal *Modern Music* he published his first article in 1925, was in part a response to a variety of objectionable practices on the part of the ICG. It speaks of Chávez's undeniable musical talents, determination, and diplomatic skills that he succeeded in working

Figure 6.1. Affiliations of select early Guggenheim fellows

Fellow	Guggenheim Year(s)	Pulitzer	Boulanger	Damrosch	Copland	Yaddo	Surette	Bloch	Goldmark	Varèse	Schoenberg	Luening	Hanson	Goossens
Aaron Copland	1925, 1926	1945	●	●					●					
Leopold Damrosch Mannes	1926			●										
Roger Sessions	1926, 1927	1974, 1982	●		●	●		●						
Roy Harris	1927, 1928, 1976		●		●	●								
Carl McKinley	1927, 1928								●					
Bernard Rogers	1927, 1928							●						
Theodore J. Stearns	1927		●	●										
Robert Russell Bennett	1928, 1929		●			●								
Quinto Maganini	1928, 1929	1927	●	●										
Robert Mills Delaney	1929, 1930		●				●							
Quincy Porter	1929, 1930	1954				●		●						
Randall Thomson	1929, 1930						●							
Carl Bricken	1930			●										
Ruth Crawford	1930									●				
Otto Luening	1930, 1931, 1974				●	●	●							
Mark Wessel	1930, 1932			●							●			
George Antheil	1932, 1933		●		●	●		●						
Adolph Weiss	1932			●							●			

Fellow	Guggenheim Year(s)	Pulitzer	Boulanger	Damrosch	Copland	Yaddo	Surette	Bloch	Goldmark	Varèse	Schoenberg	Luening	Hanson	Goossens
Juan José Castro*	1933				⊙									
Paul Nordoff	1933, 1935	1940							⊙					
Douglas Moore	1934	1951	⊙									⊙		
William Grant Still	1934, 1935, 1938									⊙			⊙	⊙
Dante Fiorillo	1935, 1936, 1937, 1938				⊙	⊙	⊙							
Walter Piston	1935	1948, 1961	⊙			⊙	⊙							
Ross Lee Finney	1937, 1947	1937	⊙			⊙								
Robert McBride	1937						⊙					⊙		
Carlos Chávez*	1938, 1956		⊙		⊙					⊙				
Paul Creston	1938, 1939		⊙											
David Diamond	1938, 1941, 1958		⊙			⊙								
Ernst Bacon	1939, 1942, 1964	1932											⊙	
Anis Fuleihan	1939													⊙
William Schuman	1939, 1940	1943, 1985			⊙									
Marc Blitzstein	1940, 1941		⊙			⊙								
Alvin Etler	1940, 1941, 1963													
Earl Robinson	1940, 1941				⊙									

* Awarded through the Latin American Program.

with both Varèse and Copland, who were often perceived as representing different factions.[11] He also benefited from good timing: Chávez came to the fore just prior to and during the "golden age" of Pan-Americanism.[12] *Modern Music* and later Cos Cob Press became forums for Guggenheim insiders' efforts.

INNER AND OUTER RINGS

Of the six awardees discussed in this chapter, three—Copland, Sessions, and Antheil—come from the innermost circle of the network, and three—Crawford, Still, and Chávez—represent a more distant set of associations, although Chávez challenges the simple dichotomy of inner and outer circles. All fellows were appointed to pursue "creative work in music composition." There was no requirement that composers submit the work for review when it was done, nor was there a penalty if they did not finish or even start what they had described in their applications, as Sessions's and Antheil's cases prove. As a condition of the appointment, however, fellows agreed to submit annual reports summarizing their accomplishments over the course of their careers. Performances and publications were measurable events and opportunities to credit and advertise the foundation. Moe enjoyed listing the fellows' accomplishments in the annual reports he created for the board. When awardees fell behind with their reports Moe sent reminders. He was not above inquiring whether others knew of a delinquent fellow's whereabouts or checking to make sure that performances people claimed to have taken place had, in fact, occurred.

Although foundation administrators wanted their investments to pay dividends, no one was chastised for not producing. Extant letters attest that Moe remained understanding even with the least productive or responsive fellows: There is no expression of disappointment or reprimand in writing. The likelihood of being renewed or awarded a subsequent fellowship might diminish if one did not show signs of serious effort, but that was not a certainty, and neither was there any guarantee that finishing what one had proposed would result in another award. Favored as he was in the Guggenheim network, for instance, Copland, who asked to have his fellowship renewed for a third year in 1927, was denied despite his having produced the ambitious list of creative projects he had described in his original application. Other worthy applicants, it was explained, deserved fellowships. It was rightly assumed that Copland's career had been successfully launched, as was the Paris feeder system that his award initiated. Denying Copland an additional renewal appears to have motivated him to explore other sources of support, with the foundation's help, which he did immediately. In the fall of 1927 Paul Rosenfeld voluntarily relinquished his teaching position at the New School for Social Research in order to give it to Copland, thus initiating a decade-long association with the New School that guaranteed Copland a steady, if modest, income.[13] The next year Copland and Roger Sessions began their Copland-Sessions Concerts. By 1929 Copland, along with Louis Gruenberg and Emerson Whithorne, was one of three founding advisors to Alma Morgenthau Wertheim's Cos Cob Press, which would publish numerous Copland compositions over the years. Though it denied Copland a third award in 1927, the foundation was generous to other composers that year, granting five composition fellowships including a renewal for Roger Sessions and awards to Roy Harris, Carl McKinley, Bernard Rogers, and Theodore J. Stearns.[14]

Copland, Sessions, and Antheil shared multiple associations, but what might not be obvious is the degree to which Copland championed these colleagues' causes while simultaneously concentrating his own influence. In January 1925 Copland's brief article about George Antheil appeared in the *League of Composers' Review*, the precursor to *Modern Music*; he cited the publication in his original handwritten Guggenheim application.[15] That article was followed by additional references to "this extremely talented young American composer" a year later in another article in the same journal, and then a decade after that in a third article.[16] With the 1926 publication of his article "America's Young Men of Promise" in *Modern Music*, Copland assumed the role of spokesperson for a group of neoclassical-leaning modernist composers seeking to distinguish themselves from their peers. In letters written that same year to Nicolas Slonimsky and Israel Citkowitz, Copland mentioned Antheil, his "humble colleague" and "that young genius."[17] Copland's tongue-in-cheek characterization of his contemporary as "humble" revealed his awareness of the self-promoting behaviors that Antheil displayed while he was in Germany and France building a reputation as an avant-garde personality, pianist, and composer.[18]

Copland supported Sessions as well, beginning with his original suggestion that Sessions apply to the foundation for an award; he later coaxed him to write for *Modern Music*.[19] Although the exact date and occasion of the two men's introduction is not certain, Copland recalls meeting Sessions formally for the first time in the spring of 1926 "at one of Mademoiselle's afternoon teas."[20] It's likely their paths crossed earlier, perhaps at a Boston Symphony Orchestra concert sometime in the late teens prior to Copland's leaving for Europe in 1921,[21] or during the summer of 1924, when Sessions and six of his colleagues from the Cleveland Institute spent the months from June to September in Europe. It was in the first week of his trip that Sessions met Boulanger, thanks to an introduction by Theodore Chanler, a good friend, colleague, and eventual Guggenheim winner (1944, 1956). In the brief encounter with Boulanger, Sessions played a piano reduction of his recently composed *Black Maskers*. The importance of Boulanger was obvious to Sessions, as was her enthusiasm for Igor Stravinsky's music. Over the summer, Sessions heard multiple works by Stravinsky and members of Les Six. This first taste of Europe convinced Sessions that it was where he needed to work, and with his award it was where he went. In 1926 Copland's and Sessions's fellowships overlapped, and in 1928 the two joined forces and lent their names to a concert series that was created to support and encourage "the younger generation of American composers . . . and develop a strong sense of solidarity among the creators of a growing American music."[22] Copland's willingness to share the masthead with Sessions was generous given how little the latter did to organize, administer, or contribute to the series, a reality that Sessions recognized. Having won a Prix de Rome, which took him away for three years, Sessions was of limited practical help on the ground.[23] In two letters written in March 1928 Copland informed Sessions of the first and second programs of the concerts he had arranged. They included works by himself and Sessions, as well as by Piston, Chávez, Delaney, Antheil, and Porter. (By 1938 all of them would be named Guggenheim Fellows and, except for Piston, eventually win two awards.) Ten concerts held over a three-year period, eight in the United States and one each in Paris and London, introduced works by more than two dozen composers. When Copland expressed concern to Sessions regarding Antheil's ability to complete his string quartet in time for the second concert, scheduled for April 29, 1928, Copland postponed its performance. Copland acknowledged that Antheil was busy pursuing his European career and was only in the United States on occasion in the 1920s. The work premiered a few months later at the third concert in the series on December 30, 1928, at the Little Theater.[24] Sessions would have similar difficulties meeting deadlines or finishing his own works, an issue that remained for his entire professional career, but because he was firmly inside the circle, it didn't cost him Guggenheim support.

Copland wasted no opportunity to network or promote; his naturally disarming personality and steady energy made him the perfect agent and ambassador for a group of youthful American composers across the pond and on both sides of the U.S.—Mexico border. As a result of his early cultivation of Slonimsky in 1926, the critic wrote entries about Sessions, Piston, and Cowell for the 1933 book *American Composers on American Music: A Symposium*, edited by Henry Cowell, while Copland, himself, wrote an essay on Chávez for the same volume.[25] Copland understood how to employ personal connections and all available media to advance the cause of American music, and he encouraged others to do the same.

Sessions and Antheil had associations outside the concert series as well. Both had studied with Ernest Bloch, the Swiss-born American composer who had come to the United States in 1916, taught at the Mannes School of Music from 1917 to 1920, and become a citizen in 1924 before moving to the Cleveland Institute. When Boulanger came to the United States in 1925 she visited Bloch, her friend from time spent together in Paris. Later that year, Bloch's daughter Suzanne traveled to

Paris to study composition with Mademoiselle.[26] Different as Copland, Sessions, and Antheil were in their pedigrees, personalities, productivity, and impacts on twentieth-century American music, they all benefited from the Guggenheim network.

THE INNERMOST CIRCLE

AARON COPLAND, 1900–1990

As the first music composition fellow, Aaron Copland established a handful of precedents enjoyed by many subsequent awardees. The first of these was the option to spend part or all of the fellowship year in the United States rather than go abroad if that was not most conducive to completing one's work. While staying in the United States was not encouraged, Copland's experience meant that it was possible. This was significant given Surette's well-known disapproval of musical training in the United States. With Surette as music advisor, European (and preferably French) travel was assumed for composer fellows, although it was not for awardees in other categories.

Unlike the Rhodes Scholarship, which mandated study at Oxford University, a Guggenheim Award was intended to honor a recipient's decision regarding where he or she needed to work. Copland's recent three years of study on the continent, where he had been based in France but spent months in Berlin and Vienna as well as visiting England, Italy, and Belgium, argued against the necessity of using his fellowship to expand his worldly perspective by going abroad: it was already significantly expanded at the time he applied. With the undeniable success of his New York and Boston premieres in early 1925 and a list of international references whose expertise and prestige were unassailable, Copland proposed six months based in New York followed by six months in Europe. Although Educational Advisory Board member Charles Homer Haskins of Harvard University expressed concern that living close by one's family undermined the spirit of the fellowship, Surette didn't challenge the heady European company or bona fides Copland enjoyed and advised in his favor. He argued for Copland's patriotic value as a composer citizen. When Copland requested renewed support to investigate contemporary European music in a number of European cities *and* New York, Surette argued that given how much the young composer had already accomplished, he should be allowed to work wherever he preferred.[27] Despite any prejudices that Surette may have harbored regarding Copland's ethnic identity, a logical surmise given that he regularly noted the Jewishness of applicants to his Concord Summer School, no references to Copland's being Jewish appear in the correspondence made available to me. No references to his sexual orientation appeared, either, although its absence would not have been unusual at the time.

Surette respected Copland's professional connections, achievements, and ambition and didn't get in his way. In return, Copland recognized Surette's commitment to amateur music making and appears not to have recorded any opinion regarding its value; he left Surette to it while he dedicated himself to the professionalization of "American" high-art music and the cultivation of its composers. Given Copland's near-ubiquitous presence in musical matters related to the foundation in the early years, his avoidance of both the Concord Summer School and Black Mountain College, where Surette's amateur-focused music agenda was most obvious and impactful, is noteworthy.[28] When it came to choosing where to take one's fellowship year, through the mid-1930s most composers elected to go abroad, and most of them elected to go to Paris, but at least Copland's action provided a model and left them an option for doing otherwise.

The second precedent Copland established was a pattern of renewed fellowships, which, though not restricted to music composition winners, characterized a majority of awards in that category in the early years. Of the fifteen categories in which awards were made in 1925, a total of five noncomposer fellows received a second award the following year and two others received second awards, but theirs were separated by at least two years.[29] Recipients in the eight other categories never received more than a single award.[30] By comparison, eighteen of the first thirty-five music composition fellows received consecutive awards.

The Guggenheim family's support for music was evident in the number of renewals earned by composers. That number, however, also signaled the small pool of applicants personally known to and approved by Surette and, by extension, Moe. Whereas advisors in other award categories had university colleagues and academic affiliates to supply applicants and expertise, when it came to music composition awards, the foundation depended on founders' knowledge, connections, previous awardees, and their close relationships. Surette's personal practices were not ideally suited to handle an operation the size of the Guggenheim Foundation, although no one questioned them outwardly. The challenge continued through the 1930s, as evidenced by a letter that Moe wrote to Sessions in late 1938 asking the former fellow to recommend "Guggenheim Fellowship timber" and help him "in this difficult business."[31] He invited Sessions to send names any time in the future as well. Although many organizations regularly invite previous winners to recommend and encourage future applicants, the practice is seldom their exclusive means of generating an applicant pool.

The third precedent Copland set for early music composition fellows was related to the previous one and involved his almost immediate promotion from the role of fellowship recipient to that of applicant evaluator. With Surette's limited knowledge of contemporary music or musicians he, and Moe, by extension, relied on newly minted fellows' assessments of applicants' scores and statements regarding their projects, although Surette asserted his advisor's authority (and tastes) when making final approvals. Herein lies one explanation for Copland's meteoric rise in influence in a few short years after returning from France in 1924; Surette and Moe needed qualified applicants and knowledgeable reviewers, and Copland was a one-stop shop for both. It also explains how the circle of winners remained largely inbred in the early years.

Copland was twenty when he left for France in 1921 and only twenty-four when he received his first fellowship; he was not yet the heir apparent to any kind of privileged position among his U.S. peers that he always seems to have been from our twenty-first-century vantage point. In fact, Sessions, with his family's Revolutionary War lineage, Ivy League credentials, successful premieres of works in the early twenties, and the hyperbolic endorsements of Paul Rosenfeld starting in 1923, might have been a more logical leader. Rosenfeld wrote an adoring assessment of the twenty-seven-year-old Sessions in his book *Port of New York* based on his hearing Sessions's *Black Maskers* performed by a poorly prepared college ensemble: "The music to *The Black Maskers* is no happy hit such as many slight talents make once in their lives; accidents likely as not never to repeat themselves again. The author is an artist."[32] But starting in 1925, Sessions left the country for an extended European sojourn that kept him away most of the time through 1933, and he produced very little. In addition, his personality turned decidedly inward rather than outward. His nervousness, shyness, and lengthy periods of nonproductivity, as well as his inability to manage money (which meant he was frequently in debt to his friends) or to meet deadlines or follow through on promises, would have prevented him from inspiring others to action. Despite Sessions's head start and obvious intellectual and musical gifts, by the time Copland turned thirty in late 1930, a majority of successful Guggenheim composition award applicants had some connection to him, Boulanger, Damrosch, or Yaddo, not to Sessions. What some perceived to be a dismaying preponderance of "Coplandites" at the first two Yaddo festivals reflected the younger composer's impact.

It is difficult to imagine another American composer at the turn of the twentieth century who could have amassed such influence in such a brief period of time, particularly without the benefit of a prestigious academic appointment or conservatory propping him up. Despite their affiliations, neither John Knowles Paine at Harvard University, nor George Whitefield Chadwick at the New England Conservatory, nor Daniel Gregory Mason or Edward MacDowell at Columbia University could have established or claimed the hold that Copland had on American music culture in their time. MacDowell might have had the best shot given the popularity of his music, but his heavily Europeanized aesthetic, his retiring temperament, and his health were not conducive to organizational work on the scale Copland achieved. The Guggenheim Foundation, emerging in the aftermath of World War I, provided the essential unaffiliated but broadly connected institutional framework for Copland's down-to-earth, go-getter style and his unprecedented rise in influence and prestige. The timing was right; there was an opportunity, and with the foundation's help, he grabbed it.

Beyond a winning public presence, however, Copland's productivity gave him credibility. In seeking a renewal of his award in March 1926, he enumerated his accomplishments since the fall of 1925. At the time of his original application, he had already composed several pieces and published multiple essays, demonstrating his skills as a writer of both music and prose. By early 1926 he had completed the five-movement suite "Music for the Theatre," which premiered in November with Serge Koussevitzky conducting the Boston Symphony Orchestra, and the one-act ballet *Grohg*, which was being reviewed by the Metropolitan Opera Company.[33] In truth, Copland had worked on *Grohg* since 1922 while in France, but he was able to claim completion of its first draft during his first fellowship year. For the 1926 application Copland stated that he had also begun a multi-movement work for violin and piano, hoped to start an oratorio and a chamber ballet, and had plans to begin incidental music for a play by Waldo Frank titled "Malva," which Frank had written in 1924–1925 for the American actress Katharine Cornell.[34] The play was never staged.

Copland's reference to Frank, a literary presence within the artists' circle at Alfred Stieglitz's 291 Gallery, which dominated New York's modernist art scene from 1905 to 1917, speaks to the composer's having made inroads into the most forward-thinking creative posse in the city just two years after returning from Europe. Frank, who was a close friend and supporter of Leo Ornstein, who had also been active in the artists' circle, was a respected champion of the most progressive element of American modernist culture. Years later Copland credited Waldo Frank and the music critic Paul Rosenfeld, also a friend and champion of Ornstein, with "introducing him to the ideas and personalities of American modernism."[35] While securing a place in the nation's consciousness, Copland spread the foundation's name, strengthened ties with composers across the Americas, and consolidated what would become his position as the country's most well-known composer-citizen. Over the years he would become increasingly aware of his historical role.

Although still a young man enjoying the honor and fruits of his first Guggenheim award, Copland began to evaluate Guggenheim composer applicants during his second fellowship year. In January 1927 Moe asked Copland, on behalf of Surette, to review Antheil's symphony and string quartet, the quartet that Copland ultimately programmed for the third Copland-Sessions concert in 1928.[36] Antheil had unsuccessfully applied for fellowships previously, so Moe's request was in response to Antheil's reapplication in 1927. Moe rightly assumed that Copland knew something about the composer's work given his article on Antheil for *the League of Composers' Review* in 1925. Copland became the first of many Guggenheim music composition fellows to assess their peers' musical works, sometimes while they were themselves applicants for award renewals, as would be the case with Otto Luening.

Starting in the late 1920s and continuing through the mid-1980s Copland confidentially evaluated hundreds of applications. I consulted 110 letters he had written, all of whose subjects were eventually awarded fellowships.[37] In each case, Copland was either enthusiastically in support of an applicant and recommended an immediate fellowship or suggested that an applicant was "worth watching." Within the latter category, Copland showed himself to be evenhanded and professional in explaining his hesitations and concerns.

Despite seeing only positive evaluations, one can develop a sense of Copland's aesthetic values and musical preferences by noting the qualities he regularly praised. His basic standards remained remarkably consistent over the years, even as he composed in different styles himself. Most important to him was a clear, identifiable voice, a distinct musical personality. Copland would likely have heard Boulanger express a similar priority in his years of study with her. In her letter recommending Copland, Boulanger noted his "quite exceptional" musical personality. She also focused on the "exceptionally personal" quality of Sessions's first works and his "truly original" personality.[38] Over the decades Copland expressed a desire to hear the "personal" composer, "real" emotion, and true feeling. He also noted those whose voices were not fully developed, whose musical scores showed flair or mere cleverness (signs of immaturity), or who were suppressed by overwhelming allegiance to academic trends—the mind over the musical impulse. He wanted proof of a composer's ability to handle the large forms but had no tolerance for gratuitous intellectualism. Still, when he was hopeful that the composer would mature, he said so.

Copland was particularly sensitive to Stravinsky's influence and encouraged applicants to trust their feelings, not technical mastery. Considering Boulanger's personal closeness to Stravinsky and Copland's regard for her, as well as his own healthy exposure to the Russian's musical language during his studies in Paris and Stravinsky's impact on the neoclassical composers, it is worth noting that he is the only composer Copland cites in these letters as potentially exerting a damaging degree of influence on younger composers. Perhaps Copland was speaking from experience, or maybe just warning young Americans away from aping the most identifiable contemporary *European* voice on the airwaves. Without doubt, Stravinsky's distinctive personal style made him an easy target. In addition, his being from the continent and closely associated with European modernist aesthetics would have lessened his appeal to a composer who increasingly valued the Americas and their cultures.

Although Copland demanded "technical assurance" and fine workmanship and valued seriousness, perseverance, and the ability to write articulately (both prose and music)—and he noted all three when they were present—he sought, above all, evidence of "vital," "alive" music that originated in feeling. Given Copland's oft-remarked-on reticence when it came to showing his own deepest emotions, it is again revelatory how much he valued "intense," "passionate," "moving" music written by others.[39] Copland praised Stefan Wolpe on more than one occasion for his original voice and the passion of his music. Perhaps he valued especially what he found difficult to reveal himself.[40]

Over the decades, Copland's focus remained identifying and cultivating composers who he believed could build a national, if not nationalistic, musical culture. He referred to an "American School of Composition" in his comments on applications from Irving Fine, Virgil Thomson, W. O. Smith, and Samuel Adler, although he never specified what an American School encompassed or how the composers' music was particularly American, or even what "American" delineated. Copland's broad musical tastes meant he endorsed composers working in a wide variety of styles, but he did not support projects with primarily pedagogical goals that were aimed at younger students.[41] He sought to build an environment for American music makers equivalent to that which nurtured European composers. This may be one reason why Copland was not involved with the Concord Summer School or Black Mountain College, where Surette's domestic (and overwhelmingly Christian) music ethos held sway. He envisioned the Guggenheim Foundation cultivating a different kind of musical culture than Surette promoted: a fully professional and secular one.

With thousands of pages of scholarly prose devoted to Aaron Copland and his music, many of them written by the composer himself, and well over a hundred musical works, of which dozens are firmly in the canon, Copland's place is secure. He is a most successful Guggenheim Fellow by any measure and arguably the foundation's most famous music composition awardee. But his greater impact may lie outside his ballets, film scores, songs, or solo instrumental, orchestral, or chamber works, expertly crafted, engaging, popular, and profound as many are. Copland may have left his most lasting mark with his community-building, culture-shaping organizational work. He used the platform that the Guggenheim Foundation network provided and built another that served himself, his circle of colleagues, and the nation's nascent concert-music culture. He made good on a dream he shared with Harold Clurman: "We both knew when we returned from Europe in 1924 that we wanted to be spokesmen of our generation in American arts."[42] Thanks to essential early and continual support from the Guggenheim network, Copland became that spokesperson. The foundation picked Aaron Copland and then made him a winner.

ROGER SESSIONS, 1896–1985

Roger Sessions, a fellow Brooklynite four years Copland's senior, tacked a different course and left an imprint on the nation's musical culture in another domain: teaching. From the beginning, Sessions actively and continuously pursued patronage. In his application to the Guggenheim Foundation he sought two or three years' support *or more* for composition. Later he referred to desiring an indefinite duration of study.[43] As much as he pursued a composer's life in Europe and conscientiously avoided and derided the distractions of American academia for almost a decade, Sessions's greatest impact was made by teaching composition to others in the academy. Copland's and Sessions's experiences with the foundation provide a comparative study of the range of benefits that accrued to fellows in the early years. Both men's careers were shaped by the John Simon Guggenheim Memorial Foundation network and the decades-long boost it supplied. Without it, however, it is questionable whether Sessions would have achieved the success he did. The complete absence of any mention of the foundation in Frederik Prausnitz's biography of Sessions, which the author culled from years of interviews with the composer, is extraordinary. One is left to wonder whether Sessions forgot, was burdened by a sense of failure to produce during his fellowship years, was unwilling to revisit a frustrating time, or was signaling a long-held grudge that the foundation didn't do more to make him a marquee figure comparable to his friend Copland.[44]

Sessions's music was characterized by his contemporaries as extremely modern and advanced, with the implication that it was difficult for the casual listener. That said, his *Black Maskers Suite* (1923) is by turns playful, energetic, and foot-tapping, and then tension-filled, lyrical, captivating, and tender. A twenty-minute, four-movement orchestral suite written when Sessions was twenty-seven for a Smith College graduation production of Leonid Andreyev's play, it is arguably his best-known piece. The French influence is audible throughout in the instrumentation, as well as in Stravinskian rhythmic asymmetries. Sessions knew *Petrushka* and *Le Sacre du Printemps* for almost a decade in their four-hand piano arrangements and acquired the orchestral versions as soon as they were published in 1922. Although he would dismiss allegiance to any aesthetic movement, *Black Maskers* makes it easy to assume that early on Sessions was a member of a loosely configured neoclassical school associated with Boulanger; by 1926 he would be more comfortable with that association though never willing to be grouped with others. But beyond contemporary French-inflected practices, *Black Maskers*' organum-like textures evoke centuries-old Notre Dame sounds; deep, thundering drones and huge orchestral climaxes anticipate Howard Hanson's

Symphony No. 2, "Romantic" (1930); and sinewy parallel dissonant lines preview Virgil Thomson's wrong-note aesthetic as heard in *The Plow That Broke the Plains* (1936). To twenty-first century ears, the *Black Maskers Suite* sounds of a time and place in American high-art musical culture a century ago while also revealing a deep pool of resources. Sessions didn't discard earlier musical practices but, rather, he absorbed and personalized them, a neoclassical practice to be sure.

Sessions had a distinctive voice—a strong musical personality—that remained true throughout his career, even in his late serial works, although modern listeners know little of it. Unlike Copland's music, Sessions's is seldom played. But like Copland, Sessions was also a productive scholar whose essays and reflections were widely circulated and read. Sessions's style, however, tended toward the philosophical rather than the popular and was more appropriate, perhaps, for the academy, where he would spend the rest of his career. His freedom from any single aesthetic orthodoxy allowed him to encourage the personal voices of the very different students he taught at a total of fourteen different colleges, institutes, universities, and schools in a combination of full- and part-time positions.[45] John Adams, Milton Babbitt, David Del Tredici, David Diamond, John Harbison, Lejaren Hiller, Conlon Nancarrow, Frederic Rzewski, and Ellen Taaffe Zwilich are a few of the widely recognized composers who claim Sessions as their teacher. The range of their compositional voices and styles reflects Sessions's reputation for cultivating individuals rather than clones. He taught a similarly impressive and eclectic list of theorists and music scholars including Edward T. Cone, Jonathan Kramer, Fred Lerdahl, David Lewin, and Eric Salzman. Sessions provided space for students to discover themselves.

In his 1985 contribution to "In Memoriam Roger Sessions," composer Gordon C. Cyr, a graduate student who worked with Sessions at Berkeley, described a typical lesson:

> The usual procedure was for Sessions to read the score silently. Occasionally he would put questions to the composer concerning some ambiguity, whether of tempo, dynamics, phrasing, or other musical intention imprecisely stated. Once in a while, Sessions would play a few notes, a single chord, or an isolated melodic fragment, after which another long period of silent reading would ensue.
>
> The process would continue for several minutes. . . . Only . . . after all of the instructor's questions had been answered to his satisfaction—did Sessions then speak about the student's work. The suggestions he offered extended from purely practical considerations of instrumental and vocal choices and limitations to the thornier, more controversial areas of development, balance and contrast . . . Never did Sessions impose his own style or methodology, but made every effort to deal with the student's work in terms of that student's own compositional manner.[46]

Zwilich described a similar early experience with Sessions at Juilliard: a slow and silent examination of her work punctuated by occasional questions. After two full lessons of near-wordless encounters that left Zwilich puzzled and increasingly impatient, Sessions announced: "Ah! I hear what you're doing." Thereafter, lessons commenced.[47]

In toto, the music and ideas of Sessions's students are better known than their teacher's, which is, perhaps, how the most dedicated pedagogues would have it be. It's hard to believe, however, that the man who single-mindedly pursued a career as a composer for most of a decade would have voluntarily chosen a life consumed by teaching others to do what he had imagined doing himself. Copland had returned from Europe to a nation ripe with opportunities; nine years later Sessions inherited a different set of circumstances, and they were less auspicious. Returning in the early thirties to a nation with an economy flattened by the Depression and a musical culture that had left behind modern and ultramodern experimentalism for a more pragmatic and populist agenda argued against anyone, even the most productive composer, pursuing the life of the independent concert-music creator. The academy provided the kind of security and validation that Sessions, but not Copland, required.

Sessions's and Copland's career trajectories speak to the Foundation's varied impacts. Copland never held a full-time position at any university or conservatory, although he spoke at many, arranged and delivered lecture series over the course of decades, and taught students privately. His most consistent teaching took place in the weekly lectures at the New School and during the summers at the Berkshire Music Center (Tanglewood) starting in the 1940s, where Serge Koussevitzky was conductor-in-residence.[48] Through the 1940s Copland was a free agent whose income came from commissions, short-term assignments, the patronage of Alma Morgenthau Wertheim, and the efforts of Koussevitzky, who continued to program Copland's compositions and encourage his career. Copland ultimately enhanced the reputation of the Guggenheim Foundation with his music and the indefatigable energy he directed at building networks, forging international cultural alliances, and spreading the word about young American composers' music, all activities that were in line with the original intentions of the Guggenheim family. Thanks to Copland's appointment in 1925, the Guggenheim Foundation became a powerful player in determining the nation's concert-music culture. As in the best of reciprocal relationships, Copland helped make its reputation as it made his.

In the case of Roger Sessions, however, benefits derived by the foundation are harder to measure. In truth, the Guggenheim network supported Sessions for six years with little return from his "creative work in music." After his first application to the foundation failed in 1925, his disappointment was mitigated by a year's sojourn in Italy funded by his father. On his successful second application, thanks to Copland's championing, Sessions ultimately won support from three organizations in the network: The Guggenheim Foundation awarded Sessions two consecutive fellowships for work in Florence (1926–1928); Moe's advocacy, along with recommendations from Koussevitzky, Boulanger, and Roy Welch (of Smith College), resulted in Sessions's receiving a Walter Damrosch Fellowship to study at the American Academy in Rome for a three-year residency (1929–1931);[49] and then Moe's connections with the Carnegie Foundation smoothed the way for support of another year abroad, which Sessions took in Berlin (1932–1933).

Correspondence between Moe, Circuit Court Judge Julian Mack, and Mack's former law clerk Milton Katz, both of whom enjoyed associations with the Carnegie Foundation, shows the importance of network connections and the extraordinary efforts exerted on Sessions's behalf by Guggenheim Foundation personnel.[50] Starting in the late spring of 1931 and continuing through December 1932, Mack and Moe considered additional options for supporting Sessions. Familiar names were floated: The Oberlaender Trust of the Carl Schurz Foundation and Elizabeth Sprague Coolidge, whom Moe admitted he didn't know. Ernest Bloch, Sessions's teacher, had received a commission from Coolidge in 1919 for his Viola Suite, so he provided a potential connection. The Julius Rosenwald Fund was mentioned as well. Founded in 1917 and designed to close its operations when the original monies were depleted, it was ultimately dismissed as an option, but not until letters were exchanged and possibilities pursued. In that regard, on September 8, 1931, Moe went so far as to write to Edwin R. Embree, president of the Rosenwald Fund and one of the former vice presidents of the Rockefeller Foundation (with which Frank Aydelotte had been associated), to inform Embree that the "distinguished jurist" Julian W. Mack would be writing to him on behalf of an American composer, Roger Sessions, who was seeking a grant. Moe endorsed the composer in a distant way, explaining that he trusted that Sessions was "first-rate" based on others' judgments, although he didn't say who the others were. Surette's name didn't come up. At its founding, the Rosenwald Fund had focused its philanthropic energies on building rural schools for African American children in the South. In its last two decades, 1928 to 1948, the fund concentrated on supporting African American artists and intellectuals.[51] It is hard to imagine how this well-placed white composer believed he should qualify for a Rosenwald Fund award, except perhaps because of his connections to board members, in this case Moe.[52] He was turned down. In December 1932, a Western Union telegram from F. P. Keppel to Mack closed the door for good on further support from the Carnegie Corporation as well, despite the number and depth of connections that existed.[53] Before becoming president of the Carnegie Corporation, Keppel had attended and then served as dean of Columbia University. On retiring from the corporation, he became vice president of the members-only elite American Philosophical Society in Philadelphia. Despite Sessions's entreaties, his Carnegie Corporation award was not renewed. Thus his string of personal subsidies dried up and he was forced to return to the United States in June 1933.

Although it took a couple of years to make the connection, starting in the summer of 1935 Sessions embarked on a commission from Elizabeth Sprague Coolidge to write a choral work for the Harvard Glee Club to perform at the college's tricentenary in September 1936. In December 1935, however, Sessions declared his lack of sympathy for the male voice and proposed a string quartet instead. Because he failed to meet any of the deadlines, and then delivered movements for a work completely different from the one she had commissioned, Coolidge threatened to withhold the $500 commissioning fee. According to Andrea Olmstead, Coolidge told Sessions, "[I] renounc[e] all 'authority or rights of performance,' as it really no longer belongs to me for the event for which I commissioned it." Sessions tried to turn the tables, however, responding that he didn't understand her reasoning. He explained that his "first responsibility was that of any artist worthy of the name—that of producing the best work of which [he] was capable." Surely, he chided, she would understand that he couldn't send her "something second-rate" and "accept either [her] money or [her] support."[54] Sessions declined responsibility for not delivering what he had originally promised and attempted to shift the burden to Coolidge to accept his failure to produce what they had agreed on and to reflect on her own alleged unreasonableness. Regardless of his conscious intentions, Sessions proved himself to be a skilled manipulator of people and situations who pulled the artist card when helpful.

Whether in response to his letter or with ulterior motives of her own, however, Coolidge reconsidered her action and, as Olmstead characterized it, "shrewdly elicited more from Sessions than she gave." Before paying the composer anything, she "obtained the right to give the quartet to whomever she wanted to premiere it."[55] Ultimately it would be played for the first time in April 1937 at Coolidge's own Eighth Festival of Chamber Music in Washington, DC. Sessions dedicated the quartet to her, and in 1938 she subsidized its publication.[56]

Despite a pattern of squandered opportunities, poor financial management, an inflated sense of self, a practice of relying on others for grants and loans, many of which went unrepaid, a seeming inability to get work done, and a divorce from his first wife followed by a quick marriage to a former student, which scandalized a number of his acquaintances—Boulanger most especially—Sessions frustrated Moe more with his failure to provide regular annual updates than with his slow or nonexistent creative work, his inaccurate claims about performances, or his personal behavior.[57] Only after he exhausted the resources of the Guggenheim

Foundation and its philanthropic partners would Sessions pursue a more secure course, one within the academy, the twentieth-century institutional patron of composers *par excellence*. But even this only occurred after one final effort to have others underwrite his work.

In January 1934, shortly after his return to the United States, Sessions struck out on a new venture: the New Music School. He started by partnering with Paul Boepple's Dalcroze Institute to form an allied music educational entity on East Fifty-Ninth Street. Bloch had studied composition with Émile Jaques-Dalcroze in Geneva, as had Jean Binet, Sessions's Swiss colleague at Cleveland. Boepple had studied at the Dalcroze Institute in Geneva and taught there from 1918 to 1926 before emigrating to the United States. Sessions met Dalcroze while in Geneva in the summer of 1924.[58] In 1926 Boepple founded the Dalcroze School of Music in New York (alternately called the American Dalcroze Institute) and in 1934 established the Cantata Society, which he brought under the wing of the school, where he was director.[59] On Binet's recommendation Sessions met with Boepple, who offered him the opportunity to use the school's facilities. Sessions, however, made it clear in his initial announcement of the opening of the New Music School that the two entities were distinct, writing, "Although the school will use the facilities of the American Dalcroze Institute, it will be conducted as a separate unit. For such preparatory courses as the Dalcroze Institute is qualified to offer, its cooperation will be called upon." His patronizing stance and ungraciously worded declaration of independence from an organization that was subsidizing his endeavor revealed his unyielding sense of entitlement. He assured potential students that the New Music School's initial offerings were but the beginning of something more ambitious: "It is clear that such a school cannot be established all at once—could not be, even if funds were available. We plan to start with a very few courses, enlarging curriculum and staff gradually as conditions warrant."[60] The phrase "even if funds were available" revealed the reality of the school's and Sessions's financial situations.

For a very brief period of time, the New Music School provided Sessions with a relatively steady supply of gifted composition students: Marion Bauer, Milton Babbitt, David Diamond, Vivian Fine, Miriam Gideon, and Hugo Weisgall. But sharing space and co-director status with Boepple was not amenable to Sessions, whose time in Europe had reinforced a sense of his singular vision and superior gifts. As early as the summer of 1924 Sessions had referred to himself as a "*supremely* gifted person" who had within him "possibilities which cannot be overestimated."[61] A decade later his self-assessment hadn't changed. After collaborating for one semester, from February 5 to June 1, 1934, the two men severed their relationship because, as Sessions characterized it, "they felt I was running the place."[62] But this was not before he had bought a new car that put him in additional debt and had imagined even more elaborate class offerings for the next season. He sent a copy of the "Season 1934–1935" bulletin for the 1934–1935 season to the Guggenheim Foundation, which it received on September 10, 1934; his school, however, would never materialize.

The twenty-page joint bulletin, which continued to promote courses at both the New Music School and the Dalcroze Institute (and had an introduction by Sessions that struck a more conciliatory tone), is still worth considering as it reveals yet another instance of the closed circuit of Guggenheim awardees and the favor shown to French musical values, Boulanger's most especially. Among the New Music School faculty Sessions listed Suzanne Bloch, who studied composition with her father Ernest Bloch, Sessions, and afterward with Boulanger in 1926; Israel Citkowitz, who studied composition privately with Copland and Sessions and counterpoint with Boulanger from 1927 to 1932; and Ralph Kirkpatrick who, in addition to his many teachers in Germany, had also worked with Boulanger from 1931 to 1932. The single academic music faculty member who hadn't worked with Boulanger, Harvey Officer, studied with the Swiss composer, musicologist, conductor, and pianist Ernst Levy in Paris and also taught history and music appreciation at the David Mannes School, the institution founded by Walter and Frank Damrosch's brother-in-law. Officer's name appeared in the brochure as dean of the faculty at the New Music School.

Given the realities of the nation's economic situation and the shortage of cash in many households for the most basic necessities, it is hard to fathom what Sessions was thinking when he set fees for courses and individual lessons. His three-hour course "Composition, Including Harmony, Counterpoint, Canon, Fugue, Form and Analysis," which met once per week during the season, cost $90, but one hour of individual instruction per season cost an additional $270. "Counterpoint," a supplementary course to "Composition and Improvisation," also met once per week and cost $50. Additional individual instruction with Sessions again cost $270, but if taken "with another instructor," in this case the only other composition instructor listed, Israel Citkowitz, it cost $190. All courses taught by Sessions were similarly priced, whereas instruction with other faculty members was less costly but still an extraordinary luxury when nearly a quarter of the population was unemployed, and the average minimum wage was $.25 per hour. It is little wonder that Sessions sought outside support.

The introduction to the school's new brochure shows the focus and scope of Sessions's ideas at the time. It is thoughtful, logical, and heartfelt, and it privileges composition—"the actual creation of music"—above all other musical activities. The purpose of his New Music School was, he wrote,

> to offer to professional students and non-professional music lovers, as well as to children, exhaustive and competent instruction in all phases of music study, with composition, the most essential musical activity, as the leading subject to which

> all other musical activities—interpretation, performing techniques, etc.—are coordinated in the logical sequence of composer, performer, public.[63]

The New Music School would fold before it ever had a chance to succeed, but not without Sessions attempting to engage Moe once again. In a March 1935 letter to Moe, Sessions explained the choice that faced him: He could either continue to develop the school independently or seek a "salaried position." Many years thinking of himself as an artist deserving of support by wealthy others made the idea of a salaried faculty position unfathomable. Sessions explained that he'd much prefer the former, but that course of action required more money than he earned from teaching poor students who couldn't pay. He acknowledged the unlikelihood of the foundation's underwriting his endeavor, but he hoped to meet with Moe nonetheless to explain his belief in the utter necessity for such a "center for the training of composers." Time was of the essence, he insisted, and he didn't want to give up on his plan without exploring all possible options.[64] Moe was cordial in his refusal to consider Guggenheim Foundation support of the venture but invited Sessions to meet at the Century Club, the site of many business deals in the city then and now. Moe assured Sessions that he had shared the composer's name with students who *could* afford to pay for lessons.[65] The situation is ironic given that Boulanger lent money to Sessions while he brought his work to her and accepted her mentoring without paying for lessons. As with many of Sessions's plans for larger works, both musical and institutional, when it came to organization and execution, he lacked the discipline, sustained interest, or dedication to guarantee success.

How did the foundation rationalize its years of support of a fellow who underperformed, squandered opportunities and money, and did not deliver what he had promised? Were his self-confidence and detached demeanor so persuasive that he convinced others he was supremely gifted? Were degrees from and connections to Harvard and Yale enough to persuade Surette despite the advisor's disparagement of the American academy and Sessions's disregard for Surette? Did winning the approbation of one network member predispose others to go along with their assessments? It would take Sessions decades to produce works with any regularity: Starting in the 1950s he was increasingly productive, but this was a full twenty-five years after his first Guggenheim fellowship.

The larger situation makes Sessions's remarks to three-time Guggenheim winner and a former student of his, David Diamond, painfully incongruous. In November 1937 Diamond asked Sessions to write a letter of reference on his behalf for a Guggenheim Fellowship to study with Boulanger. Sessions assured his star pupil that he wrote a strong letter that he was confident would "work in [Diamond's] favor." But having done so, Sessions launched into a lengthy reproach of

Diamond for his lack of commitment or single-minded pursuit of his composition work. He chided him for seeking after "some kind of fairy-godmother to support you + relieve you of all the problems which every composer has to face sooner or later." Sessions was unwilling to provide any kind of "sporadic criticism" of Diamond's work, though that is exactly what Sessions had received from Boulanger. Most difficult to reconcile is Sessions's lack of reflection or awareness of his own behavior, since he explained to Diamond:

> I also feel that you are asking the world in general, and me in particular, to pay you in advance for what still is + must obviously remain for some time to come, merely a hope and a promise, and not yet a real and mature achievement. . . . But I have told you many times, mere talent and mere promise are nothing by themselves; they are not rare, and one gets quite cynical about them by the time one has seen as much as I have seen. And my time, too, is limited and valuable—I have to save it for my own obligations and for the people who really appreciate what I have to give them—+ show that appreciation not only by words but by loyal effort and work.[66]

Diamond took the reprimand *and* the Guggenheim Fellowship, his first, in 1938. Much as Sessions claimed he didn't want to be Diamond's "best friend" or "'master' or anything sentimental of that kind," he clearly wanted to be the composer's primary teacher and was unwilling to share the young man he considered his protégé.[67] Diamond immediately became an extremely productive and successful composer across multiple genres, in part because of his versatile talents and work ethic, but also because of the endorsements he received from a number of important conductors, including Leonard Bernstein, Serge Koussevitzky, Dimitri Mitropoulos, and Eugene Ormandy.

With Surette continuing as music advisor and Moe still holding his opinions in high regard, and neither man having the musical background to question Sessions's work or promise, the composer's attitude overwhelmed the evidence. There was no question of Sessions's intelligence or erudition, but as Sessions himself had written to Diamond regarding talent and promise, "they are not rare" qualities.

It could also be that once an insider was safely part of the circle, the foundation was unwilling to reconsider or change its initial assessment. With Moe's confidence in Surette's "unpredictable ability called judgment," the foundation couldn't (or wouldn't) entertain the idea that it had made a mistake.[68] Once a composer was acknowledged by one network associate, awards usually came to that composer more easily.[69] In January 1928, for instance, Sessions wrote to Moe with greetings from Boulanger and instructions from her to please pass on to Moe the names of two of her students who were applying for Guggenheim Fellowships. Her advocacy produced results. Robert Russell Bennett and Robert Mills Delaney each received two awards: Bennett in 1928 and 1929 and Delaney in 1929 and 1930. She also asked Sessions to speak on behalf of a renewal for Roy Harris, which Sessions did, and Harris's award was renewed.[70] The network took care of its own. One can only imagine which or how many unsuccessful applicants to the Guggenheim Foundation, the American Academy, or the Carnegie Corporation might have used the thousands of dollars the network invested in Sessions (or others) to devote time to their own creative work in music, to make their careers, to become winners. In the case of Roger Sessions, the network made a different kind of winner than he or it had imagined: a pedagogue. Even then, with Sessions it took decades to see results.

GEORGE ANTHEIL, 1900–1959

The foundation's file on George Antheil contains documents from both his unsuccessful and successful applications. Cordial correspondence between the composer and Henry Allen Moe, the last letter written by Antheil in December 1956 in response to Moe's request that he send names of possible composer applicants, sheds light on their relationship over the course of three decades. None of the formal application materials speak directly to why the foundation changed its mind when it did about awarding the composer a fellowship and then renewing it, but reasons might be inferred on the basis of other sources. What is clear is that Surette disapproved, unequivocally, of recommending Antheil for fellowships based on his 1925 and 1926 applications. Regarding Antheil's first bid, Moe's handwritten comment on the cover page of the application notes Surette's "thorough" investigation of Antheil's work in the United States and Europe and mentions that Surette conveyed Leopold Stokowski's and Ernest Bloch's assessments of Antheil's originality as superficial and his preoccupation with fame as distracting. In his final sentence Moe conveys the music advisor's dismissal of the majority of Antheil's literary and socially well-placed references as lacking qualifications or discrimination. Surette relied on his taste, and Moe relied on Surette. Moe's cryptic notes from Surette on Antheil's next application, dated October 1926, don't expand on reasons why he was denied beyond the brief phrase "on merits"; the application was eliminated "without discussion." The composer had reapplied using the same materials and was similarly unsuccessful. It appears that Surette spent little time reconsidering Antheil's case. That Antheil was ever awarded a Guggenheim Fellowship for music composition illuminates the power of Surette's opinion, and the range and dynamism of relations between the foundation, its personnel, and its awardees, even among applicants like Antheil who enjoyed relatively close ties to Aaron Copland. Antheil's eventual admission to the self-selecting community of intellectual and artistic elites testifies to the composer's dawning awareness of the importance of personal dynamics, deference to expected codes of behavior, and recognition of what was considered creative work in music. The music Antheil composed in the 1920s, with its clear evocations of American ragtime and jazz—both racialized, vernacular styles of music associated with entertainment—on one hand, and abstract explorations of sound, silence, and time and an embrace of a French Dadaist machine aesthetic, on the other, was more challenging to Surette's musical tastes than any composed by successful fellows to that point.

There's no mistaking any early work by Antheil for the music of Sessions or Copland. Pieces as diverse as his Symphony No. 1, "Zingareska" (1923), "Mechanisms" for solo piano (1923), and the genre-challenging, abstract theatrical piece *Ballet mécanique* (1924), arguably his most famous work, sound unlike those of his close colleagues though all three owe a debt to Stravinsky. Antheil, however, was unique among them, not least for composing music that made an audible nod to Leo Ornstein, the Russian American futurist composer-pianist who had taken Europe and the United States by storm a decade earlier. Antheil played Ornstein's works alongside his own at his concerts and knew the composer's harmonic, textural, and voicing vocabulary as only a fellow pianist could; he also admired his reputation as a notorious *enfant terrible*, although in 1926 Antheil denied belonging to the ultramodern school of composition, where he placed Ornstein. When the latter left concertizing to concentrate on composing in 1922, Antheil surmised that Ornstein's manager, Martin H. Hanson, would be "in the market for a young pianist, of the fiery ultramodern Leo Ornstein variety."[71] He diligently applied himself to assuming that role by relentless practicing and preparation and secured Hanson's services. With Surette deciding which applicants received awards, however, comparisons to Ornstein would not have enhanced Antheil's chances.

Antheil's move to Europe in 1922 argued against his needing the fellowship to expand his horizons beyond the U.S. border; he was fully immersed in European, and especially Parisian, culture. In this regard, Antheil was in a position similar to Copland's in 1925, when he had just returned from three years of study in Europe. But rather than reference what he'd learned in Europe or what he hoped to accomplish, in his first Guggenheim application the twenty-four-year-old Antheil boasted that he was the only American composer who was taken seriously on the continent. In order to substantiate his claim he quoted the January 1924 Paris edition of the *New York Herald Tribune*, whose writer saw in Antheil "the composer who, for the first time, has broken with European traditions and created an American national music."[72]

Antheil had listed his early studies in fugue and composition with Uselma Clarke Smith at the Sternberg School of Music in Philadelphia from 1919 to 1921, composition and orchestration studies with Bloch in 1921, piano studies in 1922 with Artur Schnabel while in Berlin, and then informal work with Boulanger to provide the professional lineage needed to promote himself as the composer America had been waiting for.[73] Antheil also noted "intimate friends, a number of indisputable geniuses or great men," among whom were Constantine von Sternberg, Igor Stravinsky, and James Joyce.[74] Pointing to his broad reading habits and the great men he knew, Antheil argued that there was no better education; he was a proud autodidact who "never graduated from any school."[75] Unlike Sessions, who could rely on the prestige of his Ivy League credentials to assure adjudicators of his worth, Antheil had no institutional pedigree on which to lean; his reviewers provided the credentials.

Antheil's exuberant, supersized persona permeated his application. Well beyond the basic information requested by the foundation there were addenda and handwritten explanatory notes on the sides and bottoms of pages. He used marginalia to explain money he had received from others and why it should not count as scholarships and claimed not to have sought other fellowships, though he admitted to having applied for and been denied a Prix de Rome. He argued that it shouldn't count, either, given the judges' baseless assessment that his Symphony No. 1 was unplayable when it had been played in Berlin "with great success" that very year.[76] It is curious, given the award category designed to promote "creative work in music," that is, composition, that Antheil identified himself as "Concert-Pianist, Composer" in his application. His performer's abilities were noteworthy among the early field of music composition fellows, but privileging them might have weakened his application or suggested he was unfocused or unaware of what he was applying for. Anyone looking for reasons to eliminate Antheil could cite his performer's profile and move on to a prospect more focused on composing. Unsympathetic reviewers need little justification to eliminate applicants from consideration, so applicants are wise not to serve it up unthinkingly.

In relation to the foreign language competencies asked about in the application, Antheil claimed that he spoke, read, and wrote German "perfectly" and, as a result of having lived in France for two years, was fluent in French as well. Appearing to subscribe to the belief that more is more, Antheil included a copy of Ezra Pound's book *Antheil* and his own "Manifest de Musico Mecano" (in German) to attest to his scholarly attainments and the regard in which he was held. He provided separate lists of musical works and publications, annotated personal reference lists, two pages explaining past and future productions of his work, quotations from published critiques, and a three-page statement he titled "Merely a Suggestion About Oriental and Primitive Music," which enumerated plans for a study he hoped to undertake, not without pointing out, however, that the plan was beyond what was required of him to stake his claim as deserving a fellowship.[77] He considered that he'd already proven his worth. The "Suggestion," however, portrayed Antheil as a music scholar intent on a research project, further complicating exactly who he was or how his proposal related to traditional notions of creative work in music.

The quantity of materials Antheil included in his application bordered on the overwhelming. "A Separate Document Giving a Number of Reasons Why I Believe That a Fellowship Should be Awarded Me," however, provides the most concentrated evidence of George Antheil's understanding of himself and his position in modern music culture; in addition, it offers a commentary on the state of that culture and its practices at the time. It is included in full in figure 6.2.[78]

It is not surprising that Antheil critiques the many ways the United States funded the arts. Starting with two brief numbered statements claiming his uniqueness as a composer and his singular status as a purebred American working on behalf of the nation's music, by the third point Antheil slips into something more emotional and baiting.[79] With some sentences underlined and others in all caps, it's easy to make comparisons with futurist manifestos of the previous decade. His rationale for deserving a fellowship devolves into a foot-stomping performance by an exercised twenty-five-year-old who lectures unnamed institutions on the poor distribution of their endowments, the unfairness of his expatriate status in France—which, he claims, deprived him of financial support available to his European colleagues, although on other occasions he spoke of receiving greater support in Europe—the blindness of American culture to his primary importance, and the "cultural catastrophe" that all of the above represented.[80] With no lack of hubris, Antheil framed himself as the great hope of American music, a moniker that would be applied later to Roy Harris with the substitution of "white" for "great."[81]

In different circumstances, Antheil's lack of typical institutional credentials, coupled with his disparagement of American ways of doing things and his European imprimatur, might have garnered Thomas Whitney Surette's sympathies. But the temperamental distance between the staid, ultraconservative, older aspiring Concordian and the impatient young New Jersey native from the working-class manufacturing city of Trenton didn't bode well.

Positioning himself as "American" was essential to Antheil as it had been to Copland and to Sessions, who had frequently reported that his presence on the continent was gradually convincing Europe of the seriousness of the nation's composers. In a letter to Mary Curtis Bok, Antheil proudly quoted from the 1924 *New York Herald Tribune* article he had cited in his first Guggenheim application. Sessions had pointed to the Copland-Sessions concerts that took place in Paris in June 1929 and London in December 1931 as evidence of his success championing American music abroad. Antheil's Americanist tack was significantly different, although, like Sessions, he believed he could do more for "the cultural standard of America" while in Europe, at least early on.[82] In the 1920s he chose to convince

A Separate Document Giving a Number of Reasons Why I Believe That a Fellowship Should Be Awarded Me.

1. Because I am the solitary American composer taken seriously by the great artists and critics of Europe, excepting no one, living or dead.

2. Because I am American-born, and American-bred, and American educated. Because beyond my music, I am a typical American.

See note ⊛ 3. Because no American has ever contributed one cent towards my European concerts. I, a citizen of the richest country on earth, have been financed by Europeans, because Europeans have been the first to see the cultural value of my music, just as they have always been the first to see the cultural value of a new music. Europe has never tried to produce culture wholesale, by endowment of institutions solely, but has had the superior courage and intelligence to endow individuals for it is only through the individual that a culture can be made. The former princes of Europe knew where to concentrate their money. Genius and culture, or even talent, cannot be produced en gros.

A million dollars to endow an American conservatory for composers, will be a million dollars' worth of mediocrity.

In a word, some day America MUST awake to the fact that it must use more intelligence in its distribution of endowments ......and certainly more courage!......or take its cultural place at the tail-end of nations. Whether it does so with me or not is a matter of indifference to me: I will go on, and in a small way, my future is assure, in regard to the production of my works. But certainly I am hindered by the fact THAT I AM NOT A EUROPEAN, AND BECAUSE OF THIS I CANNOT SECURE QUITE ENOUGH MONEY TO FUNCTION AS A NATIVE BORN EUROPEAN COMPOSER OF MY STANDING WOULD. In a word, being an * American is a financial handicap in the production of my works.

Without exaggeration, I can say that scarcely a month goes by without the printing of a long cable report in the largest American newspapers about me. Unbelievable amounts have been printed in the magazines in America about me, despite the fact that I have not given a concert for over a year. STILL America turns a deaf ear to my appeals for help....during the past three years. This often, during times, when I have almost literally starved to death. The situation is absolutely unbelievable. More has been written about me during the past year than almost any young composer living, still I scarcely know where to turn from time to time for my next few hundred francs.

I can give you the addresses of four of the greatest modern critics living. You can write to them, and they will tell

note ⊛ An exception! Once an American woman gave a lot of money to a European concert manager for concerts of mine in Europe. This money was instantly misappropriated by this manager. I never had the slightest benefit therefrom. This would have not been the case had she put the money into my hands. She also knew the man was dishones

Figure 6.2. George Antheil, "A Separate Document Giving a Number of Reasons Why I Believe That a Fellowship Should Be Awarded Me," Paris, August 10, 1925. Reproduced with kind permission of Arthur McTigue, executor of the Antheil estate.

you that in several years I will be among the very very foremost of living composers, and among the foremost influences. Not of America but of the world of music.

At this time I shall be able to say (unless something is done very quickly)......"All this I have accomplished despite having been completely abandoned by my native land."

America, the richest country on earth, with billions to endow upon better or worse mediocrity, had not a penny to help, or better cooperate with a young composer who was the solitary young artist to be recognized by the most distinguished circles of culture in Europe, since the time of Pound, Whistler, Poe, and Whitman.

In a word, another cultural catastrophy. How many more can we STAND in America.?

George Antheil
Paris,
August 10, 1925

by provocation. References to Antheil's carrying a gun in a holster just in case he needed to shoot his way out of a concert to escape irate audience members were part of his showman's strategy. There is no record of its ever having been needed or used. By characterizing himself as a "bad boy," however, the phrase he used in the title of his autobiography, Antheil capitalized on his youthful mien (although he was the same age as Copland, and both men were just four years younger than Sessions) and a Barnumesque sense of promotion and theater. He reveled in being "the new darling of Paris" and understood the power of the right advocates. According to Antheil, "I was notorious in Paris, therefore famous. . . . The endorsement of Satie made it fairly certain that my career in Paris was a settled matter, at least for the next three or four years."[83]

Almost immediately on his arrival in Paris in June 1923 Antheil became part of an artistic crowd that included Sylvia Beach, the American bookseller, publisher, and owner of the English-language bookstore Shakespeare and Company, over which Antheil lived; Ernest Hemingway, the American journalist and novelist whose 1964 memoir *A Moveable Feast* captured his years in 1920s Paris; and Ford Madox Ford, the celebrated British writer and critic whose 1915 book *The Good Soldier* secured his reputation as a master of twentieth-century English literature. The expatriates formed their own network, and Antheil profited from it.[84] His 1925 Guggenheim application listed all three of the literati along with Georg Herzog, the American anthropologist and musicologist who would win Guggenheim Fellowships in anthropology and cultural studies in 1935 and 1947, and Ernest Bloch, his former teacher, who, when Antheil was leaving for Europe, had given him $320 on oath that he would "never . . . teach for money . . . or turn away a talented young person."[85] Altogether, eight of Antheil's original seventeen references had Parisian addresses. Additional referees included Carlos Salzedo; Eugene Goossens, the English conductor and composer who would lead the ill-fated 1927 Carnegie Hall premiere of Antheil's *Ballet mécanique*; and Mary Louise Curtis Bok, the patron who lent her family name to the Curtis Institute of Music in Philadelphia when she founded the school in 1924. Three years earlier Curtis Bok had begun her nineteen-year patronage of George Antheil. It was her monthly subvention of $150 starting in 1921, along with numerous additional monetary gifts over the years, that supported his trip to Europe and kept him afloat for decades.[86] Curtis Bok is most likely the "American woman" Antheil referenced at the bottom of his "Separate Document."[87] As David Savran observed, "Although Antheil and his patron frequently clashed, Bok's largesse freed him to pursue a career as a willful, self-consciously revolutionary, and (some would say) megalomaniacal artist."[88] In reality Curtis Bok's money allowed Antheil to, in Savran's more generous assessment, "live out the avant-gardist dream[;] he aspired to turn life into art and art into life."[89] This was more true of his early years than his later ones.

Given Antheil's established European residence, his ongoing financial arrangement with Curtis Bok, his productivity as a writer, concertizer, and composer, and his frequently controversial and widely reported theatricalized performances, the applicant presented a unique but potentially risky figure to the new foundation. Still trying to establish itself as a serious and responsible philanthropic organization, endorsing the young provocateur could have been perceived as an incautious move and may be one reason he was denied. In light of the overwhelmingly negative reception given the Carnegie Hall premiere of *Ballet mécanique* in 1927, which resulted in Curtis Bok's chastising the composer and recalculating her financial assistance downward, the foundation might have congratulated itself, in hindsight, on its wise call. The decision, however, sent the first of multiple unspoken messages to potential composer applicants that despite an expressed commitment to supporting a range of musical and artistic projects, the John Simon Guggenheim Memorial Foundation was most comfortable awarding a tamer, more broadly sanctioned brand of creative musical work, that which Thomas Whitney Surette understood and valued. Between 1925 and 1940, Moe's allegiance to Surette's judgment kept the foundation's music fellowships in check, and George Antheil would not be alone in feeling the effects.

Antheil showed some awareness of possible missteps he'd made with his earlier application in a letter to the foundation from Paris in November 1926. Wanting to be reconsidered for an award the following year and apparently wising up to the more conservative ethos of the music advisor, Antheil objected to having been characterized as a "radical" by the press and protested the epithet as "untrue," which he underlined twice. He also accused whoever had impugned his reputation of not having "investigated!," a second word he underlined. Some of the visual qualities of Antheil's previous manifesto-like style remained, although now they served an argument that he led a "model home life." He also used the power of Copland's name and invoked the phrase "your own appointee" when he quoted Copland's reference to himself as "the greatest talent among all the young American composers," though it was not Copland's exact wording.[90] Antheil continued to press his point in a letter sent from Budapest in January 1927, when he insisted on being considered a composer above all else. He named Walter Damrosch, Copland, and Sessions as knowledgeable about his recent work and then listed his string quartet and a piano concerto as well as pieces still in progress as evidence of his seriousness. The final two paragraphs consisted of an extended apology for the "arrogant" tone of his previous application and an entreaty not to be punished for what should be "certain periods of disrespect" allowed creative artists.[91] Antheil's evocation of the artist operating outside social norms complicated his earlier alignment with modernists, part of whose stance included negating and distancing themselves from nineteenth-century Romantic values and presumptions about artistic genius. His application for support from the very kind of institution he had disparaged in his "Statement" reveals the precarity of the ideological position he and other modernists attempted to occupy in the early decades of the twentieth century. His reapplication for a fellowship was no more successful than the original one.

Given the realities of who did and didn't win awards, when Antheil inquired once again in the summer of 1931 regarding a 1932 fellowship, he presented himself as a more traditional, even subdued, candidate. In a handwritten cover letter, he assumed the role of the supplicant thanking Moe for his kindness and advice, which he "deeply appreciate[d]." All signs of the swaggering twenty-five-year-old were erased and replaced by a continuously bowing petitioner. Antheil's official application statement reflected his matured understanding of how to apply to the Guggenheim Foundation to maximize his chances of success.[92]

He listed his occupation simply as "Composer" and his plan "for creative work in musical composition abroad," using the language typical of other applicants' proposals. There was no confusion as to his profession or his intentions. He proposed two projects: a historical opera focused on George Washington and a book, *The Modern Opera Movement in Germany*, which, he noted, was under contract with the London publisher Chatto and Windus. He also suggested the possibility of composing a shorter piece, perhaps a string quartet. Antheil directed reviewers to the June 1931 issue of *Modern Music* for a complete list of his works and a "sympathetic estimate" of his music by Randall Thompson; he also mentioned the score of his opera *Transatlantic*, which he had sent separately.[93] Despite having stated at the top of the application that he sought a fellowship to work abroad, in the body of the letter Antheil rationalized that the historic American topic of the opera argued for his remaining in the United States. He clarified, however, that he would not "press" that point.[94] He closed his three-page statement-letter with the names of references, all music-related figures this time: the head of Universal Edition in Vienna, various opera administrators and directors in the United States and abroad, the president of the Juilliard Foundation, a music critic from a New York paper, and a composer. Not listed but present in the background was Copland, on whom Antheil depended to put in a good word, which he had already done multiple times in articles, reviews, and performance opportunities. The new application bore no resemblance to the strutting harangue of the earlier ones, although his statement that he wouldn't press the point about remaining in the United States suggested that he might not have fully accepted the reality of the power dynamic that existed: He was powerless.

Moe contacted references, asked them to assess Antheil's abilities, and on January 26, 1932, requested that the composer "come to see Mr. Surette and me" at the foundation offices on Saturday, January 30. With Antheil living just a short train ride away and able to satisfy the summons, he went. While Moe completed additional background checks, Antheil continued his campaign to win an award by updating Moe about his opera on Washington. Given the innumerable parades, plays, pageants, and reenactments that accompanied Washington's birthday bicentennial in 1932 and Moe's frequent references to the nation's first exemplary citizen in lectures and talks he gave over the years, Antheil's choice of topic was smart.[95] Twice in February 1932 Antheil updated Moe regarding the difficulties he and his librettist, prize-winning poet William Carlos Williams, were experiencing in selecting the right episodes to focus on in the life of "the great and heroic figure," but he promised to write the work if he were awarded a fellowship.[96] Taking advantage of every opportunity to make a positive impression, Antheil closed his February 5 letter to Moe recalling the sincere and great honor and pleasure it was to meet him and Surette the previous week. And in his February 23 letter Antheil "positively" promised to write the opera.

On February 26, 1932, Moe sent official notification to Antheil that he had been awarded a Foundation Fellowship with a twelve-month stipend of $2,000 and a start date to be determined. The same day, Moe wrote a quick note to Antheil apologizing that the stipend wasn't more and noting that the amount reflected the foundation's available funds.[97] He also invited Antheil to come to see him again. In truth the Guggenheim Foundation was affected by the Depression and adjusted down the number and size of awards for a few years, but the reduced amount of Antheil's stipend might also have reflected Surette's tempered enthusiasm for the composer. Notes in other composers' files show that Surette often divided available monies between approved candidates without providing a written explanation of his criteria or rationale. In other cases he withheld funds completely from approved candidates and returned monies to the foundation. Again he did not provide a written rationale for his actions. Antheil's request to remain in the United States was denied. He wrote an acceptance note three days later that was filled with thanks and promises to work to his utmost ability and be a credit to the foundation. Mindful of the opera project he'd promised, Antheil made a quick reference to Williams's libretto and offered to bring what he had to Moe. The letter was, in true Antheilian fashion, replete with hyperbole; this time, however, excesses were reserved for expressions of gratitude.

Between February and June, when he finally sailed for Europe, Antheil wrote multiple letters to Moe updating him on the slowly evolving opera plot line and his early ideas for its music; he also reported on a charity concert he'd given from which he donated all the box office receipts to the local orthopedic hospital, perhaps in an effort to establish his own good citizenship. Letters from "Bill" Williams to Antheil show the two men working together to shape the storyline, with Antheil cheering the poet on: "Your pages have the very essence of music, and this period. You are a real poet, and you have the sweep and the swell and the essence."[98] He also frequently apologized to Williams for failing to progress on the music for their project. Before setting sail, Antheil had performed the premiere of his Sonatina for Violin and Cello or Pianoforte, which he had dedicated to Copland, and three other pieces at the first Festival of Contemporary Music at Yaddo. With the April 1932 Festival the first Guggenheim music composition appointee, Copland, provided the newest composition fellow, Antheil, with a showcase sendoff to Europe.[99]

Without access to the complete two-way correspondence between Moe and Antheil it is impossible to know whether Moe requested frequent detailed updates on his work, which would have been unusual, or whether Antheil simply provided them. Antheil sought Moe's and Surette's approval of the project, and Moe encouraged and advised him. Through January 1933 Antheil continued to supply lengthy descriptions of the state of the opera, the causes of its many delays, and his decision to pursue other pieces when he felt "more symphonic than operatic."[100] But the more Antheil protested his dedication to the opera and blamed Williams for its delays, the less likely it seemed the project would materialize, and it never did; neither did the other two works Antheil had proposed in his application.[101]

Moe's centrality to the operation of the foundation grew increasingly obvious throughout the 1930s. He became the go-to contact, a one-person switchboard for all communications from established fellows as well as those eager to benefit from the foundation's largesse. In March 1933, while Antheil was abroad, Williams wrote Moe to arrange his own meeting with the foundation secretary and to explain that Antheil had done nothing with his libretto. Williams hoped the project could be given to someone he had in mind and proposed that the other composer would require fellowship support, like that offered by the Guggenheim, to leave his current duties and devote time to the project.[102] Ever the professional, Moe agreed to meet with Williams, but not to discuss personal arrangements that had been made between the poet and Antheil. He welcomed learning the names of possible fellowship candidates, however. Unswayed by Williams's complaints about Antheil or by Antheil's increasingly obvious lack of productivity, the foundation stood by its man and in May 1933 renewed Antheil's request for an additional fellowship. It would be in effect from May 25, 1933, to May 25, 1934, this time with a stipend of $1,200.

In June, Antheil wrote a lengthy letter to Moe to express his "deepest and most heartfelt thanks." He led with news that his opera *Helen Retires*, which he'd written prior to his Guggenheim Fellowship to a libretto by John Erskine, was in rehearsal at the Juilliard School, where Erskine was president.[103] He hoped that the performance would redound to the glory of the foundation, although such would be the case only because it was written by a recent Guggenheim Fellow, not because it was written while the composer was supported by a fellowship. Among a list of ongoing projects, Antheil devoted a paragraph to his Washington opera, of which, he reported, he had finished one act. He returned to the opera and specifically to his fraught relationship with Williams in a postscript that took up half a single-spaced typed page. Antheil explained the slow progress and his preoccupation with a new ballet and a series of piano preludes; he characterized his situation with Williams as typical of composer-librettist relationships and recommended that Moe read the correspondence between Hugo von Hofmannsthal and Richard Strauss to understand what he was referring to. Much as Antheil struggled to keep in check the ego that had overwhelmed his earliest application, it always threatened to escape, as reflected in the breezy comparison of himself to Richard Strauss, the most famous contemporary German opera composer. Among Moe's many skills was his refusal to question or correct his "supremely gifted" creative artists despite their frequent inability to see themselves in historical context or deliver what they promised.

Although Antheil had not wanted to return to Europe, he accepted the conditions of the award: He had no choice given that Curtis Bok's support had stopped. On September 7, 1933, however, he wrote to Moe to inform him that he had been "home" (in the United States) for several weeks.[104] The pretext of returning early was to oversee the Juilliard performance of *Helen Retires*, which, he explained, was to be given in the first week of December, but now he realized he needed to stay stateside to raise additional funds, as the $1,200 stipend was insufficient to support the rest of his time in Europe. Given the incessant updates Antheil had sent to Moe in the spring, his September notification of his return to the country in mid-August smacks of either a misbehaving child hoping to sneak past his parents, a proud man embarrassed by his desperate financial straits, or both. Antheil's letter cautiously balanced informing Moe of his having ignored the fellowship's condition that he work abroad against the risk of possibly having his award revoked for having done so. He gambled that forgiveness was easier to secure than permission, and it appears he was right.

Nonetheless, Antheil requested $700 more to help him through the year, if not from the foundation, then from someone who had more assets than he. He understood Moe's position in relation to potential sources of support and took his case to the man at the center of the network. Amidst Antheil's list of what he had accomplished, which included a ballet set in New Orleans, a collection of short piano preludes that he was scheduled to perform at Yaddo at the end of the month, a sonata for violin and cello, work toward a grand fugue for orchestra, and a group of songs, he included a brief paragraph reporting that he'd given up on the George Washington opera project; he cited the incompatibility of Williams's libretto and his music and left it at that.[105] Given the opera's importance to Antheil's 1932 application and his regular references to its progress over a period of eighteen months, his casual mention of its demise is anticlimactic but not unexpected.

Letters exchanged between Antheil and Moe in late 1933 and through 1934 testify to the uncertainty of Antheil's living conditions. Having moved with his wife to his parents' New Jersey home, Antheil explained that the four of them survived on three to five dollars a week for food. Extreme as this sounds, it is likely that his situation was not worse than that of many Americans struggling in the depths of the Great Depression and may actually have been somewhat better given the guaranteed support he had from the Guggenheim Foundation with no strings attached.[106] Still, Antheil unabashedly sought more and reminded Moe of the small size of his stipend compared to awards previously made to Copland, Cowell, Sessions, and Thompson, who had received the standard $2,500. He failed to note, however, that all of them had been awarded fellowships prior to the stock market crash. He brought up Paul Nordoff, a student of Rubin Goldmark, who had received a $1,500 stipend with his 1933 award and challenged Moe to explain how he was worth any less than Nordoff. Antheil referred to the desperate moment he found himself in, his dependence on performances and tours that may or may not materialize, and the pressures his financial worries placed on his ability to do creative work. In a December 1933 letter thanking Antheil for his assessments of current applicants, Moe informed him of a $100 increase in his stipend, but he didn't spare the composer a clearly worded reminder of the explicit terms of his renewal award, which had assumed he would remain in France only as long as the amount of the stipend allowed. In a January 1934 letter Antheil thanked Moe for the additional $100, which was "really swell," but reminded Moe that he had hinted at the possibility of still more money coming. The most generous reading of Antheil's incessant, insistent requests for money acknowledges the desperate conditions the Depression foisted on people. A less generous reading questions the composer's sense of entitlement and his expectation, not unlike Sessions's, that others should support him. In reality, Antheil had been trained to expect nothing less from his years of patronage by Curtis Bok and the Guggenheim Foundation. Assumed privilege seemed to be an occupational hazard for certain fellowship winners. No letters in Antheil's papers indicate that Moe found any additional support. It was not until Antheil pursued film music and established contacts with Fox Films and Paramount Pictures starting in December 1933 that his perilous financial situation improved and eventually reversed. He became a successful Hollywood and television composer, although years later he would write to Moe saying that he didn't prefer the music business, remunerative as it was.

Antheil's application and fellowship experiences reinforce a number of realities that characterized the music composition award process in the earliest years of the Foundation's existence. Among the most important was Surette's preference for a personal way of doing things and his decisive influence over the awarding of fellowships. Proximity to downtown Manhattan was essential to meeting with Surette. Closeness to network insiders also improved one's chances of being awarded a fellowship, but it did not guarantee it. Staking one's claim as "American," as distinct from European, was as valued in the 1930s as it had been in the mid-1920s when Copland first announced his desire to foster an American music culture, this despite Surette's disparagement of American musical training and those charged with its execution. Antheil's appeal to the foundation with plans for an opera about George Washington when the first president was being commemorated throughout the country reflected the importance of the national agenda of the foundation, but it also pointed to Antheil's understanding that capitalizing on the cultural moment could be a winning strategy.

Perhaps the most instructive lesson contained within Antheil's experience with the Guggenheim Foundation involved his learning how to shape an application and persona to appeal to the advisor and the times. A darling of avant-garde Paris in the roaring 1920s, he became one of millions impacted by the quotidian realities of Depression-era America in the early 1930s; thanks to the foundation and Moe's work on his behalf, he fared better than many. By the mid-1930s Antheil was on his way to becoming a beneficiary of a burgeoning film and television industry that would explode in the 1940s and 1950s. The foundation could proudly claim him as one of its own, although his productivity while a Guggenheim Fellow was, like that of Sessions, wanting.

A MORE DISTANT CIRCLE

RUTH CRAWFORD, 1901–1953

Unlike Antheil, Ruth Crawford would never shape her work or her persona to satisfy Surette or to move easily within the circle of insiders; she could never become one of them. That Crawford was, at the time of her original application in 1929, an accomplished composer and a recognized participant in American (writ large) music culture was indisputable. Referees writing from California, Chicago, New York, and Paris made that point. That she was chosen to receive a fellowship at all in 1930—the only one that she would win and the only one that was awarded to a female composer in the first twenty-one years of the foundation's existence—reveals both the size of her talent and the near impossibility of her situation as an independent modernist whose qualifications eclipsed those of many of the previous male winners when they applied.[107] There was no precedent or playbook for gifted female composers in the late 1920s and early 1930s. It would take the death of Thomas Whitney Surette in 1941 to begin to lift the aesthetic and gender embargos that the entrenched advisor imposed on the foundation's music composition awards.

Crawford was born in East Liverpool, Ohio, to an itinerant Methodist minister father and a pianist mother with whom she took early lessons. Her midwestern roots, something she shared with Aydelotte and Moe, would be her only commonality with early foundation personnel. Crawford never cultivated the favor or friendship of the founders. She didn't attend Surette's summer school and couldn't have afforded to take the time off or pay the costs of doing so had she been inclined; she never attempted to form close alliances with the advisor or the growing group of those who did. She did not dedicate any pieces to him. Instead, between 1921 and 1928, Crawford earned multiple certificates and degrees, all with honors, from the American Conservatory in Chicago, where she studied piano, harmony, counterpoint, and composition. While there, she was awarded three consecutive Juilliard Musical Foundation Scholarships (1926, 1927, and 1928) for the study of composition and orchestration, and in 1928 she won the Adolf Weidig Gold Medal in Composition. Weidig was the German-born American composer at the American Conservatory who served as vice president and associate director of the school.

While in Chicago, Crawford became part of a small modernist musical scene nurtured by her teacher, mentor, and Scriabin disciple Djane Lavoie Herz. The city and its university had become a hub for progressive philosophical thought through the work of John Dewey, and Herz's home was the site of cultural exchanges among the most forward-thinking residents and visiting musicians and artists.[108] It was via Herz's tutelage that music replaced Methodism as Crawford's new theology, and she met Henry Cowell and Dane Rudhyar.[109] All three became advocates for the gifted composer.

With Rudhyar's advance work and encouragement, on July 1, 1929, Crawford wrote to Moe expressing her desire to apply for a Guggenheim Fellowship and to meet with Surette, as Moe had advised Rudhyar she should do. Because Surette was busy with his summer school and then would be in Europe on his regular yearly tour from August through late fall, Crawford suggested a winter meeting when both she and he would be in New York. With her advocates' encouragement Crawford moved to New York and took up residence at Blanche Walton's West Sixty-Eighth Street home, the Manhattan location of Walton's informal hostel-salon for composers, performers, and visiting artists. The address gave Crawford easy access to the city's music scene, which she believed was essential to broadening her exposure to currents in musical thought, and to working with Charles Seeger, whom Cowell advised she should seek out. Seeger was initially reluctant to teach composition to a woman, but with Cowell's encouragement and Walton footing the bill for lessons, he acquiesced on a trial basis. He was quickly won over by her obvious gifts and her potential usefulness to realizing his own projects.

Crawford sent an official application to Moe on November 14, 1929, and again expressed hope that she could meet with the music advisor. To date, I have found no evidence of a personal meeting between Crawford and Surette. In a January 22, 1931, letter to Moe, Crawford referred to a conversation with the foundation secretary that she had had the previous spring, but she did not mention the advisor. It is odd that she did not name him had he been there. Typically, Moe attended meetings with Surette and composer hopefuls since they used his office at the foundation, but it is possible Surette was not able to attend. Much as Crawford had wanted a meeting with Surette, it appears never to have happened.

Crawford's application listed her musical accomplishments including published pieces, performances, works written between 1925 and 1929, and a full page of copied press comments that captured laudatory excerpts from articles appearing in the *New York Herald Tribune*, the *Chicago Evening Post*, the *Los Angeles Times*, *Modern Music*, *Musical America*, and the *Musical Courier*. More than one spoke of the virile, masculine quality of her music as among its strengths. Given the broadly shared assumption that women could not compose in the serious, extended, and abstract forms, and the near phobic fear shared by many men that the nation's musical culture had become too feminized, in part thanks to the ubiquity and power of women's music clubs, this "young Chicago girl's violin sonata" was valuable and noteworthy because it sounded manly.[110] According to her application statement, Crawford's plans for study included work on a composition for full orchestra, a piece for string orchestra, a sonata for cello, and various smaller compositions. She acknowledged her desire to study orchestration in greater depth but concluded that her most pressing need was simply time to devote to composing. Moe responded on December 18, requesting copies of what she considered her best work, and Crawford obliged with her quintet for strings and a wind sextet among other pieces. Moe contacted the references Crawford had named and asked them to submit letters on her behalf, which they did.

In his letter of recommendation, Adolf Weidig spoke of her outstanding musical gifts and cited the Juilliard scholarships as evidence. His was one of fourteen letters of support written by composers, conductors, performers, academics, music critics, dancers, and poets from across the nation and abroad that included Marion Bauer, Adolf Bolm, Richard Buhlig, Henry Cowell, Rudolph Ganz, Louis Gruenberg, Djane Lavoie Herz, Arthur Honegger, Dane Rudhyar, Carl Sandburg, Frederick Stock, Edgard Varèse, and Carleton Washburne.

Recurring themes appeared in their letters: references to the rarity of Crawford's creative gifts among her contemporaries, the constant financial stresses she endured earning a living for herself and her mother Clara, whom she supported until Clara's death in 1928, and the opportunity a Guggenheim Fellowship would provide for Crawford to devote herself to compositional work relieved of inescapable quotidian responsibilities. Referees spoke of her intelligence, her flawless character, and her perseverance in the face of nearly insurmountable financial odds. They understood the unique value of a year to concentrate on creative musical work for this woman who had never experienced the luxury of time free from obligations to others. Unlike Sessions, she had no family money to support a year abroad, and unlike Antheil, she had no patron sending her regular checks, although Walton provided inexpensive lodging and paid for Crawford's lessons with Seeger. Crawford lived on what she earned. If Surette could criticize Antheil's original list of references for its scarcity of knowledgeable musicians, he would have to find other reasons to dismiss Ruth Crawford. Except for Carl Sandburg they were all practicing musicians, but with the publication of Sandburg's 1927 folk music collection *The American Songbag*, even he could qualify. It is possible that the appearance of the word "modern" multiple times in the referees' letters raised concerns for Surette and undermined Crawford's chances for a renewal a year later, but the same term hadn't impeded Sessions, who succeeded despite being typed an ultramodernist. It was Crawford's gender and her identification as a composer that presented the greatest challenge to all concerned. Even the publicly politic Moe couldn't contain his incredulity at the idea of a female composer when he queried Rudhyar, who had first suggested Crawford for a Guggenheim award, "Is there such an animal?"[111] In a climate where even her supporters commented on the *un*likelihood that a woman could be a serious composer, it was an easy excuse for those negatively inclined or dubious from the start to assume her efforts didn't deserve subsidizing, not as much as a man's, even one who hadn't proved himself or didn't deliver.

Despite the number and prestige of her fourteen referees, none of them had close connections to Boulanger or her atelier, and Surette sought assurance from a network insider whose aesthetic he embraced. To that end, on February 11, 1930, he had Moe contact Howard Hinners, a Harvard graduate, a former Boulanger student, a close associate of the pedagogue, and at the time a professor of organ and choral music at Wellesley College. Moe offered him an honorarium of $50 to comment on Crawford's music.[112] Hinners was active with the American Guild of Organists, whom Boulanger had addressed at their meeting on January 1, 1925, and had been present when she played Copland's Organ Symphony. He edited three lectures titled "Modern French Music" that she delivered at Rice Institute (later University) in February 1925 and so was fully versed in Boulanger's thinking and values. In response to Moe's inquiry Hinners reviewed what Crawford submitted and on February 28, 1930, typed two single-spaced pages of observations of her violin sonata, select piano preludes, the Suite for Five Wind Instruments and Piano, and the Suite No. 2 for Strings and Piano. Not intimidated by or dismissive of what he took to be affinities with Schoenbergian atonal vocabulary—neither had Boulanger been—he cited numerous details of harmonic, contrapuntal, and rhythmic behaviors and pronounced the applicant to be a gifted, original composer of intense music.[113] He applauded the "technical mastery," "extraordinary vigor," and "astonishingly mature . . . contrapuntal architecture" of the final movement of Suite No. 2. Hinners concluded that the suite alone merited a fellowship for the composer. With his unequivocal endorsement and nothing critical to use against her application, Surette approved it, and on March 7, 1930, Moe informed Crawford that she had been appointed to a fellowship for twelve months starting November 1, 1930, with a stipend of $2500.

Likely encouraged by her years of study with the Hamburg-born Weidig and more recent work with the German-trained Charles Seeger, Ruth Crawford elected to go first to Berlin rather than Paris.[114] As promised, she used the early months of her fellowship to immerse herself completely in composing and described herself in a letter to Moe as being something of a hermit. Unlike Guggenheim fellows who had gone to France and were immediately swept up in the ready-made fraternity of Boulanger students, their routines, and the larger cultural offerings with which Surette was familiar, Crawford focused on composing. In a brief report to Moe dated October 21, 1930, typed within weeks of her arrival in Berlin, Crawford commented on the conduciveness of the city to her work and noted that she had accomplished more than ever before in a similar period of time.[115] She planned to stay there until spring, when she would travel to Paris and elsewhere. Three months later, on January 22, 1931, Crawford provided Moe with a three-page, single-spaced typed report on what she had done. Trained by a life of frugality, Crawford knew how to stretch the foundation's gift of time *and* money, and so she began her letter with an assurance that she was using her stipend responsibly: She had recently located cheaper accommodations and was preparing to move.[116] The letter provides a detailed look into the first months of Crawford's Guggenheim experience.

Crawford explained that to date she had attended inspiring concerts in Berlin, where she got to hear live performances of works that she had only read or heard about previously, and had taken in the International Festival of Contemporary Music in Liege in September, but found it disappointing.[117] She reported on writing a set of choral pieces for Gerald Reynolds, who had commissioned them for his University Women's Glee Club of New York, finishing a suite for two cellos and a piano study (the Piano Study in Mixed Accents) and on composing additional materials in preparation for the orchestral work she had discussed with Moe the previous year.[118] Reynolds had studied with Boulanger and founded and conducted the Glee Club, whose members had sung in the vocal ensembles of their northeastern colleges when they were students and so had experience with traditional choral literature; he was especially supportive of contemporary composers.[119] His commission became Crawford's *Three Chants*, an a cappella SSA work written in a densely dissonant contrapuntal style that had no equal for decades, perhaps not until György Ligeti's *Lux Aeterna* for mixed choir (1966). Whereas Ligeti had set the Latin communion antiphon from the Roman Catholic Requiem Mass in such a slowly unfolding setting that the words were all but unintelligible, Crawford created her own text by inventing sung sounds that evoked what she imagined as some vaguely Eastern language suggestive of that used in the *Bhagavad Gita*.[120] Nothing about her chants was typical. The idea of a *polyphonic* chant disputed the notion of the ancient genre as axiomatically monophonic. The combination of a wholly invented text with an unheard-of approach to choral composition, one that used a harmonic structure based on dissonant counterpoint and unrelenting tone clusters, created an otherworldly sonic experience unlike any traditional religious or spiritual choral works yet composed. They were more reflective of, perhaps, the mystical sensibilities that Crawford had absorbed from Herz's theosophically inclined circle.[121]

If the title prepared listeners to expect something vaguely religious, the three chants, "To an Unkind God," "To an Angel," and "To a Kind God," tested notions of appropriate Christian music genres—hymns, anthems, cantatas, or oratorios.[122] No conventional theology was communicated in Crawford's chants. Neither Surette's summer school attendees, taught to appreciate Bach cantatas and Classical-period choral masterworks, nor the chorale-loving guests at the Drinkers' Sunday gatherings would have known what to do with such sounds. This was not music to read through easily. The crowded, one-to-a-part chords, which in the third chant required fourteen individual singers, demanded professional-level musicians and meticulous attention to pitch, tuning, and rhythm. Anyone expecting traditionally comforting, conventionally transporting sounds would be perplexed, disappointed, or perhaps outraged. On the other hand, *Three Chants* announced the breadth and creativity of the twenty-nine-year-old Crawford's musical imaginary and her ability to harness already mature composition skills to its expression. With their SSA setting the *Chants* also foregrounded women, a group that Crawford knew only too well were more often silenced than encouraged to speak in either churches or composers' circles. Crawford must have welcomed the commission and promise of performances from Reynolds. Although *Three Chants* is recognized today as among the most forward-looking early twentieth-century contributions to choral literature, ninety years ago the pieces no doubt stretched the understanding and ears of even those predisposed to its ultramodern language.

Crawford completed the rundown of her recent accomplishments for Moe: She had devoted December to copying parts and writing the last song of her set *Three Songs to Poems by Carl Sandburg* for contralto, oboe, piano, and percussion, which were needed by the New Music Society of San Francisco for an upcoming performance. She was just hitting her stride, she explained, but took the opportunity to formally ask Moe to accept her request for a renewal of her fellowship. If given another year, performances that were scheduled would become realities and she would use the letters of introduction he had provided to venture out and meet composers, critics, and theorists. Having accomplished what she had in the fall, she explained, she now felt justified in presenting herself as a composer to her peers in Europe, which she would do in the spring. Unlike Sessions or Antheil, Crawford never suffered a surfeit of self-confidence or entitlement. A combination of her Methodist upbringing, societal expectations of female modesty, and a temperament that was more reflective than performative kept her ego in check.

In the same January 1931 letter, Crawford shared ideas about pieces she wanted to compose in the hoped-for renewal year: a large work for mixed chorus, a string quartet, and small contrapuntal suites. The large choral work did not materialize, but the quartet would become her celebrated String Quartet (1931). The four-movement work showcased Crawford's rhythmic sophistication and intensity, her understanding of the expressive range of the string family, her appreciation of the timbral richness of both compressed and expansive spacings and octave doublings, and the inexhaustible possibilities of dissonant counterpoint and serialized techniques to shape and form the continuous eleven-minute piece. Spinning lines that passed between voices and compact, closely spaced tone clusters that vibrated through *Three Chants* now sizzled on the strings. At times the quartet seems to dance, and at others to inhale and exhale, to gasp and pant: an extension of the performers' breathing, perhaps. There is a living, human quality to it. Listeners hear Crawford at her most exposed. At other times, the music is more matter-of-fact and clinical in its discharge of the underlying schema. Crawford used serialized techniques and palindromic structures to organize pitches, rhythms, and dynamics at micro and macro levels and in ways that anticipated the practices "first" deployed decades later by the integral serialists. But her focus on the continuous line, a concern she shared with many of her contemporaries, distinguishes her music from that of later practitioners. Today Crawford's String Quartet (1931) is regarded by performers, scholars, and audiences alike as among the most innovative, moving, and valuable contributions to the quartet repertoire written in the first half of the twentieth century. It easily takes its place among quartets by Bartók, one of her heroes, and those of Shostakovich, Ives, Debussy, and Ravel.

Crawford closed her January letter with what sounds like an apology. She explained to Moe that her singular focus on composing meant she had little to report about performances of her pieces. Nonetheless, she proceeded to list works she expected to be programmed by the *Novembergruppe* in collaboration with the Pan-American Association of Composers, an event with the Internationale Gesellschaft für Neue Musik, two performances at the New School in New York, a concert by the League of Composers, another by the New Music Society, and a possible one by Howard Hanson at the Eastman School of Music. She mentioned the publication of one of her works in the *New Music Quarterly*, Cowell's journal of new music scores that was underwritten by Charles Ives, and alerted Moe that Charles Seeger would be writing to him about her work on his *Treatise on Modern Composition and Manual of Dissonant Counterpoint*, which had consumed the summer before she sailed for Berlin. Crawford invited Moe to ask any questions he might have about her work or to request scores of the pieces she completed while abroad if he wanted to look over the manuscripts. Having extended the invitation, Crawford awaited word from Moe for such a request. On February 4 he acknowledged receipt of her renewal request but asked for nothing. On February 7 Seeger wrote a letter to Moe explaining Crawford's summer work on the *Treatise on Modern Composition* and expressed his hope that her renewal request would be granted. On February 10 Moe acknowledged receipt of Seeger's letter with a one-sentence letter saying just that and nothing more.

Unlike other fellows, who saw their award years as opportunities to combine work with travel, networking—what Crawford referred to as "making 'connections'"—socializing, broadening their horizons in musical and extramusical ways, and soaking up continental culture, Crawford envisioned her year with a kind of singular focus: a unique chance to do creative musical work.[123] The foreignness of Berlin became an advantage: Given her rudimentary knowledge of German, opportunities for informal socializing were limited. No ready-made social circles distracted her. Today we can be grateful that Crawford cloistered herself as long as she did. Her 1930–1931 fellowship year was her only opportunity for such concentrated work and would be responsible for the majority of pieces for which she is remembered today.

Crawford's unsuccessful bid for a fellowship renewal defies a charitable reading of Surette's actions or the foundation's practice of deferring to his judgment. As if deciding that he had erred in approving Crawford's first fellowship in 1930, Surette took extraordinary measures and time to deny her a second one in 1931. Over a period of months, Crawford was involved in what appears to have been a gratuitous and ultimately futile one-way correspondence with Moe to demonstrate her worthiness. Although second-year renewals had become all but business-as-usual in the early years of the Foundation, with nothing additional required of the fellow but a letter asking for continuation, Crawford's request was treated differently. Since ten of twelve previous composition fellows had received renewals between 1925 and 1929, she had every reason to assume she, too, would receive one. But with Moe's brief February 4 letter acknowledging Crawford's renewal request, written communications from the foundation office seem to have ceased. There are no copies of correspondence from Moe in the file, and if he wrote, she never received anything to which she responded. Nothing appears in the Crawford files to suggest that he sent anything.

Assuming that she was still being considered for a renewal, on May 15, 1931, Crawford wrote Moe a lengthy letter bringing him up to date on all that she had done since her January report. Though fellows had been asked to submit reports annually, Crawford had provided them in October, January, and May. She would write two more in June. In the May report she spoke of concerts she had attended and music she'd heard, including Stravinsky's *Oedipus Rex* and works by Haba, Malipiero, Krenek, Kaminski, Zoellner, Herrman, Hindemith, Honegger, Egk, Monteverdi, Cavalieri, Beck, and Orff. She talked of a half-dozen composers she had met and with whom she'd discussed contemporary trends in European and U.S. music. But she saved her most enthusiastic comments for Bela Bartók, whom she believed was "the greatest Hungarian . . . and perhaps the greatest composer" of the day. After Bartók, Alban Berg impressed her most: "a towering personality both physically and musically."[124] Crawford enclosed a copy of the program of the April 8 *Novembergruppe* concert on which her Diaphonic Suite for viola and cello, which she had written that spring, was performed, and she referred to a representative of the Hamburg International Society for New Music who had contacted her regarding programming one of her works the next season. In a couple of handwritten lines that she scribbled on the side of the first typed page, Crawford noted that her cello and violin suite had been performed and she'd be forwarding the program when her bags arrived from Berlin. She assured Moe that her Berlin address would always forward her mail as it had done since she arrived on the continent.

Still Crawford heard nothing from Moe about renewals or anything else, and no copies of letters addressed to her appear in the Guggenheim's Ruth Crawford file or anywhere else.[125] Brief notes from Moe to Gerald Reynolds and to Quinto Maganini, a California-born composer, flutist, and conductor and another Boulanger student, written between May 23 and June 1, however, show the foundation secretary asking both men to share their opinions of Crawford's *Chants* based on Reynolds's March performance of the second chant, "To an Angel," with the Women's University Glee Club. Reynolds commented on the experimental nature of the work but conveyed the "very favorable" reactions from other musicians.[126] If a letter Charles Seeger wrote to Ruth Crawford on May 9 accurately captures Reynolds's handling of the piece, the conductor was extremely nervous when performing the work. According to Seeger, Reynolds had worked very hard at getting the pitches right, but the tempo and dynamics suffered. Balance was off, homophonic sections didn't come across, and too often what were supposed to be sevenths became octaves. To Seeger, the work sounded more like a solfeggio than a piece, which may explain Reynolds's characterization of the work as experimental: It was an experiment for him, if not for the composer.[127] Drawing on his memory of the concert, which had taken place two months earlier, Maganini pronounced Crawford's work "genuinely good," a piece with "real conviction behind it" far beyond "the outbursts of dissonance that many of the ultra-moderns are putting on paper."[128] In what would become an ironic remark, Maganini praised the foundation's original decision to award Crawford a fellowship and acknowledged it had been justified.

It was only in a telegram that Crawford received from Seeger on May 5, 1931, which she mentioned in a letter she wrote to Moe on June 2, that she had learned her renewal request had not yet been decided and that Moe had been expecting her to send him scores. Seeger explained that he would be giving him more of her compositions.[129] Moe and Surette wanted to review evidence of her accomplishments—scores of the works she had created while in Berlin and lists of performances that had occurred during her award year thus far (the fall of 1930 to the spring of 1931). While between European cities, Crawford scrambled to locate scores to send to Moe. She set about copying two parts of her *Songs to Poems by Carl Sandburg* and pointed Moe to scores for the *Chants* and Diaphonic Suites that he could secure from Seeger. Clearly concerned that Moe did not communicate personally with her and had never responded directly to her earlier offer to send him music, she assured him she would have been glad to provide him whatever he wanted, had she only known he wanted it. She enclosed a review of the *Novembergruppe* concert that appeared in the *Berliner Zeitung* and gently bragged that the review was as long as the Klemperer concert notice.

Two days later, on June 4, having still not heard anything from Moe about a renewal, she wrote to him again, this time after having met with Adolf Weiss, who was in Paris in connection with the Pan-American concert that was taking place (he would win a single Guggenheim composition award in 1932). Weiss, like Seeger, informed Crawford that Moe had talked with him about her request and wondered why she had not sent him her music. How Moe succeeded in communicating with so many others but not with Crawford about her own case is not easily explained. At the very least it casts doubt on the sincerity of the foundation's efforts to support her. Given the even-tempered and cordial tone of letters that Crawford had previously written to Moe, she sounded palpably distressed in her June 4 communiqué. But she was unwilling to let Moe off the hook. Despite relatively constant travel over the course of her fellowship, she had used the same address since arriving in Berlin and had successfully received mail all along, and she told him so. Crawford also referred to the February 4 letter Moe had written acknowledging receipt of her January renewal request, which she received at the Berlin address. She wouldn't countenance any suggestion that her itinerancy was the cause of the difficulties in communication. She also used the occasion to note the unusual nature of the request for materials given what she had learned of renewal practices from other fellows. None had been asked to provide scores or evidence of what they had produced halfway through their fellowship year.

Crawford beseeched Moe to give her additional time to copy the first movement of her string quartet, which Seeger had suggested was a good work to send, and promised that when her suitcase arrived, she would send additional movements. She assured Moe that Seeger, who was in New York, would get him scores for the choruses and Diaphonic Suites. Crawford explained that much of the responsibility for organizing the *Novembergruppe* concert had fallen on her shoulders, and it had consumed her energies; the fragments of time she had for work prevented her from concentrating on the larger orchestral piece. Crawford offered a "condensed calendar" of the last eight months' work, much of it reviewing what she had already written to Moe in January, May, and the earlier June letters. She looked forward to the summer months, when she could relocate to a quiet place away from the city, but most of all hoped that a decision regarding her renewal could be delayed six weeks to two months, during which time she could turn her attention to the orchestral work. She closed the June 4 letter to Moe asking to hear just a few words from him and reiterated her distress at the thought that she had not known he had been waiting for her to send him music.

There is no copy of a response from Moe to this letter or to the ones she had written in May or June, or to the brief handwritten note she sent him on June 13 and which was stamped received by the foundation on June 19. In it, Crawford reported that her suitcase with the music had arrived and she would be sending everything to him within the week. Unfortunately for Crawford, Moe and Surette had already sent scores of Suite No. 2 for four strings and piano, as well as four suites for various instruments, to Otto Luening for his review. Although not a student of Boulanger, Luening was a close associate of Moe's and Surette's and had attended the latter's summer school. He knew both men from his time in New York as a freelance composer just before being awarded his first fellowship in 1930, the same year Crawford won hers. Luening had stayed close to Moe and Surette throughout the 1930s while he sought and, through their intercession, secured a series of academic positions. Although Luening was qualified to assess

Crawford's scores by dint of his training with Ferruccio Busoni at the University of Zurich and a number of chamber works he had written to that time, he himself had requested a renewal of his fellowship and so was in the questionable position of judging the work of another composer applying for the same consideration he was seeking. He was, in effect, asked to judge his competition. The conflict did not seem to bother any of the principals, as Luening's renewal had likely been decided, if not officially acted on, as early as March.

Luening provided a two-page review of Crawford's materials characterized by abstract criticisms of the music and not a few ad hominem attacks regarding the shortcomings of the composer. He cited the lack of invention, an idea he repeated four times without elaboration, and the weak form. He called various movements of Suite No. 2 monotonous and depressing and described the composer as "undeveloped in almost every way." Luening decided the composer was "thin blooded," and the music was a bore, or dull, uninteresting, or banal. Altogether Luening determined that the composer possessed a "negative artistic personality." In a parenthetical question at the top of the first page, before he listed the works' failings, he asked: "Is it a woman?" Given his closeness to the inner circle, Luening almost certainly knew exactly whose work he was reviewing. The likely disingenuousness of the question aside, that Luening committed it to print betrays the acceptability of such a query and the thinking behind it. Why it should matter when one is evaluating music defies logic, except in a culture where women were assumed to be incapable of composing. In such a thought world, all the shortcomings Luening enumerated could be attributable to the composer's sex, and using a form of circular logic, confirm the belief that women could not compose. His assessment was received by the foundation office on June 20.[130]

Today Luening is best known for co-founding Composers Recordings, Inc., in 1954 with 1934 Guggenheim awardee and Boulanger student Douglas Moore, and for his work with two-time Guggenheim composition awardee Vladimir Ussachevsky (1956, 1960), including their founding of the Columbia-Princeton Electronic Music Center in 1958. These institutions and the students he taught at Columbia and Juilliard have earned Luening a place in U.S. music history. With the exception of his opera *Evangeline*, written during his Guggenheim fellowship years, and a handful of songs, most contemporary musicians know nothing of his musical output before the 1940s despite his writing approximately four hundred pieces, eighty of them songs. What most musicians associate with Luening are the small number of pieces for tape, synthesizers, and various electronic manipulative techniques that he wrote beginning in the 1950s. It is an unfortunate reality that few musicians can name a single work by Otto Luening written prior to his Columbia-Princeton years, and yet his assessment of Crawford's 1930 works determined her fate as a Guggenheim Fellow and her life as a composer ever after.

On July 8 Surette sent a brief typed letter to the treasurer of the foundation detailing his final decisions for the distribution of music composition and research monies for the following year: Of the $6,500 allotted him for renewals he awarded $2,500 to Luening for music composition and $2,500 to Roy Dickinson Welch (1885–1951) for research focused on writing a general study of music in relation to art and social history that never appeared.[131] He noted that Carl Bricken, a 1930 composition awardee, had withdrawn his request for a renewal. Rather than award the remaining money to Crawford, Surette chose to return the $1,500 to the foundation, claiming that he had decided her music did not meet the foundation's standards.[132] Later that same day the foundation sent a Western Union "Night Letter" to Crawford with an eight-word message: "Regret Your Request for Fellowship Renewal Not Granted."

Although Moe sent the telegram and most likely would have been a part of the discussions, the final decision was Surette's alone, as handwritten comments on Crawford's original application page make clear. As early as March 4, 1931, the Committee of Selection had *approved* Crawford's reappointment, simply leaving the stipend amount and period of time for the award up to Surette. On March 13 the Trustees so ordered. But four months later Surette did not approve. In hindsight, it is no surprise. The surprise was that Crawford received an award in 1930. It was likely impossible for Surette to imagine a woman in any role but that of teacher, or a woman as a composer representing U.S. music culture on the continent.

Crawford's gender, her unyielding modernist aesthetic, her choice to work on her own in Berlin and not in Paris, where she would have been within Boulanger's orbit and under her watchful eye, and Surette's choice of Luening as a reviewer doomed her chances: She would never be more than a one-year fellow. Regarding Crawford's modernist aesthetic, Carleton Washburne had identified it as a likely roadblock to her successful bid in his December 1929 letter of recommendation. Noting that Crawford was an excellent, creative, original, decidedly talented candidate for a fellowship, he nonetheless doubted her chances given the "strongly classical" bent of the advisory group and the improbability of Surette's approval. He allowed that he might be doing Surette an injustice, and her 1930 award almost suggests that he did. But all that transpired in the following year suggests that her modernist aesthetic was only part of the problem.

In the third decade of the twenty-first century, Crawford's treatment by Surette, Moe, and the foundation raises the specter of gender discrimination, not of the overt variety, which takes place less frequently, but of the more subtle and insidious kind, which occurs regularly: seemingly unintended exclusions, communications gone astray, inappropriate comments exchanged between insiders, and the unequal treatment of applicants in effect creating a hostile atmosphere where women are not welcome, supported, or encouraged. Crawford's experience reveals the vulnerability of any organization, however progressive and well-intentioned its founders are, to the people entrusted to execute its charge. As long as Surette was music advisor, the Guggenheim Foundation's commitment to supporting "women as well as men" would be realized only once in the music composition and music research categories. Although Moe went along with Surette, the number of women awarded fellowships in other categories argues against Moe's being primarily responsible for Crawford's treatment, although he appears not to have questioned Surette or taken the initiative to reach out to Crawford as he had to other fellows seeking renewals. The dearth of correspondence is damning. In other categories Moe administered advisors' choices; he did not presume to possess their expertise or have a significant voice in determining winners. Of the six composer fellows surveyed in this chapter, Ruth Crawford stood farthest outside the circle of music composition winners even after she secured an award *because* she was a woman, and women were not supposed to be composers.

There is no written evidence in the file to suggest that Crawford objected to or challenged the decision, as Antheil had when the amounts of his two awards were not what he expected, claimed he needed, or comparable to what others received. Instead, in a letter she wrote from Paris on September 4, Crawford asked Moe to return the string quartet she had forwarded to him in June and to send all other manuscripts to Seeger in care of the Harvard Club. We will never know what Crawford might have accomplished as a composer if her request for a renewal had been granted and she got another year abroad to cultivate her craft and develop relationships with peers, something that nurtures all artists. She acknowledged receiving Moe's telegram, which had been forwarded to her from Berlin, and expressed her appreciation to the foundation for the privilege of the fellowship year. Crawford would be right about the uniqueness of that year: In the two additional decades that she lived, she would never have more than a few scattered days to focus exclusively on cultivating her musical gifts. Crawford made no waves, remained pleasant, and went away quietly, just as women and others outside privileged inner circles were, and still are, expected to do. That reality makes the denial of her renewal request all the more stinging.

WILLIAM GRANT STILL, 1895–1978

William Grant Still's Guggenheim fellowship experience differed from Ruth Crawford's in almost every way, despite their sharing outsiders' status. Although Crawford's gender undermined her being taken seriously as a composer and an applicant, and her association with modernist aesthetics worked against her, his race placed Still even further beyond the experience or imagination of the innermost circle of white power players in interwar U.S. art music: His being "Negro" was cited frequently in correspondence in foundation files, likely because of Still's assumed exceptionalism. The foundation's leaders had no connections to the Black music community beyond what Still brought to them. There is no evidence that foundation personnel would have cultivated associations with Black composers without the incentive of the Foundation's mission statement. Though he was far from the only African American musician accomplished in the high-art genres, with the foundation's help Still became *the* marquee name and one of a very small handful of professional Black composers who would slowly be recognized by white culture for their achievements.[133] From the beginning, however, Howard Hanson's advocacy, Still's assiduous cultivation of foundation personnel, and Surette's and Moe's support played pivotal roles in securing Guggenheim awards for him in 1934, 1935, and 1938. Thanks to Moe's continued interventions and his presence on the Rosenwald Foundation's board, Still also won two Rosenwald Fellowships immediately following the last of the three Guggenheims (1939, 1940).

Although Hanson was not a Guggenheim insider—his location in Rochester precluded that, and his full-time faculty position meant he didn't need a fellowship—he was part of a large group of U.S. Americanists and a highly respected force in promoting the nation's music culture. His appointment, along with those of Leo Sowerby and Randall Thompson, as the first music fellows at the American Academy in Rome in 1921 had secured for him the credibility he needed to be appointed director of the Eastman School of Music at the conclusion of his three years' residency at the academy in 1924. He remained at Eastman for forty years. Access to a steady stream of hundreds of well-trained instrumental and vocal student-performers enabled him to mount large works. Hanson provided a champion for William Grant Still, and Eastman supplied a laboratory, a workshop, and a stage for many of his compositions. Hanson and Eastman premiered Still's *Afro-American Symphony* in 1931. Multiple daily trains running between Manhattan and Rochester made attending events at the school relatively convenient for the New York crowd, as Surette's presence at performances of Still's pieces testifies. Hanson never flagged as Still's advocate, and Moe and Surette sought out and listened to Hanson.

Like Crawford, Still had years of traditional academic musical training, although unlike Crawford he never earned any formal degrees. Still attended Wilberforce University, the nation's oldest private historically Black university, from 1911 to 1915 and took courses at Oberlin before and after World War I. He studied privately for a few months with George Whitefield Chadwick at the New England Conservatory in the summer of 1922, and then with Edgard Varèse in New York City from 1923 to 1925. Still also played and arranged for W. C. Handy, self-anointed Father of the Blues, and was regularly contracted by Paul Whiteman as an arranger. Still's musical expertise was far-reaching and his talents were well known, and he crossed comfortably between classical and popular idioms as he sought acceptance in the white concert hall. While experience within the popular music realm might have cast suspicion on white composer-applicants and hindered their chances of being taken seriously—read as a sign of slumming, perhaps—in the eyes of foundation administrators such fluency was likely interpreted as an "honest" reflection of Still's roots (and hence expected), and worked to his advantage. In their eyes Still's musical Blackness was authentic and not easily dismissed. Widespread assumptions that all Black musicians were knowledgeable about and associated with popular music styles to the exclusion of familiarity with high-art styles and genres were as pervasive as the common wisdom that no women were capable of composing in the large forms.[134]

Still, however, refused to be confined by others' assumptions—musical, personal, societal, or political—and ultimately his finely honed genre-crossing abilities made him attractive to foundation personnel. With a musical background that included learning spirituals from his maternal grandmother, the formerly enslaved Anne Fambro, singing traditional Protestant hymns at the Presbyterian church his family attended, enjoying the concerts of touring Black artists, and his life-altering exposure to the sounds of opera thanks to a collection of Red Seal recordings owned by his stepfather Charles B. Shepperson, Still could be acceptable to white establishment taste-makers even while remaining a doubly exotic other: exotic primarily because of his Blackness, but also because he was thoroughly trained and fluent in the language of white Western European art music practices.[135] He inhabited and negotiated multiple worlds.[136] His musical polylingualism could legitimize and authenticate his creative work across genres and styles. Although Still sought a Guggenheim Fellowship to carve out time away from his obligations to the commercial music industry, and the foundation wanted to support those efforts, it also wisely cultivated Still in order to realize its own goals. He could supply the music composition award category with the racial diversity the larger foundation claimed it valued in its mission statement, but which had yet to be demonstrated. All this boded well for Still's chances to secure a fellowship when he first applied in 1932.

Still met with Surette and then with Surette and Moe in May 1931, and again in January and February 1932, and he presented glowing letters from Howard Hanson, flutist and conductor George Barrère, and Frank Patterson, a *Music Courier* staff writer, with his application.[137] On February 26, 1932, however, just three weeks after meeting with Moe a final time, the latter wrote and informed Still that his application for a fellowship was not granted, although Moe encouraged him to apply again the following year.

The rejection might be explained, in part at least, by events that took place on February 5. At a personal meeting with the composer, Moe suggested that Still contact the Rosenwald Fund, the organization dedicated to expanding educational opportunities for African Americans. On February 15 Still wrote to Moe thanking him for contacting Mr. Arthur of the fund on his behalf. In that same letter, however, he expressed concern about the requirements of the award, which included spending additional time in school: At almost thirty-seven years of age, he did not want to take time away from composing. Whether Moe assumed that Still would take his advice, apply to the Rosenwald Fund, and win an award from it, thereby preserving Guggenheim Foundation funds for other applicants, is unknown.[138] Trying to save funds would be wise stewardship of the Guggenheims' money, although it would not fulfill the mission statement that boasted a commitment to supporting men and women without account of their race.[139]

A cryptic note by foundation staff at the bottom of Still's unfunded 1932 Guggenheim application offered the official explanation of why he was denied a fellowship: Surette had decided that the libretto for Still's proposed opera project was "ill-considered." Still had mentioned two unnamed potential operas in his application, the first set in Africa and the second in the southern United States. For the second work Still suggested he would use the "musical idiom of the American Negro." His dedication to nurturing and setting plots focused on Africans and African Americans—stories that venerated African cultures and religious heritages and tracked enslaved people's passage and diasporic experiences throughout the Americas—placed him in the center of pan-artistic Harlem Renaissance thinking and practice.[140] Surette's "ill-considered" seems a curious reason for rejecting Still's application, especially in light of the consistent interactions the composer had enjoyed so close to final decisions being made and Surette's knowledge of what the composer had in mind for his opera. But Surette wasn't required to explain his thinking more fully. It is hard to imagine Surette exercising such detailed oversight or presuming such authority over an operatic libretto, or micro-managing a proposal from Copland or Sessions. It was a given that fellows' proposals were merely starting points for their creative work. It is more likely that Still's plans for operas focused on African music, customs, and rituals and on Black Americans' experiences and religious practices were beyond what Surette could understand: He would be out of his depth or comfort zone. It was not so much that Still's libretto was poorly considered, but that Surette couldn't consider it. The Wagner-venerating lecturer who knew little about U.S. music culture at all was likely even less prepared to understand or evaluate operatic plot lines rooted in traditional cultures originating on the African continent. For 1933, Surette approved first-time music composition fellowships for Juan José Castro and Paul Nordoff and a partially funded renewal for George Antheil.

Following Moe's advice to reapply the next year, Still wrote on May 9, 1933, to express his intention to do just that and to assure Moe that the story Surette had found wanting the previous year was now stronger. He also mentioned meeting with Surette at Rochester a week earlier, when the music advisor had seen a performance of Still's ballet *La Guiablesse* at the Eastman Theatre and made some "encouraging remarks" about the work. On May 10, in Moe's absence, his secretary responded and assured Still that a new application was not necessary if he simply wanted to write a letter confirming his continuing interest in a fellowship. In this regard the foundation willingly treated Still's second application as a renewal of his unsuccessful first bid and required minimal materials. The relaxed requirement and informality of the process as applied to Still suggests that in his case, despite having been denied a fellowship the first time, an award was almost guaranteed the next year barring the discovery of something disqualifying. (George Antheil's experience in the late 1920s argued that such assumptions should not be made.) Still elected, however, to take no chances and to avoid appearing presumptuous. He submitted a whole new application and listed three new references in addition to Howard Hanson. Eager to secure an award, Still mailed his re-application form on June 9, 1933, a full five months before the November 1 deadline.

Still listed his accomplishments including published works and live and broadcast performances that had taken place between 1924 and 1933: In 1924 C. C. Birchard had published *Darker America* and in 1926 G. Schirmer had published two songs, "Winter's Approach" and "The Breath of a Rose." Howard Hanson had conducted nine of twenty-one live performances, and Barrère had conducted three; Goossens had conducted two. John Tasker Howard oversaw an NBC radio performance in 1933. Strengthening his case for his opera project, Still offered a statement explaining his familiarity with dramatic technique and "Negro" music and spoke of a special interest in instrumentation. His work as an arranger would have given him ample experience solving orchestration and balance problems. Still referred to his choral ballet *Sahdji* and the ballet *La Guiablesse*, both premiered by Hanson, and his twenty-two-year preparation for composing an opera, the genre he aspired to create beyond all others and the best suited to tell the story of African diasporic peoples. He summarized his plans for the twelve-month fellowship year: three months studying voodoo culture, ceremonies, and music as practiced in southern states, and the rest of the time writing the opera. His preferred location to take the award was California, which he found conducive to creativity and with which he was familiar given his commercial work. If going abroad was a requirement, he could expand his research to include the West Indies, a logical destination given the subject of his opera.[141] Still listed three new referees: composer John Alden Carpenter, *New York Times* music critic Olin Downes, and Boston publisher C. C. Birchard.

All three referees mentioned Still's race in their letters. Birchard judged him to be the most competent of the "Negro" composers but also one of the best equipped musicians among the entire younger group of American composers. Carpenter acknowledged a decade-long relationship with Still and his recent work in Chicago assisting in the production of *La Guiablesse*. He cited Still's rarity as a technically trained "Negro" composer who "retained his race pride" and refused to "go white." Carpenter's racialized assessment extended to praising Still, the man, for maintaining the warmth and freedom that were part of his heritage. His nostalgia-laced stereotypical assumptions about the temperamental characteristics of Still's heritage come close to evoking the "happy darky" prototype made famous in Stowe's *Uncle Tom's Cabin*.[142] His preference that Still pursue something other than a voodoo topic for his opera was likely shared by many who were made uncomfortable by what they didn't understand and so disparaged African, Afro-Caribbean, and African American syncretic religious practices by referring to them as "cults." Even so, he predicted that whatever Still did would bring honor to the foundation.[143] Carpenter was likely a sympathetic referee in part because he enjoyed another, if more distant, connection to the composer. He had been a member of the inaugural Fellowship Selection Committee of the American Academy in Rome that chose Howard Hanson for the first three-year residency in 1921. He remained on the committee through 1933. So it was Carpenter who had launched Hanson, and Hanson who would help launch Still with the financial assistance of the Guggenheim Foundation. There were concentric circles of winners within the larger institution.

Downes also spoke of his prior history with the composer; he had judged the orchestral composition competition at the Eastman School, whose award was publication of the winning work: Still's *Darker America*. Downes pronounced Still a "Negro composer of unquestionable talent." He had no doubts about Still's ability or promise, although like Carpenter, and Surette before him, he questioned the opera project Still proposed. Unlike Surette, however, Downes didn't allow it to prevent him from endorsing Still's candidacy; he believed the composer would deliver what he promised.[144] Not fully satisfied with three endorsements, Moe sought someone with dance or theatrical expertise to review Still's application. In late November, on the advice of Thomas Dabney Mabry, field secretary representative for Fisk University, Moe solicited a review from Lincoln Kirstein, a Harvard graduate and recent co-founder of the School of American Ballet. If Kirstein responded in writing, it is not among the papers in the foundation's William Grant Still file that were made available to me. Hanson's review, as before, praised Still's gifts.

Despite knowing the composer for more than a year, Moe wrote to Still on Monday, February 26, 1934, asking him to come see him again at his office the following Saturday. Still's proximity made it possible, and he agreed to the suggested day and time. Because Moe did not mention Surette's name in the invitation it is unlikely that the music advisor planned to be there, but Surette had already weighed in. A note at the bottom of Still's re-application shows that as early as February 15, Surette had "strongly recommended" in his favor and the standing committee had approved Still's appointment. When the nomination went to the board on March 16, once again Surette wanted it noted that he "strongly recommended" Still's appointment, and it was recorded as such. The trustees appointed Still on March 22 and the foundation received Still's acceptance four days later. What changed Surette's mind in the intervening year or why he was adamant about being on record two times in 1934 as strongly recommending Still isn't apparent in the existing files. Perhaps it was procedural, or he sought to appear involved and in charge. The advisor's preference to conduct business in person rather than via letter, except with his Concord Summer School "children," to whom he wrote frequently, means there are few archival documents written by Surette. Regardless of the thinking behind Surette's changed vote, Still clearly benefited from the unanimity of opinion and Surette's endorsement. As Crawford had learned two years earlier: As Surette went, so went the composition awards.

Correspondence between Still and Moe shows a composer eager to express his gratitude. When Moe funded a quick trip to Rochester for Still in early May 1934 that allowed him to hear a performance of his ballet *Sahdji* before the official start of his fellowship year, Still sent a handwritten thank you. When he arrived in Los Angeles later that same month, Still typed a single-page letter to Moe assuring him how much the fellowship opportunity meant and promised to compose something worthy. In July Still sent a progress report on his opera *Blue Steel*, which he had been working on with composer, writer, and librettist Harold Bruce Forsythe to a story by actor and screenwriter Carlton Moss.[145] He enclosed a copy of the chant "Whence come the drums" for Moe's opinion, not understanding that Moe possessed no musical training or expertise on which to base a judgment. That Still didn't know this may suggest that the close interactions composers witnessed between Moe and Surette were perceived as their sharing equal musical competencies. To his credit, Moe acknowledged his musical ignorance and forwarded the score to Hanson; he explained that were it not for Surette's illness he would have sent the music to the advisor.[146] Beyond any health issues Surette might have been experiencing, the advisor was preoccupied with his summer school, which was in session at the time, was finishing plans for his annual European sojourn, and was overseeing a variety of issues associated with music at Black Mountain College, which would consume increasing amounts of his attention over the next few years. Throughout 1934 and 1935, Still's letters regularly stated his commitment to writing music that was broadly appealing to Americans and "not cerebral music," a not-too-subtle declaration of his awareness of the unofficial anti-modernist aesthetic preferences of the advisor and hence the foundation. For Still, "cerebral" was code for left-leaning "politically minded" music that he associated with intellectual types who he would later equate with communists.[147] He subtly expressed a political ideology that he carried through his composing career and well beyond the music he composed while a foundation fellow.[148]

For the extremely busy Moe, who made it a habit to respond to all fellows' letters, Still's frequent notes and updates were both welcome and burdensome. After additional correspondence from Still detailing his progress, in November 1934 Moe thanked him, but then gently reminded the composer that he was not obligated to provide such reports; his only obligation was to his work.[149] The large quantity and friendly tone of the Moe-Still correspondence is in stark contrast to that between Moe and Crawford, which was minimal and purely businesslike on Moe's end. Though he never discouraged Crawford from writing detailed reports on her work, Moe appears never to have responded. Perhaps he assumed that his communications with Seeger found their way to Crawford, which would betray a paternalistic and disrespectful stance on his part toward the Guggenheim appointee. Perhaps Still's constant engagement with Moe, including his expressions of gratitude and emphasis on his appealingly American, not-cerebral, music were wise and strategic moves.

In late December Still wrote inquiring about a six-month "extension" of his fellowship to compose a ballet based on the Uncle Remus African American trickster stories. The idea had been suggested to him by the Black dancer Katherine Dunham, who had performed in the Chicago production of *La Guiablesse*.[150] Still reminded Moe that it would be an opportunity to write something wholly American in character.[151] Just months later, however, the project was dropped when Dunham apparently lost interest, but that wouldn't be known to Moe when he first considered Still's request. Still reported on the progress he had made on *Blue Steel* thanks to the foundation's generosity, promised a piano reduction of a good portion of the work soon, and took advantage of the opportunity to remind Moe that the opera, like the ballet, was based on an American topic. His constant references to the Americanness of his work speaks to his desire to be known as something more than a Negro composer, but it also suggests his embrace of an assimilationist politics that appealed to a particular stratum of Black Americans at the time. Along with the country's eventual move away from overtly nationalistic musical aesthetics, Still's strong pro-American (anti-Communist) political allegiances, which he articulated publicly and often, and his cooperation with Senator Joseph McCarthy's hearings before the House Un-American Activities Committee, would contribute to the decline of his popularity in his later years.[152]

Moe responded immediately, assuring Still that when it came to an extension, which Moe characterized as a "renewal," all he needed to do was write a letter requesting a renewal that was received by the foundation before February 1. He explained that Still should summarize what he had accomplished to date and state his plans for future work. Moe suggested that Still send examples of his scores and Dunham's libretto. It took Still two months to complete the piano score to *Blue Steel* that he had mentioned in the December letter, but in a lengthy typed update stamped as received by the foundation, once officially on February 11 and a second time on February 20, Still acknowledged that what remained to be done could easily be completed before the expiration of his current fellowship.[153] He admitted that he didn't need the extension to complete the previous fellowship project. There is no explanation why his materials arrived after the deadline, and there are no notes on existing application forms detailing how his request was received, processed, or approved by the advisory committee, the music advisor, or the Board of Trustees.

Still now pursued a fellowship extension to set a text by a certain "Mr. Trask," a typed summary of which he attached, titled *A Negro Etude*. Still reminded Moe that he had discussed the text the previous year with him and Surette and that "Mr. Surette preferred it" to *Blue Steel*.[154] Unwilling to leave Moe wondering about the wisdom of the foundation's investment in the *Blue Steel* project, which Still now seemed to be dropping, he characterized his work on that project as good experience for "achieving more satisfactory results" with *A Negro Etude*. The pages he attached to his application included an outline of the fifteen scenes from Trask's text with occasional editorial comments by Still.

He didn't disguise or object to the racialized characterizations and musical markers that Trask included in what Surette had encouraged him to set, which may reflect the complex and compromised position a Black composer and fellowship applicant inhabited in 1930s America. He described the opening of scene 1 as set in Africa with "Dancing natives in war bonnets" and the scene's close as accompanied by "furiously beating tom-toms."[155] A succession of tableaux in scene 2 includes "black Mammies" and "Brawny, bronze-colored Angels." Scene 5 is set on the levee, with stevedores singing work songs, and scene 6, though "devoted largely to dialogue," permits "the introduction of themes of the Jazz type (not commercial Jazz however)." Still told Moe that scene 8, with its "Symbols of America," must "be read to be appreciated," that scene 13 is a minstrel show, and that scene 14 takes place in "The Afro-American Church," where the music will include spirituals. The final scene is "The Octoroon Ball," which, Still observes, provides "an opportunity for a brilliant conclusion." Careful to avoid endorsing musical styles known to offend Surette, whether of the high modern and cerebral type or the too-low popular type, Still assured Moe that the jazz of scene 6 would avoid the commercial type.[156] Successfully pursuing funding from the Guggenheim Foundation for a high-art music project, while maintaining ties to the commercial music industry that paid most of his bills, illustrates how deftly and deliberately Still navigated the multiple musical worlds he inhabited.

As Moe had done in the case of Ruth Crawford, he turned to Otto Luening for an expert evaluation of Still's music, and on March 12, 1935, Luening obliged with a lengthy review, this time in a Western Union telegram sent from Bennington, Vermont, where Moe and Surette had secured a faculty position for him at the recently founded college there.[157] Working without an orchestral score, Luening commented on the libretto, which was "adequate": While it reminded him of Eugene O'Neill's 1920 play *Emperor Jones*, he found it occasionally "stilted." Although the melodies had a Broadway- or Hollywood-like character and suggested "a sort of Negroid Puccini," Luening allowed that it might be a popular success. He mentioned "certain banalities" without specifying them and foresaw possible problems with the balance between the orchestra and vocalists, although that was uncertain since he was working with what he acknowledged was a vocal score. Sticking to abstractions and generalities, much as he had with his assessment of Crawford's music, Luening commented on the proportions and pacing of the acts, which were not completely satisfactory, but in a final remark determined that the work was a "significant step in Negro music and opera." Luening's review was far from a rousing endorsement. Using many of the same descriptors for Crawford's works had meant that her music didn't meet the foundation's standards. That Still's work could be similarly problematic but nonetheless a positive step for "Negro music and opera" exposes the questionable expectations and flexible standards with which Luening operated. It is impossible to ignore the patronizing tone and racialized foundation of his conclusions. Luening's hubris is even more offensive given his limited experience with writing opera of any type. His single work in the genre, *Evangeline*—a sixty-five minute, three-act work—was the result of his 1930 and 1931 Guggenheim awards, excerpts of which were performed in 1932. (A reduced-score version of *Evangeline* was performed in 1948, but the work has never been performed as Luening wrote it.) The confidence with which the thirty-four-year-old passed faux-critical judgment on Still's opera-in-the-making would be remarkable were it not completely predictable.[158] Like Surette's, Luening's belief in the soundness and infallibility of his judgment grew as the foundation gave him chances to exercise it. Moe, operating from a position of ignorance of the field, accepted both men's opinions, as he was charged to do. They formed their own self-validating recursive circle of music composition award judges.

On March 20, 1935, Moe sent an official letter informing Still of a six-month reappointment with a stipend of $1,200. Still continued his pattern of writing regular reports and expressions of gratitude to Moe through the tenure of his second award. But starting in late summer, the focus of their correspondence shifted to both men's efforts to get *Blue Steel* performed. Having taken on the role of promoter, Moe informed Still that he had heard nothing from the Metropolitan Opera Company regarding the opera, and Still confided that Chicago Opera hadn't accepted it. In early October Moe wrote to Still that he was delighted to learn from Langston Hughes, a 1935 Guggenheim awardee in fiction writing, that he and Still had met. Moe didn't disguise his hopes for a match between these two marquee Black fellows.

Moe increasingly assumed agential duties for William Grant Still: He wrote to Arthur Rodzinski, conductor of the Cleveland Orchestra, suggesting that he consider *Blue Steel*, a work by a composer who, he might be interested to know, "is a Negro." Moe cited the enthusiastic reception Still's music enjoyed when conducted in Leipzig by Howard Hanson. When Rodzinski rejected *Blue Steel*, the conductor asked for information on the *Afro-American Symphony* based on Hanson's experience in Germany and turned to Moe to obtain a score; unfortunately, it was unpublished at the time. But that didn't keep Moe from suggesting that Rodzinski might be interested in Still's 1924 piece *Darker America*. When Franco Autori, a conductor of a Works Progress Administration relief orchestra, asked Moe about playing one of Still's works, Moe contacted the composer inquiring whether any recent pieces were available and then volunteered to get scores and parts to Autori. In October, Moe informed Still of the NBC Composition Contest, which Still assured him he would enter.

Correspondence between the two men continued in 1936 with Still confirming that he had not given up on *Blue Steel*, although he would eventually drop the project after additional rejections. Aborted projects were not uncommon. In March the composer updated Moe on works he had written, conducted, and published, and reported that he and Hughes were working on a project that he was certain would be more successful than *Blue Steel*; this opera, unnamed at the time, became *Troubled Island*.[159] Collaborative projects between fellows were always desirable; a project between two African American awardees from different disciplines would be a sure sign of the foundation's commitment to that part of its mission.

But Still's studio work kept him thoroughly occupied, and in May 1937 he wrote to Moe inquiring whether it was possible to apply for another Guggenheim award, which would allow him to complete the new opera. In June Moe responded that because Still had received only a year and a half of fellowship support and the foundation's practice was granting awards for up to two years, he believed it was entirely in order for the composer to request another six months.[160] Moe reiterated what he'd written to Still when the composer asked for his first extension, but his language was more succinct this time. Moe also acknowledged more direct responsibility for deciding renewals. He wrote that when it came to renewals, *he* wanted a statement of what Still had accomplished since his last application, and a second statement of the proposed project. The February 1 deadline held, and awards would be announced in March. There was no mention of Surette.

In December Still assured Moe that had there been any source of income to finance his creative work he wouldn't apply for "a further extension of [his] earlier Guggenheim Fellowship," but nothing had materialized. By characterizing his proposed project as an "extension" of work for which he had already received support, Still emphasized the idea of continuity and the prospect of completion, this despite the newest project being different from the one he had started in 1934. Still explained that commercial opportunities had dried up and he had been without work since October. In answer to Moe's request for a list of accomplishments, he reported what he had composed since his first award and proposed completing an opera titled *Troubled Island* based on a libretto by Langston Hughes.[161] Sticking with storylines that foregrounded diasporic Africans' experiences in the Americas, Still explained that the opera told the story of Emperor Dessalines of Haiti and that he had already composed part of the first act and finished the orchestral score through page 43.[162] Moe acknowledged receipt of the request on January 5, 1938, and assured Still of his pleasure in taking Still's request to Surette and the selection committee.[163] On March 21, Still learned of his reappointment for another six months at a stipend of $1,200. He responded with letters of gratitude and assurances of this new opera's superiority to *Blue Steel*.

But Still wasn't as close to insolvency as his December letter to Moe suggested. On July 29, 1938, an article titled "Work by Negro Chosen as Fair Theme Music" appeared in the *New York Herald Tribune*. On August 5 Still wrote to Moe explaining that *after* he had applied for the Guggenheim renewal, the "World's Fair people" had written asking him to compose music for the theme building "Democracity" but to keep the matter secret. Concerned that the foundation might feel he hadn't been completely honest about possible additional sources of income, Still assured Moe that he already had a sketch of the music "before [his] Fellowship began" and that he wouldn't be paid for some months. All that was left related to the World's Fair commission, Still clarified, was to score the work, which wouldn't require much time. Working again with the assumption that it was easier to ask for permission after the fact, he inquired whether Moe objected to this arrangement and assured him that he wouldn't want to act contrary to his or the foundation's wishes. Moe's response is not among the William Grant Still papers, but in light of the good publicity Still's World's Fair commission would bring the Guggenheim Foundation, and the fact that Still's music was heard at the months-long event, it is hard to imagine Moe disapproving. He might even have admired Still's financial planning and entrepreneurial spirit and appreciated the free advertising for the foundation.

In late October 1938 Still acknowledged receipt of the last of his Guggenheim checks and expressed gratitude to the secretary for the "fruitful creative period" the award had made possible. Letters from Still to Moe in 1939 and 1940 thanked him for securing a Rosenwald Award and then its renewal for the composer. Altogether, Moe and Surette had secured five awards for Still. In recognition of Moe's constant support Still asked if he could dedicate his large work for chorus and orchestra, "And They Lynched Him on a Tree," to him. The text by Katherine Garrison Chapin (poet and playwright, and wife of President Roosevelt's solicitor general, Francis Biddle) was, in Still's words "a simple statement of fact, without any trace of bitterness or any attempt to propagandize."[164] Still regularly avoided suggesting that he had suffered personally or was embittered because of racial prejudice. He appeared to downplay race and cast himself as beyond race, or perhaps that was his coping strategy when dealing with the white power structure of the foundation and the larger society. Moe accepted the dedication "with great appreciation."[165]

Long after Still's final award, Moe continued to work on behalf of the composer. When in August 1940 Howard University sought to hire Still as its dean of the College of Music, Moe responded to their request for a letter of recommendation with an endorsement of his personal character and musical abilities, the latter of which he based on the reports by "eminent" musicians. Knowing he wanted to focus on composition, however, Still did not accept the position. In April 1942 Moe wrote to Still commenting on having heard Stokowski conduct "his" piece ("And They Lynched Him on a Tree") and thanked the composer for calling his attention to the performance. Throughout the war years the two men stayed in contact, with Still sending yearly reports and Moe requesting the names of possible foundation fellows. In a letter dated October 3, 1944, Still recommended Ulysses Kay, "a young Negro composer now in the service," and Still's friend "Sargent Johnson, the Negro sculptor, who has done such outstanding work in San Francisco."

In a letter to Moe in 1939, Still had expressed his desire to "accomplish something toward the betterment of humanity and—especially—to show certain people of color how to think constructively."[166] Still did not provide a detailed explanation of what either goal would require or acknowledge the degree to which his sense of constructive thought might entail the acquiescence of "certain people of color" to unacknowledged white power structures. Readers are left to imagine that he believed his path provided a reasonable model. While it is unfair to impose twenty-first-century sensibilities on this iconic twentieth-century Black figure, it is impossible to ignore the ramifications of Still's thinking for the development of a vital Black arts culture, especially amid the Harlem Renaissance and its decades-long efforts to showcase Black accomplishments. Whether Still saw his recommendations of Kay and Johnson as part of a larger effort to better humanity or to promote people of color, the men he named attained successful careers within both white and Black cultural establishments. With Still's support, Kay studied with Hanson at Eastman and later with Luening at Columbia. Over his lifetime Kay won Fulbright, Rome, and Rosenwald awards and then a Guggenheim Fellowship in 1964. He was appointed Distinguished Professor of Music at Lehman College, a campus of the City University of New York, in 1968 and remained there until his retirement in 1988. Although Johnson never received a Guggenheim Fellowship, he achieved a level of national acclaim and recognition among the Harlem Renaissance creative network as a multimedia artist, ceramist, and sculptor who was influenced by modernist and Africanist techniques and themes.[167] His dedication to creating dignifying artistic images of African Americans in general and African American women in particular became Johnson's own contribution to promoting people of color. Johnson's 1938 drawing of Still titled *Lenox Avenue*, after Still's piece, is among the most often reproduced images of the composer.

Although Still's Guggenheim experience was unique, it also repeated a number of practices established by Aaron Copland a decade earlier. Still received multiple awards, including an immediate renewal; he took his fellowship in the United States with apparently no resistance or insistence that he go abroad; he was asked to recommend possible awardees; and he dedicated a composition to one of the men he credited with his successful applications. Both men maintained relationships with the foundation through Henry Allen Moe long after their award years were complete. The Guggenheim Foundation's circle of winners, which had begun coalescing in the late 1920s, grew slowly in the 1930s and continued to champion its most favored, chosen ones.

CARLOS CHÁVEZ, 1899–1978

Carlos Chávez was a thirty-nine-year-old internationally recognized Mexican composer and conductor when he received his first Guggenheim Fellowship in 1938, the same year William Grant Still won his third award. Chávez did not require the foundation's help to launch his career as had other awardees. It was not assistance of the start-up kind, although the fellowship helped solidify his reputation and especially his U.S. portfolio of accomplishments. Chávez had been to Europe in 1922 and 1923, spent time in Paris, met Paul Dukas, who encouraged him to value his own nation's musical culture, and made trips to the United States starting in December 1923, after which he returned to Mexico.[168] He stayed through March 1924 before locating to Manhattan for eighteen months, from September 1926 through June 1928. Chávez was fluent in English and comfortable in New York. Early in his U.S. sojourns he met Edgard Varèse. Their encounter led to performances of two of his works, a song cycle titled *Tres exágonos* (*Three Hexagons*) and his symphonic ballet *Caballos de vapor* (*H.P.*, or *Horsepower*), at concerts sponsored by Varèse's International Composers' Guild in February of 1925 and November of 1926 respectively.[169] Showing masterful diplomatic abilities, Chávez maintained his friendship with Varèse while developing a deep and abiding relationship with Copland, whom he also met during his extended stay in Manhattan.

In April 1928 Chávez was a featured composer on the first of the Copland-Sessions concerts, and in the same year, he, along with Varèse and Cowell, founded the Pan-American Association of Composers. In May 1928 Copland published a brief article in the *New Republic*, "Carlos Chávez—Mexican Composer," and later contributed the piece to Cowell's 1933 edited collection *American Composers on American Music*.[170] The same volume contained an article by Chávez ("The Music of Mexico") and contributions by the Cuban composers Alejandro García Caturla ("The Development of Cuban Music") and Amadeo Roldan ("The Artistic Position of the American Composer").[171] The PAAC focused heretofore unprecedented attention on Latin American and modernist music and caused no small amount of consternation among the more conservative set who reviewed its concerts. Boston-based music critic Philip Hale fretted over the impression left on the ears of European audiences by "the wild-eyed anarchists" whose music he feared would be considered representative of the nation.[172] New Yorker Paul Rosenfeld, on the other hand, turned his pen to championing Chávez and continued writing propaganda for the modernists' cause. As Carol Hess observed, Rosenfeld imagined Chávez as "the embodiment of 'rampant Pan-Americanism.'"[173] And that was a good thing. Copland believed that Chávez had succeeded in creating a music that overcame stultifying fealty to European influences.[174] By the early 1930s Copland had shifted his gaze away from Europe as well. The two men shared their newfound musical emancipation in a series of letters: "I am through with Europe Carlos" were strong words from Boulanger's most famous student.[175]

Chávez invited Copland to visit his home country. In response, Copland traveled to Mexico for the first time, arriving on September 2, 1932, and spent four months there. He returned multiple times in the 1930s and on behalf of the U.S. government in the 1940s.[176] Chávez toured the United States as a conductor starting in 1935, the trip coinciding with the composition of his second symphony, *Sinfonía India*. He conducted the work with the Columbia Broadcasting System Orchestra in January 1936 for a radio performance and then for its first live performance in April with the Boston Symphony Orchestra, one of the two orchestras that had launched Copland's career eleven years earlier. For better or worse, more than any other work, *Sinfonía India* unequivocally established Chávez's credibility and reputation as a composer in the United States. It quickly became his most famous piece and, with the help of a group of U.S. composers eager to anoint Chávez the franchise player within musical pan-Americanism (Copland principal among them), marked him as the archetypal Latin composer. That said, Copland and Cowell recognized that Chávez was more timeless and "ur-classical" than could be contained by nationality.[177]

Considering that the Guggenheim Foundation's Latin America and Caribbean Program was established in 1929 and Chávez was already a familiar figure in the United States before its creation, it is worth noting that he didn't apply for a fellowship until 1938. The first non-U.S. music composition fellow was the Argentine composer-conductor Juan José Castro. The 1933 award provided Castro with time to both finish a ballet titled *Mekhano* (*Machine*) and compose his second symphony, *Sinfonía Argentina*, in 1934. That Castro and Chávez both used *Sinfonía* in their titles may suggest that the men thought it prudent to clearly identify with their native cultures as part of an effort to draw attention to their Latin Americanness in the period of high Pan-Americanism, what Hess dubs its "golden age."[178] Their similar-but-different works could be heard as challenging notions of Latin America's musical-cultural sameness.[179] Although Chávez wrote his work before winning his award and Castro, who frequently employed neoclassical idioms, was, as Garcia Muñoz described the situation, leery of the "abuses of folklore" and its deployment in consciously nationalistic works, both composers understood that they benefited from associations with their Latin American roots at the time.[180] Both men would have been keenly aware of the United States's Good Neighbor policy, officially established as part of Franklin Delano Roosevelt's larger foreign policy in 1933. It became central to the Guggenheim Foundation's efforts to encourage Pan-American cultural exchanges. It is unknown, however, whether or how much Castro and Chávez or other Latin American Program fellows considered the Guggenheim family's mining business interests in Central and South America or the economic and environmental impacts they had on their native countries and cultures. Given the very public nature of the Guggenheims' global activities, it is hard to imagine that the composers were unaware of their benefactor's exploitative business practices.

While Castro focused his 1933 Guggenheim fellowship year on the composition of two works, Chávez was building a career in his home country. In December 1928 he began a five-year term as director of Mexico's National Conservatory of Music and of the Mexico Symphony Orchestra. His positions at the head of state-sponsored cultural institutions allowed him to design an infrastructure for Mexican music and art that embraced the range of his personal aesthetic values. He created a platform to support popular, indigenous, and new music. Chávez accomplished in Mexico what Copland and Harold Clurman had discussed doing for the United States, and Copland envied him his opportunities, achievements, and "clout."[181]

Sinfonía India assured that Chávez would be closely associated with indigenous musical sources, Mexican Indian music, and Latin American percussion instruments in particular, but it did more than that. Chávez, who was Mexican Indian himself, was equally committed to using those materials along with traditional high-art musical forms and exploring newer developments including electronic music, as his 1937 book *Toward a New Music* would make clear.[182] Varèse and Cowell were not the only composers "dreaming of new instruments obedient to their thought" or eager to explore "new musical resources"; the three men, with Charles Ives a constant presence in the background, encouraged each other's efforts to write new "American" music.[183] When, in 1938, Chávez won a five-month Guggenheim Fellowship for creative work in music, specifically to support composition of a piano concerto, the foundation chose a composer-conductor whose musical gifts, international reputation, and unquestioned productivity guaranteed it a reliable representative.[184] They also chose an applicant with no pressing financial need. Chávez completed a short score of the work by the end of the fellowship year and finished it in 1940. His single piano concerto was premiered in the United States by Dimitri Mitropoulos and the New York Philharmonic with Eugene List as soloist in January 1942. The Chilean pianist Claudio Arrau performed in the Mexican premiere in August 1943 with Chávez conducting the Orquesta Sinfónica de México. Chávez made good on his plan, and with acknowledged virtuosi introducing his work across the Americas, the foundation demonstrated the soundness of its choice. This was not inconsequential in 1938, when Dante Fiorillo was awarded the last of his four fellowships and the foundation was still trying to put the unpleasantness associated with his tenure behind it.

In selecting Chávez it also rewarded a man who had already done work for the foundation. In December 1930 Chávez had written on behalf of Cowell, his friend from the PAAC, who had applied for a music research award. Cowell became the third recipient of an award in that category in 1931.[185] Chávez's letter was one of nearly two dozen written to support Cowell's study in Berlin, the same year Ruth Crawford was denied a renewal of her music composition award, which she would have taken in that same city. In hindsight, it appears that the foundation could support only one known musical high-modernist at a time, despite Crawford's and Cowell's very different projects. Chávez's identity as a Latin American composer, his extremely close association with Copland, and his uniformly praised gifts as a conductor of a vast repertoire could overshadow his work as a musical modernist.

Chávez was a unique applicant in 1938. His administrative work and scholarly accomplishments had already qualified him to support Cowell's ethnomusicological research project. His compositions through the mid-1930s had informed, among other developments, Copland's turn away from predominantly European musical idioms and his synchronous move to a more populist and decidedly Latin-tinged style. The high-modernist Copland of the *Symphonic Ode* (1929), *Piano Variations* (1930), and *Short Symphony* (1931–1933), the last of which was dedicated to Chávez, took a back seat for the next few years to the composition of more accessible, "populist" works, at least until *Connotations* (1961–1962) and *Inscape* (1967).[186]

Chávez's acknowledged stature and secure position in international musical circles raised some questions, however: What purpose was served by directing the foundation's limited financial resources to an established figure? Who, beyond the composer himself, benefited from his being named a Guggenheim Fellow? Chávez appears to have won an award in 1938 based on his achievements rather than his need for monetary support, the latter of which had been one of the essential criteria for securing a foundation award. It was the reason cited most frequently by Moe when explaining why an applicant's request for a renewal was denied. In an ironic twist, Chávez would receive such an explanation from Moe when he inquired about the possibility of another award years later.

Documents in the Carlos Chávez folder at the foundation office affirm the specialness of his treatment in 1938. Although Chávez eventually received a second award, in 1956, the following discussion focuses primarily on his first award, earned within the chronological confines of this study, 1925–1940, with a few brief remarks about his attempts to secure additional support from the foundation before his second successful bid. The discussion of Carlos Chávez concludes with his successful request for a "renewal" within the context of a changed political landscape.

World War II, and tensions between the United States and its wartime ally the Soviet Union that consumed the 1940s and grew immediately after signing the Potsdam and Paris peace treaties, changed all aspects of the social, political, cultural, and aesthetic landscapes. Pan-Americanism faded from its central focus as the cold war came to the fore. The debilitating stroke that Surette suffered in December 1938 after a fall semester at Black Mountain College and his death in May 1941 ended the first period of the Guggenheim Foundation's music composition awards and coincided with the complete upheaval of the experimental college in North Carolina. Although Surette retained his advisor's title until his death, his active engagement with foundation's music award business had ceased earlier. A different study can unravel how the foundation slowly adopted a more professional than personal process for attracting qualified music composition applicants and choosing fellows. Chávez's experience reveals the Guggenheim's music composition fellowship competition in an extended moment of transition.

Unlike applications from the previous composers surveyed, many of which threatened to bury the foundation's offices in the volume of paper that accompanied them, Chávez's 1938 application was minimal: It included no references' names and hence no letters of solicitation or responses. Copies of newspaper articles reviewing his 1937 concerts in Pittsburgh, Columbus, and Cleveland, as well as a copy of the table of contents from the October 1936 issue of the *Musical Quarterly* listing Herbert Weinstock's eleven-page article "Carlos Chávez," stood in for typical referees' letters and lists of accomplishments. Together they attested to the seriousness with which Chávez was taken on the international stage. He hardly needed an introduction, and chances were he was not in the habit of providing one or justifying himself. Along with missing reference letters, there is no evidence that he was asked to submit musical scores for consideration or did so, and hence no mention of reviewers' having been asked to assess them. The whole process appears to have been pro forma in the extreme. Surette's name, with the honorific title "Dr.," appears once in the entire file: It was typed by a secretary at the bottom of the application's cover page with the brief note that Dr. Thomas Whitney Surette recommended that Chávez's application be granted. Whether that was after serious consideration of the request or something more cursory is unknown, but the latter is likely. Between January 20 and 21, 1938, while Surette was acting as guest faculty and then on leave at Black Mountain College, he exercised his Guggenheim Foundation music advisor's prerogative, devoid of adverbs or explanations this time, and provided his imprimatur to Chávez's application. Nothing like the typical assessment of application materials occurred. Surette's name on the cover page remains as one of the last vestiges of his personal way of doing business.

Given the exceptionally close professional relationship and friendship between Chávez and Copland, however, which resulted in each composer's dedicating multiple works to the other over a period of decades, and Copland's growing influence over the nation's New York–centered high-art music culture, it is not hard to imagine who encouraged Chávez to apply or championed his cause when he did. With Surette's presence diminished, Moe increasingly turned to the foundation's first music composition fellow for guidance. He was present, handy, and well connected, and unlike Surette, was a recognized and active practitioner of his craft. Although Copland's personal biases favored certain applicants, there was no question about his musician's credentials. Over the next few years, the foundation took increasing advantage of having trained, productive composers participating in the selection process although their tight relationships to each other and the Foundation limited a diversity of opinions or perspectives. With Copland and his cohort's regular assistance, the philanthropy professionalized its selection process for awards in music composition.

Moe wrote to Chávez on February 1, 1938, easily six weeks earlier than the late March date when applicants were typically notified, informing him that he'd been awarded a $2,000 stipend for a period of not less than five months to be taken sometime between the date of the letter and the following November. Chávez would dedicate the five months to the composition of a concerto for piano. There is no evidence suggesting that the location of his fellowship period, which had been an issue for Antheil and Still, was discussed. As a Mexican, Chávez could take his award in the United States and address Foundation preferences that composer fellows take their awards abroad, if that were an issue with this prestigious applicant: it seems not to have been.

All this being the case, it was Chávez's financial situation that caused Moe to revisit the decision, but only after he had informed the composer of his award. In March 1938 Moe learned that Chávez had signed a contract to conduct the NBC Orchestra at a series of concerts. In a letter dated March 17 Moe asked Chávez to clarify the "persistent rumors" of "exceedingly high compensation" for conducting and an assurance from him that the foundation would not be diverting monies from deserving "youngsters." Moe explained that he was willing to continue his endorsement of Chávez if the composer used the fellowship to free himself from other "money-making activities" to write the work he had promised; Moe had to think about policies, precedents, and appearances. In addition to the honor Moe understood Chávez could bring to the foundation, the secretary was also painfully aware that a well-heeled celebrity fellowship recipient might present an opportunity for embarrassment of the foundation; with the Fiorillo episode still hovering, Moe needed to avoid any whiff of questionable judgment when announcing award recipients. At a private, in-person meeting that Moe arranged with the composer, Chávez assured him (as had William Grant Still regarding the World's Fair commission) that he would do as he said and devote the needed time to the concerto's composition. Moe, once again, supported the applicant.

Delivering on his promise, Chávez wrote his single piano concerto, a continuous thirty-five-minute, three-movement work of unrelenting energy, emotional range, and contrapuntal complexity. The concerto is theatrical in every way, from the Allegro agitato that explodes out of the introductory Largo to the breathless final Allegro movement that likely left early audiences feeling euphoric if gut-punched. For listeners unfamiliar with Mexican musical markers, it might have been difficult to untangle Chávez's specifically native threads from the dense, dissonant, modernist web of sound that characterizes all but the Molto lento middle movement. Occasionally, prominent pentatonic and modal melodic fragments recall folk roots. The presence of a large variety of percussion instruments, the predominance of brass and woodwinds, and unexpected doublings (piano and bassoon in the second movement) also evoke traditions beyond those tapped in the works of other famous concerti composers of the era—Rachmaninoff, Bartók, Ravel, Prokofiev, and Shostakovich to name just some of his near contemporaries who wrote oft-played works in the genre.[187] Harp and celesta lend an other-worldly quality to the sound and suggest a brush with Debussy, perhaps. But when the piece concludes with an unapologetic *fortissimo* F-sharp major chord in the piano and lower orchestral instruments that is simultaneously and unequivocally challenged by a sustained A-natural in the upper orchestral instruments, it is hard not to believe that this is where the music was heading all along: a shimmering, shaking, sonic avalanche that consumes all in its wake and refuses to confine itself to anyone's idea of how it should behave. This is neither purely native nor modernist music. It is, on the other hand, clearly the work of a consummate composer and mature musical mind. On his five-month Guggenheim Fellowship Chávez composed an extraordinary work; it could be argued that the concerto more than justified the special treatment his application received.[188]

From the beginning of the 1938 application process there was a different tone in Moe's letters to Chávez than was present in his letters to the other applicants discussed in this chapter. He was obviously aware of Chávez's stature when he spoke of hoping that he "may" have "the pleasure of seeing [him]." A version of the solicitousness audible in William Grant Still's letters to Moe is here, but now it's moving in the opposite direction. Rather than summoning this applicant to a meeting, as was his practice, Moe wrote that he would be "obliged" if Chávez could find the time "at [Chávez's] convenience" to meet.[189] Seventeen months later, in August 1940, when Moe wrote Chávez following up on an initial request for his annual activity report, which the composer hadn't sent, Moe politely asked permission to "reinforce [the] plea" and signed the letter "with highest regards." These are small matters, to be sure, but combined they suggest a different relationship between the typically self-assured foundation administrator and Sessions, Antheil, Crawford, and Still, for instance, and the one that emerges in the tone of his letters to Chávez.

In other official situations, Moe communicated in more typical ways with Chávez, as when he asked him to advise the foundation on prospective fellows, each of whom had named the composer as a potential referee. What is significant about Moe's January 19, 1940, letter in the context of others discussed in this chapter and Moe's efforts to secure expert reviewers for applicants is the secretary's request that Chávez advise the foundation on behalf of a Mexican film director and two Mexican painters, as well as a composer. Moe explained that the single musician named in his request, the Mexican composer Silvestre Revueltas, had not referred Moe to Chávez, but Moe took the initiative to ask his judgment nonetheless. The two composers had had a falling out, so there was good reason that Revueltas had not named Chávez; it is possible that Moe didn't know of the situation.[190] Moe and the petitioners seemed to assume that Chávez's Mexican birth made him expert in all aspects of Mexican culture; his position as head of a national school of arts may have reinforced that idea. Although it speaks to Chávez's stature in his native land, it is hard to imagine a similar situation occurring in the United States, where a famous composer or conductor would be asked to formally assess the work of a film director or visual artist for something as consequential as a major financial award if he or she were not involved in the project being proposed. In another situation, as was standard practice with other composer fellows who provided lists of yearly accomplishments in their personal reports, Moe sought confirmation of performances that Chávez claimed took place by writing directly to orchestra directors; he explained that the foundation sought to list such events in its composite annual report on fellows' achievements.

Despite instances of routine communications, through the early 1940s Moe treated Chávez with a kind of formal respect unusual among the composers discussed in the present study, and this is the case even when the Moe delivered unwelcome news. Although there is nothing in the foundation's Chávez papers regarding a formal request in 1941 for another fellowship, on June 4 of that year, far outside the typical application and decision window, Moe informed Chávez that he had taken the idea of another grant for Chávez to the committee the day before.[191] Moe's wording suggests an inquiry of an informal nature, which would have been in keeping with Chávez's original application. With monies already allocated, Moe explained the foundation's need to preserve funding for "young men" who aspired to "attain the eminence that now is yours." That, he clarified, was its primary duty.[192] Moe's continued gendered assumptions that it would be "young men" who were awarded composition fellowships speaks to the difficulty of dislodging long-held thought habits, both his own and the larger society's. His acknowledgment of Chávez's eminence just three years after approving the composer's initial award, when he was arguably similarly eminent, once again raises the question of why Chávez was granted a fellowship in the first place, one that clearly diverted Foundation funds to an established figure.

The outbreak of World War II, the changing status of the United States on the international stage, and the consolidation of competing Western Pan-Americanist ideologies, complex and dynamic as they always were, provide an additional backdrop for Chávez's experiences with the Guggenheim Foundation. In September 1939 Hitler had invaded Poland; seven months later Germany invaded Norway and began its occupation of Denmark. In May 1940 Hitler marched into Paris, and in June 1941 his forces invaded Russia, all in an effort to expand German cultural dominance on the continent. When Germany's ally Japan bombed Pearl Harbor six months later, all the world's attention was turned away from Latin America and toward Europe and the East and how the United States would reply. Over the next five years, everything, including perhaps Chávez's stature, changed in the eyes of the Guggenheim Foundation.

All composition fellows, starting with Copland, were impacted by the economic, political, and cultural conditions that defined the years of their awards. But from the beginning Chávez's appointment appears to have been especially affected by global political factors. More than a few scholars have devoted themselves to troubling simplistic notions of what constituted Pan-Americanism and when and how these morphing ideas served and were served by composers and their music.[193] The Guggenheim family's private business interests in Central and South America combined seamlessly with U.S. economic policies designed to favor aspects of trade with other countries and efforts to expand the notion of "American" by employing cultural diplomacy to that end. These factors complicate Chávez's fellowship experiences in ways that distinguish him from other music fellows and are beyond the scope of this study to tease out or treat fully. A few words about his postwar interactions with the foundation will suffice to close out this chapter.

Chávez received a second fellowship in 1956, but only after overcoming serious difficulties securing a visa to travel to the United States. At the root of the controversy was the Mexican government's official toleration of Communism while it maintained close relations with the United States. Five articles in Chávez's Guggenheim files clipped from the *New York Times* and published between March 1952 and August 1954 confirm how closely the foundation monitored the activities of its former fellow. At a time when reckless accusations by U.S. politicians bent on flushing out suspected Communist operatives threatened and destroyed the lives of individuals and institutions alike, the Guggenheim Foundation recognized that it was not immune from investigations of its practices, and that included its choices of awardees.

The headline of the first article, dated March 10, 1952, announced, "Rivera Mural Too Red, Says Mexico."[194] As director of the government-sponsored Museum of Fine Arts, Carlos Chávez was squarely in the middle of a dispute involving the outspokenly Communist-sympathizing muralist Diego Rivera. Because Rivera had created the sets for Chávez's symphonic ballet *H.P.* in 1932, there was no denying that the men had worked together. The article, however, which mentions Chávez's name multiple times, explained why the Mexican government, which had commissioned the mural and had already advanced 10,000 of the promised 40,000 pesos, had decided against sending Rivera's 33' × 15' triptych "The Nightmare of War and Dream of Peace" to Paris for the exhibition of Mexican art scheduled to take place there.[195] Without denouncing Communism or Rivera's work outright, Chávez was quoted as saying, "It contains grave political charges against various foreign nations with which our Government maintains friendly relations."[196] Rather than state his personal position regarding Communism or name the United States outright as a friendly nation, Chávez responded to Rivera's accusations of censorship as a government official.[197] He chided the painter: "You better than anyone know that the Mexican Government does not profess or impose an anachronistic creed of static purism."[198] For any U.S. politician eager to find reasons to suspect Chávez of Communist sympathies, the composer's explanation that "the Mexican Government is bound by 'international courtesy and traditional respect for foreign countries and foreign governments'" instead of a clear condemnation of Rivera's politically charged work would be sufficient. Chávez's apparently even-handed assessment of the situation and assurance that "the Government would feel and act the same way about a painting that praised other countries and insulted the Soviet Union"[199] was likely the equivalent of a guilty plea for those seeking evidence of his questionable loyalties. Additional articles published in the *Times* in March 1952 and filed in Chávez's folder kept the composer's associations with Rivera and the barred mural in New Yorkers' consciousness.

An article that appeared in the *Times* on June 16, 1954, two years after Chávez had left his official governmental posts, reported that Chávez's visa had been cancelled and the conductor's entry into the United States forbidden until a security clearance study could take place. Two months later, on August 17, 1954, the *Times* reported that his visa had been approved. What back-room negotiations caused the reversal are unknown. According to the unnamed reporter of the article, just an hour before press time a State Department spokesperson had cited immigration laws that made Chávez *in*eligible for a temporary visa. But something changed, and ultimately "the conductor was permitted to enter the United States . . . out of consideration for United States' relations with Mexico, especially in view of Señor Chávez's firm denial that he is now or has ever been a Communist."[200]

Given the many affiliations and affinities shared by Copland and Chávez, it is not surprising that Copland experienced similar challenges to his patriotism and, more specifically, difficulties securing a passport to travel abroad around the same time as Chávez.[201] And this was within a decade of his having been engaged by the U.S. State Department to lecture on American music culture in Latin America (1941, 1947) and in Italy (1951). During the 1940s Copland had traveled through nine Latin American countries on government-sponsored goodwill tours. While his sense of what constituted appropriate representations of Latin America in music had surely expanded beyond his touristic *El salón México* of 1936, (what Virgil Thomson had characterized as his "borderland fling")[202] or even *Danzon Cubano* of 1942, Copland's much-applauded work cultivating good neighbors was now suspect, in part because of his activities in the 1930s.[203]

Copland, like many musicians at the time, had had close interactions with creative people across the arts who subscribed to progressive social and political beliefs. Among them were committed Communists, socialists, fellow travelers, and sympathizers. His most obvious work on their behalf was a song he wrote for a competition sponsored by the Composers Collective for publication in the leftist weekly *New Masses* to celebrate May Day 1934. The title, "Into the Streets May First," with words adapted from Alfred Hayes's poem of the same name, charged "comrades" to "shake the midtown towers / crash the downtown air." If Copland's use of Hayes's summons to shake and crash "the roaring square" wasn't revolutionary enough to argue that he had composed a protest song designed to accompany a Communist workers' rebellion, the song's references to "shops and factories," "the sickle and hammer," and the piece's being "a tool" removed any doubt.[204] The composer had a network of associates and an award-winning song to explain to anyone who questioned his loyalty to American democratic principles. Whereas Chávez had inherited the ambiguous reality of his nation's accommodating stance toward Communism, Copland, like the Mexican government Chávez described, was not burdened by political "purism." Both men's situations speak to the multiple intricate networks of relationships that exist between individuals, artworks, nations, cultural organizations, and political conditions that should provide the context in which later generations understand actions and events. They also expose the unexpected ways that powerful educational and philanthropic institutions with economic and political interests of their own can become entangled in webs beyond the obvious and intended ones. That the Guggenheim Foundation was aware of the tenuousness of the political situation is evident in materials found in its Chávez files, especially those pertaining to his activities in the 1940s and 1950s.

Ultimately Chávez was permitted back into the United States to conduct concerts in Los Angeles with the Hollywood Bowl Orchestra on August 24, 1954, and in Portland, Oregon, with the Portland Symphony Orchestra in October 1954, but only after "Señor Chávez' firm denial that he is now or has ever been a Communist."[205] The decision appears to have cleared the air of possible political controversies associated with the composer-conductor, enough, at least, for Chávez to ask Moe about another Guggenheim Fellowship. In a letter dated April 14, 1955, he began the process by explaining his long-held desire to write a cantata on a Whitman poem, "perhaps the Song to The Open Road"; he eventually proposed writing a cantata for chorus, soloists, and orchestra to a text in English without naming a poet or work. Ever the businessman, Chávez explained how much money he "expected" ($3,000) was needed to be able to devote six months to the project if he stayed in Mexico. The amount would "increase considerably" if he had to take his award in the United States. Moe responded on May 9, addressing his letter "Dear Don Carlos," with regrets that Chávez's request was too late to be acted on in the current cycle, but to please consider applying next year. On

June 28 Chávez requested consideration for the next year, and on July 6, James F. Mathias, newly appointed associate secretary of the Foundation, responded explaining, as Moe had done many times before, that no forms were needed for applications coming from previous fellows. The eighteen years between Chávez's 1938 and 1956 awards would be considered a continuation of assistance, what Moe would refer to in his own correspondence with the composer as a "renewal."

The foundation received Chávez's formal application on August 2. This time he listed A. Copland and V. Thomson as references. Others referees asked to weigh in included Otto Luening, Douglas Moore, Quincy Porter, Robert Ward, and William Bergsma, all five men active composers and former Guggenheim music composition fellows.[206] A handwritten note added to the application by administrative staff explained that although Chávez was a Mexican citizen, he requested permission to take his award in his home country as he had done previously, or, as the applicant would clarify later, in another place with favorable exchange rates.[207] Chávez attached a two-page typed list of compositions he had written and published since his previous award. Moe wrote to Chávez in August 1955 acknowledging receipt of his materials and promising action by the Committee of Selection in the following spring, including a decision on whether he could take the award, were it to be granted, somewhere other than the United States. When Moe reported the Foundation's favorable decision on April 12, 1956, he notified Chávez that he'd been awarded a $4,000 grant to be taken over a twelve-month period starting from any date in 1956. Mathias responded to Chávez's acceptance letter, extending all good wishes from Moe and adding, "It is good to have you aboard again."[208] Postwar prosperity impacted the foundation, and 1956 proved to be a good year for music composition fellows: Chávez, Theodore Ward Chanler, Bohuslav Martinu, and Julia Amanda Perry all received renewals in that year, and there were ten first-time awardees: Chilean composer Carlos Boto Vallarino, Carlisle Floyd, Edmund Thomas Haines, Earl Kim, Ezra Laderman, Jan Meyerowitz, George A. Rochberg, Seymour J. Shifrin, Vladimir Alexis Ussachevsky, and Rickard Kenelm Winslow.

In his biography of Copland, Howard Pollack devotes a paragraph to summarizing the composer's relationship with Chávez.

> Copland's friendship with the Mexican composer Carlos Chávez, which lasted more than fifty years, was extraordinary: more enduring than with Sessions or Harris, more intimate than with Thomson or Piston, more coequal than with Blitzstein, Diamond, or any number of young composer friends. Chávez, for his part, had no better friend than Copland, at least among composers. That they became the most venerated composers of their respective countries made the association all the more remarkable. In an essay on the subject, Robert Parker emphasized its

> wide-ranging aspects, pointing out that although both men were "first and foremost composers" they were also "pianists, conductors, teachers, entrepreneurs, writers, lecturers, administrators, and statesmen for the arts."[209]

Beyond the insightfulness of Pollack's observation, it is worth noting that every composer he named was a Guggenheim Fellow, and all but Chávez had studied with Boulanger. The case of Carlos Chávez reveals the degree to which the John Simon Guggenheim Memorial Foundation reached across cultural and political borders to share its wealth and extend its influence. But it also speaks to the importance of personal associations and the close, some would say closed, circles they can form. Starting with the insular Guggenheim family business and then enlarging that circle to include Rhodes Scholarship winners whose ideas and oversight shaped the foundation, in 1925 the circle expanded to include the early winners of music composition fellowships, almost all of whom were connected to a handful of people and institutions—Copland, Boulanger, and the Conservatoire Américain chief among them. Motivated by a tragic personal loss, Simon and Olga Guggenheim used it and their business interests and ambitions to create a philanthropic institution whose fellowships are still widely sought and prized. Since 1925, the foundation has awarded more than four hundred million dollars to eighteen thousand fellows, and each of their lives was changed as a result.[210]

CONCLUDING THOUGHTS

It is axiomatic that large scholarly projects morph. The longer the gestation process, the more possibilities for growth and change. The slow evolution of *Circle of Winners* has provided an expansive moment to consider what is most important to say about the early years of the Guggenheim Foundation's music composition awards and to reflect on their impact on the nation's music culture. It has also convinced me of the value of institutional studies. Original goals for this book transformed as unexpected discoveries and irresistible forces shifted my attention and priorities. In addition, the opening decades of the twenty-first century presented extraordinary opportunities for enlarging my own self-awareness, and that experience has left its imprint.

Prior to the new millennium I wasn't actively thinking about the pervasive whiteness of my scholarly perspective, although I was aware of the absence of others' voices and the overwhelming maleness of the music I had been taught, the histories I had read, and the ideas that had dominated my thought world. As a female I knew I inhabited a different space than what I studied, but I hadn't gone far beyond acknowledging that situation in relation to my own experience to interrogate its specific impact or consequences for others. Witnessing Ruth Crawford's treatment as a woman-who-composed in a culture that had little experience with such "an animal" deepened my sense of the inextricable links between institutions and the societies that spawn them. I understand with new clarity that the prejudices of those in power prevail unless they are challenged and changed.

The John Simon Guggenheim Memorial Foundation emerged at a propitious moment and established a new type of systematic institutional patron of the arts. But its first fifteen years would bring growing pains. Despite the uniquely encompassing idealistic vision of Simon and Olga Guggenheim and its implementation in many fellowship categories starting in 1925, when it came to music composition fellowships, the man tasked with their oversight lacked the expertise, experience, or imagination needed to embrace their potential. Thomas Whitney Surette's limitations affected the assessment of many composers' applications; with regard to Crawford, Surette cost her a fellowship renewal. He also initially impeded William Grant Still, whose African and African American opera subjects tested Surette's capacity to conceive of plots that went beyond European locales or narratives, but Still fared better because he had a well-placed champion whom Surette respected: Howard Hanson. In both cases, the assumed exceptionalism of Crawford and Still based on gender and race denied them and those like them the naturalness and legitimacy of their work. They were treated as outside the white, male norm and judged against different standards. But both women and African Americans compose, and sometimes women who are African American compose, as Julia Amanda Perry proved when she won Guggenheim Fellowships in 1954 and 1956. It would take many decades before women and African Americans won composition fellowships with some regularity.

Surette's values played out in less obvious ways, but they were equally impactful. His insistence on a personal way of doing things that typically included Saturday morning meetings at the foundation's New York offices—sometimes scheduled with only a couple of days' notice—potentially restricted the geographic diversity, educational experiences, cultural influences, and musical practices of awardees. It was not unheard-of for hopeful composers to move to New York to better their chances of winning an award. The city that had been, along with Boston, one of two centers of high-art music in the nineteenth century consolidated its influence in the early twentieth century in no small part because of the Guggenheim Foundation and its nearby network partners. Surette's disparagement of popular music idioms also meant that composers felt they needed to avoid them or rationalize references to jazz or vernacular styles and downplay their commercial qualities.[1] This while Paris was devouring them. For an advisor responsible for supporting young U.S. composers, his disdain for jazz or anything that smacked of independent or experimental thought meant that applicants had to remake themselves and hew closely to his conservative, heavily Europeanized aesthetic or fail in their fellowship bids. Copland successfully worked around Surette largely by avoiding him, but that was only after he was safely inside the Guggenheim winners' circle.

Applicants dismissed Surette's aesthetic preferences at their peril. Apart from Crawford, another case in point is Harry Partch, who applied unsuccessfully for fellowships in 1933 and 1934, likely without fully appreciating the futility of his efforts at the time. In a rare show of independence from the music advisor's judgment, Moe pursued support for Partch from another Guggenheim network associate he had cultivated, the Carnegie Corporation. In June 1934 the Institute of International Education, which administered the Carnegie grant, informed Partch of his $1,500 award.[2] It is impossible to know whether Moe's actions were part of his own strategy to preserve foundation funds for Douglas Moore and Still, whether Surette had been consulted, or whether Moe supported Partch simply because he believed in his application and Surette didn't. That Partch hadn't been approved the previous year, when multiple awards were made, suggests that Surette was not involved. Two years after Surette's passing, Partch's 1943 Guggenheim application was enthusiastically encouraged by Moe and endorsed by Virgil Thomson, Otto Luening, and Douglas Moore. Although Copland, who had taken over the advisor's role vacated by Surette, was not especially enamored with Partch or his work, his own catholic tastes and wide-ranging accomplishments allowed him to support the innovative California-born contemporary for a fellowship, which he won.[3]

In the foundation's early years, Surette's association with Nadia Boulanger and his use of her musical atelier to supply winning applicants resulted in a steady migration of young composers to and from Fontainebleau, all eager to learn their craft from the French pedagogue or at least to claim they had worked with her. The preponderance of Boulanger-trained fellowship winners between 1925 and 1940 speaks to Surette's friendship with her but also perhaps to his ignorance or dislike of other composition teachers. A French connection was a good thing, especially in the decade between the wars, when Germany had lost its favored status as the training ground for would-be composers, but more especially when France was Surette's favored destination for his yearly trips abroad. Well into the twenty-first century, composers, conductors, and theorists list their studies with Boulanger as a sign of their pedigree. Among the continuing effects of the Guggenheim Foundation on U.S. music culture is the prestige and power accorded an American musician's association with Mademoiselle, however brief or informal. Since Boulanger's death in 1979, however, that has begun to change.

As Surette juggled responsibilities to the Guggenheim, his Concord Summer School, and eventually Black Mountain College, the foundation's Latin American Program geared up. Latin America assumed increased importance in response to the Guggenheim family's continually expanding mining interests in that part of the world, Roosevelt's Good Neighbor policy, which was made official in 1933, and—as regards the music composition awards—in relation to Aaron Copland's shifting his attention southward, encouraged by Carlos Chávez. Copland's associations with the region were formalized when the U.S. State Department sent him there on tours in the 1940s. No evidence exists in any of Surette's lectures, texts, or song collections that he was familiar with or valued Latin American,

Indigenous, or Spanish music cultures.[4] On the contrary, he expressed his disdain for Helen McGraw's all-French and -Spanish piano recital at Black Mountain College. Surette's brief statement recommending Chávez's 1938 application was, however, a sign that he would not be left out of the fellowship loop. Surette remained music advisor to the foundation until he died.

From the distance of a century it is hard to fathom the power that was vested in Thomas Whitney Surette to pick one composer instead of another, to actively advance and invest in one person's career prospects and withhold support from and impede another's: to *make* a winner. Despite Frank Aydelotte's expertly crafted and comprehensive start-up plan for the foundation, the pressure to quickly name an advisor for an award category of special importance to the Guggenheims, along with the absence of established philanthropic models to provide guidance regarding arts fellowships, Aydelotte's and Moe's ignorance of music, and Moe's youthful eagerness to embrace what he believed was an older man's wisdom and experience meant that Surette's availability earned him the position.[5] Aydelotte overrode his own initial hesitancy to accept Surette as a member of the advisory board and listened to Moe. It's likely that few expected the sixty-two-year-old advisor to remain in the position as long as he did.

The dearth of fellowship opportunities in the arts in the early decades of the twentieth century meant that the John Simon Guggenheim Memorial Foundation had a unique opportunity to support young composers, and it did. It identified a need and filled it, much as Meyer Guggenheim had done when he first came to the United States. Beyond supplying a need, however, thanks to Henry Allen Moe's cultivation of a network of associates, the foundation enlarged its sphere of influence. By engaging its network partners, it was able to access additional resources and expand its reach beyond what it could have delivered on its own. It also increased the impact of winning a Guggenheim Fellowship, because an award from the foundation often led to awards from other organizations in its network. It upped the stakes. Although awards attracted awards, it was more than the imprimatur of a Guggenheim that predisposed network members to look kindly on an applicant; it was Moe's active intercession on behalf of select fellows that secured additional support for them. Roger Sessions benefited from Moe's efforts, as did Otto Luening, William Grant Still, and Dante Fiorillo. Sometimes the support was in the form of additional fellowships, and at other times it was in the form of academic positions that secured a fellow's career and well-being for life.

Without underestimating the value of Copland's associations with Walter Damrosch and Serge Koussevitzky or the cachet he enjoyed as a result of their conducting the debuts of his Organ Symphony, as the first composition fellow Copland did not so much benefit from an existing Guggenheim Foundation network as help establish it. In addition, his connections with Boulanger, with Yaddo, and with multiple early winners (through Boulanger, Rubin Goldmark, the League of Composers, the Copland-Sessions concerts, Tanglewood, and the MacDowell Colony) made him as much an agent of the Guggenheim's munificence as a beneficiary. That said, it was the John Simon Guggenheim Memorial Foundation that gave him his initial platform. Its quick elevation of him from applicant to fellow to reviewer increased his power. If over the years Copland's closest friends profited from their association with him, so, too, did the foundation. He was its most visible and compelling composition fellow in the early years and became its marquee name. His fame redounded to them. He worked tirelessly to build the nation's art music culture, just as he told Harold Clurman he planned to do. If few knew Surette, everyone knew Copland. It would be hard to argue with Copland's credibility or impact even if a number of individuals outside the inner circle resented his connections and power. Copland brought the music composition fellowship selection process closer to that practiced in other foundation award categories: He professionalized the composition award by dint of being a celebrated composer himself. His good works were theirs. It is unfortunate that Senator Guggenheim didn't live to see this change take place. He died in November 1941, just six months after Surette.

If at the start of this project I hadn't appreciated the foundation's support of artists and composers as unique at the time—or the breadth of Boulanger's and Copland's roles in identifying and promoting Guggenheim composition fellows, or the impact of its parochial music advisor—I also hadn't thought deeply about the sources of our largest philanthropies' wealth or the costs of the business practices that fed those fortunes. Today almost 4 billion of the planet's 7.9 billion people live in a dozen resource-rich countries. We know that the benefits derived from those resources seldom find their way to the workers whose physical labor extracts, transports, and refines them and brings them to production. We also know that in the United States since the nineteenth century, the titans of the railroads and extractive industries have been the greatest patrons of the arts and educational initiatives.

The connection between the arts, education, philanthropy, and natural resource exploitation in the United States seems to be as inevitable as it is irrefutable. Early on, this natural bounty was what distinguished the nation from Europe. It was used as evidence of our collective virtue and superiority. But plenitude invited profiteering. The Guggenheims, for instance, started mining and smelting operations in Colorado, Nevada, and Utah, and spread to the Yukon and the Pacific Northwest to create the Alaska Syndicate. When resources and operating costs became irresistible in Mexico, the family looked beyond national borders and soon controlled what Harvey O'Connor observed was "the biggest economic factor in Mexico—the price of silver." It was "officials of Asarco [the Guggenheims' American Smelting and Refining Company] who represented the Mexican government in international silver conferences."[6] Guggenheim moved into Chile when that nation's wealth in copper and nitrates was discovered. Promises of cooperation and mutual benefit between the family business and the government never materialized, although the Guggenheims prospered.[7] Similar stories played out in Cuba and the Congo (today the Democratic Republic of Congo).

In 1937, as the nation crawled out of the Depression and the Dust Bowl, and Hitler laid plans to advance across Europe, O'Connor published *The Guggenheims: The Making of an American Dynasty.* The book traces the systematic creation of a business empire by Meyer Guggenheim's Swiss-Jewish immigrant family. In that regard it is a supersized American success story. But O'Connor didn't gloss over the politics, practices, or human costs of that achievement. The portrait was often brutal in its matter-of-fact honesty, but it was also generous in its recognition of the good done by the family. O'Connor lauded the Guggenheim family's philanthropic work, but he reserved special approbation for the Senator and the foundation named for his son:

> Simon was pre-eminent among his brothers for the munificence of his philanthropy—the John Simon Guggenheim Memorial Foundation for fellowships. By 1937 it was estimated that he had given away nearly half his fortune. In his own lifetime hundreds of creative practitioners of the arts and sciences were to remember him kindly for help given them—without strings. If he walked plainly and simply in his way of life, at least it could not be said that he had been unhonored. The University of Colorado conferred on him the degree of Doctor of Laws while remembering his gifts of some $230,000.00 to the state's colleges; and the press and learned leaders never ceased to praise his intelligently devised scholarships.[8]

It is impossible to deny the good done by the Guggenheim Foundation and the opportunities it has provided for composers, specifically, in the United States, Canada, Latin America, and the Caribbean. But that doesn't address or eliminate questions about how that good was funded. How does knowledge of the sources of the Guggenheims' wealth affect prospective fellowship applicants whose consciences are troubled by ever-threatening environmental crises, many of which are the direct result of the exploitation of natural resources? Is there a statute of limitations on the shadow cast by extractive industries and their questionably sought gains regardless of the contemporary, humane uses to which those gains are put? How does a potential recipient proceed knowing that present actions don't erase past practices and a personal protest won't make a difference if another applicant accepts a fellowship that he or she declines? These are no small issues for scholars, composers, artists, or musicians who need financial support to do their work but cannot easily override their principles.

Institutional studies force a confrontation with the realities of relationships and their impacts, both immediate and long-range. They expose the intimate and the extravagant interactions that bind organizations to each other and, perhaps unexpectedly, to agents outside their obvious purview. They allow deep explorations of specific players and broader understandings of the interdependencies that develop as individual interests overlap and goals combine. Stepping back from the John Simon Guggenheim Memorial Foundation to see its place inside a network of institutions reveals connections that might have remained hidden had the focus remained exclusively on the foundation. Knowing that Black Mountain College's early life was significantly different from that made famous by the brief residencies of John Cage and company, or that the initial plans for the college were proposed by Frank Aydelotte's brother-in-law, that his sister was among its incorporators, and that the college's first mailing address was Moe's foundation office, invites scholars to reimagine the breadth of the foundation's associations, formal and informal. The time-consuming involvements of Moe, Surette, and the secretarial staff of the foundation in mundane aspects of the college's operations and the cleanup efforts required to address the crisis created by one Guggenheim Fellow who resided there point directly to the ways in which studies of institutional networks can expose activities hidden from view and forgotten by history. That Moe, the Oberlaender Trust, and Black Mountain College joined forces to assist scholars and artists displaced by world events points to the inextricable connectedness of their interests with the times.

The foundation was born into and operated within a specific social and cultural moment: all pervasive antisemitism, accepted racialized attitudes and rhetoric, and gendered assumptions about who could and should do what, informed those tasked with realizing Olga and Simon Guggenheim's mission. The effects of one war just ended and another on the horizon, along with a booming economy followed by an unprecedented depression, can be tracked in the foundation's ability to support awardees, the locations where fellows spent their time, and the projects they pursued. Although this book focuses on the complexities of the early years of the foundation's music composition awards specifically, it also talks about the nation and the world in which those fellowships emerged.

One hundred years after its founding, a different nation and time frame the foundation's work. In the spring of 2022, viewers of the New Music Box website can see an announcement: "12 Composers Among Recipients of 2021 Guggenheim Fellowships."[9] The statement mentions the three thousand applicants across all categories and the "rigorous peer-review process" that winnowed them down to 184 winners. It also boasts that "close to 60 Fellows have no full-time college or university affiliation," a condition that described all six of the composers discussed in this study when they won their awards. Times change. Full-time faculty positions in music composition became more typical later in the twentieth century and characterized fellows' profiles accordingly. Today the number of such positions has diminished as funding of the arts, including faculty lines, has contracted in a STEM-seized, corporatized academy. The foundation's support of nonacademic artists and musicians is especially important in this environment. Beyond reflecting broad, nationwide employment realities, however, the list of 2021 composer awardees reflects several significant internal changes, the most encouraging of which are those that speak to assumptions regarding *who* can compose, and *what* qualifies as fellowship-worthy "creative work in music."

Notable in the 2021 list are seven women: Zosha Di Castri, Sky Macklay, Miya Masaoka, Nkeiru Okoye, Helen Sung, Katherine Young, and Nina C. Young. It had taken almost fifty years (1925 to 1972) to award seven women fellowships in music composition. The number of female awardees in this category in 2021 likely reflects the greater number of women pursuing advanced music composition training in general, the number of women applying, and changes in foundation sensibilities. That these women engage in a range of sound art practices, from electro-acoustic to more traditional vocal and orchestral composition techniques, suggests an enlarged notion of what meets "Foundation standards," the phrase Surette used when informing Crawford that her request for a renewal had been denied.

There are eight people of color, including fellows born in Pakistan, Iran, Brazil, and Cuba and Asian Americans born in Washington, DC, New York, Houston, and Berkeley. Three of the twelve awardees are listed with international addresses: Ashkan Behzadi (Canada), Sky Macklay (France), and Ming Tsao (Germany), although Macklay and Tsao have U.S. roots. Another fellow, Igor Santos, is a native of Brazil, but he currently lives in Illinois. Nkeiru Okoye is an American-born composer who draws on her African American and Nigerian roots to write operas taken from American history, especially works about racial issues. Her 2014 opera *Harriet Tubman: When I Crossed That Line to Freedom* centers the work of one heroic Black female. She wrote her 2017 work, *Invitation to a Die-In*, in memory of Trayvon Martin. William Grant Still would welcome Okoye's attention to both the heroic and the horrific experiences of African Americans in her music, although her critical stance might make him uncomfortable.

Given Surette's aversion to jazz or contemporary music styles, it is also significant that four of the twelve winners are jazz musicians: Rez Abbasi, Helen Sung, Elio Villafranca, and Katherine Young. That two of the jazz composers are women points to the foundation's recognizing the presence of women in all strata of the nation's music culture. They were always there, but not necessarily acknowledged or encouraged. Another change concerns the average age of composer fellows; of those listed for whom birth dates are available, the average age is forty-six. This differs significantly from the foundation's original assumption that fellows would be between the ages of twenty-five and thirty-five. A final change has to do with renewals. Whereas two years of support was the norm for composition fellows in the early years, recipients now enjoy a single year of support. This simultaneously spreads the wealth and avoids potential abuses of privilege. Correcting for inflation, the average award stipend has remained the same: The sum of $2,500 in 1925 is equivalent to approximately $40,000 in 2022. All these changes are welcome and reflect the more enlightened attitudes and more equitable educational and mentorship opportunities afforded women and people of color, as well as a more eclectic understanding of what constitutes U.S. music culture.

What haven't changed, however, are the regional and institutional biases that characterized composer fellows in the earliest years, when Surette's personal approach to identifying worthy applicants held sway. It is hard to dismiss charges of a New York bias when seven of the composers listed in the 2021 announcement live in New York and an eighth, Donnacha Dennehy, an Irish-born contemporary classical music composer, teaches at Princeton University in New Jersey, an hour's drive away from the foundation's offices. Beyond what appears to be a tightly drawn geographic circle, a long-established institutional bias also continues: Columbia University remains a favored academic affiliate, with four of the fellows named having studied there. It's little wonder that there's great skepticism among those outside the Northeast that music composition fellowships are equally accessible to everyone. It is, of course, impossible to know the pool from which the winners are selected because unsuccessful candidates' names are not publicized, and there is a small chance that very few composers from outside the New York metropolitan area applied. If that is the case, however, it suggests a different kind of problem. Do potential applicants disqualify themselves because of their suspicions that the world of Guggenheim Fellows is a closed circle of winners?

The John Simon Guggenheim Memorial Foundation invites and rewards serious study of its practices, associations, interests, and impacts. It also suggests the value of research into institutional practices across the arts. This study has focused on one aspect of the foundation's cultural work, and within that, on a single fellowship award category—music composition—as it was conceived in the foundation's first fifteen years of operation. I make no claim to having written the whole story of this institution or its effects on music culture; it is too sprawling a project and too many materials remain off-limits, or unknown, or "disappeared."[10] What I can offer is an extended effort to understand the ways one high-culture philanthropic institution came into being, envisioned and enacted its mission, nurtured, supported, and empowered a group of select awardees, and shaped the nation's music culture in the years 1925–1940, a time of intense social, political, and economic change. That said, I'm confident in the hard-won belief that the greater story of U.S. music culture lies beyond the confines of the

Guggenheim Foundation and its music composition fellows. Large and impactful as the foundation's legacy is, it is just one part of a much fuller, more diverse, and more complex history. It is one rooted in a rich variety of networks of people and organizations operating in different geographic, economic, and aesthetic spheres across the nation, many of them hidden in the shadows and only coming into the light. In their own ways each is dedicated to diffusing knowledge, encouraging understanding, and cultivating the appreciation of beauty, however that is defined. We benefit from and live with the largesse of all of them.

Notes

Introduction

1. See "Charter: March 26, 1925," in *The John Simon Guggenheim Memorial Foundation, 1925–2000: A Seventy-Fifth Anniversary Record*, ed. G. Thomas Tanselle, Peter F. Kardon, and Eunice R. Schwager (New York: John Simon Guggenheim Memorial Foundation, 2001), 22 (hereafter Tanselle). This book includes the texts of official documents related to its origin, a basic chronology of events related to the foundation, lists of trustees, officers, and advisers, assorted statistics, the names of recipients and their projects that received publication subventions, a bibliography of publications by and about people related to the foundation, prizes won by Guggenheim fellows, and most important for this study, a chronologically arranged record of fellowship winners by field.

2. See Tanselle, 20.

3. For an early expression of awareness regarding the tragic consequences of depleting the nation's natural resources see Susan Fenimore Cooper's 1850 book *Rural Hours* (ed. Rochelle Johnson and Daniel Patterson [Athens: University of Georgia Press, 1998]). As stated in Rochelle Johnson's introduction, "*Rural Hours* . . . offers readers insights into the environmental concerns of an educated mid-nineteenth-century woman" (ix). Cooper's book pre-dated Thoreau's similarly structured journal-like series of seasonal observations, *Walden*, by four years.

4. It is ironic that the Guggenheims were even excluded from being listed among the nation's "titans of industry" by Matthew Josephson in his 1934 book *The Robber Barons: The Great American Capitalists, 1861–1901*. The only Jew on his list of more than thirty men was the investment banker Joseph Seligman, whose family was turned away from vacationing at the Grand Union Hotel in Saratoga, New York, in 1877 despite their having stayed there in previous years. It may be that Josephson considered the Guggenheims' rise to robber-baron status to have occurred beyond the forty-year focus of his study, but that is hard to argue given the accumulation of their wealth starting in the 1880s.

5. By "multitextuality" Born references Dave Laing's understanding of the concept as "the analysis of meaning as operating through many simultaneous, juxtaposed, and interrelating symbolic forms or mediations." See Georgina Born, *Rationalizing Culture: IRCAM, Boulez, and the Institutionalization of the Musical Avant-Garde* (Berkeley: University of California Press, 1995), 16–17. In truth, Born's study was not the first to focus its lens on a single institution devoted to high art: see Martin Duberman, *Black Mountain: An Exploration in Community* (Evanston, IL: Northwestern University Press, 1972) for a previous undertaking. It might not meet Born's criterion of an institution devoted exclusively to music, which it was not. A similar argument could eliminate Bridget Falconer-Salkeld, *The MacDowell Colony: A Musical History of America's Premier Artists' Community* (Lanham, MD: Scarecrow, 2005) and Martin Brody, ed., *Music and Musical Composition at the American Academy in Rome* (Rochester, NY: University of Rochester Press, 2014); both residency programs served multiple artistic practitioners. See Michael Sy Uy, *Ask the Experts: How Ford, Rockefeller, and the NEA Changed American Music* (New York: Oxford University Press, 2020) for a study devoted to three philanthropic institutions and their impact on music culture in the United States. George E. Lewis's comprehensive study *A Power Stronger Than Itself: The AACM and American Experimental Music* (Chicago: University of Chicago Press, 2008) is unique and invaluable for its focus on a powerful Black arts institution that has cultivated, supported, and nurtured African American musical talent with a singleness of purpose for over fifty years.

6. Born, *Rationalizing Culture*, 32.

7. Born, *Rationalizing Culture*, 35. In the case of this study, "confidentiality" prevented me from seeing full files for the early organizational days of the foundation or any of the composers I discuss in Chapter 6.

8. The most recent information provided on the Guggenheim Foundation site explains that 175 awards are distributed among the 3,000 applications they receive. See https://www.gf.org/about/fellowship.

9. The current website for IRCAM links to Profellow, a fellowship database and resource that announces: "Fellowships enhance your resume and provide networking opportunities with leaders in your career field. A fellowship might be your best opportunity to travel abroad, be your own boss, attend graduate school or publish a piece of work." See https://www.profellow.com/what-is-a-fellowship.

Chapter 1. The Family

1. See John H. Davis, *The Guggenheims: An American Epic* (New York: William Morrow, 1978) for basic biographical information about the patriarch Simon and his son Meyer Guggenheim. Davis draws on archival documents and interviews with Guggenheim family members.

2. Any list of U.S. captains of industry reveals the overwhelming importance of railroads and natural resources to the early industrialists' fortunes, and the Guggenheim family was no different in that regard.

3. Davis, *The Guggenheims*, 58.

4. Ironically, Jews in Lengnau were prohibited from engaging in the smelting industry, which is where Simon Guggenheim's family would make its fortune sixty years later.

5. This is not to ignore or minimize the Quakers' robust participation in the slave trade before the Revolution, again like the Puritans. See https://philadelphiaencyclopedia.org/archive/immigration-and-migration-colonial-era/ for a discussion of the Quakers trafficking in African and Caribbean slaves as early as 1684.

6. See Mark Lewis, "Doing Business the Quaker Way," in *Forbes*, October 9, 2009, https://www.forbes.com/2009/10/09/quaker-business-meetings-leadership-society-friends.html#36c271b29fa1. The Wharton School of Business regularly ranks in the top three business schools in the nation. Although not a Quaker institution, the University of Pennsylvania was among the earliest diversified large institutions. It admitted its first African American students in 1879, and women were admitted to the graduate school from its inception in 1882. See https://archives.upenn.edu/exhibits/penn-history/brief-history for additional information on the school's founding.

7. At Swarthmore, African American students waited until 1945 to be admitted. It is hard to reconcile Swarthmore's early racial policy given its other progressive attitudes regarding education. In 1835, the private Presbyterian institution known since 1850 as Oberlin College admitted its first African American male students. See Dwayne Mack, "Oberlin College (1833–)," BlackPast, October, 25, 2010, https://www.blackpast.org/african-american-history/oberlin-college-1833.

8. Davis, *The Guggenheims*, 60.

9. Ibid., 60–61.

10. Ibid., 61. Davis explained that "Benjamin, the first Guggenheim to go to college, left Columbia University's School of Mines to become the A. Y. and Minnie's bookkeeper. William, upon graduating from the University of Pennsylvania, went to work in the assay and laboratory department of the mines and later at the family's new smelter at Pueblo." Ibid.

11. In the foreword to the 1962 edition of his 1934 book *The Robber Barons: The Great American Capitalists, 1861–1901*, Matthew Josephson refers to "the embattled farmers of Kansas, who, in one of their anti-monopoly pamphlets of 1880, first applied the nomenclature of Robber Baron to the masters of railways systems" (vi). American robber barons were first alluded to in a February 9, 1859, *New York Times* editorial by Henry J. Raymond, editor of the paper, when he compared the business practices of Cornelius Vanderbilt to those of German barons poised along the Rhine. Over the years, characterizations of the nineteenth-century industrialists who made personal fortunes while simultaneously building the nation's infrastructure have ranged widely from the damning to the generous, with distinctions between the two being suggested by the more benign phrase "captains of industry" for those whose reputations have been tied tightly to philanthropy. "Captains of Industry" was coined by the Scottish philosopher, mathematician, and social commentator Thomas Carlyle (1795–1881) in his 1843 book *Past and Present*, a candid critique of nineteenth-century British society. For purposes of a study of the John Simon Guggenheim Memorial Foundation it may be relevant to acknowledge that Carlyle was a virulent antisemite. Wealth earned by Jewish businessmen in Carlyle's view was, by dint

of their race alone, lucre. Josephson discusses the barons who were most conspicuously active between 1860 and 1900. The Guggenheims' emergence as mining industry power brokers in the 1880s appears to qualify them for inclusion in this group, although they are never mentioned. A single Jewish industrial titan regularly listed among the "robber baron" group was Joseph Seligman. He made his fortune in New York in banking and railroads.

12. *Brown* as a racial descriptor goes back to the eighteenth century but has been used more frequently in common parlance, especially with increased sensitivities to the immigration of peoples from Central and South America and various countries in the Near and Middle East to the United States and their distinctiveness from people of African heritage.

13. The story covering the denial of access to the Seligmans at the Grand Union Hotel appeared in the *New York Times*, June 19, 1877. The reason given for the denial was poor business in the preceding year, which had been attributed to unhappy Christian guests who were avoiding the hotel because of the large number of Jews at the resort. It is more likely that numerous old animosities between Seligman and Hilton were the source of the act.

14. Benjamin Guggenheim (1865–1912), the fifth of Meyer's seven sons, married Joseph Seligman's niece Florette Seligman (1830–1937). She was the youngest daughter of Joseph's brother James Seligman, who was head of the banking firm J. & W. Seligman & Company. In a *New York Times* story that appeared on October 25, 1894, Benjamin is described as "the Silver Prince." Benjamin and Florette had a daughter, Peggy Guggenheim (1898–1979). Benjamin was among those who drowned when the *Titanic* sank. See https://www.encyclopedia-titanica.org/guggenheim-seligman.html.

15. Irish and Italian immigrants, tagged "Papists" by what was then the Protestant majority, endured prejudicial attitudes, especially in some northeastern cities where their numbers threatened old family Anglo-Saxons, but both groups were more quickly assimilated. It may bear repeating that in 1960 John F. Kennedy was questioned about his Roman Catholic faith and his understanding of who or what would have greater authority: the pope or the constitution. Kennedy became the nation's first Roman Catholic president when he was sworn in on January 20, 1961.

16. See https://www.guggenheimpartners.com/firm/history. According to the Guggenheim Partners website, "By the end of World War I the family controlled over 80% of the world's supply of silver, copper, and lead."

17. In her book *Representing the Good Neighbor: Music, Difference, and the Pan American Dream* (New York: Oxford University Press, 2013), Carol Hess discusses the role played by writer Waldo Frank in promoting the idea that "organic wholeness, authenticity, and originality lay just across the Rio Grande." Quoting the historian Helen Delpar, Hess refers to the "enormous vogue of things Mexican" that consumed the United States in the 1920s. This was helped by Frank's popularity as a writer. See Hess, *Representing the Good Neighbor*, 31–32.

18. See Stephanie N. Stallings, "Collective Difference: The Pan-American Association of Composers and Pan-American Ideology in Music, 1925–1945" (PhD diss., Florida State

University, 2009), 3. Stallings provides a helpful introduction to the "Pan-American Project" and the major players in its musical analogue, the PAAC.

19. Hess, *Representing the Good Neighbor*, 4.

20. See Carroll Wilson to Frank Aydelotte, February 25, 1924, Frank Aydelotte Papers, Swarthmore College, Friends Historical Library (hereafter Aydelotte Papers, Swarthmore College).

21. See C. A. Wilson to Senator Simon Guggenheim, April 10, 1924, in Aydelotte Papers, Swarthmore College.

22. *The John Simon Guggenheim Memorial Foundation, 1925–2000: A Seventy-Fifth Anniversary Record*, ed. G. Thomas Tanselle, Peter F. Kardon, and Eunice R. Schwager (New York: John Simon Guggenheim Memorial Foundation, 2001), 25 (hereafter Tanselle).

23. I am grateful to Stephanie Stallings for early discussions about multidirectional cultural flow as the phenomenon emerged in her dissertation project on the Pan-American Association of Composers.

24. Tanselle, 25.

25. Ibid.

26. Fifteen years earlier, in 1911, the Society for American Indians was formed with the purpose of unifying remaining Native peoples across the country regardless of their original tribal associations or cultural practices. The society morphed over the years as Pan-Indian groups challenged the U.S. government's treatment of Native peoples and their lands. See David Eugene Wilkins, *American Indian Politics and the American Political System* (Lanham, MD: Rowman and Littlefield, 2006).

27. Tanselle, 19. Five million dollars in 1929 is the equivalent of approximately seventy-five million dollars in 2021. See https://data.bls.gov/cgi-bin/cpicalc.pl?cost1=5%2C000%2C000.00&year1=192901&year2=201906.

28. Hess, *Representing the Good Neighbor*, 4.

29. Tanselle, 37.

30. Davis, *The Guggenheims*, 245.

31. Ibid. Davis quotes a speech made by Simon Guggenheim that was reproduced in the *Denver Post*. Senator Guggenheim served a single six-year term, 1907–1913.

32. "The Emergency Quota Act [of 1921] restricted the number of immigrants to 357,000 per year, and . . . was intended to be a temporary measure, but the National Origins Formula continued until 1965." See http://www.american-historama.org/1913-1928-ww1-prohibition-era/1921-emergency-quota-act.htm.

33. By the end of his life, Senator Guggenheim would be well acquainted with grief. His twin brother Robert died at age eleven in a horseback riding accident. John Simon, the first of two sons born to Simon and Olga Guggenheim, died in 1922, and a second son, George Denver Guggenheim, born in 1907, died by his own hand in 1939 at age thirty-two. Simon understood all too well that his family's fortune did not provide immunity to tragedy.

34. Tanselle, 23.

35. In 1937, twelve years after the founding of the JSGMF, Simon's older brother Solomon (1861–1949) started the Solomon R. Guggenheim Foundation, which had as its focused

mission "promoting the understanding and appreciation of modern and contemporary art through exhibitions, education programs, research initiatives, and publications." Multiple Guggenheim family members supported artistic and educational initiatives. See https://www.guggenheim.org/foundation for a discussion of the Solomon R. Guggenheim Foundation.

36. To be fair, the patriarch and his son Meyer were busy building the family's fortune, which the third generation of Guggenheim children, including Simon and his brothers and sisters, got to dispose of in more generous ways. This is similar to generational patterns of other successful immigrant families.

37. Given the family's devotion to business success above all else, it would be naïve to think that any Guggenheim was unaware of the public relations boon that such bequests accomplished. It would also be cynical to think that the Guggenheims were driven exclusively by self-serving motives.

38. "Millionaires Club" is a phrase often used in reference to the U.S. Congress, where, starting in 2014, a majority of members have net worths well in excess of a million dollars. In 1907 that was not the case. See https://www.opensecrets.org/news/2014/01/millionaires-club-for-first-time-most-lawmakers-are-worth-1-million-plus.

39. For the whole text of Bryan's speech and an audio clip of him reading a nine-minute excerpt, see http://historymatters.gmu.edu/d/5354.

40. Davis, *The Guggenheims*, 250. The poem was first published in the *Washington Times* on February 18, 1910, page 8. It was prefaced with "News Note: The Guggenheim interests have obtained options on about 75% of the soft coal in the country." The poem is credited to "G. H. G." although none of the people officially associated with the paper as editors, reporters, or columnists has these initials. Attempts to identify the author have failed.

41. It follows that the largest philanthropic institutions in the United States today sport such names as Carnegie (founded 1911), Rockefeller (1913), Guggenheim (1925), Ford (1936), Heinz (1941), Hilton (1944), Getty (1953), Buffett (1964), Hewlett (1966), Mellon (1969), and Gates (2000).

42. See Ashley Geer Hedrick's 2017 Ph.D. dissertation "'Music's Most Powerful Ally': The National Federation of Music Clubs as an Institutional Leader in the Development of American Music Culture, 1898–1919" for a study of the work of the early National Federation of Women's Music Clubs. Retrieved from http://purl.flvc.org/fsu/fd/FSU_2017SP_Hedrick_fsu_0071E_13773.

43. Tanselle, 28.

44. Cecil Rhodes's fortune was also made in mining, although he mined for diamonds. Rhodes founded the still-thriving DeBeers Diamond Company in Johannesburg, South Africa, in 1888. It is logical that Wilson and Guggenheim saw an attractive model in Rhodes, a fellow mining entrepreneur.

45. Tanselle, 28.

46. Ibid., 21.

47. Ibid. The same situation continues today with sabbatical salaries being inadequate on their own to support extensive research work beyond the physical confines of one's home institution. While digital collections and technology have mitigated some of the problem, they cannot simulate the totality of experiences rendered by physical interactions with archival materials.

48. See Donald Markwell, *Instincts to Lead: On Leadership, Peace, and Education* (Brisbane, Australia: Connor Court, 2013), as cited in https://www.rhodeshouse.ox.ac.uk/about/history-of-the-rhodes-trust/.

49. Tanselle, 32.

50. In another of many ironic twists, in more recent years composer-residents at the American Academy in Rome have used funds including their Guggenheim Fellowship awards to underwrite their time at the academy. As Richard Trythall explains in his essay "A History of the Rome Prize in Music Composition, 1947–2006" in Martin Brody, ed., *Music and Musical Composition at the American Academy in Rome* (Rochester, NY: University of Rochester Press, 2014), 50, "the composer-in-residence position also depended on outside support since no stipend was attached to this position. Composers-in-residence arrived on Guggenheim Fellowships, Senior Fulbright grants, or found other financial support for their stay at the Academy."

51. Brody, "Introduction," *Music and Musical Composition*, 2.

52. See the quotation from the February 2, 1920, letter of Felix Lamond in Carol Oja, "'Picked Young Men,' Facilitating Women, and Emerging Composers," in Brody, *Music and Musical Composition*, 168. Henry Walters (1848–1931) was an art collector whose father, William Thompson Walters, had made his fortune in railroads. Walters may best be remembered today for the Walters Art Museum in Baltimore, whose collection includes more than fifteen hundred artworks that were part of a palace in Rome that he purchased. Walters's preference for ancient, medieval, and classical art made him a natural sympathizer with the academy's aesthetic values.

53. Brody, *Music and Musical Composition*, provides the most thorough study of the history, aesthetic goals, and practices of the academy and is the essential resource on the institution.

54. See ibid., 2, for a description of the twenty acres of land bequeathed to the academy.

55. Oja, "'Picked Young Men,'" 160.

56. Ibid., 161, quoting from Fikret K. Yegül, *Gentlemen of Instinct and Breeding: Architecture at the American Academy in Rome, 1894–1940* (New York: Oxford University Press, 1991), 80.

57. Oja, "'Picked Young Men,'" 175. One shudders to think how Robert Schumann might have fared in trying to get past the selection committee if he had sent some of his character pieces or a song cycle.

58. Ibid.

59. Ibid.

Chapter 2. The Foundation

1. See Robert Earnest Miller, "The Raymond Walters Diaries: The Swarthmore College Days (1925–1932)," *Pennsylvania Magazine of History and Biography* 141, no. 3, Education in Pennsylvania History (October 2017): 369.

2. Ibid.

3. In the early fall of 1924 Aydelotte considered recommending Walters for the job he eventually offered to Moe. He acknowledged Walters's greater maturity and experience, but he valued Moe's temperament, which he saw as better suited to the job he envisioned.

He may also have recognized the greater malleability of the young and eager Moe, who was not as established as was Walters. Walters would eventually serve as president of the University of Cincinnati for twenty-three years, from 1932 to 1955, and Moe's name would become synonymous with the Guggenheim Foundation.

4. See Mary Douglas, *How Institutions Think* (New York: Syracuse University Press, 1986) for the origin of this phrase.

5. The importance of Wilson's role is suggested in John H. Davis, *The Guggenheims: An American Epic* (New York: William Morrow, 1978); see pages 256, 257, and 275 especially. Davis does not, however, provide the details of Wilson's involvement.

6. See Makhieba Simon, "Carroll A. Wilson: A Brief Biography," History of Special Collections @ Colby, http://web/colby.edu/csc-history-of/c-a-wilson-bio.

7. The consensus appears to be that the Guggenheims had planned for John Simon to attend Harvard, although I have not found unequivocal evidence to that effect. Restrictive quotas that controlled the number of Jewish students admitted to elite northeastern schools would have presented a challenge to his admittance to any of them were he not a Guggenheim. The size of the Guggenheim fortune and the possibility that part of it might find its way to the school John Simon attended could have offset concerns about adherence to quotas. School administrators needed only to look at the gifts the Guggenheims had made to the Colorado School of Mining and to the University of Colorado in 1905 and 1907 to make an exception and admit just one more Jewish son. The Guggenheims' second son George graduated from Harvard after a less-than-stellar tenure there.

8. See Davis, *The Guggenheims*, 55–56, for details of the educational experiences of Isaac, Daniel, Murry, and Solomon Guggenheim.

9. Aydelotte held that position for thirty-four years, 1918–1952.

10. See Carroll A. Wilson to President Frank Aydelotte, February 25, 1924, Aydelotte Papers, Swarthmore College.

11. Ibid.

12. See Carroll Wilson, "Suggestions for the John S. Guggenheim Foundation," April 10, 1924, Aydelotte Papers, Swarthmore College. Although Aydelotte's name does not appear anywhere as the author of the report, on page 26 Wilson refers to ideas "originally outlined by President Aydelotte." Given the specific information regarding academic and educational practices that are contained in the report, it is impossible to imagine that Wilson could have created it without significant input from Aydelotte, or that Aydelotte would have had the data he used without the work of Raymond Walters. All further quotations from this report are from this source.

13. Ibid. Wilson associated the West with more manly men, which would be in keeping with the American mythology that was still prevalent at the time. Later in the document he makes another reference to "full-blooded men with scholastic attainment." It is hard not to read Wilson's words as exhibiting a form of homophobia and the rampant assumption that the arts, and music especially, belonged to the feminine domain and that male practitioners were predisposed to cultivated "Eastern" (feminine) behaviors.

14. Ibid. With rare exceptions, the quality of genius was gendered as male and so would direct committee members' thinking regarding the appropriate gender of composition fellows.

15. At one point there was discussion of the foundation working exclusively with applicants from institutions that were members of the Association of American Universities. This would have reduced the number of participating institutions to only those focused on research and eliminated many art and music applicants completely.

16. See Carroll A. Wilson to Senator Guggenheim, April 12, 1924, Aydelotte Papers, Swarthmore College.

17. See Frank Aydelotte to Carroll Wilson, April 25, 1924, Aydelotte Papers, Swarthmore College.

18. See Carroll Wilson to Frank Aydelotte, May 5, 1924, Aydelotte Papers, Swarthmore College.

19. *The John Simon Guggenheim Memorial Foundation, 1925–2000: A Seventy-Fifth Anniversary Record*, ed. G. Thomas Tanselle, Peter F. Kardon, and Eunice R. Schwager (New York: John Simon Guggenheim Memorial Foundation, 2001), 29 (hereafter Tanselle).

20. Simon Flexner, "Wickliffe Rose: 1862–1931," *Science*, n.s., 75, no. 1950 (May 13, 1932): 504–506. Rose responded enthusiastically in a letter dated May 20, 1924. Copies of Rose's and Ruml's letters to Simon Guggenheim are in the Henry Allen Moe Papers, American Philosophical Society, Philadelphia.

21. See "Suggestions for Chronological Working Out of Your Ideas as to Foundation," May 14, 1924, Frank Aydelotte Papers, Swarthmore College.

22. Davis, *The Guggenheims*, 259, 256. Davis quotes Peter Lyon.

23. See Frank Aydelotte to Simon Guggenheim, July 16, 1924, Aydelotte Papers, Swarthmore College.

24. This is the equivalent of approximately $164,414 in 2022 dollars. This amount was on top of the salary Aydelotte earned as Swarthmore's president and his remuneration for being American secretary of the Rhodes Foundation. By way of comparison, when Aydelotte accepted a full professorship at M.I.T. in 1915, his salary was $2,700. As a point of contrast, the average annual U.S. income in 1924 was $2,196. For information on Aydelotte's M.I.T. salary, see Frances Blanshard, *Frank Aydelotte of Swarthmore* (Middletown, CT: Wesleyan University Press, 1970), 118.

25. I take the phrase "thinking institutionally" from the title of Hugh Heclo, *On Thinking Institutionally* (New York: Oxford University Press, 2008), and Douglas, *How Institutions Think*. .

26. See http://www.wabi.tv/content/news/Benton-Falls-Congregational-Church-begins-steeple-renovation-project-483511511.html.

27. See Blanshard, *Frank Aydelotte*, 16.

28. A collection of seven of Moe's lectures, addresses, and essays written before 1952 and discovered after his death by his wife Edith Monroe Moe bore the title "Power of Freedom." She combined them with a dozen other writings in a book titled *The Power of Freedom in Human Affairs*. It was published by the American Philosophical Society in 1977, two years after Moe's death.

29. See Tanselle, 29.

30. This criticism of Moe is ironic given that Beardsley Ruml had cautioned against a similar tendency in Aydelotte when otherwise enthusiastically recommending him to Guggenheim in May. He feared that Aydelotte might suffer from a "pro-British bias." See

Beardsley Ruml to Senator Guggenheim, May 17, 1924, Henry Allen Moe Papers, American Philosophical Society.

31. See Frank Aydelotte to Carroll Wilson, August 18, 1924, Aydelotte Papers, Swarthmore College.

32. See Frank Aydelotte to Carroll Wilson, August 19, 1924, Aydelotte Papers, Swarthmore College.

33. Tanselle, 30.

34. Ibid.

35. Ibid.

36. See W. O. Thompson to Frank Aydelotte (typed), September 8, 1924, Aydelotte Papers, Swarthmore College.

37. Ibid.

38. See Walter D. Scott to Frank Aydelotte, September 30, 1924, Aydelotte Papers, Swarthmore College.

39. See Frank Aydelotte to C. A. Wilson, September 17, 1924, Aydelotte Papers, Swarthmore College.

40. Ibid.

41. Tanselle, 33.

42. See Frank Aydelotte to C. A. Wilson, September 23, 1924, Henry Allen Moe Papers, American Philosophical Society.

43. See C. A. Wilson to Frank Aydelotte, September 24, 1924, Henry Allen Moe Papers, American Philosophical Society.

44. See the eleven-page report of October 2, 1924, Aydelotte Papers, Swarthmore College.

45. See Henry Allen Moe to Frank Aydelotte, undated, Henry Allen Moe Papers, American Philosophical Society. It was written before September 26, 1924, based on a reference to an upcoming dinner on the twenty-sixth in the final paragraph of page 2. There is a handwritten note on the top of the letter speculating that the letter was written in September or October 1924.

46. Ibid.

47. See the report dated October 2, 1924, Aydelotte Papers, Swarthmore College. The same situation holds in 2022, as this author can attest.

48. See Frank Aydelotte to Simon Guggenheim, October 6, 1924, two-page memo marked "Personal," Aydelotte Papers, Swarthmore College.

49. See Frank Aydelotte, "Endowment for Foreign Study: A Report of the Systems of Scholarships Now in Operation and on the Field Which Might Usefully be Occupied by a New Foundation," n.d., Aydelotte Papers, Swarthmore College.

50. See Frank Aydelotte to Carroll Wilson, October 15, 1924, Aydelotte Papers, Swarthmore College.

51. See Ibid.

52. See Carroll Wilson to Frank Aydelotte, October 20, 1924, Aydelotte Papers, Swarthmore College. I have not found any specific comments by Wilson regarding what qualities he found lacking in Moe. Given Wilson's encouragement to hire him, no particular trait must have been damning.

53. Henry Allen Moe, report to Frank Aydelotte, November 29, 1924, page 16 of 22, Aydelotte Papers, Swarthmore College.

54. Ibid., 17. Given the historically strong music culture in Cleveland and the location of Western Reserve University in that city, it seems logical that Vinson would be comfortable with the notion that musical and artistic abilities could be adjudicated.

55. The assumptions regarding musicians' and artists' inability to navigate basic application forms or imagine the social implications of their work suggests how far removed from the arts world and its practitioners some of those being solicited for advice stood.

56. Henry Allen Moe, November 29, 1924 report, Aydelotte Papers, Swarthmore College. Edward Asahel Birge (1851–1950) was president of the University of Wisconsin-Madison from 1918 to 1925. Robert Ernest Vinson (1876–1945) was president of the University of Texas-Austin from 1916 to 1923 and then went to Western Reserve (now Case Western Reserve University), where he was president from 1923 to 1933.

57. Ruth Porter Crawford won the first music composition fellowship awarded to a female in 1930. Louise Talma won the second and third with consecutive awards in 1946 and 1947, and Julia Amanda Perry, an African American Juilliard- and Boulanger-trained composer, was the third female music composition fellow; she received Guggenheim awards in 1954 and 1956.

58. See Virginia C. Gildersleeve to Frank Aydelotte, December 11, 1924, Aydelotte Papers, Swarthmore College.

59. Ibid.

60. Tanselle, 85–86.

Chapter 3. The Advisor

1. Henry Allen Moe, "The Only Great Decider," Address to the American Academy of Arts and Sciences, Boston, Massachusetts, April 11, 1945, reprinted in *The Power of Freedom in Human Affairs* (Philadelphia: American Philosophical Society, 1977), 25. Beyond Moe's claim, it is impossible to ascertain that Surette could read and hear a score whose music he did not know, especially if it didn't follow musical rules from the common practice era. Surette's reliance on others to review scores may suggest that he was not confident in those skills. The absence of any written evaluations or detailed comments by Surette regarding applicants' compositions means that there is no evidence to consult.

2. Daniel Gregory Mason, "Is American Music Growing Up? Our Emancipation from Alien Influences," *Arts and Decoration* 14, no. 1 (November 1920): 40. Italics are mine.

3. Daniel Gregory Mason, *Tune in America: A Study of Our Coming Musical Independence* (New York: Knopf, 1931), 160. Italics are mine. In a letter written May 16, 1933, to the music editor at the *New York Times* and published five days later, Mason expressed distress that "certain statements in my book, 'Tune in America,' are being misinterpreted as anti-Jewish propaganda, and even as friendly to jingoism and Hitlerian nationalism." See *New York Times*, May 21, 1933, ProQuest Historical Newspapers, p. X5. It is hard to fathom that Mason was surprised that his sentiments were read as anti-Jewish. He was not shy about "othering" Jews, and his characterization of Jewish music as "an alien art" leaves little room for misinterpretation. See Mason, *Tune in America*, 160–161.

4. Their names might have been mentioned in private conversations among Guggenheim, Wilson, and Aydelotte, although no written evidence that I have consulted addresses this issue.

5. Mason, *Tune in America*, 161–162. Mason's us-them sensibility was on full display in his remarks about Bloch. The composer, Mason observed, "capped his dealings with *us* by the grim jest of presenting to *us* a long, brilliant, megalomaniac, and thoroughly Jewish symphony—entitled *America*. (In calling attention to this irony, it is hardly necessary to state that no 'anti-Jewish propaganda' is intended.)" Mason continued that it was Bloch's "subservience to fashion" that most distressed him. Italics are mine. Bloch had composed "America" in 1927 for a contest sponsored by the magazine *Musical America*. The piece won first prize.

6. In 1933, in just one of a lifetime of noxious remarks, Carl Ruggles famously referred to the musicians associated with Juilliard as "that filthy bunch of Juilliard Jews . . . cheap, without dignity, and with little or no talent." See Marilyn J. Ziffrin, *Carl Ruggles: Composer, Painter, and Storyteller* (Urbana: University of Illinois Press, 1992), 136.

7. See Jerold S. Auerbach, *Unequal Justice: Lawyers and Social Change in Modern America* (New York: Oxford University Press, 1976), 127, for a reference to Drinker's remarks.

8. Henry S. Drinker, *Legal Ethics* (New York: Columbia University Press, 1953).

9. Henry S. Drinker's repeated attempts to have Surette awarded an honorary degree from the University of Pennsylvania ultimately succeeded in 1934. I am grateful to the Honorary Degree Records Office at the University of Pennsylvania for sharing information about Drinker's nomination and to the Historical Society of Pennsylvania for making available family papers from the Dr. and Mrs. Henry Drinker Collections. On Surette's death, the Drinkers hosted a memorial service in his honor at their Merion, Pennsylvania, home. For a complete list of the more than sixteen hundred participants who joined in the Drinkers' "sings" over their thirty-year course, see *Accademia dei Dilettanti di Musica (1930–1960)* by Henry S. Drinker and Sophie H. Drinker. I'm grateful to Ruth Solie for sharing this document with me. Multiple members of the Drinker family had been awarded honorary degrees by the University of Pennsylvania. Germaine to a study of the John Simon Guggenheim Memorial Foundation, Frank Aydelotte was also awarded an honorary doctorate (Litt. D.) in 1924 by the University of Pennsylvania, strengthening his Philadelphia connections and providing another connection for Surette, if one was needed.

10. See Kathleen Uhler Adams, *Thomas Whitney Surette: A Crusader for Good Music* (Cambridge, MA: Windflower, 1983), 8.

11. See https://concordlibrary.org/special-collections/fin_aids/social_circle. See the cover image of the Social Circle centenary celebration of Ralph Waldo Emerson, 1903.

12. Given the historical hostility of the Roman Catholic Church toward Freemasonry and vice versa, and the social impossibility of a Protestant Shattuck marrying a Catholic Surette, it is assumed that Louis-Athanase had converted on marrying Frances Jane.

13. "Defalcation" was the word used in the minutes of the trustees' meeting of June 15, 1874, where the Honorable George M. Brooks was chosen to replace Louis A. Surette as trustee and treasurer of the Sleepy Hollow Cemetery Fund. Defalcation is a specific form

of embezzlement in which the person who is misappropriating funds has a fiduciary responsibility to the people or organization from which he or she has stolen. The sum in question, $3,000, is the equivalent of over $70,000 in 2022. See Thomas Whitney Surette Papers, William Munroe Special Collections, Concord Free Public Library, Concord, Massachusetts. I am grateful to Leslie Perrin Wilson, curator of the William Munroe Special Collections, for making available papers related to Surette and the Concord Summer School of Music.

14. See Louis A. Surette to Mr. Munroe Esq., July 22, 1873, Surette Papers, Concord Free Public Library.

15. Louis-Athanase Surette to unknown, November 18, 1873, Surette Papers, Concord Free Public Library. It is not clear where the money to pay creditors would come from if not from Frances Jane Shattuck's family.

16. "To the Hon. George M. Brooks Treas of the Sleepy Hollow Cemetery Fund" (report), Surette Papers, Concord Free Public Library.

17. Biographical information about Louis-Athanase Surette and Thomas Whitney Surette comes from a variety of sources including archival materials at the Concord Free Public Library, but an essential resource is Charles W. Heffernan, "Thomas Whitney Surette: Musician and Teacher" (Ph.D. diss., University of Michigan, 1962).

18. I have not been able to find corroborating evidence that Sarah Surette studied with Lang beyond Adams's assertion that that was the case. See Adams, *Crusader for Good Music*, 10.

19. Heffernan, "Thomas Whitney Surette," 16. Heffernan drew on articles found in newspapers located at the Concord Free Public Library. The most important materials related to Surette that are housed at the library are scrapbooks that focus on the Concord Summer School.

20. Henry Drinker referred Surette's work at Harvard and assigned him a class, '94, in his nomination for an honorary doctorate from the University of Pennsylvania in 1934. The same information was repeated in Surette's 1941 obituary.

21. Heffernan observed that Thomas Whitney Surette's Wagner lecture, which he gave multiple times over the years, followed exactly N. J. Corey's Lyceum lecture on Wagner, given December 18, 1889. Heffernan, "Thomas Whitney Surette," 28.

22. Surette was fond of Gilbert and Sullivan, a musical taste he didn't try to hide.

23. Heffernan, "Thomas Whitney Surette," 30.

24. Ibid., 35. For Heffernan's comment on Surette's trite melodies see ibid., 66.

25. See ibid., 33–58, for a discussion of Surette's foray into composition and his later disavowal of his works.

26. Beth E. Levy discusses the community music movement on many occasions in her book *Frontier Figures: American Music and the Mythology of the American West* (Berkeley: University of California Press, 2012).

27. I have not learned how the Concord-based Surette heard of this position in Pennsylvania, but his work close by Philadelphia would prove fortuitous.

28. Adams, *Crusader for Good Music*, 22. Adams names June 20 as the date, but the *New Rochelle Pioneer* of Friday, June 24, 1899, refers to Surette's marriage as taking place

on "Tuesday last." The previous Tuesday was June 21. See *New Rochelle Pioneer*, 41, no. 14, front page under "Personal," http://fultonhistory.com/Newspaper4/New%20Rochelle%20NY%20Pioneer/New%20Rochelle%20NY%20Pioneer%201899%20-%201903%20Grayscale/New%20Rochelle%20NY%20Pioneer%201899%20-%201903%20Grayscale%20-%200126.pdf. Although Adams refers to a large wedding with many prominent guests, attempts to locate a wedding announcement in any Philadelphia paper, where the marriage purportedly took place, have thus far failed. The *New Rochelle Pioneer* story similarly lacks any references to a large event.

29. See information about the Cooperative State Research, Education, and Extension Service at https://www.usda.gov/topics/rural/cooperative-research-and-extension-services.

30. American Society for Extension of University Teaching, "General Announcement for 1906–1907," listed Frederick B. Miles as president of the board. https://www.google.com/books/edition/General_Announcement/wsQ2AAAAMAAJ?hl=en&gbpv=1&dq=General+Announcement+of+the+American+Society+for+Extension+of+University+Teaching+1906–1907&pg=PA1&printsec=frontcover. As an indication of the benefits that would accrue to Thomas Whitney as a result of his marriage, Mr. and Mrs. Thomas W. Surette are listed with the name "Miles" in parenthesis in the New York Social Register of 1916. A Concord address is also given. In the New York Social Register of April 1917, after Frederick B. Miles had died, there is a listing that shows the continuing importance of the Miles connection. It reads: "Mr. and Mrs. Thom W. Surette (Ada E. Miles)." *Social Register, New York* 1917, p. 645. Surette's name is followed by "H'94," indicating that Surette graduated from Harvard in 1894. This was, however, not the case. See https://babel.hathitrust.org/cgi/pt?id=njp.32101045650635&view=1up&seq=7.

31. American Society for Extension of University Teaching, "General Announcement," 1.

32. Ibid., 6.

33. Ibid., 9.

34. Ibid., 4.

35. Frederick Basil Miles had connections to the University of Pennsylvania through his son Basil Miles, who earned a degree there. The relationship between the university and principal figures active in the extension service and later with the Drinkers and with Aydelotte made Surette's nomination for an honorary degree from the university a logical one.

36. Thomas Whitney Surette, "What Constitutes Good Church Music?," *Protestant Episcopal Review* 20, no. 1 (October–November 1896).

37. The term *courses* was used freely and could refer to as few as a pair of lectures or a brief series of talks but should not be confused with modern uses of the term as it applies to semester-long university offerings.

38. American Society for Extension of University Teaching, "General Announcement," 16.

39. See *Who's Who in New York* 1905, 872, for an entry for Surette, Thomas Whitney. Available at https://www.google.com/books. The register contains "authentic biographies

of New Yorkers who are leaders and representatives in various departments of worthy human achievement." Surette's entry lists his membership in the Folk-Song Society (London), St. Botolph Club (Boston), and the Players Club (New York).

40. Mason encouraged a national musical style based on Anglo-Celtic musics. Surette didn't undertake any additional public projects with D. G. Mason beyond their single co-authored text although their friendship remained intact, as evidenced by Mason's gift to the Surettes of a Mason and Hamlin grand piano, which the Surettes kept in the "glamorous" music room of their Concord house, and by the exclusive use of Mason and Hamlin pianos by the Concord Summer School. See Adams, *Crusader for Good Music*, 40–41.

41. *The Appreciation of Music* focuses on traditional musical forms (suite, rondo, variation, and sonata forms) and devotes chapters to folk song, dance, Bach's polyphony, and Beethoven's fifth symphony.

42. See Elizabeth Crouch Fitts, "Aspects of American Musical Life as Reflected in *The New Music Review and Church Music Review*, 1901–1935," Ph.D. diss., University of Maryland, College Park, 2009, 4. As Fitts explains, H. W. Gray continued to represent Novello.

43. Ibid., 252–253.

44. Ibid., 5.

45. Ibid., 17.

46. Ibid., 241.

47. For information on the Ancoats Brotherhood see http://www.wcml.org.uk/contents/creativity-and-culture/leisure/ancoats-brotherhood.

48. See "Towers Entertain Germany's Rulers," *New York Times*, March 14, 1908. Accessed at *NYT* online.

49. Students supported by The Music Fund went to Paris to study. The Surettes' yearly visits allowed them to check on the recipients of the private funds. During the 1930s the Surettes brought favorite students with them to Europe on their summer sojourns.

50. Heffernan, "Thomas Whitney Surette," 73–74.

51. Other members of the committee included Daniel Bloomfield, Mabel Daniels, Percy Atherton, and "John P. Marshall, organist of the Boston Symphony Orchestra." For a detailed list and discussion of the committee's recommendations see Adams, *Crusader for Good Music*, 35–38. Although Davison was the only committee member with a university connection, it is likely that well-ensconced resistance by town to gown didn't endear the idea of the committee's recommendations to the teachers. Surette's minimal formal music education might also have alienated teachers who wouldn't have enjoyed being lectured to by a person with no experience in a public classroom setting.

52. Information on the source, size, or mission of The Music Fund beyond brief references to it has evaded the author of this study. It's likely, however, that the source of the fund was money inherited by Ada Miles Surette on the death of her father in 1916.

53. See Heffernan, "Thomas Whitney Surette," 83, quoting from *Proceedings of the School Committee of the City of Boston* (City of Boston: Printing Department, 1915), 63.

54. Heffernan, "Thomas Whitney Surette," 175.

55. Ibid., 115.

56. Summer school prospectus for 1915, Surette Papers, Concord Free Public Library. By 1917 the school's name had been shortened to "Surette Summer School of Music, Concord, Massachusetts."

57. The first twelve students included Miss Black, Miss Miriam Cochrane, Mrs. Robert Currier, Miss Marie Denervaud, Miss Edith Freeman, Miss Corinne Harmon, Mrs. Frederick Lowell, Mrs. K. S. Pray, Miss Marion Richardson, Miss Bertha Scholl, Miss Harriet Spofford, and Miss Anna Jansen. Of those listed, Mrs. Robert Currier would attend Surette's summer school a total of thirteen times between 1915 and 1930.

58. See Adams, *Crusader for Good Music*, 49–50. The italics are original to Mrs. Surette's letter as it appears in Adams's book. The issue of the presence of women compromising the perceived seriousness of a musical undertaking would be front and center when Ruth Crawford was prevented from attending a 1930 meeting of the New York Musicological Society (later the American Musicological Society) by founding male members for fear that her presence might "confuse [the endeavor] with a Women's Club" and suggest the amateur nature of those gathered. See Judith Tick, *Ruth Crawford Seeger: A Composer's Search for American Music* (New York: Oxford University Press, 1997), 121–122.

59. Concord Summer School of Music, 1916 flyer, Surette Papers, Concord Free Public Library.

60. Ibid. Surette appears to have been unaware of Bach's having studied Arcangelo Corelli's scores and of his public admiration of the composer's concerti grossi. All phrases in quotation marks come from the "Historical Outline" and are part of the 1916 flyer.

61. "Salon" is a negative word in Surette's lexicon.

62. Concord Summer School of Music, 1916 flyer.

63. Ibid.

64. Ibid. Debussy was still alive at the time Davison wrote his thesis and Surette compiled his flyer. It is possible that Surette's visits to Europe in the early years of the twentieth century made him more open to developments occurring in music in those years, although his own musical preferences would not change.

65. Concord Summer School of Music, 1916 flyer, final unnumbered page of 1916 course materials.

66. Concord Summer School of Music, 1920 flyer, Thomas Whitney Surette Papers, Concord Free Public Library.

67. Adams, *Crusader for Good Music*, 95–96. See also Emily Coakley, "Joseph Lee, Father of the Playground Movement," May 26, 2017, http://2day.sweetsearch.com/joseph-lee-father-of-the-playground-movement. The National Recreation Association was one of the sponsors of the songbook that Surette insisted be used by Black Mountain College, discussed in Chapter 5.

68. See Henry Allen Moe to Frank Aydelotte, January 14, 1925, Aydelotte Papers, Swarthmore College. All quoted passages that follow come from this single lengthy letter.

69. The "boy" was Walter Piston. Piston visited Surette's Concord Summer School in 1919, entered Harvard in 1920, graduated in 1924, won a John Knowles Paine Traveling Fellowship, and went to Paris to study with Nadia Boulanger from 1924 to 1926. He won a Guggenheim Fellowship in 1935 and two Pulitzer Prizes, the first in 1948 and the second in 1961.

70. Italics are mine. Although the foundation's charter explicitly articulated impartiality based on sex, Surette's personal biases, which, letters prove, include a disparaging attitude toward female composers, would impact his judgment and the distribution of awards. Surette clearly thought of composers as being male.

71. Frank Aydelotte to Charles Homer Haskins, April 18, 1925, Aydelotte Papers, Swarthmore College. The Emerson being referred to is William Emerson, head of the Department of Architecture at MIT at the time.

Chapter 4. The Network

1. See the cover of *Time*, June 5, 1933.

2. See Simon Guggenheim to Frank Aydelotte, April 8, 1931, Frank Aydelotte Papers, Swarthmore College.

3. See Frank Aydelotte to Simon Guggenheim, April 21, 1931, Frank Aydelotte Papers, Swarthmore College.

4. Bernard Rogers, Quinto Maganini, Mark Wessel, and Ernst Bacon received Pulitzer Traveling Scholarships in 1918, 1927, 1930, and 1932, respectively. Wessel appears not to have accepted his scholarship, given that he received the first of his two Guggenheims in the same year. In 1943, Columbia University would cease awarding Pulitzer Traveling Scholarships and name a single Pulitzer Prize winner in music, an award not intended to support travel abroad, necessarily, but to recognize compositional achievement. Of the pair, the Guggenheim Foundation had assumed responsibility for supporting American composers' travel abroad.

5. See Hanns Gramm, *The Oberlaender Trust, 1931–1953* (Philadelphia: Carl Schurz Memorial Foundation, 1956), 46, for the definitive study of this short-lived, focused philanthropy of which Henry Allen Moe was a founding member.

6. Simon, "Carroll A. Wilson: Brief Biography." See https://web.colby.edu/csc-history-of/c-a-wilson-bio/ for the online article from which the quotation comes. Wilson would serve as a board member or part owner of various mining-related businesses within the Guggenheim empire. As explained by Simon, Guggenheim's chief counsel "worked as director of Chilean Nitrate Sales Corporation and Pacific Tin Consolidated, along with several other companies. Later he was elected vice president of the American Smelting and Refining Company."

7. Emily Pope-Obeda recognized immigration and deportation policies as tied to (manual) labor needs and the nation's desire to define itself with regard to race. Concerning the latter she noted that immigrants in the early twentieth century were often turned away because of a "weak physique," which she observed was "a label often used particularly against eastern European Jewish immigrants." Emily Pope-Obeda, "This Deportation Business: 1920s and the Present," *Against the Current*, May/June 2016, https://solidarity-us.org/atc/182/p4640.

8. Gramm, *Oberlaender Trust*, 41.

9. See Mary Emma Harris, *The Arts at Black Mountain College* (Cambridge, MA: MIT Press, 1987), 6.

10. Martin Duberman, *Black Mountain: An Exploration in Community* (Evanston, IL: Northwestern University Press, 1972), 350. Quakers had a history of establishing highly

respected schools and colleges in the United States as early as the seventeenth century. In the nineteenth century alone, Friends founded Haverford College (1833), Guilford College (1837), Earlham College (1847), Swarthmore College (1864), and Bryn Mawr College (1885), among others. Friends' involvement in Black Mountain College could have been a good portent of success had other conditions been more conducive.

11. The Yaddo Records (1870–1980) are held by the Humanities and Social Sciences Library, Manuscripts and Archives Division, New York Public Library. An excellent source discussing the materials contained in the Yaddo Records is Micki McGee, ed., *Yaddo: Making American Culture* (New York: Columbia University Press, New York Public Library, 2008). It contains contributions by nine authors including one by Tim Page that is especially relevant to this study: "The Trailblazer: Aaron Copland and the Festivals of American Music," 31–40. A thorough study of the musical life at Yaddo is still to be written. It, like this project, will reveal networks of individuals and institutions that together helped shape American culture.

12. Leopold Damrosch Mannes was the son of Clara Damrosch Mannes, the nephew of Frank Damrosch (Clara's brother) and the grandson of Leopold Damrosch.

13. The current foundation offices are at 90 Park Avenue, just a few blocks away from the original headquarters.

14. I am exceedingly grateful to my graduate assistant, Hannah Crider, who compiled the exhaustive list of Guggenheim Foundation advisors and their institutional affiliations on which I base my observations.

15. See Kathleen Uhler Adams, *Thomas Whitney Surette: A Crusader for Good Music* (Cambridge, MA: Windflower, 1983), 27. Adams offers no information about the lectures beyond a list of topics with which students were supposed to familiarize themselves. It is likely that the lectures were offered to the general public and similar to those Surette had perfected during his time as a staff member of the Philadelphia-based American Society for the Extension of University Teaching.

16. See *The John Simon Guggenheim Memorial Foundation, 1925–2000: A Seventy-Fifth Anniversary Record*, ed. G. Thomas Tanselle, Peter F. Kardon, and Eunice R. Schwager (New York: John Simon Guggenheim Memorial Foundation, 2001) (hereafter Tanselle), 117–122.

17. For a discussion of the "power of the accumulation of advantage" see Abigail J. Stewart and Virginia Valian, *An Inclusive Academy: Achieving Diversity and Excellence* (Cambridge, MA: MIT Press, 2018), 201–216, esp. 213.

18. The phrase is often credited to Winston Churchill, although no indisputable evidence exists to confirm the attribution. Another possible if less attractive source is Hermann Göring. For additional sources see Matthew Phelan, "The History of 'History Is Written by the Victors,'" *Slate*, November 26, 2019, https://slate.com/culture/2019/11/history-is-written-by-the-victors-quote-origin.html.

19. The foundation was ahead of the college with its more even-handed treatment of applicants of different races. See Elizabeth Weber's article "The First Admission of Negro Students to Swarthmore College" in the school's newspaper, *The Phoenix*, April 12, 1996, available at http://www.swarthmore.edu/library/friends/Smorehistory/Negro.admissions

.html. Beyond equality, other basic Quaker tenets include commitments to community, simplicity, stillness and quiet, peace, personal integrity, and stewardship. It is likely that the Guggenheim family's experiences with discrimination inspired their mission and actions more than a commitment to or awareness of Quaker beliefs. Aydelotte's knowledge of and sympathy with those beliefs, however, could have strengthened their implementation at the foundation, where he set the tone of the organization.

20. Among those identifying as Quakers are Friends who believe in Christ and the trinity, and also those who reject such fundamental Christian tenets. Others reject the existence of God. There is no single doctrine or statement of beliefs to which all those identifying as Friends subscribe.

21. See Frances Blanshard, *Frank Aydelotte of Swarthmore* (Middletown, CT: Wesleyan University Press, 1970), 181. Even Aydelotte's biographer was a member of the inner academic network. Blanshard earned her bachelor's degree at Smith and her master's and PhD degrees at Columbia. She also pursued non-degree studies at Oxford. In 1925 Blanshard joined the Swarthmore philosophy faculty and later served as a dean at the college. It is worth noting that Heinrich Jalowetz, often cited as the most beloved faculty member at Black Mountain College, was described much as Aydelotte was. Listening and cultivating consensus were behaviors shared by the two men.

22. See ibid., 155, 294.

23. See ibid., 154.

24. In order of their award years they include Aaron Copland (1925, 1926), Roger Sessions (1926, 1927), Roy Harris (1927, 1928, 1976), Bernard Rogers (1927, 1928), Robert Russell Bennett (1928, 1929), Quinto Maganini (1928, 1929), Robert Mills Delaney (1929, 1930), George Antheil (1932, 1933), Douglas Stuart Moore (1934), Walter Hamor Piston (1935), Ross Lee Finney (1937, 1947), Paul Creston (1938, 1939), David Diamond (1938, 1941, 1958), and Marc Blitzstein (1940, 1941). Delaney and Piston, along with Randall Thompson and Otto Luening, also studied with Surette at his Concord Summer School. Leopold Damrosch Mannes (1926), Theodore J. Stearns (1927), and Carl Bricken (1930) all enjoyed connections to Walter Damrosch. See Tanselle, starting at page 147, for a complete list of music composition fellows through 1999.

25. See Kendra Preston Leonard, *Conservatoire Américain: A History* (Lanham, MD: Scarecrow, 2007), xviii. Leonard's book provides a carefully researched study of the school from its conception through the twenty-first century. Its many appendices supply information about attendees and awards from which readers can draw numerous conclusions about the culture and focus of the school.

26. According to the U.S. Army Band website: "The U.S. Army Band 'Pershing's Own' was formed on January 25, 1922 by order of General John J. Pershing: 'You will organize and equip The Army Band.' General Pershing believed that bands played a vital role in troop morale and efficiency and was convinced that America needed a premier band to surpass those of Europe." See https://www.usarmyband.com/history.

27. See Leonard, *Conservatoire Américain*, xix.

28. The importance of the Leipzig Conservatory to American music culture, and especially to American college and university music programs, is well documented in studies

by E. Douglas Bomberger and Joanna Pepple. See Bomberger "The German Music Training of American Students, 1850–1900" (PhD diss., University of Maryland—College Park, 1991), and Pepple's "Americans at the Leipzig Conservatory (1843–1918) and Their Impact on American Music Culture" (PhD diss., Florida State University, 2018).

29. See Kendra Preston Leonard, "Excellence in Execution and Fitness for Teaching: Assessments of Women at the Conservatoire Américain," *Women and Music* 11, no. 1 (2007): 29–50, for insights into the varied reasons why a range of women sought admission to the Conservatoire, many of which made it difficult for those most interested in advanced music studies to be taken equally seriously as their male peers.

30. See Leonard, *Conservatoire Américain*, appendices F and G, "Selected Notable Students of the Conservatoire Américain" and "Diplomas and Awards of the Conservatoire Américain." The proportion of students of pedagogy (general music education), solfège, or earning diplomas associated with teaching particular instruments or voice, is overwhelmingly female. In 1927, the first year a prize was awarded in composition, all three awardees were females: Helen Roessing (first prize), Hedy Spielter (second prize), and Margaret Kenney (third prize). In 1933 the only two diplomas given in the category "Harmony" went to Virginia Mackie and Louise Talma. In 1937, the next year composition prizes were awarded, no first prize was given, but four males shared second and third prizes: Livingston Gearhart, Andrew Imbrie, Floyd Morgernstern, and Frederick Werle. Of these four, only Imbrie won Guggenheim awards, and those much later, in 1953 and 1960. It might be argued that he is the only broadly recognizable composer. Prizes in all categories were awarded intermittently in the forty-six years for which records are available, 1927–1973. See Leonard, 205–250.

31. See Kathleen Uhler Adams, *Thomas Whitney Surette: A Crusader for Good Music* (Cambridge, MA: Windflower, 1983), 75. Adams was a regular attendee of the Concord Summer School. Her biography veers towards hagiography, but to be fair it makes no claims to be a scholarly account. There are no citations for any of Adams's assertions.

32. See Thomas Whitney Surette to Dorothy Smith, January 10, 1926, Dorothy Smith Dushkin Collection, SSC-MS-00243, Sophia Smith Collection, Smith College, Northampton, Massachusetts. It is hard to know what differences Surette was thinking of, or how detailed his knowledge would have been of any composition courses or programs at Harvard, Yale, or Columbia, to name just three universities with recognized composers on their faculties at the time. Dorothy Smith met David Dushkin in Paris when he studied at the Conservatoire Américain in 1925. David Dushkin earned a Diplome d'Aptitude à l'Enseignement (Teaching). They were married in 1930. See Leonard, *Conservatoire Américain*, appendix G (210–213), for a list of all students earning a diplome in that year.

33. See Thomas Whitney Surette to Dorothy Smith, March 17, 1926, Sophia Smith Collection, Smith College. "Flambulgent" doesn't exist in any dictionary (English or French) that I consulted. I read the word as a hybrid of flamboyant and refulgent, the latter the word Emerson used in the opening of his Divinity School address of 1838: "In this refulgent summer, it has been a luxury to draw the breath of life." See "An Address to the Senior Class in Divinity College, Cambridge, July 15, 1838" in *Ralph Waldo Emerson: Essays and Lectures* (New York: Literary Classics of the United States, 1983), 75. Surette turns Emer-

son's reference to the bright, shining beauty of the season into a sarcastic commentary on the American professoriate.

34. See Nadia Boulanger to Sophia Smith, April 25, 1926, Sophia Smith Collection, Smith College. The letter confirms that Surette had contacted the pedagogue on Smith's behalf. As a result of his advocacy, Boulanger wrote assuring Smith that she looked forward to having her as a pupil.

35. See Thomas Whitney Surette to Dorothy Smith, February 18, 1927, Sophia Smith Collection, Smith College. Despite his enthusiasm for Smith's staying in Paris, it doesn't appear that Surette supported her with monies from The Music Fund. I found no mention of it in their correspondence.

36. Ibid.

37. See Duberman, *Black Mountain*, 92. Duberman attributes an overriding concern with developing the individual to the man who would become the first rector of Black Mountain College, Frank Aydelotte's brother-in-law, John Andrew Rice.

38. Surette to Smith, November 14, 1927.

39. See Henry Allen Moe to [Aaron Copland], February 23, 1925, Aaron Copland files, John Simon Guggenheim Memorial Foundation. The requirement that fellows go abroad was immediately challenged by Copland, who, having just returned from three years in Europe, argued successfully that he be allowed to spend part of his fellowship year in the United States.

40. See Aaron Copland to Thomas Whitney Surette, March 1925 letter (no more precise date given), Aaron Copland files, John Simon Guggenheim Memorial Foundation. Surette was never a trustee of the foundation, but such distinctions were likely beyond the young Copland, who had little exposure to institutional hierarchies and their titles at the time.

41. See Aaron Copland to Thomas Whitney Surette, April 15, 1925, Aaron Copland files, John Simon Guggenheim Memorial Foundation.

42. See Howard Pollack, *Aaron Copland: The Life and Work of an Uncommon Man* (New York: Henry Holt, 1999), 137–138. Copland's action was the first of many dedications that fellows would make to each other and to foundation personnel.

43. If the foundation's initial award announced its belief in Copland's promise, its unstinting support for decades and its network of connections provided the framework for his career. His success was used as evidence that it knew how to pick winners. Left unspoken is the role the foundation played in engineering and assuring his success.

44. See Alex Ross, *The Rest Is Noise: Listening to the Twentieth Century* (New York: Farrar, Straus and Giroux, 2007), 268, for Thomson's quote, taken from *Virgil Thomson: An Autobiography* (New York: Dutton, 1985), 254.

45. See Leah Weinry Grohsgal, "Chronicling America's Historic German Newspapers and the Growth of the American Ethnic Press," National Endowment for the Humanities blog, neh.gov, July 2, 2014, https://www.neh.gov/divisions/preservation/featured-project/chronicling-americas-historic-german-newspapers-and-the-grow. For specific studies of German singing societies in the United States see Mary Sue Morrow's essay "Somewhere Between Beer and Wagner: The Cultural and Musical Impact of German Männerchöre in New York and New Orleans," and Suzanne G. Snyder's essay "The

Indianapolis Männerchor: Contributions to a New Musicality in Midwestern Life" in *Music and Culture in America, 1861–1918*, ed. Michael Saffle and James R. Heintze (New York: Garland, 1998), 79–110 and 111–140.

46. See Gramm, *Oberlaender Trust*, 41.

47. Ibid., 39. It is possible that Moe interpreted this goal as potentially encroaching on Guggenheim Foundation efforts, but unlikely. By the 1930s there were always more applicants than Foundation fellowships, and his presence on the Oberlaender board would have assured that no trespassing occurred.

48. Among his friends was Albert Stuercke, who worked for William Steinway of Steinway & Sons. Stuercke got Oberlaender a job at the firm, where he helped Steinway with his German correspondence. See Gramm, *Oberlaender Trust*, 25.

49. Two years after his death in 1936, the trust initiated an ambitious scholarly project that continued Oberlaender's investment in music. Originally the goal had been a catalogue of autograph manuscripts by German masters held by American institutions, but over the years it grew to become *A Census of Autograph Music Manuscripts of European Composers in American Libraries*; Otto E. Albrecht, professor of music at the University of Pennsylvania, was put in charge. Fifteen years later, in 1953, the same year the trust ceased operation, the book was published by the University of Pennsylvania Press. Oberlaender had been a trustee of the University of Pennsylvania Museum in Philadelphia, and the institution was close to his heart.

50. Gramm, *Oberlaender Trust*, 46.

51. Ibid.

52. Ibid.

53. See https://www.penncharter.com/about-us/quaker-education.

54. Gramm, *Oberlaender Trust*, 41.

55. Ibid., 43.

56. Ibid.

57. All quoted passages come from the January 21, 1935, *New York Times* article "Schurz Relatives Fight Nazi Link." For a concise study of the situation see Rennie W. Brantz, "German-American Friendship: The Carl Schurz Vereinigung, 1926–1942," *International History Review* 11, no. 2 (May 1989): 229–251.

58. Gramm, *Oberlaender Trust*, 48.

59. Ibid., 65. The use of the male pronoun reflects not only common practice of the time, but also the reality of the situation. As can best be ascertained by the appearance of "Miss," "Mrs.," or full first names in Gramm's history of the Oberlaender Trust, only approximately 13 percent, or 32 of 245, displaced scholars were female. Making grants to institutions allowed the trust to get around government regulations that prohibited awards from individuals to individuals for the express purpose of supporting their emigration to the United States.

60. Gramm, *Oberlaender Trust*, 65.

61. See Harris, *Arts at Black Mountain College*, 75.

62. See Gramm, *Oberlaender Trust*, appendix B, 114–128, for a complete list.

63. Ibid., 83. The American Music Center was founded in 1939 by Otto Luening and Aaron Copland along with Marion Bauer, Howard Hanson, Harrison Kerr, a less well-known student of Boulanger, and Quincy Porter.

64. Bennington College was founded as a progressive women's college in 1932 and became co-ed in 1969. It was the first such institution to include the visual and performing arts as credit-generating components in a liberal arts curriculum. Martha Graham and Aaron Copland created *Appalachian Spring* in 1944, the final year of Luening's tenure at the college. By then Graham had received three Guggenheim Fellowships for choreography, in 1932, 1943, and 1944. Together Copland, Luening, and Graham received a total of eight Guggenheim Fellowships.

65. See Otto Luening to Douglas Moore, April 26, 1938, Otto Luening Papers, Music Division, New York Public Library.

66. Moore had taught at Columbia's sister school, Barnard, prior to his Guggenheim Fellowship, and so was known to the larger institution.

67. See Otto Luening to Thomas Whitney Surette, May 6, 1937, and Mary 24, 1937, Otto Luening Papers, Music Division, New York Public Library.

68. The other three, Marion Bauer, Howard Hanson, and Harrison Kerr, never received fellowships, although it is impossible to know from available records at the Guggenheim Foundation offices whether they applied. Bauer and Kerr had studied with Boulanger, and Hanson was among the first recipients of a fellowship to the American Academy in Rome, so all three enjoyed connections within the larger Guggenheim network of associations.

Chapter 5. The College

1. Bruno Latour, *Reassembling the Social: An Introduction to Actor-Network-Theory* (Oxford: Oxford University Press, 2005). John and Nell Rice divorced soon after his resignation from Black Mountain in 1940.

2. See Mary Emma Harris, *The Arts at Black Mountain College* (Cambridge, MA: MIT Press, 1987), 6, for additional information about investors and incorporation. Dreier was friends with Malcolm J. Forbes. Although Frank Aydelotte did not sign on as one of the official incorporators, the reality of his sister's and brother-in-law's tenuous financial situation meant that he contributed to their upkeep when financial needs exceeded the couple's means. Money problems grew when the Rices separated and then divorced. Aydelotte subsidized Nell, who continued to work at the college.

3. Stephen Forbes attended Black Mountain College between 1935 and 1938 and again between 1940 and 1942.

4. In the case of the Aydelotte and Rice families, their involvements were of a different kind: Despite John's eventually being forced out of his position as rector, Aydelotte's sister Nell served as college librarian for a time and remained at Black Mountain until 1955, when she went on permanent leave. John and Nell Rice's son Frank (named for his uncle) taught German there from 1947 to 1949. Aydelotte and Black Mountain paid the expenses for the Rices' daughter Mary to attend Swarthmore College in 1939–1940 and covered unpaid fees from previous semesters that John had failed to settle. After more than a year of being on leave or on sabbatical, John Rice officially resigned from Black Mountain February 17, 1940. Although John Rice and a few friends had been responsible for the original idea of the college, now the institution, but especially Frank Aydelotte, assumed financial responsibility for his sister's family's well-being after John left. The few thousands of dollars that the college spent to cover John Rice's debts constituted an

enormous financial burden for the struggling institution, whose faculty compensation often included only room and board, and an occasional nominal salary.

5. Harris, *Arts at Black Mountain*, 4. The French family also enjoyed a kind of dynastic relationship to educational thought. The senior French's son, Boston-born John R. P. French Jr. (1913–1995), was a Harvard-educated expert on social psychology. French Jr. received his doctorate in 1940 and became a program director at the University of Michigan Institute for Social Research in 1947. The French family's work in education and group psychology provided a useful resource for Rice as he imagined an open educational community.

6. See Harris, *Arts at Black Mountain*, 6. Although never stated outright in any correspondence between Black Mountain College personnel, it seems apparent that its founders held out hope that Surette would make some kind of financial gift to the school. When he passed away, he bequeathed his substantial library to them, but that was all.

7. See Ibid., xx.

8. See Martin Duberman, *Black Mountain: An Exploration in Community* (Evanston, IL: Northwestern University Press, 1972), 94. Including illustrious thinkers on its Advisory Board was one way the college attempted to increase its prestige in the early years; this remains established practice today. In later years Albert Einstein was named an advisor, as were Franz Kline and William Carlos Williams, among others. Duberman characterized the new board as "strictly *pro forma*, but nonetheless dazzling in its array of names" (see 535 n65).

9. Theodore (Ted) Dreier to John Dewey, July 13, 1940. Dewey responded July 18, providing an endorsement along the lines of Dreier's suggestion. See the John Dewey Papers, 1937–1947, within the Theodore Dreier Papers, Western Regional Archives, State Archives of North Carolina, Raleigh.

10. See Duberman, *Black Mountain*, 323. For a list of donors as named in a 1942 letter from Fred Mangold to Ruth O'Neill, see ibid., where Mangold explains: "Most of our really large donations come from friends of the College in New York and Massachusetts who wish to remain anonymous. However, such people have helped us considerably as Dr. Frank Aydelotte of the Institute of Advanced Study, Mrs. Marcy C. Draper, Mr. and Mrs. H. Edward Dreier of Brooklyn, New York, Mr. Marshall Field of New York, Mrs. Daniel P. Rhodes of Brookline, Massachusetts, Mr. Edward Warburg of New York City, etcetera" (483). Given the close involvement of Guggenheim personnel, it is no surprise that the majority of the college's supporters came from the same geographical region as the foundation's closest associates.

11. Dreier's paternal aunt, Katherine Dreier, was a painter and member of modernist art and literary circles. In 1920 she, along with Marcel Duchamp and Man Ray founded the Société Anonyme. It became the first museum devoted to modern art in the country, pre-dating the Museum of Modern Art by eight years.

12. As early as November 18, 1937, William Morse Cole, auditor for the college, expressed his concern to Dreier, who was treasurer at the time, regarding "the one-sided curriculum and faculty." He found the imbalance in favor of the arts "quite excusable" in the early years but questionable if the school was to function as a liberal arts college, as it had originally announced it would in 1933. See William Morse Cole to Theodore Dreier, November 18, 1937, Western Regional Archives, State Archives of North Carolina.

13. See *Remembering Black Mountain College*, the exhibition guide curated by Mary Emma Harris in 1995, based on recollections gathered from approximately one hundred attendees at the October 28, 1995, reunion. *Remembering Black Mountain College* (Black Mountain, NC: Black Mountain College Museum and Arts Center, 1996).

14. Surette would distinguish his goals from those of the larger community music movement, however, which he believed were more social than musical.

15. I am grateful to Esther M. Morgan-Ellis for sharing the text of her paper "Sounding Whiteness in the American Community Singing Movement," which she delivered at the March 2022 conference of the Society for American Music.

16. See Theodore Dreier to Thomas Whitney Surette, September 10, 1933, Western Regional Archives, State Archives of North Carolina.

17. The most detailed description of the fund was provided by Surette in a letter to Theodore Dreier dated April 14, 1934, Western Regional Archives, State Archives of North Carolina. Dreier explained that he knew nothing about the fund and wondered whether the college could join. Surette explained: "The Music Fund is a foundation of which I am the trustee, which was instituted some years ago to provide money to further the kind of teaching I stand for. The income of this fund, like that of most foundations, has been considerably reduced, and I now spend the money to help individuals who are preparing to teach music or who are teaching it to get more training."

18. Musicologist Amy C. Beal has written extensively about John Evarts and his roles as the coordinator of music officers and a cultural administrator in postwar Germany in her article "Negotiating Cultural Allies: American Music in Darmstadt, 1946–1956," *Journal of the American Musicological Society* 53, no. 1 (Spring 2000): 105–139, and in her book *New Music, New Allies: American Experimental Music in West Germany from the Zero Hour to Reunification* (Berkeley: University of California Press, 2006), 30–46. Evarts may be better known and appreciated for his impact on music culture in Germany than in the United States. The Federal Republic of Germany awarded John Evarts its Distinguished Service Cross in 1986 for his role in reestablishing German musical culture after World War II, despite his having been dismissed from his U.S. military position because of his homosexuality. See Beal, *New Music, New Allies*, 31–32.

19. For information about the Progressive-era organization Better Homes in America and especially its campaign to encourage prospective home buyers to consider the people living in a neighborhood before building or purchasing there, see Eric Wycoff Rogers, "Planning the Family: The Better Homes in America Campaign and the Economics of the Household," https://www.academia.edu/9664776/Planning_the_Family_The_Better_Homes_in_America_Campaign_and_the_Economics_of_the_Household. Without stating outright the desirability of segregated neighborhoods, the message is clear, and it is directed at white homeowners.

20. See Theodore Dreier to Thomas Whitney Surette, September 10, 1933, Western Regional Archives, State Archives of North Carolina. This is not unlike the situation in many smaller music programs today, in which instrumentalists also teach academic courses without specialized training in those areas.

21. See Thomas Whitney Surette to Theodore Dreier, September 14, 1933, Western Regional Archives, State Archives of North Carolina. Given Surette's practice of listing a

student's Jewishness on the cards he kept on all official Concord Music School students, one wonders if in this instance the young man's Jewishness was enough to raise concerns about whether he would fit in.

22. See Drier to Surette, September 10, 1933.

23. See Henry Allen Moe to Fredrick Mangold, April 15, 1940, Western Regional Archives, State Archives of North Carolina.

24. See Theodore Dreier to Thomas Whitney Surette, November 8, 1933, Western Regional Archives, State Archives of North Carolina.

25. Theodore Dreier to Thomas Whitney Surette, September 24, 1933, Western Regional Archives, State Archives of North Carolina.

26. Ibid.

27. Ibid. Surette's lack of earned educational credentials wasn't widely known at the college, not even by officers who were present at its founding. When creating a new college catalogue announcing faculty for the 1938–1939 school year, Frederick Mangold, secretary of the Black Mountain Board, asked Surette to provide a list of his degrees. I haven't found any evidence of a response to Mangold's inquiry. Surette was to be appointed professor of music and poetry for the following academic year, but a stroke that he suffered in December 1938 cut short his appointment. Frederick Mangold to Thomas Whitney Surette, April 19, 1938, Western Regional Archives, State Archives of North Carolina.

28. Dreier to Surette, September 24, 1933.

29. Ibid.

30. See Thomas Whitney Surette to Theodore Dreier, September 28, 1933, Western Regional Archives, State Archives of North Carolina.

31. Together Shawn and St. Denis created the legendary dance festival in Becket, Massachusetts, in the Berkshire Mountains, that would morph into Jacob's Pillow. In 2003 the property formerly belonging to Ted Shawn was declared a National Historic Landmark District. It was cited for being "an exceptional cultural venue that holds value for all Americans." According to the Jacob's Pillow website, "The Denishawn Company had popularized a revolutionary dance form rooted in theatrical and multicultural traditions rather than those of European ballet." See http://www.jacobspillow.org /exhibits-archives/history.

32. Theodore Dreier to Thomas Whitney Surette, January 26, 1934 ("rousing college songs"), and February 14, 1934, Western Regional Archives, State Archives of North Carolina.

33. Elizabeth Ames to Alexander Byer, October 4, 1933. Byer, a painter, had befriended Fiorillo and was concerned for his well-being. Marion Sheffeld's Northampton, Massachusetts, home became a regular retreat for Fiorillo in the years immediately following his Yaddo residency. Yaddo Records, New York Public Library.

34. Fiorillo's lack of traditional academic credentials mirrored Surette's, although the latter never endured the impoverished living conditions Fiorillo did. Despite Surette's having patched together educational experiences at prestigious institutions, it is possible that he felt some empathy with Fiorillo.

35. Dante Fiorillo to Elizabeth Ames, March 1935, Yaddo Records, New York Public Library.

36. It is another of many ironies that *American* music and contemporary composers were foreign to Surette, who was responsible for supporting them in his role as Guggenheim music advisor. Surette's limitations were shared by many others, however, which made the Yaddo festivals all the more important to young American composers.

37. Quoted words and phrases come from Copland's letter of recommendation, which was stamped received by the Guggenheim Foundation on two occasions, Nov. (?) 29 (?), 1933, and January 8, 1934. In a letter to Moe, Luening volunteered his enthusiasm for Fiorillo as well as remarking on his "unusual talent" and his own willingness to "stake what reputation I have on this fellow and throw in my shirt to boot." See Otto Luening to Henry Allen Moe, August 2, 1935, Otto Luening Papers, New York Public Library.

38. In 1935 the Board of Trustees included the original seven members named in the foundation's charter: Simon and Olga Hirsh Guggenheim, Charles Earl, Carroll A. Wilson, Charles D. Hilles, Francis H. Brownell, and Roger W. Straus. See *The John Simon Guggenheim Memorial Foundation, 1925–2000: A Seventy-Fifth Anniversary Record*, ed. G. Thomas Tanselle, Peter F. Kardon, and Eunice R. Schwager (New York: John Simon Guggenheim Memorial Foundation, 2001), 76. Given their presence on the board, Simon and Olga Guggenheim themselves approved the financial arrangement.

39. See Harris, *Arts at Black Mountain College*, 35. According to Harris, Moe advised Dreier that Fiorillo "required two quarts of milk a day in addition to the regular meals and a thermos of warm milk should be placed by his bedside each night." Surette explained to Dreier that he was writing to Moe regarding clearing up Fiorillo's debts. In mid-November Moe was still trying to get information from Fiorillo regarding his debts and the location of his manuscripts. See Thomas Whitney Surette to Theodore Dreier, October 22, 1935, letter from Surette to Dreier, Western Regional Archives, State Archives of North Carolina.

40. A September 30, 1935, letter from Moe to Luening regarding Fiorillo's passport troubles explains that the foundation had proved Fiorillo's citizenship to the satisfaction of the State Department, but now he wouldn't be going abroad because his mother was ill. It's possible that Fiorillo's passport problems began with questions related to his precise birthdate and year. Although his death certificate lists his birthdate as July 4, 1905, the 1930 U.S. Census lists his birth year as "ab[ou]t 1905." The 1940 census estimated his birth year as "ab[ou]t 1907." Household members named at the bottom of the 1940 census list Dante Fiorillo's age as 33, which would be consistent with a 1907 birth year. Just weeks earlier, in an August 2, 1935, letter from Luening to Moe, Luening had expressed his hope that Dante would stick to the most recent plan of action and visit Germany in December, but that never happened. Letters quoted courtesy of André Bernard of the John Simon Guggenheim Memorial Foundation. Luening had become increasingly involved in musical matters at the foundation as early as 1930. In November 1934 Surette and Moe asked Luening's advice about two works by Virgil Thomson. Prior to soliciting Luening's input, Surette had asked Robert Delaney to comment. Delaney won Guggenheim composition awards in 1929 and 1930.

41. In a letter to Dreier, Moe explained that Thomas Whitney Surette acknowledged (presumably to Moe) that Dante Fiorillo was at Black Mountain College at Surette's instigation. Henry Allen Moe to Theodore Dreier, October 10, 1935, Western Regional Archives, State Archives of North Carolina.

42. See Thomas Whitney Surette to Theodore Dreier, July 20, 1935, regarding Edith Vail; Theodore Dreier to Thomas Whitney Surette, July 23, 1935, stating that he regarded Sly as a "great find" both in Western Regional Archives, State Archives of North Carolina. Efforts to locate information about Edith Vail have not yielded any results. Vail does not appear in any records for the Concord Summer School, and she is not indexed in the Duberman, *Black Mountain*, or Harris, *Arts at Black Mountain College*, although Harris lists her in "Faculty and Other Teaching Positions" (268) and in "Faculty and Student[s]" (276). It is possible that she had attended Surette's summer school and her records have been lost.

43. See Duberman, *Black Mountain*; Anna Hines, "Music at Black Mountain College: A Study of Experimental Ideas in Music" (PhD diss., University of Missouri, 1973); and Harris, *Arts at Black Mountain College*.

44. See Harris, *Arts at Black Mountain College*, 36. The author quotes from Ted Dreier's Black Mountain College papers, as well as a conversation with Sly of September 12, 1981.

45. See Harris, *Arts at Black Mountain College*, 47.

46. Allan Sly Tape 3, quoted courtesy of Western Regional Archives, State Archives of North Carolina. All passages from the Allan Sly tapes are quoted courtesy of Western Regional Archives, State Archives of North Carolina.

47. Allan Sly Tape 3.

48. Allan Sly Tape 2. While at Black Mountain, Sly recalled seeing Fiorillo leave a meal to go "down to the music cottage where he knew [manuscripts of various piano works] were on a shelf and took them away and I never saw them again." Quoted from Allan Sly Tape 3. In a letter of April 29, 1937, Sly asked Fiorillo to please return scores that the composer had borrowed before leaving Black Mountain College. They included four of Fiorillo's piano suites and the two-piano reduction of the concertino that Sly was preparing for the Toronto performance.

49. See Harris, *Arts at Black Mountain College*, 35, quoted from an interview Harris had with Sly on July 21, 1978. Fiorillo's mastery of established musical customs, idioms, and forms would have argued in his favor for Thomas Whitney Surette.

50. Regarding Fiorillo's introducing him to Yaddo, see Allan Sly Tape 2. The remainder of quoted passage is from Allan Sly Tape 3.

51. Sly recalled talking with Sir Thomas Beecham and the English-Scottish piano duo Bartlett and Robertson, attempting to interest them in his colleague's music. See Allan Sly Tape 3.

52. Allan Sly Tape 1.

53. Ibid.

54. Ibid. McGraw had studied chamber music with Jacques Gordon, the founder of the Gordon String Quartet, with whom Allan Sly would play. Promoting less frequently heard works was a hallmark of McGraw's career.

55. Allan Sly Tape 1.

56. Locating evidence to corroborate what is repeated in various sources has been extremely difficult. Redacted files, missing documents, and the refusal of those familiar with the situation to speak have combined to produce an effective, if not systematically orchestrated, effort to suppress research into this episode. I leave it to other scholars to pick up the trail and persevere. The goal is not to expose or shame possible wrongdoers; it is to consider how resilient networks respond to crises and endure.

57. Allan Sly Tape 1. Heinrich Kaminski published a total of twenty-nine works with Universal Editions. Once Hitler assumed the German chancellorship in 1933, Kaminski's Jewish heritage prevented his works from being programmed and heard. It is logical to think that he might have welcomed the chance to send his music abroad if he thought it would get a hearing.

58. Ibid.

59. Ibid. The Austrian composer wrote orchestral works, chamber music, choruses, and numerous pieces for solo piano and voice, about sixty pieces altogether, many of them large, multi-movement works. By the 1930s he had won multiple prizes for his works, some of which were published by Universal Editions. It's possible the fantasy-like piece in question was Kornauth's Fantasy in E♭, op. 10, 1912—1915 [arr. orch], or the Sonata in A♭, op. 4, 1912. See Gerald W. Gruber, "Kornauth, Egon," *Grove Music Online*, edited by Deane Root, http://www.oxfordmusiconline.com.

60. Allan Sly Tape 1.

61. See Lisa Hardy, *The British Piano Sonata, 1870—1945* (Suffolk, UK: Boydell & Brewer, 2001), 42–48.

62. Ibid. Hardy acknowledges the structure's similarity to Tchaikovsky's Piano Trio.

63. Allan Sly Tape 1.

64. Ibid.

65. Ibid.

66. Henry Allen Moe to Otto Luening, September 28, 1936. Quoted courtesy of André Bernard of the John Simon Guggenheim Memorial Foundation.

67. Henry Allen Moe to Otto Luening, November 13, 1936, quoted courtesy of André Bernard of the John Simon Guggenheim Memorial Foundation.

68. Otto Luening to Henry Allen Moe, December 2, 1936, Otto Luening Papers, New York Public Library.

69. Randall Thompson to Henry Allen Moe, November 24, 1936, John Simon Guggenheim Memorial Foundation. Quoted courtesy of André Bernard of the John Simon Guggenheim Memorial Foundation.

70. Goldschmidt learned from Karl Amadeus Hartmann, another German composer, that he had "received similar offers from Fiorillo" to get his music published. See Colin Matthews, "Berthold Goldschmidt: Orchestral Music," *Tempo*, n.s. no. 148 (March 1984): 12 n3.

71. Otto Luening to Henry Allen Moe, January 18, 1937, Otto Luening Papers, New York Public Library.

72. Henry Allen Moe to Ted Dreier, February 1, 1937, Western Regional Archives, State Archives of North Carolina.

73. Ibid.

74. Theodore Dreier to Henry Allen Moe, February 4, 1937, Western Regional Archives, State Archives of North Carolina.

75. Ibid.

76. Henry Allen Moe to Theodore Dreier, February 6, 1937, Western Regional Archives, State Archives of North Carolina.

77. See Aydelotte Papers, Swarthmore College.

78. See the report on Dante Fiorillo's renewal, March 18, 1937, Aydelotte Papers, Swarthmore College.

79. See Minutes of the Annual Meeting of the Board of Trustees, May 6, 1937, Aydelotte Papers, Swarthmore College. In 2022 dollars, $506 is the equivalent of $10,076 and $750 is the equivalent of $14,935.

80. See Otto Luening to Henry Allen Moe, July 26, 1937, Otto Luening Papers, New York Public Library.

81. On May 16, 1938, Sullivan and Moe arranged for Fiorillo's passage on the *Transylvania* at a cost of $260 for passage and $112 for room and board. They included some pocket money in their budget. Two days later Moe instructed Helen Daugherty to assure Sullivan that he would "attend to passage money," but knowing Fiorillo's propensity for changing plans, and not wanting to lose money, Moe requested an exact figure for "a deposit." On July 2, 1938, seven weeks later, the composer sailed to Glasgow, Scotland. From there he traveled to Cornwall, England, and then to Germany. He returned to New York on August 17, 1938, having sailed on the S.S. *Columbus* from Bremen, Germany.

82. See http://psychology.iresearchnet.com/counseling-psychology/history-of-counseling-psychology for a history of the emergence of psychological counseling. See https://dictionary.apa.org/interpersonal-theory for a brief explanation of Henry (Harry) Stack Sullivan's "interpersonal theory" and his foundational work in the field.

83. All quotations in this paragraph and the next come from John H. Davis, *The Guggenheims: An American Epic* (New York: William Morrow, 1978), 253–254. Davis cites interviews with Gladys Guggenheim Straus, M. Robert Guggenheim Jr., and James F. Mathias, a vice-president of the John Simon Guggenheim Memorial Foundation, as his sources. See 562 n1.

84. See "Guggenheim Heir Ends Life by Shot: Son of Simon Killed by Rifle Bullet in Hotel Room Here—Suffered Nervous Disorder," *New York Times* obituary, November 10, 1939. The story provides additional information about George Guggenheim's life, behavior, and last hours.

85. See "Lincoln Play Wins a Pulitzer Award," *New York Times*, May 2, 1939, 1. I have not been able to ascertain whether Fiorillo took advantage of European instruction with his scholarship.

86. The Institute of Musical Art had been founded in 1905 by Frank Damrosch. By the mid-1920s it had combined its board with that of the Juilliard Graduate School and in 1926 changed its name to the Juilliard School of Music. Referring to the Institute of Musical Art in 1939 suggests that adjudicators from outside the Columbia University music teaching faculty did not come from the Juilliard Graduate School faculty. See https://www.juilliard.edu/school/brief-history for a concise history of the early years of the school.

87. See the May 18, 1938, summary of foundation office activity created for Henry Allen Moe by his secretary, Josephine Leighton, who refers to Mrs. Daugherty's list of specific events related to Dante Fiorello including conversations with Fiorillo's wife Mary and with Sullivan, and Mary's report that pages of Fiorillo's Partita were missing. Daugherty wrote that Dante was being advised to sue Howard Hanson, to which Moe responded that he hoped Sullivan could dissuade Dante from that course. The range of crises provoked by Fiorillo can be suggested with the evidence that still exists, although a complete account is likely impossible to construct. See Henry Allen Moe Papers, American Philosophical Society.

88. See Thomas Whitney Surette to Theodore Dreier, October 22, 1935, Western Regional Archives, State Archives of North Carolina.

89. See the March 3, 1937, summary prepared for Moe by Jennifer Leighton. Henry Allen Moe Papers, American Philosophical Society.

90. See Ralph Vaughan Williams to Thomas Whitney Surette, March 13, 1937, William Munroe Special Collections, Concord Free Public Library.

91. Attempts to locate correspondence between Vaughan Williams and Surette or Fiorillo in the Vaughan William papers at the British Library have turned up nothing. I appreciate the help of Fiona McHenry, reference specialist at the British Library, who searched on my behalf.

92. See Ralph Kirkpatrick's article "The Challenge of the Harpsichord," reprinted in "Concert Bulletin of the Boston Symphony Orchestra, Sixty-Sixth Season, 1946–1947," originally appearing in *Modern Music* (Fall 1946), 550, http://worldcat.org/digitalarchive/content/server15982.contentdm.oclc.org/BSYMO/PROG/TRUSVolume6/Pub411_1946-1947_BSO_Subscription_Wk09.pdf.

93. See "Composers Give Concerts: Music of Homer and Fiorillo Is Heard at Forum-Laboratory," *New York Times*, January 8, 1940, 12.

94. See "3D Winners Series at Carnegie Hall," *New York Times*, January 25, 1942.

95. See "1,600 Youngsters See Dixon Conduct: He Directs the Philharmonic in an Elementary Program Before Alert Audience," *New York Times*, November 20, 1949, 83.

96. See "Music Prize Winners Led by Mitropoulos," *New York Times*, March 18, 1950, 8; "Camelia Memorial Held: 25 Colleagues of Late 'Cellist Give Free Concert as Tribute," *New York Times*, May 22, 1950, 28.

97. See Robert L. Simon, "Whatever Happened to Dante Fiorillo?" in *ComposerUSA* (Fall 2003), 5, 14. Simon took weekly lessons with Fiorillo from 1946 to 1948. *ComposerUSA* is the bulletin of the National Association of Composers, U.S.A., a nonprofit organization that succeeded the National Association of American Composers and Conductors. A response to Simon's article that appeared in the Winter 2003–2004 issue of *ComposerUSA* named four others who had studied with Fiorillo.

98. Attempts to talk with one of Fiorillo's relatives came to a sudden halt when it became known that I was a researcher working on a project focused on the early history of the Guggenheim Foundation. The family member was advised by an unidentified person not to communicate with me. I encountered another dead end at the Concord Free Public Library when consulting a scrapbook belonging to Thomas Whitney Surette. A small envelope that was labeled as containing four pieces of correspondence from Dante Fiorillo was empty except for a postcard. No record of its contents or their location exists.

Chapter 6. The Winners

1. David Mannes, founder of the Mannes School of Music, was married to Clara Damrosch, daughter of Leopold Damrosch and sister of Frank and Walter Damrosch. Roger Sessions's work with Boulanger was unofficial: He never enrolled in the Conservatoire Américain or paid her for private lessons although he regularly sought her advice regarding his compositions. Andrea Olmstead, Sessions's biographer, argues that Boulanger had loaned Sessions money and so knew that he couldn't afford to pay. Olmstead concludes that based on their longstanding relationship and interactions "Sessions was indeed a Boulanger student." See Andrea Olmstead, *Roger Sessions: A Biography* (New York: Routledge, 2008), 216.

2. Although not discussed in this project, the same principle of associations held for winners of the Guggenheim Fellowships in Music Research, first awarded in 1927, which were also overseen by Surette in the early years. Its first awardee, Nicholas G. Ballanta, received two consecutive awards (1927, 1928) based on the recommendations of Walter and Frank Damrosch, George Peabody of Yaddo, and Franz Boas of Columbia University. I am grateful to Anna Maria Busse Berger, a Guggenheim fellow herself, for sharing a draft of her chapter on Ballanta to be published in *A Search for Medieval Music in Africa and Germany, 1891–1961: Scholars, Singers, Missionaries* (Chicago: University of Chicago Press, 2020). The Guggenheim Foundation's Music Research Fellowships deserves its own systematic study.

3. The pronoun "his" is used purposely given the sex of all but one of the music composition fellows in the first twenty-one years of the foundation's existence.

4. This is the text from the act of incorporation of the John Simon Guggenheim Memorial Foundation as it appears in *The John Simon Guggenheim Memorial Foundation, 1925–2000: A Seventy-Fifth Anniversary Record*, ed. G. Thomas Tanselle, Peter F. Kardon, and Eunice R. Schwager (New York: John Simon Guggenheim Memorial Foundation, 2001), 32 (hereafter Tanselle).

5. The question of whether people of Jewish heritage should be considered white given different attitudes toward the meaning of "race" and the importance of the issue to the Guggenheim family is not trivial. For purposes of this study, however, the more contemporary understanding of "race" as a signifier of color in general, and Black and brown people more specifically, will be used.

6. Additional types of relationships may also have influenced the selection process. More than one informal observer of Guggenheim composition fellows has noted the predominance of gay males, but the same might be said of New York's music and art culture more generally, in which case Guggenheim composers would be a subset of a larger local population.

7. In 1942 Copland, Castro, and Chávez were among seven composers to contribute choral arrangements of folk tunes collected by Kurt Schindler (1882–1935) for a New York Schola Cantorum concert memorializing the late composer and ethnomusicologist. Afterward these composers' paths appeared to cross regularly. See Howard Pollack, *Aaron Copland: The Life and Work of an Uncommon Man* (New York: Henry Holt, 1999), 374.

8. The tightness and strength of Copland's circle was apparent at Yaddo. After the first two Festivals of Contemporary American Music in 1932 and 1933, which Copland had organized, critic Paul Rosenfeld observed that "too many Coplandites" were controlling the agenda. When the festivals were discontinued and then resumed in 1936 as "Music Periods," the organizing committee consisted of Otto Luening, Quincy Porter, Richard Donovan, and Ralph Kirkpatrick, all but Donovan Guggenheim Fellows. Kirkpatrick received a Guggenheim Fellowship in music research in 1936. While none of the composers would likely welcome the sobriquet "Coplandite," three of the four were still closely associated with the Guggenheim network. Donovan was a professor of music at Yale University and president of the American Composers Alliance. In the late 1920s he was affiliated with the PAAC and served as director of the Yaddo Corporation. For the phrase "too many Coplandites" see Tim Page, quoting Rosenfeld, in "The Trailblazer: Aaron Copland and the Festivals of American Music" in *Yaddo: Making American Culture*, ed. Micki McGee (New York: Columbia University Press, 2008), 36. See https://archives.yale.edu/repositories/6/resources/10620 for information on Richard Donavan.

9. Along with Varèse and Cowell, composer members of the PAAC included George Antheil, Charles Ives, Wallingford Riegger, and Carlos Salzedo. Ives provided financial support, and Nicolas Slonimsky conducted the majority of orchestral performances, with Adolph Weiss conducting the remaining multi-instrumental works. Imre Weisshaus and Stephanie Schenatowitsch performed the pianist's duties.

10. See David Nicholls's review of *Edgard Varèse: Composer, Sound Sculptor, Visionary*, ed. Felix Meyer and Heidy Zimmermann (Woodbridge, Suffolk, UK: Boydell, 2006), in *Music and Letters* 88, no. 4 (November 2007): 704.

11. Carol Oja nuances the situation by demonstrating that the Copland-Sessions concert series was more eclectic in its programming choices than was the ICG, at least in the second year of its three-year existence. The reputation that the series had for favoring neoclassicists is more justified if one looks at the composers included in the first concert: the Paris-based cohort plus Chávez. The second year, however, included works by Crawford, Weiss, and Rudhyar, composers labeled "ultra-modern." See Carol J. Oja, *Making Music Modern: New York in the 1920s* (New York: Oxford University Press, 2000), 196–197.

12. Carol Hess uses this phrase frequently to characterize the 1930s and 1940s in *Representing the Good Neighbor: Music, Difference, and the Pan American Dream* (New York: Oxford University Press, 2013). See page 4 for the first of many references.

13. See Aaron Copland and Vivian Perlis, *Copland: 1900 Through 1942* (New York: St. Martin's, 1984), 138.

14. I am grateful to the John Simon Guggenheim Memorial Foundation, and especially to André Bernard, for providing me a degree of access to the foundation's files on the six subject composers and finding a place for me to work. The crowded foundation offices were not designed to accommodate researchers, and I appreciate the unique opportunity that was accorded me. All composer files that I consulted there had been reviewed by Vice President Bernard, prior to my seeing them; he redacted any pages he considered potentially compromising. The foundation's admirable commitment to confidentiality,

even of files that are nearly a century old, makes easy or thorough research difficult. The numerous expurgations forced me to identify and explore over a half-dozen additional sets of papers related to Guggenheim personnel and fellows located in other collections. Ultimately, those collections provided a more complete and nuanced picture of what I was researching than I would have achieved had I depended exclusively on the foundation files. I am grateful to all the keepers of those collections, whose cooperation made this project possible.

15. See *League of Composers' Review* 2, no. 1 (January 1925): 26–28.

16. Ibid., 26. See Copland's later remarks on Antheil in "America's Young Men of Promise," *Modern Music* 3, no. 3 (1926): 13–20, and in "Our Younger Generation Ten Years Later," in *Modern Music* 8, no. 4 (1936): 3–11. Copland's positioning himself as judge of "younger" composers is noteworthy given that he was the same age as many of them, including Antheil. Antheil, born July 8, 1900, was actually four months older than Copland, who was born November 14 that same year.

17. See Aaron Copland to Nicolas Slonimsky, March 3, 1926, and Aaron Copland to Israel Citkowitz, July 12, 1926, in the Aaron Copland Collection, Library of Congress.

18. George Antheil titled his autobiography *Bad Boy of Music* (New York: Doubleday, Doran & Company, 1945), which speaks to a degree of self-conscious branding.

19. See Olmstead, *Roger Sessions*, 219, where she states that "it was Copland, with his ambition and savvy, who helped Sessions more than any single other person was to do." Despite the difficulty of quantifying "help," it can't be denied that Henry Allen Moe also exerted enormous effort to secure financial support for Sessions during his six years in Europe. The Roger Sessions files at the John Simon Guggenheim Memorial Foundation provide incontestable evidence of Moe's herculean efforts in that regard.

20. See Copland and Perlis, *Copland: 1900 Through 1942*, 125.

21. See Olmstead, *Roger Sessions*, 172. Olmstead refers to a letter from John Burk that mentions getting a Boston Symphony Orchestra ticket for "Copeland [*sic*]" (see 391n13), in Roger Sessions Collection, Library of Congress.

22. Quoted by Oja from a manifesto printed in the series's inaugural program. See "Celebrating the Copland-Sessions Concerts," https://www.americancomposers.org/copland_sessions_oja.htm. See also Oja, *Making Music Modern*, 235.

23. See Copland and Perlis, *Copland: 1900 Through 1942*, 144–145.

24. See Oja, *Making Music Modern*, 368. The December 30 concert also included works by Blitzstein, Cowell, Nikolai Lopatnikoff, and Bernard Wagenaar.

25. See "Carlos Chávez—Mexican Composer" in Henry Cowell, ed., *American Composers on American Music: A Symposium* (New York: Frederick Ungar, 1933), 102–106.

26. See Leonie Rosenstiel, *Nadia Boulanger: A Life in Music* (New York: W. W. Norton, 1982), 188.

27. See the remarks by Surette of April 6, 1926, and September 13, 1926, in the Aaron Copland files, John Simon Guggenheim Memorial Foundation.

28. Copland was not alone in recognizing that his mission was different from Surette's. Sessions biographer Andrea Olmstead observed that "Sessions . . . did not take Surette's ideas too seriously." See Olmstead, *Roger Sessions*, 270.

29. Harold William Thompson received awards in English Literature in 1925 and 1927; Clark Harris Slover received awards in Medieval Literature in 1925 and 1931. See Tanselle, 196, 205.

30. These awardees were concentrated in the social sciences and what are now known as the STEM fields: botany, chemistry, math, medicine, neuroscience, political science, and psychology.

31. Henry Allen Moe to Roger Sessions, August 11, 1938, Roger Sessions files, John Simon Guggenheim Memorial Foundation.

32. Paul Rosenfeld, *Port of New York* (Urbana: University of Illinois Press, 1966), 146, 148 (originally published in 1924 by Harcourt, Brace and Company). Given that *The Black Maskers* is likely Sessions's best-known piece and the only one by him that many musically knowledgeable people can name, some might question Rosenfeld's conclusion that it was "no happy hit." Rosenfeld was an enthusiast, and over the course of his career wrote panegyric prose about Ornstein and Chávez as well.

33. *Grohg* was revised significantly in 1932 and given its first complete performance in 1994.

34. See Copland's handwritten letter to Moe dated March 1, 1926, in the Aaron Copland files, John Simon Guggenheim Memorial Foundation. It is possible that "Cortège Macabre" (1923) and "Dance Symphony" (1929), both excerpted from *Grohg*, were what he was referring to when he mentioned a chamber ballet. "Two Pieces" ("Nocturne" and "Ukulele Serenade") were written in 1926 for violin and piano, and "Vitebsk" (Study on Jewish Themes) for piano trio was composed in 1928. The only oratorio per se in Copland's oeuvre is a reference to "Selections from an Imaginary Oratorio," which appears on page 12v of the "Notebook 1," which he kept while working with Rubin Goldmark. Gayle Murchison calls this "Copland's biblical oratorio." See Murchison, *The American Stravinsky: The Style and Aesthetics of Copland's New American Music, the Early Works, 1921–1938* (Ann Arbor: University of Michigan Press, 2012), 18.

35. See Copland and Perlis, *Copland*, 125.

36. See Henry Allen Moe to Aaron Copland, January 27, 1927, Aaron Copland files, John Simon Guggenheim Memorial Foundation.

37. As with other materials at the John Simon Guggenheim Memorial Foundation offices, I was allowed to see select files. I had no access to letters that Copland wrote for applicants who did not eventually win awards. It is impossible to know how he characterized the applications he rejected out of hand or found unacceptable or wanting for any specific reason.

38. See Nadia Boulanger, addressed to "Gentlemen," April 17, 1925, Aaron Copland files, and Nadia Boulanger to Henry Allen Moe, September 10, 1925, Roger Sessions files, both in the John Simon Guggenheim Memorial Foundation files.

39. In his sourcebook on Copland's Emily Dickinson songs, Larry Starr comments on Copland's setting of "Heart, we will forget him." He observes that "writing of this nature is the more effective for being employed sparingly." See *The Dickinson Songs of Aaron Copland*, CMS Sourcebooks in American Music 1, ed. Michael Budds (Hillsdale, NY: Pendragon, 2002), 34. In reference to Copland's 1944 work *Letter from Home*, Howard

Pollack, *Life and Work of an Uncommon Man*, commented on Copland's "characteristic detachment" (388).

40. Starr also spoke of Copland's "eminently practical and friendly public profile [which] flew in the face of the traditional Romantic imagery and mythology concerning composers." In quoting the composer when talking about the *Twelve Poems of Emily Dickinson* Starr singles out Copland's remark, "Encouraged, I could fall in love with all of them!" and notes, "This is one of the strongest emotional statements Copland allowed himself in print about any of his compositions." See Starr, *Dickinson Songs*, 4. For the Copland quotation see Aaron Copland and Vivian Perlis, *Copland: Since 1943* (New York: St. Martin's, 1999), 162.

41. In Copland's report on the 1969 re-application of Robert M. Lombardo, which described two projects, he endorsed the first, which referred to composing an opera, but not the second, which concerned teaching pieces for young students. Copland believed that the pedagogically focused project was not in keeping with the aims of the foundation's music composition fellowship program.

42. See the Harold Clurman interview recounted in Copland and Perlis, *Copland: 1900 Through 1942*, 60.

43. Roger Sessions files, John Simon Guggenheim Memorial Foundation.

44. Given the extraordinary effort exerted by Henry Allen Moe on behalf of Roger Sessions and the thick file of correspondence that was exchanged between the two men over a period of years, the silence is deafening. Frederik Prausnitz's biography of the composer, *Roger Sessions: How a "Difficult" Composer Got That Way* (New York: Oxford University Press, 2002), has no entry for Moe or the John Simon Guggenheim Memorial Foundation in its index. The Carnegie Corporation and the American Academy in Rome are mentioned only in passing.

45. Sessions provided a comprehensive list of positions held to date in the application he submitted to the Guggenheim Foundation in September 1951. He withdrew the application in November on the recommendation of Moe, who informed him that the foundation discouraged former applicants from seeking third awards. Sessions's list of full-time academic appointments included Smith College (1917–1921), Cleveland Institute of Music (1921–1925), Princeton University (1936–1945), and the University of California (1945–). Among part-time positions he listed were the Boston University School of Music (1933–1936), the New School for Social Research (1933), Malkin Conservatory, Boston (1933–1934), the New Music School and Dalcroze Institute (1934–1935), the New Jersey College for Women (1935–1939), the Summer Schools of the University of California, Berkeley (1935, 1936, 1941), Colorado College (1939), Columbia University (1940), the Juilliard School (1949), and the University of Southern California (1950).

46. See Gordon C. Cyr, "Roger Sessions at Berkeley: A Personal Reminiscence," *Perspectives of New Music* 23, no. 2 (Spring–Summer 1985): 131–132.

47. Personal conversation with Ellen Taaffe Zwilich, confirmed by email July 5, 2020. Zwilich won a Guggenheim Award in 1980 and a Pulitzer Prize in 1983.

48. With Koussevitzky at Tanglewood, the two men continued a relationship they had started two decades earlier. Tanglewood and Koussevitzky became essential players in Copland's personal network.

49. According to Olmstead, none of the letters of recommendations survive in the American Academy in Rome archives file in New York. See Olmstead, *Roger Sessions*, 396n1.

50. In 1931–1932 Milton Katz served as Mack's law clerk. Katz later became chairman of the Carnegie Foundation.

51. See Henry Allen Moe to Edwin R. Embree, September 8, 1931, Roger Sessions files, John Simon Guggenheim Memorial Foundation. The Rosenwald Fund supported some of the most accomplished African American artists and intellectuals of the twentieth century including Marian Anderson, Maya Angelou, Rita Dove, Katherine Dunham, and Langston Hughes.

52. The Julius Rosenwald Fund remains under-researched by music scholars, although a study of the African American visual artists it supported, published to accompany an exhibit at the Spertus Museum, is an invaluable guide to one aspect of this remarkable early twentieth-century philanthropist. See *A Force for Change: African American Art and the Julius Rosenwald Fund*, ed. Daniel Shulman (Chicago: Spertus Institute of Jewish Studies and Northwestern University Press, 2009).

53. See telegram of F. P. Keppel to Julian Mack, December 20, 1932, Roger Sessions files, John Simon Guggenheim Memorial Foundation.

54. See Andrea Olmstead, *The Correspondence of Roger Sessions* (Boston: Northeastern University Press, 1992), 253.

55. See ibid., 242.

56. For significant correspondence regarding Sessions's commission from Coolidge see ibid., 248, 251–252, 252–254, 266–269, and 309–310.

57. See Henry Allen Moe to Lazare Saminsky, February 16, 1938, Roger Sessions files, John Simon Guggenheim Memorial Foundation. Moe asked Saminsky to verify when and where he had conducted a performance of Sessions's *Black Maskers* in Europe the previous summer. Saminsky wrote back that Sessions had failed to get the piece to him in time for a performance. Saminsky explained that he played Sessions's *Suite for Flute* at a lecture recital dedicated to "Music of the Two Americas" in Paris on June 6, [1937]. It was, unfortunately, not unusual for Sessions to fail to deliver a score that he promised or to report a performance that didn't take place.

58. See Olmstead, *Roger Sessions*, 175.

59. See https://www.bach-cantatas.com/Bio/Boepple-Paul.htm.

60. See *First Bulletin of the New Music School* (in conjunction with the American Dalcroze Institute), Roger Sessions files, John Simon Guggenheim Memorial Foundation. The address is listed as 9 East Fifty-Ninth Street, New York. Roger Sessions's and Paul Boepple's names are listed, in that order, in the center of the masthead. The Dalcroze Institute was referred to as the American Dalcroze Institute in the following year's bulletin.

61. See Sessions's letter to his first wife Barbara, September 6, 1924, quoted by Andrea Olmstead, *Roger Sessions*, 181. The italics appear in the original.

62. Sessions, quoted in Prausnitz, *Roger Sessions*, 147. It's unclear whether they parted amicably or whether Sessions was invited to leave.

63. See New Music School and Dalcroze Institute Season 1934–1935 Bulletin, 1–2, Roger Sessions files, John Simon Guggenheim Memorial Foundation. Under "Management," Paul

Boepple is listed as president, Roger Sessions as vice president, and Joseph H. Wechsler as treasurer. Ruth Wertheim is the executive assistant.

64. See Roger Sessions to Henry Allen Moe, March 13, 1935, Roger Sessions file, John Simon Guggenheim Memorial Foundation.

65. See Henry Allen Moe to Roger Sessions, March 16, 1935, Roger Sessions file, John Simon Guggenheim Memorial Foundation.

66. See Roger Sessions to David Diamond, November 17, 1937, reprinted in Olmstead, *Correspondence*, 288–290.

67. Ibid. Diamond had remained a close friend of Sessions and his second wife Lisl throughout their affair and attended their very private wedding despite others' distancing themselves from the composer. Sessions clearly felt abandoned by the young student he had befriended and cultivated when Diamond expressed an interest in studying with Boulanger.

68. See Moe's comments on Surette in Henry Allen Moe, "The Only Great Decider," Address to the American Academy of Arts and Sciences, Boston, Massachusetts, April 11, 1945, reprinted in *The Power of Freedom in Human Affairs* (Philadelphia: American Philosophical Society, 1977), 25. I am grateful to Naomi André for a conversation regarding her experience as a graduate tutor at Harvard. While seeking advice regarding how to teach obviously intelligent students who didn't come to class, showed no initiative, and were earning failing grades, she was assured that despite their poor performance they would never fail. Her conclusion was, "Harvard never made a mistake. If they accept you, you'll get a degree." Given Harvard's significant role within the Guggenheim network, it is not surprising that the two institutions had similar attitudes.

69. This was the case for most fellows but not all, as Crawford's case will make clear.

70. See Roger Sessions to Henry Allen Moe, January 23, 1928, Roger Sessions files, John Simon Guggenheim Memorial Foundation.

71. See Antheil, *Bad Boy of Music*, 7, 9, 10.

72. See David Savran, *Highbrow, Lowdown: Theater, Jazz, and the Making of the New Middle Class* (Ann Arbor: University of Michigan Press, 2009), 206, 297n147. The author's name is not given.

73. Duplicate copies of Antheil's Guggenheim application materials are housed at both the foundation and at the Library of Congress. A different chronology of where Antheil studied and with whom he worked is part of the George Antheil Collection at the Library of Congress. See "Biographical Note" in the George and Böske Antheil Papers (1875–1984) Finding Aid, available at https://findingaids.loc.gov. Antheil makes clear in his autobiography that he did not formally study with Boulanger.

74. The George and Böske Antheil Papers (hereafter Antheil Papers), Library of Congress.

75. See the typed, re-created application by George Antheil, dated August 10, 1925, Antheil Papers, Library of Congress.

76. See the marginalia on page 3 of the August 12, 1925, application mailed from Paris, Antheil Papers, Library of Congress.

77. See George Antheil to Henry Allen Moe, November 30, 1925, Antheil Papers, Library of Congress. In this application letter Antheil explains how he'll use the Guggenheim award money.

78. I am grateful to Charles Amirkhanian, who put me in touch with George Antheil's nephew, Arthur Antheil McTigue, executor of the Antheil estate, who granted me permission to quote the entirety of this document and brief excerpts. I thank Robin Rausch, head of reader services, Music Division of the Library of Congress, for originally sending me to Mr. Amirkhanian and for her help accessing the Antheil papers at the Library of Congress, especially during its closure as a result of the Covid-19 pandemic.

79. Antheil does not clarify how he defines "pure-bred" beyond pointing out that others of his caliber, Varèse, Ornstein, and Bloch, were not Americans by birth.

80. See Antheil to Moe, November 30, 1925. He compares European and American support "as a mountain to a molehill."

81. John Tasker Howard's 1941 remark is quoted in Beth Levy, "'The White Hope' of American Music; or, How Roy Harris Became Western," *American Music* 19, no. 2 (Summer 2001): 131–167; see John Tasker Howard, *Our Contemporary Composers* (New York: Thomas Y. Crowell, 1941), 133.

82. See George Antheil to Mary Curtis Bok, November 20, 1925, Antheil Papers, Library of Congress.

83. See Antheil, *Bad Boy of Music*, 134. Antheil is referring to a November 1923 concert in Paris.

84. Antheil's participation in this group is not unlike Copland's being befriended by members of the Stieglitz circle, although the latter group has not been subject to as much romanticization as has the expatriate French cohort.

85. See George Antheil to Henry Allen Moe, December 26, 1956, George Antheil file, John Simon Guggenheim Memorial Foundation. Antheil suggests names of possible Guggenheim fellows but takes time to explain "a little Scholarship" of his own that he provides to needy composition students. He attributes the idea to Bloch and Sternberg who taught him gratis. I'm grateful to Arthur Antheil McTigue for permission to quote from his uncle's papers.

86. The sum of $150 in 1921 is the equivalent of over $2,000 in 2022, a generous subvention for an artist. In addition, its buying power was considerably greater in Paris than New York at the time.

87. Bok removed all but the monthly allowance after the 1927 Carnegie Hall premiere of *Ballet mécanique*.

88. See Savran, *Highbrow, Lowdown*, 188.

89. Ibid., 206.

90. Copland's precise remark was: "Antheil is all they claim and more; one needn't be particularly astute to realize that [Antheil] possesses the greatest gifts of any American now writing." See *League of Composers' Review* (*Modern Music*) 3, no. 3 (Spring 1926): 15, for Copland's remarks about Antheil.

91. George Antheil to "Mrs. Rossell," January 4, 1927, George Antheil file, John Simon Guggenheim Memorial Foundation. Eva D. Rossell was just the third person hired by Simon Guggenheim. She joined the foundation on April 1, 1925, to provide secretarial help for Moe. On September 10, 1928, Josephine Leighton became Moe's assistant and the foundation's office manager. She stayed until April 1963, passing away only weeks before Moe's retirement that same month. See Tanselle, 33.

92. See George Antheil's handwritten statement of application received July 22, 1931, George Antheil file, John Simon Guggenheim Memorial Foundation, and in duplicate materials at the Library of Congress.

93. Randall Thompson had won a Prix de Rome from the American Academy in Rome in 1922 and was considered a thoroughly conservative composer.

94. In his 1945 autobiography Antheil is more forthcoming about the reasons he preferred to stay in the United States. He and his wife Böski had just moved to Greenwich Village. As he explained: "I was notified that I had been given a Guggenheim scholarship for study abroad. It was not entirely welcome. It was a *European* scholarship. We knew, now, that we should go back to Europe for at least a year longer, for, at my present speed, it would take at least that much longer to finish the actual composition of 'Helen Retires,' put it into full orchestral score; yet now, after the beginning of the third symphony, we longed to live in New York for just once, even though it was only a few months before the time the Guggenheim award stipulated I must be in Europe." Antheil, *Bad Boy of Music*, 263.

95. The nation undertook a serious bicentennial celebration of its first president that included the formation of a commission. Among the many resources it provided was an instruction booklet created by Esther Willard Bates on how best to honor "the greatness of Washington" in pageant form. For references to Williams's identification with Washington and his desire to create an opera with Antheil, see Paul R. Cappucci, "A Libretto in Search of Music: The Strain of Collaborative Creation in William Carlos Williams's The First President," *Journal of Modern Literature* 36, no. 2 (Winter 2013): 84.

96. See George Antheil to Henry Allen Moe, February 5 and February 23, 1932, George Antheil file, John Simon Guggenheim Memorial Foundation.

97. The typical Guggenheim Fellowship had carried a $2,500 stipend, the amount Surette had suggested when he was first engaged as music advisor, but Surette was free to adjust the award figure and divide available resources at his discretion.

98. Quote in Cappucci, "Libretto in Search of Music," 89, from the William Carlos Williams Collection, Box 1, File 23, Beinecke Rare Book and Manuscript Library, Yale University, New Haven, CT. Antheil's solicitous praise of Williams, seventeen years his elder, suggests a lack of awareness on his part of Williams's established position in American literature. Williams hardly needed Antheil's endorsement or assessment. The poet would go on to win the National Book Award in 1950 and be a finalist for the same six other times, be named U.S. Poet Laureate in 1952, win the Bollingen Prize in 1953, and win the Pulitzer Prize and the American Academy of Arts and Letters Gold Medal in 1963.

99. See Linda Whitesitt, *The Life and Music of George Antheil, 1900–1959* (Ann Arbor: UMI Research Press, 1983), 222. Other Antheil works played at the concert included *Death of Machines*, *Sonata Sauvage*, and *Airplane Sonata*.

100. See George Antheil to Henry Allen Moe, January 3, 1933, George Antheil file, John Simon Guggenheim Memorial Foundation. I'm grateful to Arthur McTigue, executor of the George Antheil estate, for permission to quote from his uncle's materials.

101. Antheil application, July 22, 1931. For information about Antheil's not meeting the book contract deadline, see Whitesitt, *Life and Music*, 303. It was never published. No string quartet appears to have been written in 1932, either, although a holograph score

and parts for Six Little Pieces for String Quartet are housed at the library of the Curtis Institute of Music. Whitesitt mentions a premiere taking place in August or September 1931 in Woodstock. There appears to be no evidence that it took place but only a reference to it in a letter from Antheil to Bok. If the dates given are correct, the work would have been completed and performed two months, at most, after Antheil proposed it as a project to be undertaken the following year. See ibid., 222. In a typed letter dated September 7, 1933, Antheil regretfully informed Moe that he had to abandon the Washington opera. See the George Antheil file, John Simon Guggenheim Memorial Foundation.

102. Starting in May 1933 Tibor Serly, a Hungarian-born composer and friend of Ezra Pound, attempted to work with Williams on the opera, but their collaboration failed when Serly suggested that Williams submit his ideas to a real librettist to fashion them into a form suitable for an opera. See Cappucci, "Libretto in Search of Music," 89–90. Antheil wasn't the only composer challenged by Williams's prose.

103. Antheil announced that the opera was scheduled to be performed in December 1933, but according to Whitesitt (*Life and Music*, 243), the premiere took place February 28, 1934, at the Juilliard School of Music. As is still true today, performances, and especially premieres, are often rescheduled to later dates, and sometimes they never occur at all.

104. This would mean Antheil had been in Europe for approximately two months of his fellowship before returning to the United States.

105. Among the evidence for the existence of the opera Whitesitt (*Life and Music*, 243) lists only a reference to it in a letter from Antheil to Bok dated April 21, 1931.

106. In 1933, 25 percent of the nation's workers were unemployed and verged on various degrees of destitution. In response, in 1935 the federal government enacted the Social Security Act.

107. In order to contextualize the situation regarding female award recipients in music composition and music research before and after Surette's tenure as music advisor, it helps to know that Crawford was the single woman named in either category during Surette's tenure. Between 1946 and 1966, however, three female composers, Louise Talma, Julia Perry, and Peggy Glenville Hicks, each won two awards, and nine women won a total of twelve music research awards: Helen Margaret Hewitt, Isabel Pope Conant, Angela Diller, Eta Harich-Schneider, Carleen M. Hutchins, Carol Cook MacClintock, Sylvia W. Kenney, Maria Ester Grebe Vicuna, and Janet Knapp.

108. The Chicago school of thought, led by John Dewey at the University of Chicago, would put the city on the philosophical map in the first decade of the twentieth century. For a brief explanation of the school see William James, "The Chicago School," *Psychological Bulletin* 1 (1904): 1–5, http://www.uky.edu/~eushe2/Pajares/jachicago.html. .

109. For Crawford's responses to Rudhyar and Cowell, see Judith Tick's essential biography, *Ruth Crawford Seeger: A Composer's Search for American Music* (New York: Oxford University Press, 1997), Chapter 4, "New Ways of Knowing," esp. 48–51. In the time since its publication, Tick's book has not been bested for its thorough research or its sensitive handling of her complex subject.

110. See reviews in the *New York Herald Tribune*, February 14, 1927, and *the Chicago Journal*, February 9, 1928. Crawford was described in one review as "the greatest woman composer of the day." See also the *Los Angeles Times*, March 18, 1928. Charles Seeger

was so concerned with the common perception that music was "women's work" that he purposely excluded Crawford from the meeting at which the New York Musicological Society was founded. See Ellie M. Hisama, *Gendering Musical Modernism: The Music of Ruth Crawford, Marion Bauer, and Miriam Gideon* (New York: Cambridge University Press, 2001), 18n8, for Seeger's recollections of his and others' thinking and motivations.

111. See Tick, *Ruth Crawford Seeger*, 110. Moe's remarks are taken from an interview with Dane Rudhyar by Sorrel Hays, March 19, 1984.

112. This is the only reference to a reviewer's being paid an honorarium that I came across in my research on the Guggenheim Foundation (granted, my project is limited in both numbers and types of subjects and the period of time considered). Lincoln Kirstein was not offered an honorarium when asked to review William Grant Still's application in 1933 although he was not a named referee in Still's application and never received a fellowship himself. The majority of other letter writers were named referees or former fellows. If money was exchanged for their reviewing services, it was not mentioned in correspondence I accessed.

113. As Barrett Ashley Johnson demonstrates in his 2007 dissertation "An Original Composition, *Galleria Armonica*, Theme and Variations for Piano, Harpsichord, Harp and Orchestra and A Comparative Study Between the Pedagogical Methodologies of Arnold Schoenberg and Nadia Boulanger Regarding Training the Composer" (PhD diss., Louisiana State University, 2007), although Boulanger became closely associated with Stravinsky and so positioned by history as opposed to the Viennese master's musical thought, Boulanger taught Schoenberg's music, and her pedagogical practices shared many traits with his.

114. Charles Seeger graduated from Harvard University in 1908 and then studied music and conducting in Cologne, Germany, before returning to the United States. It could be that his German connections influenced Crawford's choice of destination as well.

115. See Ruth Crawford to Henry Allen Moe, October 21, 1930, Ruth Crawford file, John Simon Guggenheim Memorial Foundation.

116. See Ruth Crawford to Henry Allen Moe, January 22, 1931, Ruth Crawford file, John Simon Guggenheim Memorial Foundation.

117. Ibid.

118. Ibid.

119. See Tick, *Ruth Crawford Seeger*, 113, for information about Gerald Reynolds.

120. The *Bhagavad Gita*, among the most famous Hindu spiritual texts, contains seven hundred verses of scripture and is traditionally attributed to the compiler Vyasa.

121. Crawford's friend and supporter Dane Rudhyar was among the most ardent theosophists in the group.

122. The most dissonant-sounding sacred choral work written prior to Crawford's *Three Chants* is probably Charles Ives's eight-part piece for mixed chorus *Psalm 67*, whose polytonal opening and closing sections likely tested the capacity of congregations in the 1890s for harmonic experiments in the sanctuary, although the clearly articulated text would have at least provided an anchor of some kind for listeners. See James B. Sinclair, *A Descriptive Catalogue of the Music of Charles Ives* (New Haven: Yale University Press, 1999),

270, for information on dating the work. Given that *Three Chants* received its premiere in New York in 1937 and was published in 1939, it is not known whether Crawford was aware of the earlier work or how she might have learned of it, although her closeness to Henry Cowell and his to Ives doesn't rule out that possibility.

123. See Crawford to Moe, January 22, 1931. Crawford set off the word "connections" with single quotation marks.

124. See Ruth Crawford to Henry Allen Moe, May 15, 1931, Ruth Crawford file, John Simon Guggenheim Memorial Foundation.

125. This could be because they were redacted from the file, although all other evidence points to the lack of letters. There are none in the Library of Congress materials. The dearth of correspondence from Moe is striking when compared to other files I consulted.

126. See Gerald Reynolds to Henry Allen Moe, May 29, 1931, Ruth Crawford file, John Simon Guggenheim Memorial Foundation.

127. See Charles Seeger to Ruth Crawford, May 9, 1931, Seeger Family Collection, Library of Congress. I am grateful to Robin Rausch for providing access to this collection during the Covid closures.

128. See June 1 handwritten note from Maganini at bottom of Moe's June 1 typed letter to him asking his opinion. Ruth Crawford file, John Simon Guggenheim Memorial Foundation.

129. See Charles Seeger to Ruth Crawford, May 5, 1931, telegram, Seeger Family Collection, Library of Congress.

130. Thomas Whitney Surette to Otto L. Myers, July 8, 1941. See Otto Luening papers, New York Public Library. Myers was the foundation's treasurer.

131. It is likely that Welch's application appealed to Surette. Welch had written a book very much like Surette's co-authored text of 1907. Welch's *Appreciation of Music* (1927) showed a similar focus on common practice forms and values. Unlike Surette's and Mason's earlier book, however, the later text included review and test questions, an indication that the volume was intended for use in classrooms. Welch's appointment at Smith College and his summer teaching at Harvard University from 1923 to 1930 would have provided an outlet for the book's adoption. His participation in the Music Teachers' National Association put Welch in a pedagogical orbit similar to Surette's. He never published a book based on his projected Guggenheim project.

132. See Thomas Whitney Surette to Otto L. Myers, treasurer of the foundation, July 8, 1931, Ruth Crawford files, John Simon Guggenheim Memorial Foundation. It is doubtful that Surette reviewed any of Crawford's music or would have been capable of doing so.

133. And even then, recognition has been late in coming. Only in the late decades of the twentieth century did the names of African American musicians and composers other than William Grant Still begin to attract serious scholarly attention: Harry T. Burleigh, Margaret Bonds, William Levi Dawson, Theodore Drury, Harry Lawrence Freeman, Eva Jessye, Sissieretta Jones, Scott Joplin, Undine Smith Moore, Julia Amanda Perry, Zenobia Powell Perry, Florence Price, and George Walker are just a few of the dozens of classically trained, practicing Black musicians whose work is only now being brought out of the shadows. I am grateful to Tammy Kernodle for conversations with her regarding Black

music communities and their distance from the world of the early Guggenheim administrators and advisors.

134. See the colloquy "Shadow Culture Narratives: Race, Gender, and American Music Historiography," Naomi André and Denise Von Glahn, convenors, in the *Journal of the American Musicological Society* 73, no. 3 (Fall 2020): 711–784, for a collection of essays illuminating other Black musicians and musical events seldom showcased in traditional music histories.

135. See Gayle Murchison's essay "New Paradigms in William Grant Still's *Blue Steel*" in *Blackness in Opera*, ed. Naomi André, Karen M. Bryan, and Eric Saylor (Urbana: University of Illinois Press, 2012), for multiple references to Still's early musical experiences, and especially pages 145–146 for the impact that opera recordings had on Still's love for the genre. Murchison's essay is invaluable for the insights it provides into many aspects of Still's life and works, and especially the dilemmas he faced negotiating the Black and white worlds he inhabited.

136. The "double consciousness" that W. E. B. DuBois identified as a requirement of successful Black Americans was essential for Still in his negotiations with the Guggenheim Foundation. See DuBois's article "Strivings of the Negro People," *Atlantic Monthly* (August 1897), and the better-known *The Souls of Black Folk* (Chicago: A. C. McClurg, 1903) for DuBois's discussion of this concept.

137. Barrère had been enticed to come to the United States from his native France on the invitation of Walter Damrosch, who wanted him as a flutist for the New York Symphony Orchestra. Once in the country he founded the Barrère Ensemble of Wind Instruments and then the Little Symphony Chamber Orchestra. Barrère was the dedicatee of Edgard Varèse's *Density 21.5*. With close connections to Damrosch and to Varèse, Barrère was firmly within the Guggenheim network.

138. See William Grant Still to Henry Allen Moe, February 15, 1932, William Grant Still file, John Simon Guggenheim Memorial Foundation. Encouraging Still to seek funds elsewhere would not be an unwise move on the part of the foundation, which understood its role as part of a larger network supporting promising young talent. Moe's early argument to Senator Guggenheim that his presence on other foundations' boards could advantage the Guggenheims' enterprise was likely a part of his effort to encourage Still to apply to the Rosenwald Foundation.

139. A music composition award to Juan José Castro in 1933 recognized a nonwhite composer, but his fellowship was part of the Latin American Program initiative that had begun in 1929.

140. See Naomi André, introduction to *Blackness in Opera* (Urbana: University of Illinois Press, 2014), 6–7, for a summary of the many ways Black stories and Blackness were depicted on the stage.

141. See ibid., 6, for André's argument regarding the critical role Haiti played for artists associated with the Harlem Renaissance.

142. Harriett Beecher Stowe's 1852 novel *Uncle Tom's Cabin: or, Life Among the Lowly* provided the origin for a number of derogatory stereotypes applied to Black Americans starting in the mid-nineteenth century including the "happy darky," "the mammy," "the tragic mulatto," and the "Uncle Tom" character.

143. See John Alden Carpenter to Henry Allen Moe, October 16, 1933, William Grant Still file, John Simon Guggenheim Memorial Foundation. Carpenter expressed dismay that Still was pursuing an opera that dealt with "the voodoo cult," which, he noted, had "tinctured quite a bit of his past work."

144. See the Olin Downes report received by the foundation on December 6, 1933, William Grant Still file, John Simon Guggenheim Memorial Foundation.

145. Both Forsythe and Moss were accomplished African American creatives, at home with Still's subject matter, comfortable with his operatic aspirations, and able to help him realize them.

146. Given Hanson's positive inclination toward Still, Moe's action hardly represented an effort to solicit a neutral or dispassionate evaluation. On the other hand, it might reflect Moe's lack of knowledge of composer-evaluators outside the insular circle of the foundation.

147. See Still's essay "Politics in Music" (1941) in *The William Grant Still Reader: Essays on American Music*, ed. Jon Michael Spencer (Durham, NC: Duke University Press, 1992), 144–149.

148. See letters from Still to Moe received by the foundation on May 23 and 29, July 21, and August 1, 1934. Still had the unfortunate habit of not dating most of his letters. It is fortunate that the foundation was diligent about stamping correspondence when it was received. Given the very efficient postal service at the time and the existence of multiple deliveries in a single day in many localities, many letters were sent and responded to within a very few days. When Moe and his correspondents were both in New York or close by, responses were often sent the same day the original letters were posted.

149. See Henry Allen Moe to William Grant Still, November 13, 1934, William Grant Still file, John Simon Guggenheim Memorial Foundation.

150. The Uncle Remus stories were the creation of white southern author Joel Chandler Harris, who purportedly based his stories, which he tells in dialect, on those he heard from enslaved men and women, Uncle George Terrell, Old Harbart, and Aunt Crissy. While based on African folk tales and culture, their telling by a white southerner raises questions regarding appropriation and the perpetuation of derogatory stereotypes. See https://www.georgiaencyclopedia.org/articles/arts-culture/joel-chandler-harris-1845-1908 for background on Harris and the Uncle Remus stories.

151. See William Grant Still to Henry Allen Moe, received December 24, 1934, William Grant Still file, John Simon Guggenheim Memorial Foundation. Still appears not to have questioned the veracity of the stories or their dubious depictions of the Black characters.

152. Still's rabid anti-communist rhetoric and his apparent willingness to suggest names of possible communist-sympathizing musicians and artists put him on the opposite side of the witch hunt when Aaron Copland was brought in for questioning by the committee.

153. The two date stamps may suggest when the letter was received by the foundation (the February 11 date) and when the request was approved by the Advisory Committee (the February 20 date). With no explanation, this is purely speculation. Regardless of what the dates suggest, both are well *after* the deadline Moe had stated.

154. Catherine Parsons Smith believed that the Mr. Trask referred to is one of two men, either Sherwood Trask or Willard Ropes Trask. See Catherine Parsons Smith, *William*

Grant Still: A Study in Contradictions (Berkeley: University of California Press, 2000), 93. Based on an entry by Judith Anne Still, Michael J. Dabrishus, and Carolyn L. Quin in *William Grant Still: A Bio-Bibliography* (Westport, CT: Greenwood, 1996), it seems quite clear that the Mr. Trask to whom Still refers is Sherwood Trask, an Illinois-born educator and poet. He wrote the text and scenario for a work Still called *A Negro Etude*, for which a fragment from scene 1, "The Black Land," exists. According to Judith Anne Still, "A holograph of the conductor's score of Scene 1 . . . with stage directions and vocal parts and a facsimile of the complete libretto of 15 scenes by Sherwood Trask are in the William Grant Still and Verna Arvey Papers at the University of Arkansas Libraries, Fayetteville." See p. 104, W48.

155. The centrality of drums, drumming, and tom-toms is discussed throughout André's essay collection *Blackness in Opera*, but especially in relation to Still in Murchison, "New Paradigms in William Grant Still's *Blue Steel*," 156–158.

156. See a holograph of the libretto of fifteen scenes by Trask in the William Grant Still and Verna Arvey Papers at the University of Arkansas Libraries, Fayetteville, Arkansas.

157. See Otto Luening to Henry Allen Moe, March 12, 1935, Western Union telegram, William Grant Still files, John Simon Guggenheim Memorial Foundation.

158. See https://www.nytimes.com/1985/02/13/arts/opera-a-rare-performance-of-evangeline-by-luening.html for a discussion of the second performance of Luening's single opera.

159. Eventually Hughes pulled out of the project and the libretto was finished by Still's collaborator and wife Verna Arvey.

160. See Henry Allen Moe to William Grant Still, June 25, 1937, William Grant Still file, John Simon Guggenheim Memorial Foundation. The practice to which Moe referred seemed not to apply to Ruth Crawford.

161. William Grant Still to Henry Allen Moe, dated December 31, 1937, received in the Guggenheim offices January 4, 1938. William Grant Still file, John Simon Guggenheim Memorial Foundation.

162. The opera was completed in 1939, with Still's wife Verna Arvey finishing the libretto that Langston Hughes had begun. Hughes dropped the project when he left the country to cover the Spanish Civil War for the *Baltimore Afro-American*. Although *Troubled Island* was scheduled to be premiered by the New York City Opera in 1945 and then in 1948, it was finally produced by the same company in March of 1949. It received an enthusiastic reception by the audience with twenty-two curtain calls, but mediocre to condescending reviews by critics. See "Troubled Opera," *Time*, April 11, 1949.

163. Henry Allen Moe to William Grant Still, January 5, 1938, William Grant Still file, John Simon Guggenheim Memorial Foundation.

164. See William Grant Still to Henry Allen Moe, March 8, 1940, William Grant Still file, John Simon Guggenheim Memorial Foundation. The piece called for two choruses, one white and one Black. I'm grateful to Judith Anne Still and William Grant Still Music for permission to quote excerpts from William Grant Still's letters.

165. See Henry Allen Moe to William Grant Still, May 10, 1940, William Grant Still file, John Simon Guggenheim Memorial Foundation.

166. See William Grant Still to Henry Allen Moe, May 11, 1939, William Grant Still file, John Simon Guggenheim Memorial Foundation. Still doesn't elaborate who the people of color might be, but it is likely that he was thinking of any Black leaders inclined toward a more militant separatist and less assimilationist stance.

167. I don't know whether Sargent Johnson ever applied for an award based on the papers I consulted at the foundation or other materials available to me.

168. See Pollack, *Life and Work of an Uncommon Man*, 217, for Dukas's advice to Chávez. More than two decades after its publication, Pollack's book remains the most complete reference on Copland and his music.

169. See Oja, *Making Music Modern*, 374, for a list of performances of Chávez's music by the ICG, and the PAAC and at the Copland-Sessions Concerts.

170. See Aaron Copland, "Carlos Chávez—Mexican Composer," *New Republic* (May 2, 1928), 322–323, and Aaron Copland, "Carlos Chávez—Mexican Composer" in Henry Cowell, ed., *American Composers on American Music* (New York: Frederick Ungar, 1962), 102–106.

171. See Cowell, *American Composers on American Music*. The book was originally published in 1933 by Stanford University, which is near San Francisco and Cowell's Menlo Park, California, birthplace. It is clear from the title of the book and the composers who contributed essays that Cowell's understanding of what constituted American music went beyond the United States, and from the original publisher that Cowell was not confined by the dominance of the northeastern United States when it came to imagining where the nation's musical culture resided. According to Cowell's introduction, the book functioned as a symposium on "creative music in America" (iii).

172. Deane L. Root, "The Pan American Association of Composers (1928–1934)," *Yearbook for Inter-American Musical Research* 8 (1972): 54.

173. See Carol Hess, *Representing the Good Neighbor: Music, Difference, and the Pan American Dream* (New York: Oxford University Press, 2013), 48, for her quotation of Rosenfeld from his book *By Way of Art* (1928; repr., Freeport, NY: Books for Libraries Press, 1967), 281, 274.

174. See William Robin, "Mexico's Envoy to Modernism" *New York Times*, August 2, 2015, AR 8. Robin quotes Copland on Chávez as "one of the few American musicians about whom we can say that he is more than a reflection of Europe." The passage is an excerpt from longer statement that appeared in Copland, "Carlos Chávez—Mexican Composer."

175. See Pollack, *Life and Work of an Uncommon Man*, 222, for excerpts from multiple letters Copland and Chávez exchanged on the topic between 1931 and 1935.

176. See Hess, *Representing the Good Neighbor*, 35, for Copland's impressions of Mexicans during his 1932 trip to the country.

177. See ibid., 6–9, 40, for an overview of the controversial nature of the way Chávez was branded, and the role Copland and Cowell played in marketing the Mexican composer. See also Robin, "Mexico's Envoy to Modernism," reporting on that summer's Bard Festival, celebrating Chávez.

178. Hess, *Representing the Good Neighbor*, 4.

179. See ibid., 191, for a reflective summary of different historicizations of Pan-Americanism, sameness being one of them. The first movement of Castro's *Sinfonía Argentina*,

"El Arrabal," (The Slums), evokes the tango, a dance which has come to be closely associated with Argentina and lower-class life in sections of Buenos Aries.

180. Ibid., 129, quoting Garcia Muñoz, "Juan José Castro," 21, 226n106.

181. See Pollack, *Life and Work of an Uncommon Man*, 224, for extracts from Copland's December 1933 letter to Chávez, in which he reflects on what his Mexican colleague had accomplished and the impossibility of his doing the same thing in the United States. Pollack concludes that Copland's experience in Mexico "strengthened his growing resolve to communicate with a larger public."

182. See Leonora Saavedra, "Carlos Chávez and the Myth of the Aztec Renaissance," in Carlos Chávez and His World, ed. Leonora Saavedra (Princeton, NJ: Princeton University Press, 2015), 134—164.

183. See Edgard Varèse's statement "I dream of instruments obedient to my thought and which with their contribution of a whole new world of unsuspected sounds, will lend themselves to the exigencies of my inner rhythm," first published in *391* no. 5 (June 1917), quoted in *Contemporary Composers on Contemporary Music*, ed. Elliott Schwartz and Barney Childs (New York: Da Capo, 1978), 196. *New Musical Resources* is the name of Henry Cowell's 1919 treatise, first published by Alfred A. Knopf in 1930. It may be fruitful to consider whether Varèse was already thinking of an enlarged American hemisphere when he wrote his piece *Amériques* (plural America) in the years 1918–1921. I discuss possible meanings of Varèse's pluralized title in *The Sounds of Place: Music and the American Cultural Landscape* (Boston: Northeastern University Press, 2003), 127–141.

184. The situation was reminiscent of the foundation's choosing Copland as the first recipient of a composition award. It took an easy gamble given the critical acclaim accorded the premiere of his Organ Symphony in New York and Boston in 1925. Marketing was already done for the foundation, which in its debut year provided welcome confirmation of its existence.

185. The first two awardees in music research, each of whom received immediate renewals, were Nicholas G. Ballanta (1927, 1928) and Roy Dickinson Welch (1930, 1931).

186. This is not to say that Copland's *Short Symphony* is inaccessible or unappealing. Early performances were rare because of rhythmic difficulties—asymmetrical beat divisions and polyrhythmic passages—that challenged orchestral musicians accustomed to more traditional beat divisions or at least allegiance to a sovereign meter. But Copland had anticipated such rhythmic play in his *Symphonic Ode* of 1929. He sought to secure more performances of the *Short Symphony* in 1937 by arranging the work for sextet (clarinet, string quartet, and piano), which enjoyed limited success, but the *Short Symphony* as originally written became a favorite of Copland's friend, conductor Leonard Bernstein. Today the piece is no more rhythmically difficult than many contemporary scores; Copland just got there decades earlier.

187. Chávez writes for a large percussion arsenal that includes glockenspiel, side drum, suspended cymbal, woodblock, tenor drum, crash cymbals, maracas, claves, xylophone, tambourine, bass drum, and large gong.

188. Chávez wrote a second concerto, one for violin, between 1945 and 1950 and a concerto for trombone in 1975–1796. The piano concerto is a major contribution to twentieth-century keyboard repertoire. Unfortunately, its scant performances are likely the result of

its unrelenting difficulty. It is hard not to compare what Chávez accomplished in a single five-month fellowship with what Sessions and other recipients didn't accomplish with many years of support.

189. Henry Allen Moe to Carlos Chávez, March 17, 1938, Carlos Chávez file, John Simon Guggenheim Memorial Foundation.

190. See Pollack, *Life and Work of an Uncommon Man*, 220, for a brief discussion of the relationship between Chávez and Revueltas. The latter was never awarded a fellowship, although it is impossible to know what Chávez might have said or whether he said anything at all.

191. In the cases of all composers' files, it is impossible for me to say unequivocally that no such documentation existed at some time. My conclusions are based on the materials I was able to consult.

192. Henry Allen Moe to Carlos Chávez, June 4, 1941, Carlos Chávez file, John Simon Guggenheim Memorial Foundation. In 1941 the foundation made six music composition awards: David Diamond, a Boulanger student, received the second of three awards. Marc Blitzstein, another Boulanger student, Alvin Etler, who would receive a third award in 1963, and Earl Robinson received renewals of their 1940 awards. Paul Bowles received his single Guggenheim award, and Hunter Johnson received the first of two fellowships, the second being awarded in 1954.

193. See Hess's *Representing the Good Neighbor*, essays in Leonora Saavedra's *Carlos Chávez and His World*, and Stallings's "Collective Difference: The Pan-American Association of Composers and Pan-American Ideology in Music, 1925–1945" (PhD diss., Florida State University, 2009) as three works that devote significant time to Pan-Americanism in relation to music.

194. See "Rivera Mural Too Red, Says Mexico: Pro-Soviet Coloration Will Keep It from Exhibit in Paris," *New York Times*, March 10, 1952, 4.

195. In 1952, 10,000 pesos was the equivalent of US$1,157.

196. See "Rivera Mural Too Red." The article contains a detailed description of the depictions of Premier Stalin, Chairman Mao Tse-tung, and Uncle Sam, although Chávez never mentions the various foreign nations with which the Mexican government had friendly relations.

197. In 1952 Chávez ended the fifth year of a five-year term as director of Mexico's Institute of Fine Arts. Between 1933 and 1934 he had directed the Ministry of Education's Department of Fine Arts. According to Howard Pollack's assessment of the situation, the Communist Party "became especially influential in educational and artistic affairs"; Pollack, *Life and Work of an Uncommon Man*, 217. Chávez was especially vulnerable to political tensions because of his roles in both spheres of public life.

198. See Sydney Gruson, "New Rivera Mural Barred by Museum," *New York Times*, March 16, 1952, 28. Gruson was writing from Mexico City.

199. Ibid.

200. See "Visa for Chávez Approved by U.S.," *New York Times*, August 17, 1954, 17.

201. See Pollack, *Life and Work of an Uncommon Man*, 451–460, for a discussion of Copland's interactions with HUAC, his suspect political affiliations, the banning of *Lincoln Portrait* from a performance at Dwight D. Eisenhower's inauguration, and the prohibition

on sending his music to American libraries abroad, as had been the practice before 1953. These events resulted in Copland's appearance before McCarthy's committee, continuing investigations of the composer through the mid-1950s, and his eventual "official" rehabilitation starting with the Kennedy administration and with subsequent presidents through Ronald Reagan. It is a commentary on the times that while Aaron Copland was being surveilled and censored by the U.S. government, Diego Rivera complained of being censored by the Mexican government, and Carlos Chávez, in his official role as director of the Mexican Museum of Fine Arts, was involved in an action that resulted in an artwork's being eliminated from a scheduled exhibition in Paris.

202. See Hess, *Representing the Good Neighbor*, 118–120, 190, for an overview of multiple critics' concerns with Copland's musical take on Mexico despite the composer's admission that "all [he] could hope to do was to reflect the Mexico of the tourists." See ibid., 120, for Copland's acknowledgment and Virgil Thomson's characterization of the piece.

203. For the most focused study of Copland's alignment with left-wing ideals and its manifestation in his music, see Elizabeth B. Crist, *Music for the Common Man: Aaron Copland During the Depression and War* (New York: Oxford University Press, 2005). Crist gives nuance to the many meanings of Communism during the 1930s and 1940s and provides a framework for understanding how Copland's actions might have been interpreted by 1950s redbaiters.

204. See Crist, *Music for the Common Man*, esp. 27–31, for a discussion of Copland's political anthem.

205. See "Visa for Chavez Approved by U.S."

206. Whether any of these men actively evaluated Chávez's materials is impossible to determine. I saw no correspondence to indicate they did.

207. See Carlos Chávez to James F. Mathias, July 25, 1955, Carlos Chávez file, John Simon Guggenheim Memorial Foundation.

208. See James F. Mathias to Carlos Chávez, April 26, 1956, Carlos Chávez file, John Simon Guggenheim Memorial Foundation.

209. Pollack, *Life and Work of an Uncommon Man*, 216. For Parker's remarks see "Copland and Chávez: Brothers-in-Arms," *American Music* 5, no. 4 (Winter 1987): 434.

210. See https://www.gf.org/about/history.

Concluding Thoughts

1. Surette's distaste for the commercial aspects of music is ironic given his insistence that his songbooks be adopted by Black Mountain College and purchased by its students, his assigning his own monographs to summer school attendees and pointing students to where they could be bought, and his demand that the costs of John Evarts's attendance at his summer school be at least shared by the college although Evarts was one of Surette's protégés. Surette was not averse to the world of music commerce when it came to selling his ideas.

2. See Bob Gilmore, *Harry Partch: A Biography* (New Haven: Yale University Press, 1998), 103. Gilmore devotes considerable attention to Partch's relationship to Moe and to Partch's efforts to secure a Guggenheim award.

3. See S. Andrew Granade, *Harry Partch: Hobo Composer* (Rochester, NY: University of Rochester Press, 2014) for the most recent study of Partch, which includes several references to his Guggenheim Foundation experiences. Partch was one of the composers who had moved to New York. See page 238 for Granade's comment on Copland's more catholic tastes.

4. There is a single anthem of Spanish origin in his *Concord Anthem Book*: Tomás Luis de Victoria's unaccompanied four-part chorus "Jesu dulcis memoria," which appears in Archibald T. Davison's arrangement as "O Thou Joy of Loving Hearts."

5. Henry Allen Moe was thirty years old when the John Simon Guggenheim Memorial Foundation engaged sixty-two-year-old Thomas Whitney Surette as music advisor.

6. Harvey O'Connor, *The Guggenheims: The Making of an American Dynasty* (New York: Covici Friede Publishers, 1937), 324.

7. O'Connor devotes a chapter of his book to the Guggenheims' interests in Chile, at least until 1937, when his book was published. See Harvey O'Connor, "Chilean Transmutation," in ibid., 410–421.

8. See ibid., 478.

9. See https://nmbx.newmusicusa.org/social-news/12-composers-among-recipients-of-2021-guggenheim-fellowships. The list actually includes thirteen names. None of the 2021 recipients was on the 2020 list and would therefore have been a renewal. The reason for the discrepancy is unclear.

10. This is the case of a scrapbook in the Thomas Whitney Surette papers at the Concord Free Public Library, where an envelope labeled as containing four documents related to Dante Fiorillo has been emptied with no explanation or trace.

Bibliography

Adams, Kathleen Uhler. *Thomas Whitney Surette: A Crusader for Good Music*. Cambridge, MA: Windflower, 1983.

André, Naomi. "Introduction: Representing Blackness on the Operatic Stage." In *Blackness in Opera,* edited by Naomi André, Karen M. Bryan, and Eric Saylor, 1–10. Urbana: University of Illinois Press, 2012.

André, Naomi, and Denise Von Glahn, convenors. "Colloquy: Shadow Culture Narratives: Race, Gender, and American Music Historiography." *Journal of the American Musicological Society* 73, no. 3 (Fall 2020): 711–84.

Antheil, George. *Bad Boy of Music*. New York: Doubleday, Doran & Company, 1945.

Antheil, George and Böske. Papers. Library of Congress, Washington, DC.

Auerbach, Jerold S. *Unequal Justice: Lawyers and Social Change in Modern America*. New York: Oxford University Press, 1976.

Aydelotte, Frank. Papers. Swarthmore College, Friends Historical Library, Swarthmore, PA.

Beal, Amy C. "Negotiating Cultural Allies: American Music in Darmstadt, 1946–1956." *Journal of the American Musicological Society* 53, no. 1 (Spring 2000): 105–39.

Beal, Amy C. *New Music, New Allies: American Experimental Music in West Germany from the Zero Hour to Reunification*. Berkeley: University of California Press, 2006.

Blanshard, Frances. *Frank Aydelotte of Swarthmore*. Middletown, CT: Wesleyan University Press, 1970.

Bomberger, E. Douglas. "The German Music Training of American Students, 1850–1900." PhD diss., University of Maryland, College Park, 1991.

Born, Georgina. *Rationalizing Culture: IRCAM, Boulez, and the Institutionalization of the Musical Avant-Garde*. Berkeley: University of California Press, 1995.

Brantz, Rennie W. "German-American Friendship: The Carl Schurz Vereinigung, 1926–1942." *International History Review* 11, no. 2 (May 1989): 229–51.

Brody, Martin, ed. *Music and Musical Composition at the American Academy in Rome*. Rochester, NY: University of Rochester Press, 2014.

Busse Berger, Anna Maria. *A Search for Medieval Music in Africa and Germany, 1891–1961: Scholars, Singers, Missionaries*. Chicago: University of Chicago Press, 2020.

Cappucci, Paul R. "A Libretto in Search of Music: The Strain of Collaborative Creation in William Carlos Williams's *The First President*." *Journal of Modern Literature* 36, no. 2 (Winter 2013): 80–104.

Carlyle, Thomas. *Past and Present*. London: Chapman and Hall, Strand, 1843.

Cooper, Susan Fenimore. *Rural Hours*. Edited by Rochelle Johnson and Daniel Patterson. Athens: University of Georgia Press, 1998. First published 1850.

Copland, Aaron. "America's Young Men of Promise." *Modern Music* 3, no. 3 (Spring 1926): 13–20.

Copland, Aaron. "Carlos Chávez—Mexican Composer." *New Republic* 54 (May 2, 1928): 322–23.

Copland, Aaron. "Carlos Chávez—Mexican Composer." In *American Composers on American Music*, edited by Henry Cowell, 102–6. New York: Frederick Ungar Publishing, 1962. First published 1933 by Leland Stanford Junior University.

Copland, Aaron. Collection. Library of Congress, Washington, DC.

Copland, Aaron. "Forecast and Review: George Antheil." *The League of Composers' Review* II, no. 1 (January 1925): 26–28.

Copland, Aaron. "Our Younger Generation Ten Years Later," *Modern Music* 8, no. 4 (1936): 3–11.

Copland, Aaron, and Vivian Perlis. *Copland: 1900 through 1942*. New York: St. Martin's Press, 1984.

Copland, Aaron, and Vivian Perlis. *Copland: Since 1943*. New York: St. Martin's Press, 1999.

Cowell, Henry, ed. *American Composers on American Music: A Symposium*. New York: Frederick Ungar Publishing, 1933.

Crist, Elizabeth B. *Music for the Common Man: Aaron Copland During the Depression and War*. New York: Oxford University Press, 2005.

Cyr, Gordon C. "Roger Sessions at Berkeley: A Personal Reminiscence." *Perspectives of New Music* 23, no. 2 (Spring-Summer 1985): 131–32.

Davis, John H. *The Guggenheims: An American Epic*. New York: William Morrow, 1978.

Dewey, John. Papers. Theodore Dreier Papers. Black Mountain College Collection. Western Regional Archives, State Archives of North Carolina.

Douglas, Mary. *How Institutions Think*. New York: Syracuse University Press, 1986.

Dreier, Theodore. Papers. Black Mountain College Collection. Western Regional Archives, State Archives of North Carolina.

Drinker, Henry S. *Legal Ethics*. New York: Columbia University Press, 1953.

Drinker, Henry S., and Sophie H. Drinker. *Accademia dei Dilettanti di Musica: 1930–1960*. n.p., 1960.

Duberman, Martin. *Black Mountain: An Exploration in Community*. Evanston, IL: Northwestern University Press, 1972.

DuBois, W.E.B. "Strivings of the Negro People." *Atlantic Monthly* 80 (August 1897): 194–98. Also published in DuBois, *The Souls of Black Folk: Essays and Sketches*. 2nd ed. Chicago: A.C. McClurg, 1903.

Dushkin, Dorothy Smith. Collection. Sophia Smith Collection. Smith College, Northampton, MA.

Falconer-Salkeld, Bridget. *The MacDowell Colony: A Musical History of America's Premier Artists' Community*. Lanham, MD: Scarecrow, 2005.

Fitts, Elizabeth Crouch. "Aspects of American Musical Life as Reflected in The New Music Review and Church Music Review, 1901–1935." PhD diss., University of Maryland, College Park, 2009.

Flexner, Simon. "Wickliffe Rose: 1862–1931." *Science* 75, no. 1950 (May 13, 1932): 504–6.

García Muñoz, Carmen. "Juan José Castro." *Cuadernos de Musica Iberoamericana* 1 (1996): 3–24.

Gilmore, Bob. *Harry Partch: A Biography*. New Haven, CT: Yale University Press, 1998.

Gramm, Hanns. *The Oberlaender Trust, 1931–1953*. Philadelphia: Carl Schurz Memorial Foundation, 1956.

Granade, S. Andrew. *Harry Partch: Hobo Composer*. Rochester, NY: University of Rochester Press, 2014.

Grohsgal, Leah Weinry. "Chronicling America's Historic German Newspapers and the Growth of the American Ethnic Press." National Endowment for the Humanities blog, neh.gov, July 2, 2014, https://www.neh.gov/divisions/preservation/featured-project/chronicling-americas-historic-german-newspapers-and-the-grow.

Gruber, Gerald W. "Kornauth, Egon," *Grove Music Online*, edited by Deane Root. http://www.oxfordmusiconline.com.

Hardy, Lisa. *The British Piano Sonata, 1870—1945*. Suffolk, UK: Boydell & Brewer, 2001.

Harris, Mary Emma. *The Arts at Black Mountain College*. Cambridge, MA: MIT Press, 1987.

Harris, Mary Emma. *Remembering Black Mountain College*. Black Mountain, NC: Black Mountain College Museum and Arts Center, 1996.

Heclo, Hugh. *On Thinking Institutionally*. New York: Oxford University Press, 2008.

Hedrick, Ashley Geer. "'Music's Most Powerful Ally': The National Federation of Music Clubs as an Institutional Leader in the Development of American Music Culture, 1898–1919." PhD diss., Florida State University, 2017.

Heffernan, Charles W. "Thomas Whitney Surette: Musician and Teacher." PhD diss., University of Michigan, 1962.

Hess, Carol. *Representing the Good Neighbor: Music, Difference, and the Pan American Dream*. New York: Oxford University Press, 2013.

Hines, Anna. "Music at Black Mountain College: A Study of Experimental Ideas in Music." PhD diss., University of Missouri, 1973.

Hisama, Ellie M. *Gendering Musical Modernism: The Music of Ruth Crawford, Marion Bauer, and Miriam Gideon*. New York: Cambridge University Press, 2001.

Howard, John Tasker. *Our Contemporary Composers*. New York: Thomas Y. Crowell, 1941.

James, William. "The Chicago School." *Pyschological Bulletin* 1, no. 1 (1904): 1–5.

Johnson, Barrett Ashley. "An Original Composition, *Galleria Armonica*, Theme and Variations for Piano, Harpsichord, Harp and Orchestra and A Comparative Study between the Pedagogical Methodologies of Arnold Schoenberg and Nadia Boulanger Regarding Training the Composer." PhD diss., Louisiana State University, 2007.

Josephson, Matthew. *The Robber Barons: The Great American Capitalists, 1861–1901.* New York: Harper, 1962. First published 1934.

Kirkpatrick, Ralph. "The Challenge of the Harpsichord." Reprinted in the *Concert Bulletin of the Boston Symphony Orchestra, Sixty-Sixth Season, 1946–1947*, 546–58. First published in *Modern Music* 23, no. 4 (Fall 1946).

Leonard, Kendra Preston. *Conservatoire Américain: A History*. Lanham, MD: Scarecrow, 2007.

Leonard, Kendra Preston. "Excellence in Execution and Fitness for Teaching: Assessments of Women at the Conservatoire Américain." *Women and Music* 11, no. 1 (2007): 29–50.

Levy, Beth. *Frontier Figures: American Music and the Mythology of the American West*. Berkeley: University of California Press, 2012.

Levy, Beth. "'The White Hope' of American Music; or, How Roy Harris Became Western," *American Music* 19, no. 2 (Summer 2001): 131–67.

Lewis, George E. *A Power Stronger Than Itself: The AACM and American Experimental Music*. Chicago: University of Chicago Press, 2008.

Lewis, Mark. "Doing Business the Quaker Way." *Forbes*, October 9, 2009. https://www.forbes.com/2009/10/09/quaker-business-meetings-leadership-society-friends.html?sh=5a0c85929fa1.

Luening, Otto. Papers. Music Division, New York Public Library.

Markwell, Donald. *Instincts to Lead: On Leadership, Peace, and Education*. Brisbane, Australia: Connor Court, 2013.

Mason, Daniel Gregory. "Is American Music Growing Up? Our Emancipation from Alien Influences." *Arts and Decoration* 14, no. 1 (November 1920): 40.

Mason, Daniel Gregory. *Tune in America: A Study of Our Coming Musical Independence*. New York: Knopf, 1931.

Matthews, Colin. "Berthold Goldschmidt: Orchestral Music," *Tempo*, New Series, no. 148 (March 1984): 12–16.

McGee, Micki, ed. *Yaddo: Making American Culture*. New York: Columbia University Press, New York Public Library, 2008.

Miller, Robert Earnest. "The Raymond Walters Diaries: The Swarthmore College Days (1925–1932)." *Pennsylvania Magazine of History and Biography* 141, no. 3, Education in Pennsylvania History (October 2017): 369.

Moe, Henry Allen. "The Only Great Decider." Address to the American Academy of Arts and Sciences, Boston, Massachusetts, April 11, 1945. Reprinted in *The Power of Freedom in Human Affairs*. Philadelphia: American Philosophical Society, 1977.

Moe, Henry Allen. Papers. American Philosophical Society, Philadelphia, PA.

Moe, Henry Allen. *The Power of Freedom in Human Affairs*. Philadelphia: American Philosophical Society, 1977.

Morgan-Ellis, Esther M. "Sounding Whiteness in the American Community Singing Movement." Paper presented at the Annual Conference of the Society for American Music, Tucson, AZ, March 2022.

Morrow, Mary Sue. "Somewhere Between Beer and Wagner: The Cultural and Musical Impact of German Männerchöre in New York and New Orleans." In *Music and Cul-*

ture in America, 1861–1918, edited by Michael Saffle and James R. Heintze, 79–110. New York: Garland, 1998.

Murchison, Gayle. *The American Stravinsky: The Style and Aesthetics of Copland's New American Music, the Early Works, 1921–1938*. Ann Arbor: University of Michigan Press, 2012.

Murchison, Gayle. "New Paradigms in William Grant Still's *Blue Steel*." In *Blackness in Opera*, edited by Naomi André, Karen M. Bryan, and Eric Saylor, 141–63. Urbana: University of Illinois Press, 2012.

Nicholls, David. Review of *Edgard Varèse: Composer, Sound Sculptor, Visionary*, edited by Felix Meyer and Heidy Zimmermann. *Music and Letters* 88, no. 4 (November 2007): 702–4.

O'Connor, Harvey. *The Guggenheims: The Making of an American Dynasty*. New York: Covici Friede Publishers, 1937.

Oja, Carol J. *Making Music Modern: New York in the 1920s*. New York: Oxford University Press, 2000.

Oja, Carol. "'Picked Young Men,' Facilitating Women, and Emerging Composers." In *Music and Musical Composition at the American Academy in Rome*, edited by Martin Brody, 159–94. Rochester, NY: University of Rochester Press, 2014.

Olmstead, Andrea, ed. *The Correspondence of Roger Sessions*. Boston: Northeastern University Press, 1992.

Olmstead, Andrea. *Roger Sessions: A Biography*. New York: Routledge, 2008.

Page, Tim. "Opera: A Rare Performance of 'Evangeline' by Luening." *New York Times*, February 13, 1985, C22.

Page, Tim. "The Trailblazer: Aaron Copland and the Festivals of American Music." In *Yaddo: Making American Culture*, edited by Micki McGee, 31–40. New York: Columbia University Press, New York Public Library, 2008.

Parker, Robert L. "Copland and Chávez: Brothers-in-Arms." *American Music* 5, no. 4 (Winter 1987): 433–44.

Pepple, Joanna. "Americans at the Leipzig Conservatory (1843–1918) and Their Impact on American Music Culture." PhD diss., Florida State University, 2018.

Pollack, Howard. *Aaron Copland: The Life and Work of an Uncommon Man*. New York: Henry Holt, 1999.

Pope-Obeda, Emily. "This Deportation Business: 1920s and the Present." *Against the Current*, no. 182 (May/June 2016), https://solidarity-us.org/atc/182/p4640.

Prausnitz, Frederik. *Roger Sessions: How a "Difficult" Composer Got that Way*. New York: Oxford University Press, 2002.

Robin, William. "Mexico's Envoy to Modernism." *New York Times*, August 2, 2015, AR8.

Root, Deane L. "The Pan American Association of Composers (1928–1934)." *Yearbook for Inter-American Musical Research* 8 (1972): 49–70.

Rosenfeld, Paul. *By Way of Art*. Freeport, NY: Books for Libraries Press, 1967. First published 1928.

Rosenfeld, Paul. *Port of New York*. Urbana: University of Illinois Press, 1966. First published 1924 by Harcourt, Brace and Company.

Rosenstiel, Leonie. *Nadia Boulanger: A Life in Music*. New York: Norton, 1982.

Ross, Alex. *The Rest Is Noise: Listening to the Twentieth Century*. New York: Farrar, Straus and Giroux, 2007.

Saavedra, Leonora. "Carlos Chávez and the Myth of the Aztec Renaissance." In *Carlos Chávez and His World*, edited by Leonora Saavedra, 134—64. Princeton, NJ: Princeton University Press, 2015.

Saffle, Michael, and James R. Heintze, eds. *Music and Culture in America, 1861–1918*. New York: Garland, 1998.

Savran, David. *Highbrow, Lowdown: Theater, Jazz, and the Making of the New Middle Class*. Ann Arbor: University of Michigan Press, 2009.

Schwartz, Elliott, and Barney Childs, eds. *Contemporary Composers on Contemporary Music*. New York: Da Capo Press, 1978.

Seeger Family Collection. Library of Congress, Washington, DC.

Sessions, Roger. Collection. Library of Congress, Washington, DC.

Shulman, Daniel, ed. *A Force for Change: African American Art and the Julius Rosenwald Fund*. Chicago: Spertus Institute of Jewish Studies and Northwestern University Press, 2009.

Simon, Makhieba. "Carroll A. Wilson: A Brief Biography." History of Special Collections @ Colby, https://web.colby.edu/csc-history-of/c-a-wilson-bio.

Simon, Robert L. "Whatever Happened to Dante Fiorillo?" *ComposerUSA* (Fall 2003): 5, 14.

Sinclair, James B. *A Descriptive Catalogue of the Music of Charles Ives*. New Haven: Yale University Press, 1999.

Sly, Allan. Papers. Western Regional Archives, State Archives of North Carolina.

Smith, Catherine Parsons. *William Grant Still: A Study in Contradictions*. Berkeley: University of California Press, 2000.

Snyder, Suzanne G. "The Indianapolis Männerchor: Contributions to a New Musicality in Midwestern Life." In *Music and Culture in America, 1861–1918*, edited by Michael Saffle and James R. Heintze, 111–40. New York: Garland, 1998.

Stallings, Stephanie N. "Collective Difference: The Pan-American Association of Composers and Pan-American Ideology in Music, 1925–1945." PhD diss., Florida State University, 2009.

Starr, Larry. *The Dickinson Songs of Aaron Copland*. CMS Sourcebooks in American Music, No. 1, edited by Michael Budds. Hillsdale, NY: Pendragon Press, 2002.

Stewart, Abigail J., and Virginia Valian. *An Inclusive Academy: Achieving Diversity and Excellence*. Cambridge, MA: MIT Press, 2018.

Still, Judith Anne, Michael J. Dabrishus, and Carolyn L. Quin. *William Grant Still: A Bio-Bibliography*. Westport, CT: Greenwood Press, 1996.

Still, William Grant, and Verna Arvey Papers. University of Arkansas Libraries, Fayetteville, Arkansas.

Still, William Grant. "Politics in Music." In *The William Grant Still Reader: Essays on American Music*, edited by Jon Michael Spencer. Durham, NC: Duke University Press, 1992.

Surette, Thomas Whitney. "What Constitutes Good Church Music?" *Protestant Episcopal Review* 20, no. 1 (October-November 1896).

Tanselle, Thomas, Peter F. Kardon, and Eunice R. Schwager, eds. *The John Simon Guggenheim Memorial Foundation, 1925–2000: A Seventy-Fifth Anniversary Record*. New York: John Simon Guggenheim Memorial Foundation, 2001.

Thomas Whitney Surette Papers. William Munroe Special Collections, Concord Free Public Library, Concord, MA.

Thomson, Virgil. *Virgil Thomson: An Autobiography*. New York: Dutton, 1985.

Tick, Judith. *Ruth Crawford Seeger: A Composer's Search for American Music*. New York: Oxford University Press, 1997.

Trythall, Richard. "A History of the Rome Prize in Music Composition, 1947–2006." In *Music and Musical Composition at the American Academy in Rome*, edited by Martin Brody, 42–126. Rochester, NY: University of Rochester Press, 2014.

Uy, Michael Sy. *Ask the Experts: How Ford, Rockefeller, and the NEA Changed American Music*. New York: Oxford University Press, 2020.

Vaughan William, Ralph. Papers. British Library, London, UK.

Von Glahn, Denise. *The Sounds of Place: Music and the American Cultural Landscape*. Boston: Northeastern University Press, 2003.

Whitesitt, Linda. *The Life and Music of George Antheil, 1900–1959*. Ann Arbor, MI: UMI Research Press, 1983.

Wilkins, David Eugene. *American Indian Politics and the American Political System*. Lanham, MD: Rowman and Littlefield, 2006.

Williams, William Carlos. Collection. Beinecke Rare Book and Manuscript Library, Yale University, New Haven, CT.

Yaddo Records. Humanities and Social Sciences Library, Manuscripts and Archives Division, New York Public Library, New York, NY.

Yegül, Fikret K. *Gentlemen of Instinct and Breeding: Architecture at the American Academy in Rome, 1894–1940*. New York: Oxford University Press, 1991.

Ziffrin, Marilyn J. *Carl Ruggles: Composer, Painter, and Storyteller*. Urbana: University of Illinois Press, 1992.

Index

Page numbers in *italics* refer to illustrations and tables.

DENISE VON GLAHN is a Professor of Musicology at Florida State University. She is the author of the books *The Sounds of Place: Music and the American Cultural Landscape*, *Music and the Skillful Listener: American Women Compose the Natural World*, *Libby Larsen: Composing an American Life*, and *Leo Ornstein: Modernist Dilemmas, Personal Choices*.

MUSIC IN AMERICAN LIFE

Only a Miner: Studies in Recorded Coal-Mining Songs *Archie Green*
Great Day Coming: Folk Music and the American Left *R. Serge Denisoff*
John Philip Sousa: A Descriptive Catalog of His Works *Paul E. Bierley*
The Hell-Bound Train: A Cowboy Songbook *Glenn Ohrlin*
Oh, Didn't He Ramble: The Life Story of Lee Collins, as Told to Mary Collins *Edited by Frank J. Gillis and John W. Miner*
American Labor Songs of the Nineteenth Century *Philip S. Foner*
Stars of Country Music: Uncle Dave Macon to Johnny Rodriguez *Edited by Bill C. Malone and Judith McCulloh*
Git Along, Little Dogies: Songs and Songmakers of the American West *John I. White*
A Texas-Mexican *Cancionero*: Folksongs of the Lower Border *Américo Paredes*
San Antonio Rose: The Life and Music of Bob Wills *Charles R. Townsend*
Early Downhome Blues: A Musical and Cultural Analysis *Jeff Todd Titon*
An Ives Celebration: Papers and Panels of the Charles Ives Centennial Festival-Conference *Edited by H. Wiley Hitchcock and Vivian Perlis*
Sinful Tunes and Spirituals: Black Folk Music to the Civil War *Dena J. Epstein*
Joe Scott, the Woodsman-Songmaker *Edward D. Ives*
Jimmie Rodgers: The Life and Times of America's Blue Yodeler *Nolan Porterfield*
Early American Music Engraving and Printing: A History of Music Publishing in America from 1787 to 1825, with Commentary on Earlier and Later Practices *Richard J. Wolfe*
Sing a Sad Song: The Life of Hank Williams *Roger M. Williams*
Long Steel Rail: The Railroad in American Folksong *Norm Cohen*
Resources of American Music History: A Directory of Source Materials from Colonial Times to World War II *D. W. Krummel, Jean Geil, Doris J. Dyen, and Deane L. Root*
Tenement Songs: The Popular Music of the Jewish Immigrants *Mark Slobin*
Ozark Folksongs *Vance Randolph; edited and abridged by Norm Cohen*
Oscar Sonneck and American Music *Edited by William Lichtenwanger*
Bluegrass Breakdown: The Making of the Old Southern Sound *Robert Cantwell*
Bluegrass: A History *Neil V. Rosenberg*
Music at the White House: A History of the American Spirit *Elise K. Kirk*
Red River Blues: The Blues Tradition in the Southeast *Bruce Bastin*
Good Friends and Bad Enemies: Robert Winslow Gordon and the Study of American Folksong *Debora Kodish*
Fiddlin' Georgia Crazy: Fiddlin' John Carson, His Real World, and the World of His Songs *Gene Wiggins*
America's Music: From the Pilgrims to the Present (rev. 3d ed.) *Gilbert Chase*
Secular Music in Colonial Annapolis: The Tuesday Club, 1745–56 *John Barry Talley*
Bibliographical Handbook of American Music *D. W. Krummel*
Goin' to Kansas City *Nathan W. Pearson Jr.*
"Susanna," "Jeanie," and "The Old Folks at Home": The Songs of Stephen C. Foster from His Time to Ours (2d ed.) *William W. Austin*
Songprints: The Musical Experience of Five Shoshone Women *Judith Vander*

"Happy in the Service of the Lord": Afro-American Gospel Quartets in Memphis *Kip Lornell*

Paul Hindemith in the United States *Luther Noss*

"My Song Is My Weapon": People's Songs, American Communism, and the Politics of Culture, 1930–50 *Robbie Lieberman*

Chosen Voices: The Story of the American Cantorate *Mark Slobin*

Theodore Thomas: America's Conductor and Builder of Orchestras, 1835–1905 *Ezra Schabas*

"The Whorehouse Bells Were Ringing" and Other Songs Cowboys Sing *Collected and Edited by Guy Logsdon*

Crazeology: The Autobiography of a Chicago Jazzman *Bud Freeman, as Told to Robert Wolf*

Discoursing Sweet Music: Brass Bands and Community Life in Turn-of-the-Century Pennsylvania *Kenneth Kreitner*

Mormonism and Music: A History *Michael Hicks*

Voices of the Jazz Age: Profiles of Eight Vintage Jazzmen *Chip Deffaa*

Pickin' on Peachtree: A History of Country Music in Atlanta, Georgia *Wayne W. Daniel*

Bitter Music: Collected Journals, Essays, Introductions, and Librettos *Harry Partch; edited by Thomas McGeary*

Ethnic Music on Records: A Discography of Ethnic Recordings Produced in the United States, 1893 to 1942 *Richard K. Spottswood*

Downhome Blues Lyrics: An Anthology from the Post–World War II Era *Jeff Todd Titon*

Ellington: The Early Years *Mark Tucker*

Chicago Soul *Robert Pruter*

That Half-Barbaric Twang: The Banjo in American Popular Culture *Karen Linn*

Hot Man: The Life of Art Hodes *Art Hodes and Chadwick Hansen*

The Erotic Muse: American Bawdy Songs (2d ed.) *Ed Cray*

Barrio Rhythm: Mexican American Music in Los Angeles *Steven Loza*

The Creation of Jazz: Music, Race, and Culture in Urban America *Burton W. Peretti*

Charles Martin Loeffler: A Life Apart in Music *Ellen Knight*

Club Date Musicians: Playing the New York Party Circuit *Bruce A. MacLeod*

Opera on the Road: Traveling Opera Troupes in the United States, 1825–60 *Katherine K. Preston*

The Stonemans: An Appalachian Family and the Music That Shaped Their Lives *Ivan M. Tribe*

Transforming Tradition: Folk Music Revivals Examined *Edited by Neil V. Rosenberg*

The Crooked Stovepipe: Athapaskan Fiddle Music and Square Dancing in Northeast Alaska and Northwest Canada *Craig Mishler*

Traveling the High Way Home: Ralph Stanley and the World of Traditional Bluegrass Music *John Wright*

Carl Ruggles: Composer, Painter, and Storyteller *Marilyn Ziffrin*

Never without a Song: The Years and Songs of Jennie Devlin, 1865–1952 *Katharine D. Newman*

The Hank Snow Story *Hank Snow, with Jack Ownbey and Bob Burris*

Milton Brown and the Founding of Western Swing *Cary Ginell, with special assistance from Roy Lee Brown*
Santiago de Murcia's "Códice Saldívar No. 4": A Treasury of Secular Guitar Music from Baroque Mexico *Craig H. Russell*
The Sound of the Dove: Singing in Appalachian Primitive Baptist Churches *Beverly Bush Patterson*
Heartland Excursions: Ethnomusicological Reflections on Schools of Music *Bruno Nettl*
Doowop: The Chicago Scene *Robert Pruter*
Blue Rhythms: Six Lives in Rhythm and Blues *Chip Deffaa*
Shoshone Ghost Dance Religion: Poetry Songs and Great Basin Context *Judith Vander*
Go Cat Go! Rockabilly Music and Its Makers *Craig Morrison*
'Twas Only an Irishman's Dream: The Image of Ireland and the Irish in American Popular Song Lyrics, 1800–1920 *William H. A. Williams*
Democracy at the Opera: Music, Theater, and Culture in New York City, 1815–60 *Karen Ahlquist*
Fred Waring and the Pennsylvanians *Virginia Waring*
Woody, Cisco, and Me: Seamen Three in the Merchant Marine *Jim Longhi*
Behind the Burnt Cork Mask: Early Blackface Minstrelsy and Antebellum American Popular Culture *William J. Mahar*
Going to Cincinnati: A History of the Blues in the Queen City *Steven C. Tracy*
Pistol Packin' Mama: Aunt Molly Jackson and the Politics of Folksong *Shelly Romalis*
Sixties Rock: Garage, Psychedelic, and Other Satisfactions *Michael Hicks*
The Late Great Johnny Ace and the Transition from R&B to Rock 'n' Roll *James M. Salem*
Tito Puente and the Making of Latin Music *Steven Loza*
Juilliard: A History *Andrea Olmstead*
Understanding Charles Seeger, Pioneer in American Musicology *Edited by Bell Yung and Helen Rees*
Mountains of Music: West Virginia Traditional Music from *Goldenseal* *Edited by John Lilly*
Alice Tully: An Intimate Portrait *Albert Fuller*
A Blues Life *Henry Townsend, as told to Bill Greensmith*
Long Steel Rail: The Railroad in American Folksong (2d ed.) *Norm Cohen*
The Golden Age of Gospel *Text by Horace Clarence Boyer; photography by Lloyd Yearwood*
Aaron Copland: The Life and Work of an Uncommon Man *Howard Pollack*
Louis Moreau Gottschalk *S. Frederick Starr*
Race, Rock, and Elvis *Michael T. Bertrand*
Theremin: Ether Music and Espionage *Albert Glinsky*
Poetry and Violence: The Ballad Tradition of Mexico's Costa Chica *John H. McDowell*
The Bill Monroe Reader *Edited by Tom Ewing*
Music in Lubavitcher Life *Ellen Koskoff*
Zarzuela: Spanish Operetta, American Stage *Janet L. Sturman*
Bluegrass Odyssey: A Documentary in Pictures and Words, 1966–86 *Carl Fleischhauer and Neil V. Rosenberg*
That Old-Time Rock & Roll: A Chronicle of an Era, 1954–63 *Richard Aquila*
Labor's Troubadour *Joe Glazer*

American Opera *Elise K. Kirk*
Don't Get above Your Raisin': Country Music and the Southern Working Class *Bill C. Malone*
John Alden Carpenter: A Chicago Composer *Howard Pollack*
Heartbeat of the People: Music and Dance of the Northern Pow-wow *Tara Browner*
My Lord, What a Morning: An Autobiography *Marian Anderson*
Marian Anderson: A Singer's Journey *Allan Keiler*
Charles Ives Remembered: An Oral History *Vivian Perlis*
Henry Cowell, Bohemian *Michael Hicks*
Rap Music and Street Consciousness *Cheryl L. Keyes*
Louis Prima *Garry Boulard*
Marian McPartland's Jazz World: All in Good Time *Marian McPartland*
Robert Johnson: Lost and Found *Barry Lee Pearson and Bill McCulloch*
Bound for America: Three British Composers *Nicholas Temperley*
Lost Sounds: Blacks and the Birth of the Recording Industry, 1890–1919 *Tim Brooks*
Burn, Baby! BURN! The Autobiography of Magnificent Montague *Magnificent Montague with Bob Baker*
Way Up North in Dixie: A Black Family's Claim to the Confederate Anthem *Howard L. Sacks and Judith Rose Sacks*
The Bluegrass Reader *Edited by Thomas Goldsmith*
Colin McPhee: Composer in Two Worlds *Carol J. Oja*
Robert Johnson, Mythmaking, and Contemporary American Culture *Patricia R. Schroeder*
Composing a World: Lou Harrison, Musical Wayfarer *Leta E. Miller and Fredric Lieberman*
Fritz Reiner, Maestro and Martinet *Kenneth Morgan*
That Toddlin' Town: Chicago's White Dance Bands and Orchestras, 1900–1950 *Charles A. Sengstock Jr.*
Dewey and Elvis: The Life and Times of a Rock 'n' Roll Deejay *Louis Cantor*
Come Hither to Go Yonder: Playing Bluegrass with Bill Monroe *Bob Black*
Chicago Blues: Portraits and Stories *David Whiteis*
The Incredible Band of John Philip Sousa *Paul E. Bierley*
"Maximum Clarity" and Other Writings on Music *Ben Johnston, edited by Bob Gilmore*
Staging Tradition: John Lair and Sarah Gertrude Knott *Michael Ann Williams*
Homegrown Music: Discovering Bluegrass *Stephanie P. Ledgin*
Tales of a Theatrical Guru *Danny Newman*
The Music of Bill Monroe *Neil V. Rosenberg and Charles K. Wolfe*
Pressing On: The Roni Stoneman Story *Roni Stoneman, as told to Ellen Wright*
Together Let Us Sweetly Live *Jonathan C. David, with photographs by Richard Holloway*
Live Fast, Love Hard: The Faron Young Story *Diane Diekman*
Air Castle of the South: WSM Radio and the Making of Music City *Craig P. Havighurst*
Traveling Home: Sacred Harp Singing and American Pluralism *Kiri Miller*
Where Did Our Love Go? The Rise and Fall of the Motown Sound *Nelson George*
Lonesome Cowgirls and Honky-Tonk Angels: The Women of Barn Dance Radio *Kristine M. McCusker*
California Polyphony: Ethnic Voices, Musical Crossroads *Mina Yang*

The Never-Ending Revival: Rounder Records and the Folk Alliance *Michael F. Scully*
Sing It Pretty: A Memoir *Bess Lomax Hawes*
Working Girl Blues: The Life and Music of Hazel Dickens *Hazel Dickens and Bill C. Malone*
Charles Ives Reconsidered *Gayle Sherwood Magee*
The Hayloft Gang: The Story of the National Barn Dance *Edited by Chad Berry*
Country Music Humorists and Comedians *Loyal Jones*
Record Makers and Breakers: Voices of the Independent Rock 'n' Roll Pioneers *John Broven*
Music of the First Nations: Tradition and Innovation in Native North America *Edited by Tara Browner*
Cafe Society: The Wrong Place for the Right People *Barney Josephson, with Terry Trilling-Josephson*
George Gershwin: An Intimate Portrait *Walter Rimler*
Life Flows On in Endless Song: Folk Songs and American History *Robert V. Wells*
I Feel a Song Coming On: The Life of Jimmy McHugh *Alyn Shipton*
King of the Queen City: The Story of King Records *Jon Hartley Fox*
Long Lost Blues: Popular Blues in America, 1850–1920 *Peter C. Muir*
Hard Luck Blues: Roots Music Photographs from the Great Depression *Rich Remsberg*
Restless Giant: The Life and Times of Jean Aberbach and Hill and Range Songs *Bar Biszick-Lockwood*
Champagne Charlie and Pretty Jemima: Variety Theater in the Nineteenth Century *Gillian M. Rodger*
Sacred Steel: Inside an African American Steel Guitar Tradition *Robert L. Stone*
Gone to the Country: The New Lost City Ramblers and the Folk Music Revival *Ray Allen*
The Makers of the Sacred Harp *David Warren Steel with Richard H. Hulan*
Woody Guthrie, American Radical *Will Kaufman*
George Szell: A Life of Music *Michael Charry*
Bean Blossom: The Brown County Jamboree and Bill Monroe's Bluegrass Festivals *Thomas A. Adler*
Crowe on the Banjo: The Music Life of J. D. Crowe *Marty Godbey*
Twentieth Century Drifter: The Life of Marty Robbins *Diane Diekman*
Henry Mancini: Reinventing Film Music *John Caps*
The Beautiful Music All Around Us: Field Recordings and the American Experience *Stephen Wade*
Then Sings My Soul: The Culture of Southern Gospel Music *Douglas Harrison*
The Accordion in the Americas: Klezmer, Polka, Tango, Zydeco, and More! *Edited by Helena Simonett*
Bluegrass Bluesman: A Memoir *Josh Graves, edited by Fred Bartenstein*
One Woman in a Hundred: Edna Phillips and the Philadelphia Orchestra *Mary Sue Welsh*
The Great Orchestrator: Arthur Judson and American Arts Management *James M. Doering*
Charles Ives in the Mirror: American Histories of an Iconic Composer *David C. Paul*
Southern Soul-Blues *David Whiteis*
Sweet Air: Modernism, Regionalism, and American Popular Song *Edward P. Comentale*

Pretty Good for a Girl: Women in Bluegrass *Murphy Hicks Henry*
Sweet Dreams: The World of Patsy Cline *Warren R. Hofstra*
William Sidney Mount and the Creolization of American Culture *Christopher J. Smith*
Bird: The Life and Music of Charlie Parker *Chuck Haddix*
Making the March King: John Philip Sousa's Washington Years, 1854–1893 *Patrick Warfield*
In It for the Long Run *Jim Rooney*
Pioneers of the Blues Revival *Steve Cushing*
Roots of the Revival: American and British Folk Music in the 1950s *Ronald D. Cohen and Rachel Clare Donaldson*
Blues All Day Long: The Jimmy Rogers Story *Wayne Everett Goins*
Yankee Twang: Country and Western Music in New England *Clifford R. Murphy*
The Music of the Stanley Brothers *Gary B. Reid*
Hawaiian Music in Motion: Mariners, Missionaries, and Minstrels *James Revell Carr*
Sounds of the New Deal: The Federal Music Project in the West *Peter Gough*
The Mormon Tabernacle Choir: A Biography *Michael Hicks*
The Man That Got Away: The Life and Songs of Harold Arlen *Walter Rimler*
A City Called Heaven: Chicago and the Birth of Gospel Music *Robert M. Marovich*
Blues Unlimited: Essential Interviews from the Original Blues Magazine *Edited by Bill Greensmith, Mike Rowe, and Mark Camarigg*
Hoedowns, Reels, and Frolics: Roots and Branches of Southern Appalachian Dance *Phil Jamison*
Fannie Bloomfield-Zeisler: The Life and Times of a Piano Virtuoso *Beth Abelson Macleod*
Cybersonic Arts: Adventures in American New Music *Gordon Mumma, edited with commentary by Michelle Fillion*
The Magic of Beverly Sills *Nancy Guy*
Waiting for Buddy Guy *Alan Harper*
Harry T. Burleigh: From the Spiritual to the Harlem Renaissance *Jean E. Snyder*
Music in the Age of Anxiety: American Music in the Fifties *James Wierzbicki*
Jazzing: New York City's Unseen Scene *Thomas H. Greenland*
A Cole Porter Companion *Edited by Don M. Randel, Matthew Shaftel, and Susan Forscher Weiss*
Foggy Mountain Troubadour: The Life and Music of Curly Seckler *Penny Parsons*
Blue Rhythm Fantasy: Big Band Jazz Arranging in the Swing Era *John Wriggle*
Bill Clifton: America's Bluegrass Ambassador to the World *Bill C. Malone*
Chinatown Opera Theater in North America *Nancy Yunhwa Rao*
The Elocutionists: Women, Music, and the Spoken Word *Marian Wilson Kimber*
May Irwin: Singing, Shouting, and the Shadow of Minstrelsy *Sharon Ammen*
Peggy Seeger: A Life of Music, Love, and Politics *Jean R. Freedman*
Charles Ives's *Concord*: Essays after a Sonata *Kyle Gann*
Don't Give Your Heart to a Rambler: My Life with Jimmy Martin, the King of Bluegrass *Barbara Martin Stephens*
Libby Larsen: Composing an American Life *Denise Von Glahn*
George Szell's Reign: Behind the Scenes with the Cleveland Orchestra *Marcia Hansen Kraus*

Just One of the Boys: Female-to-Male Cross-Dressing on the American Variety Stage *Gillian M. Rodger*
Spirituals and the Birth of a Black Entertainment Industry *Sandra Jean Graham*
Right to the Juke Joint: A Personal History of American Music *Patrick B. Mullen*
Bluegrass Generation: A Memoir *Neil V. Rosenberg*
Pioneers of the Blues Revival, Expanded Second Edition *Steve Cushing*
Banjo Roots and Branches *Edited by Robert Winans*
Bill Monroe: The Life and Music of the Blue Grass Man *Tom Ewing*
Dixie Dewdrop: The Uncle Dave Macon Story *Michael D. Doubler*
Los Romeros: Royal Family of the Spanish Guitar *Walter Aaron Clark*
Transforming Women's Education: Liberal Arts and Music in Female Seminaries *Jewel A. Smith*
Rethinking American Music *Edited by Tara Browner and Thomas L. Riis*
Leonard Bernstein and the Language of Jazz *Katherine Baber*
Dancing Revolution: Bodies, Space, and Sound in American Cultural History *Christopher J. Smith*
Peggy Glanville-Hicks: Composer and Critic *Suzanne Robinson*
Mormons, Musical Theater, and Belonging in America *Jake Johnson*
Blues Legacy: Tradition and Innovation in Chicago *David Whiteis*
Blues Before Sunrise 2: Interviews from the Chicago Scene *Steve Cushing*
The Cashaway Psalmody: Transatlantic Religion and Music in Colonial Carolina *Stephen A. Marini*
Earl Scruggs and Foggy Mountain Breakdown: The Making of an American Classic *Thomas Goldsmith*
A Guru's Journey: Pandit Chitresh Das and Indian Classical Dance in Diaspora *Sarah Morelli*
Unsettled Scores: Politics, Hollywood, and the Film Music of Aaron Copland and Hanns Eisler *Sally Bick*
Hillbilly Maidens, Okies, and Cowgirls: Women's Country Music, 1930–1960 *Stephanie Vander Wel*
Always the Queen: The Denise LaSalle Story *Denise LaSalle with David Whiteis*
Artful Noise: Percussion Literature in the Twentieth Century *Thomas Siwe*
The Heart of a Woman: The Life and Music of Florence B. Price *Rae Linda Brown, edited by Guthrie P. Ramsey Jr.*
When Sunday Comes: Gospel Music in the Soul and Hip-Hop Eras *Claudrena N. Harold*
The Lady Swings: Memoirs of a Jazz Drummer *Dottie Dodgion and Wayne Enstice*
Industrial Strength Bluegrass: Southwestern Ohio's Musical Legacy *Edited by Fred Bartenstein and Curtis W. Ellison*
Soul on Soul: The Life and Music of Mary Lou Williams *Tammy L. Kernodle*
Unbinding Gentility: Women Making Music in the Nineteenth-Century South *Candace Bailey*
Punks in Peoria: Making a Scene in the American Heartland *Jonathan Wright and Dawson Barrett*
Homer Rodeheaver and the Rise of the Gospel Music Industry *Kevin Mungons and Douglas Yeo*

Americanaland: Where Country & Western Met Rock 'n' Roll *John Milward, with Portraits by Margie Greve*
Listening to Bob Dylan *Larry Starr*
Lying in the Middle: Musical Theater and Belief at the Heart of America *Jake Johnson*
The Sounds of Place: Music and the American Cultural Landscape *Denise Von Glahn*
Peace Be Still: How James Cleveland and the Angelic Choir Created a Gospel Classic *Robert M. Marovich*
Politics as Sound: The Washington, DC, Hardcore Scene, 1978–1983 *Shayna L. Maskell*
Tania León's Stride: A Polyrhythmic Life *Alejandro L. Madrid*
Elliott Carter Speaks: Unpublished Lectures *Edited by Laura Emmery*
Interviews with American Composers: Barney Childs in Conversation *Edited by Virginia Anderson*
Queer Country *Shana Goldin-Perschbacher*
On the Bus with Bill Monroe: My Five-Year Ride with the Father of Blue Grass *Mark Hembree*
Mandolin Man: The Bluegrass Life of Roland White *Bob Black*
Music and Mystique in Muscle Shoals *Christopher M. Reali*
Buddy Emmons: Steel Guitar Jazzman *Steve Fishell*
Music in Black American Life, 1600–1945: A University of Illinois Press Anthology *Compiled by Laurie Matheson*
Music in Black American Life, 1945–2020: A University of Illinois Press Anthology *Compiled by Laurie Matheson*
Ballad Hunting with Max Hunter: Stories of an Ozark Folksong Collector *Sarah Jane Nelson*
Play Like a Man: My Life in Poster Children *Rose Marshack*
Samuel Barber: His Life and Legacy *Howard Pollack*
Aaron Copland in Latin America: Music and Cultural Politics *Carol A. Hess*
Stringbean: The Life and Murder of a Country Music Legend *Taylor Hagood*
Danzón Days: Age, Race, and Romance in Mexico *Hettie Malcomson*
Flaco's Legacy: The Globalization of Conjunto *Erin E. Bauer*
Circle of Winners: How the Guggenheim Foundation Composition Awards Shaped American Music Culture *Denise Von Glahn*

The University of Illinois Press
is a founding member of the
Association of University Presses.

University of Illinois Press
1325 South Oak Street
Champaign, IL 61820-6903
www.press.uillinois.edu